The Philosophy of Sri Aurobindo

Also available from Bloomsbury

Comparative Philosophy without Borders,
edited by Arindam Chakrabarti and Ralph Weber
Differences in Identity in Philosophy and Religion,
edited by Sarah Flavel, Russell Re Manning, and Lydia Azadpour
Gandhi and Philosophy,
by Shaj Mohan and Divya Dwivedi
Wisdom and Philosophy,
edited by Hans-Georg Moeller and Andrew K. Whitehead

The Philosophy of Sri Aurobindo

Indian Philosophy and Yoga in the Contemporary World

Edited by
Debidatta Aurobinda Mahapatra

BLOOMSBURY ACADEMIC
LONDON • NEW YORK • OXFORD • NEW DELHI • SYDNEY

BLOOMSBURY ACADEMIC
Bloomsbury Publishing Plc
50 Bedford Square, London, WC1B 3DP, UK
1385 Broadway, New York, NY 10018, USA
29 Earlsfort Terrace, Dublin 2, Ireland

BLOOMSBURY, BLOOMSBURY ACADEMIC and the Diana logo
are trademarks of Bloomsbury Publishing Plc

First published in Great Britain 2020
This paperback edition published in 2021

Copyright © Debidatta Aurobinda Mahapatra and Contributors, 2020

Debidatta Aurobinda Mahapatra has asserted his right under the Copyright,
Designs and Patents Act, 1988, to be identified as Editor of this work.

For legal purposes the Acknowledgments on p. x constitute an
extension of this copyright page.

Cover design: Rebecca Heselton

All rights reserved. No part of this publication may be reproduced or
transmitted in any form or by any means, electronic or mechanical,
including photocopying, recording, or any information storage or retrieval
system, without prior permission in writing from the publishers.

Bloomsbury Publishing Plc does not have any control over, or responsibility for,
any third-party websites referred to or in this book. All internet addresses given
in this book were correct at the time of going to press. The author and publisher
regret any inconvenience caused if addresses have changed or sites have ceased
to exist, but can accept no responsibility for any such changes.

A catalogue record for this book is available from the British Library.

A catalog record for this book is available from the Library of Congress.

ISBN: HB: 978-1-3501-2486-8
PB: 978-1-3501-8868-6
ePDF: 978-1-3501-2487-5
eBook: 978-1-3501-2488-2

Typeset by Integra Software Services Pvt. Ltd.

To find out more about our authors and books visit www.bloomsbury.com
and sign up for our newsletters.

Contents

Notes on Contributors	vii
Acknowledgments	x
Introduction: Foundation of a Practical Spiritual Philosophy *Debidatta Aurobinda Mahapatra*	1

Part 1   Philosophy, History, and the Global Age

1	Mapping Sri Aurobindo's Metaphysics of Consciousness onto Western Philosophies of Mind *Richard Grego*	15
2	Sri Aurobindo, Enlightenment, and the Bengal Renaissance: A Discourse on Evolution of Consciousness *Debashish Banerji*	33
3	Sri Aurobindo's Invalidation of the Aryan Invasion Theory and the Contemporary Western Archeological Evidence *Kundan Singh*	53
4	A Philosophy for the Global Age *Richard Hartz*	75

Part 2   Yoga and Metaphysics

5	The Psychic Being: Our Opening to the Divine *Marshall Govindan*	93
6	The Metaphysical Foundations of Sri Aurobindo's Vision of the Future of Humanity *V. Ananda Reddy*	107
7	The Power of Inherent Oneness *Martha Orton*	121

Part 3   Poetry, Ethics, and Education

8	Poetry at the Center of Human Knowledge *Goutam Ghosal*	137
9	Ethics and Human Evolution: A Perspective from Sri Aurobindo *Anurag Banerjee*	153
10	Integral Education: The Imperative for the Contemporary World *Partho*	167

Part 4 Human Unity

11 Cosmic Consciousness: The Metaphor of Human Unity
    in Sri Aurobindo's Writings *Sarani Ghosal Mondal* — 187
12 Sri Aurobindo's Ideal of Human Unity and the Discourse on
    International Organizations and Global Governance
    Debidatta Aurobinda Mahapatra — 203

Part 5 Vision of India

13 The Force behind the Indian Renaissance and the Crucial
    Significance of Auroville's Emergence *Aryadeep S. Acharya* — 219
14 Sri Aurobindo's Vision of India's Rebirth *Michel Danino* — 233

Index — 249

Notes on Contributors

Richard Hartz studied philosophy at Yale University and South Asian languages and literature at the University of Washington. Since 1980 he has lived in Pondicherry, India, where he is an editor at the Sri Aurobindo Ashram Archives and teaches world philosophy at the Sri Aurobindo International Centre of Education. He is the author of *The Clasp of Civilizations: Globalization and Religion in a Multicultural World* (2015).

V. Ananda Reddy is the founder-director of Sri Aurobindo Centre for Advanced Research, Pondicherry, which is at present affiliated to Hindu University, Florida, USA. He is a well-known scholar and devotee of Sri Aurobindo and the Mother. From 1958 to 1969, he had his early schooling and undergraduate studies from the Ashram School. With the Mother's blessings, he served at Auroville from 1971 to 1976 in its education sector. He has traveled widely in the United States and Europe disseminating the thought and vision of Sri Aurobindo. He is also the chairperson of the Institute of Human Study that was established by the Mother in 1965.

Martha Orton is a writer and scholar whose focus is Sri Aurobindo's philosophy. In addition to numerous journal articles on the integral yoga of Sri Aurobindo, she is the author of several books, including *The Quest for Knowledge and Mastery: A Comparative Study of Motivation in the Light of Sri Aurobindo*, and *Oneness*. Dr. Orton serves on the faculties of the Sri Aurobindo Centre for Advanced Research, Puducherry, India, and also Hindu University of America, Orlando, Florida.

Marshall Govindan is an author, scholar, and publisher of literary works related to classical Yoga, Siddhantham and Tantra, and a sadhak of Sri Aurobindo's Integral Yoga since 1970. He is the recipient of the Patanjali Award for 2014 for his outstanding service to Yoga by the International Yoga Federation. His critically acclaimed books include *Kriya Yoga Sutras of Patanjali and the Siddhas*; *Tirumandiram*; *Enlightenment: Its Not What You Think*; *The Wisdom of Jesus and the Yoga Siddhas*; and *Babaji and the 18 Siddha Kriya Yoga Tradition*. Nearly all include discussions of Sri Aurobindo's Integral Yoga.

Partho is an educator and writer. He has spent more than twenty-five years in the fields of integral education, leadership, and personal growth and has done intensive research in the principles and practices of integral and transformative yoga. He is now one of the leading integral educationists in India and is associated as mentor and consultant with many integral initiatives in India and the United States. He works with schools, universities, educators, teachers, and parents.

Anurag Banerjee is the founder of Overman Foundation, a nonprofit organization which runs India's only online research institute dedicated to the mission of Sri Aurobindo and the Mother. He was an associate professor at NexGen Institute of Business and Technology, Kolkata. He was also a faculty at Sri Aurobindo Centre for Advanced Research (SACAR), Pondicherry. He is a trustee of the Sri Aurobindo Sakti Centre Trust which runs the Sri Aurobindo Bal Mandir school in Kolkata. An acclaimed poet, essayist, researcher, biographer, and translator, he has published works that include *Achinpather Dibyapathik*; *Debotar Shrom*; *Nirodbaran: The Surrealist's Journey*; *The Alipore Bomb Trial Judgment*; *Sri Aurobindo: His Political Life and Activities*, to name a few.

Richard Grego is Professor of Philosophy and Cultural History at Florida State College. His research interests include comparative philosophy of science and religion, including cross-cultural concepts of metaphysics, mind, physics-cosmology, and cultural-intellectual history. He has, most recently, been exploring the transmission of Advaita Vedanta philosophy to the West via its neo-Vedanta interlocutors such as Sarvepalli Radhakrishnan and Sri Aurobindo.

Debashish Banerji is the Haridas Chaudhuri Professor of Indian Philosophy and Culture and Doshi Professor of Asian Art at the California Institute of Integral Studies. He is also the program chair in the East-West Psychology department. He obtained his Ph.D. in Art History from the University of California, Los Angeles. Banerji has curated a number of exhibitions of Indian and Japanese art. He has edited a book on the Indian poet Rabindranath Tagore and is also the author of two books *The Alternate Nation of Abanindranath Tagore* (Sage, 2010) and *Seven Quartets of Becoming: A Transformational Yoga Psychology Based on the Diaries of Sri Aurobindo* (DK Printworld and Nalanda International, 2012).

Goutam Ghosal is a professor of English at Visva-Bharati, Santiniketan, India. He was the chief editor of *The Visva-Bharati Quarterly* from 2005 to 2007. His major books include *The Rainbow Bridge: A Comparative Study of Tagore and Sri Aurobindo*; *Sri Aurobindo's Prose Style*; and *Sri Aurobindo and World Literature*, to mention a few. Ghosal has published more than two hundred papers and articles on Sri Aurobindo and other Indian English poets. His other areas of interest are Shakespeare, Rabindranath Tagore, Ernest Hemingway, and nineteenth-century literature. Ghosal received a D.Litt. for his study "Lord of Language: Tradition and Experiment in Sri Aurobindo's Prose Styles." He is the recipient of Sri Aurobindo Puroshkar and Nolini Kanta Gupta Puroshkar.

Sarani Ghosal Mondal is an associate professor of English in the Department of Humanities and Sciences at the National Institute of Technology, Goa. She is the author of the book entitled *Poetry and Poetics of Walt Whitman and Sri Aurobindo* and has coedited another book entitled *Indian Responses to Shakespeare*. She has collaborated in a UGC-funded project on Comparative Mysticism under the scheme of e-Pathshala. She has authored more than forty articles and papers, especially on mysticism, on various aspects of Sri Aurobindo, Tagore's plays and poetry, and Applied Linguistics. At present, she is working on a comparative study of Islamic Mysticism and Sri Aurobindo's integral philosophy.

Debidatta Aurobinda Mahapatra is the director of Mahatma Gandhi Center for Non-Violence, Human Rights and World Peace at the Hindu University of America. He has a doctoral degree from the University of Massachusetts in the area of global governance and human security. He was a recipient of the Scholar of Peace Award (New Delhi, 2007) and the Kodikara Award (Colombo, 2010). He was a Charles Wallace India Fellow at the Queen's University at Belfast in 2010. His writings and comments have been published by reputed magazines and news agencies including Reuters. His publications include *Gandhi and the World* (Lexington, 2018, coedited), *Conflict Management in Kashmir* (Cambridge, 2018), and *Conflict and Peace in Eurasia* (Routledge, 2013, edited).

Kundan Singh is a faculty at Sofia University, Palo Alto, and vice president of the Cultural Integration Fellowship, San Francisco. He has authored a book titled *The Evolution of Integral Yoga: Sri Aurobindo, Sri Ramakrishna, and Swami Vivekananda* and several book chapters in edited works such as *Beyond Mind: The Future of Psychology as Science*; *Beyond Postmodernism: Towards a Future Psychology*; *Relativism, Self-Referentiality, and Beyond Mind*, to mention a few. He has lectured extensively in the San Francisco Bay Area and has made several paper presentations at conferences in the United States and India.

Aryadeep S. Acharya has been a resident of Auroville since 1990. He has addressed Auroville's future possibilities including the unified and harmonious development of Auroville. He has written a number of papers and articles on the subject. He has edited a commemorative volume *Dear Aurovilians: Inspiration from Dr. Karan Singh's Auroville Collaboration*. His forthcoming book is on Auroville's relevance to India. It is titled *For India's Glorious Future: Relevance of a Fully Developed Auroville Universal Township with Worldwide Collaboration and Presences for India's Supreme Resurgence*. In order to further the work and vision of Auroville, he has founded Aryadeep Vision Foundation.

Michel Danino is a French-born Indian writer on Indian civilization. His writings include *The Lost River: On the Trail of the Sarasvati* (Penguin India, 2010) and *Indian Culture and India's Future* (DK Printworld, 2011). He coedited (with Prof. Kapil Kapoor) a two-volume textbook for a CBSE elective course, *Knowledge Traditions and Practices of India* (2013 and 2015). Since 2011, Michel Danino has taught at IIT Gandhinagar, where he is a visiting professor and assists its Archaeological Sciences Center. In 2017, he received India's prestigious Padma Shri award for Literature and Education.

Acknowledgments

The book is the product of a two-day international conference, on May 4 and 5, 2017, organized by the Mahatma Gandhi Center for Nonviolence, Human Rights and World Peace at the Hindu University of America, Orlando, Florida. The theme of the conference was "Relevance of Sri Aurobindo and the Grand Visions of the Ancient Indian Wisdom." The interdisciplinary conference brought together scholars from diverse fields. Twenty-six speakers from the United States and India participated in the conference and deliberated on various aspects of Sri Aurobindo's philosophy and its relevance to the contemporary world. For Sri Aurobindo, the Indian philosopher, poet, and yogi, human society has evolved throughout history and is destined to move toward a better organization. His aphorism "All Life Is Yoga" is in consonance with his spiritual philosophy that encompasses every aspect of human life. Applying his evolutionary logic neither the individual nor the groups and organizations created by individuals are the culmination of human evolution and they are bound to evolve. Following Advaita Vedanta, he believed that a fundamental unity is the very basis of existence and the foundation of all creation.

Despite the profundity of Sri Aurobindo's ideas, they remain unexplored in the West as well as the East. The conference was a modest attempt to fill this gap. This volume is a compilation of select presentations at the conference. Sri Aurobindo's extraordinary ability to work at the intersection of multiple disciplines makes his ideas relevant to varied disciplines, including, but not limited to, philosophy, politics, history, psychology, and religion. This anthology is an attempt to focus on some of his ideas on the individual, state, society, world, and beyond.

I am thankful to Braham Aggarwal, Chairman, Hindu University of America, who inaugurated the conference and read the message of Karan Singh, the noted Sri Aurobindo scholar and Indian Parliamentarian. I am grateful to Karan Singh for sending a message for the conference. The prominent guests at the conference included Suresh Gupta, CEO, Park Square Homes, M. P. Rama of JHM Hotels, and Manohar Shinde of Dharma Civilization Foundation. The conference could not have been possible without their support and I am sincerely thankful to them. I owe thanks to Santosh Krinsky and Mudit Jain for supporting the conference. I express my gratitude to Rohini Gupta for her support. Ananda Reddy delivered the inaugural address, and Richard Hartz, Rand Hicks, Debashish Banerji, and Michel Danino delivered the keynote addresses. I am sincerely thankful to all of them. I am deeply grateful to Manoj Das Gupta, Managing Trustee of Sri Aurobindo Ashram and in charge of its Copyright Department, for giving copyright permission to use the writings of Sri Aurobindo in this volume. Sincere thanks are also due to all the chapter contributors, who spent considerable time after the conference to finalize their chapters. I am thankful to Partho for his chapter. I owe warm thanks to Ved Nanda, Yashwant Pathak,

Kalyan Viswanathan, Shekhar Patel, Abhinav Dwivedi, Abhijit Pandya, and Vishwah Rajkumar for their encouragement and support. I am thankful to Meera Bhutta and Prakhar Aggarwal for their support to make the conference a success. I extend thanks to Lynn Vannucci and Asha Patel for their cooperation in organizing the conference. Lynn proofread all the chapters despite her busy schedule. She deserves my special thanks. Martha Orton went through select chapters and offered useful suggestions. I am thankful to her. I am also thankful to Yudit, Rich and Seema for their intellectual help. Last, but not least, I am thankful to Colleen Coalter and Becky Holland of Bloomsbury for being supportive throughout the publication process.

Introduction: Foundation of a Practical Spiritual Philosophy

Debidatta Aurobinda Mahapatra

In a reply to one of his disciples about being considered a philosopher, Sri Aurobindo wrote in 1934 that he began as a poet and politician, not as a philosopher. Philosophy did not even come to him during his political activism in Calcutta (Kolkata), but he knew that "a Yogi ought to be able to turn his hand to anything" (*The Complete Works of Sri Aurobindo*, hereafter CWSA 2011, vol. 35, 70)[1] and philosophy "burst out like a volcano" (CWSA 2011, vol. 35, 63) as he started writing the *Arya*, the philosophical magazine. In an essential sense, Sri Aurobindo's philosophy can be termed yogic or spiritual philosophy. Let us consider one of his bold proclamations in *The Human Cycle, The Ideal of Human Unity, War and Self-Determination* (CWSA 1997, vol. 25, 244–245):

> Man's road to spiritual supermanhood will be open when he declares boldly that all he has yet developed, including the intellect of which he is so rightly and yet so vainly proud, are now no longer sufficient for him, and that to uncase, discover, set free this greater Light within shall be henceforward his pervading preoccupation. Then will his philosophy, art, science, ethics, social existence, vital pursuits be no longer an exercise of mind and life, done for themselves, carried in a circle, but a means for the discovery of a greater Truth behind mind and life and for the bringing of its power into our human existence. We shall be on the right road to become ourselves, to find our true law of perfection, to live our true satisfied existence in our real being and divine nature.

Sri Aurobindo was of the firm belief that the current instrument and capability of intellect, of which the individual is "so vainly proud," are limited. Intellect is an insufficient guide to discovering the "greater light." Immanuel Kant, while emphasizing sense and reason as the two bedrocks of knowledge production, acknowledged there are ideas, for example, the Idea of God, which cannot be the subject of rational knowledge. In a Kantian world, "there can be no knowledge of any spatiotemporal reality at all beyond the limits of sensibility, although in cases where concepts of the understanding can be used to formulate coherent conceptions of non-spatiotemporal entities, above all God, there may be coherent belief, even if not any knowledge" (Guyer and Wood 1998, 37). Kant would not declare anything beyond the sensual-intellectual knowledge as certain and, hence, would prefer to be agnostic. Sri Aurobindo, while not undermining the significance of sense and intellect in producing knowledge, would go further and argue that yogic experience is as certain as sensory and intellectual knowledge, or even more so. The yogi in him affirmed, "form is the rhythm of the spirit" (CWSA 1997, vol. 20, 60), "Matter is the Spirit's firm density" (CWSA 1997, vols. 33 and 34, 328), and "the limbs were trembling densities of soul" (CWSA 1997, vols. 33 and 34, 676). He firmly declared that, with the transformation of the individual and the dawn of inner vision, "philosophy, art, science, ethics, social existence, vital pursuits [would] be no longer an exercise of mind and life, done for themselves, carried in a circle, but a means for the discovery of a greater Truth" (CWSA 1997, vol. 25, 245). Thus was laid the foundation of a practical spiritual philosophy.

What Is Practical Spiritual Philosophy?

What is the practical spiritual philosophy as propounded by Sri Aurobindo? To put it in a different way: can philosophy be spiritual, or must it be confined to conventional categories of epistemology and metaphysics? In order to understand Sri Aurobindo's spiritual philosophy, it is necessary to understand his concept of Integral Yoga. His yoga is key to unraveling the secret of his philosophy. Unlike the Mayavadins of Vedanta, who would prefer to term the world and worldly experiences "illusion," Sri Aurobindo would affirm the reality of this world and argue that in this world a spiritual life must flourish. In this sense, Sri Aurobindo's spiritual philosophy is a practical philosophy that does not escape the world or worldly problems. Sri Aurobindo affirmed the reality of this world and entitled one of his major works, *The Life Divine* (CWSA 2005, vols. 21 and 22). In his scheme of Integral Yoga, which encompasses all aspects of life, the goal is to divinize life in this very world. His famous aphorism "All Life Is Yoga" alludes to his integral perspective on life.

Where does materialism find a place in this scheme of Integral Yoga? From an Aurobindonian perspective, matter and spirit are the obverse and reverse of the same divine coin, both complementing each other rather than cancelling or competing against each other. In this practical spiritual philosophy, neither matter nor spirit[2] is undermined or negated; both complement each other on a collective journey to realize the inner divine and manifest it in the outer life and on earth. That is the core of the spiritual philosophy of Sri Aurobindo. Sense, reason, and all paraphernalia of matter and mind have requisite places in his scheme of Integral Yoga. For him, matter and spirit are not irreconcilable contradictions to be disputed, but necessary elements to build a harmonious divine life. Spirituality devoid of life is a castle built in the dream of mind, and materialism devoid of spirituality is like a life that is shallow, without a connection to the reality within. He would further argue that many of the conflicts in modern life have emanated from this compartmentalization. Matter is not to be abandoned, but must be seen in a new light.[3] Conflict, violence, and war have emanated from this disconnect, and from this prioritizing of material life over spiritual life, under the governance of limited ego.

Sri Aurobindo's five dreams, on the eve of India's independence in 1947, reflected on the individual, state, and society.[4] His fifth dream posited a fervent hope in human nature and its transformative capabilities. Unless there is a fundamental transformation in basic human thinking and action, Sri Aurobindo argued, human nature will be bogged down with myriad conflicts, both individual and collective. The struggling human life, as seen in myriad conflicts worldwide, the crises of religious extremism and terrorism, the geopolitical constructs of power, and the widening chasm between ideals and practices cannot continue indefinitely. The eternal optimist in Sri Aurobindo believed that there is a scope for evolution of the human condition, toward higher forms of living and thinking, from its current formulations, which are narrow, egocentric, shaped by the binaries like mine and thine, my group and your group, and my state and your state. While the English scientist Charles Darwin researched the evolution of biological species and proved that the ancestors of human beings were not humans, Sri Aurobindo argued that the human species is not the summit of evolution of Nature. There is a scope for further evolution. While Darwin did his research in the Galapagos Islands and other places, Sri Aurobindo's laboratory was the human individual, including himself, and the world.

Though modern and innovative in his approach, Sri Aurobindo would not discard the wisdom of the past. He lamented that the modern individual is not aware of ancient wisdom and its treasures. He visualized a connection between the past, present, and future through his integral philosophy, and argued that the past provides a rich source with which to connect and discover the self. He described the Veda as a record of "inner experience and the suggestions of the intuitive mind," which is beyond "mankind's ordinary perceptions and daily activities" (CWSA 1998, vol. 15, 10). Similarly, he described the Upanishads as the waning or lost knowledge recovered by Rishis through "meditation and spiritual experience" or recovery of the old truths in new forms by Rishis who used the Vedic Word as "a seed of thought and vision." For him, the Veda symbolizes "the struggle between spiritual powers of Light and Darkness, Truth and Falsehood, Knowledge and Ignorance, Death and Immortality" (CWSA 1998, vol. 15, 10). He expressed dissatisfaction that the modern individual, busy with his mundane life and outward activities, has lost interest in this ancient wisdom. He lamented, "small is the chance that in an age which blinds our eyes with the transient glories of the outward life and deafens our ears with the victorious trumpets of a material and mechanical knowledge many shall cast more than the eye of an intellectual and imaginative curiosity on the passwords of their ancient discipline or seek to penetrate into the heart of their radiant mysteries" (CWSA 1998, vol. 15, 369). What Sri Aurobindo wrote about a century ago can be viewed in the context of developments in the twenty-first-century world. In the race toward modernization, which is a controversial term as it means many things to many people, it appears that individuals are shunning their rich past and culture as if everything in the past is repugnant to their progress. India, the birthplace of Sri Aurobindo, is no exception to this trend. India's dominant intellectual class has apparently not grasped the depth of the ancient wisdom. They are, to use the Indian philosopher's words, blinded by "transient glories of the outward life" and deafened by "trumpets of a material and mechanical knowledge." The results have been hazardous. Indian school curricula, whether at the elementary or secondary or higher levels, scantly focus on the ancient gems of Indian wisdom such as Vedanta or ancient Indian scholars like Kautilya. The young Indians of the twenty-first century, hence, are not aware of the rich past and lack appreciation of the wisdom inherent in it. This issue is not the focus of this book, and it requires another book-length research to elaborate upon it.

It may be helpful to position Sri Aurobindo in a debate on metaphysics in order to understand and appreciate his philosophy. For the Cambridge philosopher A. J. Ayer, metaphysics is nonsense as it is not amenable to sensory perception and reasoning. It cannot be verified through any available means of knowledge (Ayer 1990).[5] Sri Aurobindo would argue that sense knowledge is not the only knowledge and also the current capability of sense perception is shallow. He wrote in *The Life Divine*, in the chapter "the Methods of Vedantic Knowledge," "although it is the rule that when we seek to become aware of the external world, we have to do so indirectly through the sense-organs and can experience only so much of the truth about things and men as the senses convey to us, yet this rule is merely the regularity of a dominant habit. It is possible for the mind ... to take direct cognisance of the objects of sense without the aid of the sense-organs" (CWSA 2005, vols. 21 and 22, 70).[6] He wrote in *Savitri*, "But our dwarf will and cold pragmatic sense admit not the celestial visitants " (CWSA 1997, vols. 33 and 34, 263). There is knowledge beyond sense; there is higher knowledge which is beyond the current scope of sense and rational mind. This higher knowledge is not amenable to limited modes of human thought. He would even argue, from his yogic experience, that the senses and mind are manifestations of the spirit, but due to the veil of ignorance, the individual mistakes them as something different from the spirit, from the divine. The divine who is the governing principle of the inner world and the outer world is also the governing principle of the senses. Sri Aurobindo affirmed:

> But always mental experience and the concepts of the reason have been held by it to be even at their highest a reflection in mental identifications and not the supreme self-existent identity. We have to go beyond the mind and the reason. The reason active in our waking consciousness is only a mediator between the subconscient All that we come from in our evolution upwards and the superconscient All towards which we are impelled by that evolution. The subconscient and the superconscient are two different formulations of the same All. The master-word of the subconscient is Life, the master-word of the superconscient is Light. In the subconscient knowledge or consciousness is involved in action, for action is the essence of Life. In the superconscient action re-enters into Light and no longer contains involved knowledge but is itself contained in a supreme consciousness... When the selfawareness in the mind applied both to continent and content, to own-self and other-self, exalts itself into the luminous selfmanifest identity, the reason also converts itself into the form of the self-luminous intuitional knowledge. This is the highest possible state of our knowledge when mind fulfils itself in the supramental. Such is the scheme of the human understanding upon which the conclusions of the most ancient Vedanta were built.
>
> (CWSA 2005, vols. 21 and 22, 71–72)

The limited ego, a crude reflection of I-ness, becomes a hindrance on the path of realization of human potentials. While in the case of the individual, it is based on the individual's desire to possess and be possessed, in the case of groups and larger organizations it leads to bigger problems. It leads to jingoism, war, and expansionism. In the case of states, this propels leaders to believe in the superiority of their nation and their national interest. It propels leaders to assert that their interest is just and that it must be realized at any cost. National habits, prejudices, and idiosyncrasies reflect this national ego. Applied to international politics, this perspective leads to exploitation and wars, and practices like colonialism and imperialism. Colonialism and imperialism, two of the worst forms of exploitation, were only manifestations of an exploitative substructure. The root, the ego, is intact, and its manifestation has acquired new shapes. But Sri Aurobindo would argue that the collective ego could transform when state leaders think in terms of larger human unity and harmony. The establishment of the United Nations (UN), after the failure of the League of Nations, was hailed as a right step in this direction. Sri Aurobindo termed this development an event of "capital importance." The UN was established with a promise to ensure the dignity and equality of all states. Has this happened? Sri Aurobindo was a critic of assigning permanent veto power to five states. He wrote, "a strong surviving element of oligarchy remained in the preponderant place assigned to the five great Powers in the Security Council and was clinched by the device of the veto" (CWSA 1997, vol. 25, 582).[7] The ineffectiveness of the UN to establish international peace and security is an indication of its flawed hierarchical structure, which in turn impedes the process of development of harmonious international order.

The progress of human society concerned Sri Aurobindo as it concerned seers and thinkers across ages, including Socrates and Plato, Kautilya, St. Augustine, St. Thomas, Swami Vivekananda, and Mahatma Gandhi. To use the language of political science, Sri Aurobindo was concerned with the question—can the human individual rise above Hobbesian human nature? How can he rise? What are the challenges and prospects? His endeavor, as reflected in his writings, was directed to address these questions. With a fervent hope and eternal optimism, Sri Aurobindo argued that such a transformation of human society is possible. However, this will only come to fruition through inner engineering, not purely by external mechanisms. His is a call to look out from within, rather than to look in from without. He wrote, "on inner values hangs the outer plan" (CWSA 1997, vols. 33 and 34, 186). He applied this principle to every aspect of human life. His integral approach did not leave any branch of human knowledge, human enterprise, untouched.

It is useful to apply Sri Aurobindo's spiritual philosophy to an analysis of the human needs approach. Maslow, the founder of human needs theory, argued that the physiological needs of the individual—such as food and sleep—must be met first before the individual can move to the next rung on the needs ladder (Maslow 1943). This needs ladder moves up to self-actualization at the top. The individual who has fulfilled all his needs can climb to this step and, moved by some higher goals, attain an even greater fulfillment. Maslow's theory of human needs evolved over time and he came to assert a level of need beyond self-actualization, which he called transcendence. According to Martha Orton, "Maslow asserts an inherent motivation for spiritual growth in humanity. Maslow also concludes that what he calls transcendence, which we can see as similar to Sri Aurobindo's conception of higher levels of consciousness, provides the metamotivation which drives and underlies all the lower motivations" (Orton 2008, 265). Sri Aurobindo would argue that unless there is a deeper spiritual principle governing human life, there will be chaos, contradiction, and violence. Prioritizing physiological needs over the need for a well-ordered life based on some deeper spiritual principle would be like putting the cart before the horse. In a scheme where the needs are not governed by a higher principle, there is a possibility that mechanisms like law and order would prove ineffective to control the chaos and clash of needs. This is what is happening in the age of modernization. Much of the socio-cultural chaos in present-day society, much of the violence at the individual and collective levels, can be traced to the erroneous prioritization of human needs.

Though Sri Aurobindo's primary area of activity was India, the global thinker in him was evident throughout his writings. He saw a connection between the global and the local (McDermottt 1987, 19-22). He believed that India with its rich spiritual wealth could play an effective role in the world. Among Sri Aurobindo's five dreams, the fourth was that India with its repository of knowledge and wisdom can play a role in the world as a spiritual ambassador. India as a guru can galvanize a process that can help transform human-to-human and state-to-state relations so that the relations are more harmonious and less conflictual. He cast his vision in a larger framework of the ideal of human unity, in which humans and their culture flourish in an ambience of peaceful coexistence, each flourishing and complementing the other. Such a vision, he would argue, could gather shape only when individuals and their leaders transcend narrow boundaries of ego and its elements. The increasing acceptance of yoga in the world as a method of healing and as a method of peace, the recognition of it by the premier international body, the UN, in 2014, can be considered fruition of Sri Aurobindo's fourth dream, at least partially. However, much remains to be seen and done. How far can such actions work to transform human relations, or will they merely become fads and money-generating commercial ventures, as mushrooming of yoga studios indicate? Mere symbolism would certainly not be acceptable to Sri Aurobindo.

The ideas and philosophy of Sri Aurobindo do not fare well in academic debates and discussions, and in policymaking. This is disturbing, keeping in view the nature and scope of his work. Interestingly, for the Indian philosopher, there is no discrepancy between being an academic scholar and a yogi, and an individual can be both simultaneously. Hence, it is important that in Sri Aurobindo's philosophy one finds an invocation to praxis, a praxis that demands a transformation of the individual and society. Sri Aurobindo produced more than thirty volumes including classics like *The Life Divine, The Synthesis of Yoga, Essays on the Gita,* and *The Secret of the Veda.* His epic poem *Savitri* can be considered a practical project, in which he invites individuals seeking their transformation and transformation of the human society to participate. The subtitle of this poem, "a legend and a symbol," makes it amply clear that it is not just a poem but also a symbol to explore higher realms of consciousness. In this longest poem ever written in the English language, Sri Aurobindo builds upon a story from Mahabharata and turns it into a spiritual project. In the author's note to the poem he writes that the legend is not a mere allegory and "the characters are not just personified qualities, but incarnations or emanations of living and conscious Forces with whom we can enter into concrete touch and they take human bodies in order to help man and show him the way from his mortal state to a divine consciousness and immortal life" (CWSA 1997, vols. 33 and 34, author's note). The epic poem is a call to all, who follow the methods and beliefs of his spiritual philosophy, to take this journey along with him. While most of the writings of Sri Aurobindo were completed in the second decade of the twentieth century, the work on *Savitri* continued until his death in 1950. Sri Aurobindo continued his epic poem as a yogic endeavor and as a demonstration of his spiritual philosophy. For him, yoga and philosophy are intertwined, and in order to understand his spiritual philosophy, one must fathom his yoga.

The Parts and the Chapters

The book argues that the relevance of Sri Aurobindo spans not only to the fields of yoga and spirituality but also to politics, literature, history, and many other disciplines. From an Aurobindonian perspective, these disciplines can benefit and be saved from narrowness when allowed for mutual exchange and enrichment. The increasing interdisciplinary approach to academic disciplines is a sign of acceptance of an integral approach to knowledge and knowledge production. Sri Aurobindo would argue that these disciplines must have a yogic vision at their center. Even if we take a purely rational approach, Sri Aurobindo's spiritual philosophy would prove helpful for an understanding of current human affairs and provide ways to address the root causes of the social, psychological, and political turmoil of our age. The chapters in the collected volume seek to respond to the call: Is Sri Aurobindo relevant today? How are his ideas relevant? This volume thus embarks on an ambitious journey not only in elaborating Sri Aurobindo's ideas but also in examining how these ideas are pertinent to a discourse on various problems afflicting human life and society and solutions to them. The contributors, while adopting methodological pluralism, have used their unique expertise and understanding to examine ideas and visions of the Indian yogi and philosopher to explore problems plaguing human society.

Sri Aurobindo's ideas pertain not only to India but also to the world, as his writings were primarily concerned with human life and society. This concern remained central to his writings, whether in prose or poetry, and the visionary in him could foresee developments which were hidden from view during his time. Aware of the rationalist tradition and steeped deep in the Vedanta wisdom, Sri Aurobindo synthesized both in his project of Integral Yoga, a project that made the individual being and his collectivities as the laboratory. The panacea for the problems plaguing the human society and the world, Sri Aurobindo would argue, lies in the individual and society. For this, the current scope and breadth of human understanding of the individual and his world need to be reexamined and reevaluated, in the light of the changes within the individual, in his inner and outer circumstances, which are not often amenable to scrutiny through available mechanisms. The book is a collection of chapters dealing with various aspects of Sri Aurobindo's philosophy while keeping in mind its relevance to human society. Each contributor has outlined her or his perspective on Sri

Aurobindo in unique ways and interpreted his philosophy to reflect on developments in the modern world. Although some chapters have not strictly focused on the relevance of the philosophy of Sri Aurobindo, they offer novel insights on various dimensions of his philosophy.

The book is based on the premise that Sri Aurobindo's integral philosophy offers practical solutions to human problems. In contrast to assumptions held by some scholars, Sri Aurobindo was one of the most practical philosophers to ever emerge on the human scene. The single question that most often plagued him was how to develop a human society, which is universal and operational, across national boundaries, race, color, language, and other divides? Hence, he was not detached from the reality of the daily world, and he was not concerned with a life which is not useful and valuable for the current world. He was most concerned with the current condition of human life, whether at the individual level or at the collective level. A scholar, deeply embedded in psychoanalytic theory, may not be able to fathom such a perspective, the "oceanic feeling" the practical spiritual philosophy of Sri Aurobindo evokes. In a letter to Sigmund Freud, on December 5, 1927, Romain Rolland defined oceanic feeling as something "simple and direct fact of the feeling of the 'eternal,'" which is "totally independent of all dogma, all credo, all Church organization" (quoted in Parsons 1999, 9).

The book is divided into four parts. Part One titled "Philosophy, History, and Global Age" deals with the historical context of Sri Aurobindo's philosophy and its relevance to the global age. While Richard Grego compares and contrasts Sri Aurobindo's ideas, particularly related to mind and consciousness, with the Western philosophy of mind and consciousness, Debashish Banerji juxtaposes Sri Aurobindo's philosophy with Enlightenment and post-Enlightenment philosophy. Kundan Singh examines the contested Aryan invasion theory in the light of Sri Aurobindo, whereas Hartz adopts a broader approach and makes a case for reevaluation of Sri Aurobindo's philosophy and its relevance to addressing the maladies of our global age.

Grego in his chapter, "Mapping Sri Aurobindo's Metaphysics of Consciousness onto Western Philosophies of Mind," argues that though the Indian philosopher made original contributions to the philosophy of mind and consciousness, Western philosophers paid scant attention to these contributions. Although his ideas have a place in disciplines like comparative psychology, and his role as an original interpreter of Vedanta has gained acceptance, the Indian philosopher still has not gained due acceptance in the West. Grego seeks to address this gap. In his chapter titled "Sri Aurobindo, Enlightenment and the Bengal Renaissance: A Discourse on Evolution of Consciousness," Banerji examines Renaissance and Enlightenment and their aftermaths, and how they shaped the nationalist movement in India. He focuses on Bengal national movement, and some of its prime movers and inspirers, including Sri Aurobindo. He examines the fusion between the Western ideas with the Indian ideas in shaping the Bengal nationalist movement. He examines Sri Aurobindo's contribution to post-Enlightenment modernity and reflects on how "his critique illuminates some of the fundamental problems and phenomena of our times and moves towards possible solutions."

Singh in his chapter, "Sri Aurobindo's Invalidation of the Aryan Invasion Theory and the Contemporary Western Archeological Evidence," examines Aryan Invasion Theory and Sri Aurobindo's refutations of this theory. He focuses on the recent archeological research to argue that findings do not support these invasion theories. These theories, he argues, had certain motives like expansion and consolidation of colonial rule, to undermine the cultures and philosophies of the East. Richard Hartz in his chapter "A Philosophy for the Global Age" argues that though globalization as a concept has found a place in the academic lexicon recently, Sri Aurobindo anticipated the rise of the forces of globalization long ago. He argues that Sri Aurobindo's philosophy is not just a system of metaphysics, nor is it confined to Indian thought and traditions. His writings were addressed to the world and, hence, could be termed an attempt toward evolving philosophy for the global age.

Part Two titled "Yoga and Metaphysics" deals with Sri Aurobindo's yoga and metaphysics and their contemporary relevance. Marshall Govindan examines the concept of psychic being in Sri Aurobindo's philosophy and finds similar ideas in other Indian traditions. V. Ananda Reddy explores Sri Aurobindo's metaphysics and argues that there is a linkage between Sri Aurobindo's yoga and metaphysics, the former shaping the latter. This yoga, which can be termed an evolutionary enterprise, is not crude asceticism or for individual salvation because it calls for the transformation of the whole human nature and society. Martha Orton explores the idea of inherent oneness in Sri Aurobindo's philosophy.

Govindan in his chapter, "The Psychic Being: Our Opening to the Divine," emphasizes a truer understanding of the term psychic being in order to understand the authentic import of Sri Aurobindo's yoga and philosophy. He also examines the steps in this yoga, and how by following these steps, one can progress and bring psychic being to the forefront of action. Reddy in his chapter "The Metaphysical Foundations of Sri Aurobindo's Vision of the Future of Humanity" explores, as the chapter title suggests, the metaphysical foundations of Sri Aurobindo's philosophy. He explores how Sri Aurobindo, who started as a poet and a politician, could make original contributions to philosophy owing to his yogic experiences. Reddy emphasizes that irrespective of controversies about Sri Aurobindo's philosophy, his writings and ideas to address the evolutionary crisis that human society confronts are relevant. Orton in her chapter "The Power of Inherent Oneness" elaborates how the Indian philosopher explains the Oneness of All and writes from this realization. Oneness or unity of all forms is a central element of Sri Aurobindo's philosophy. He elaborated his vision in his writings such as *The Life Divine*, *The Synthesis of Yoga*, and in his letters to his disciples. For Sri Aurobindo, the goal is not just the liberation of the individual from the world's misery but a fundamental realization and transformation of the individual being in the light of divine consciousness. This realization can culminate in the realization of Sachchidananda, the higher divine in the form of truth-consciousness-bliss. Such an upward journey and realization of Oneness can be helpful in addressing conflicts and apparent divisions in human society, argues Orton.

Part Three is titled "Poetry, Ethics, and Education." The chapters in this part, though cover different themes, are woven around the integral philosophy of Sri Aurobindo. Goutam Ghosal in his chapter, "Poetry at the Center of Human Knowledge," focuses on the poetry of Sri Aurobindo and how his poetry is an "exploration of the soul." He argues that, for Sri Aurobindo, poetry ignites spiritual fire in the seeker, and guides him in his inner adventure, which has also a connection with the outer world. In Sri Aurobindo's scheme of integral yoga, the inner and the outer do not cancel each out but complement each other in the evolutionary process. The author makes a case that Sri Aurobindo's spiritual poetry not only draws "a new map for the future" but also offers solutions to the problems of the world. Anurag Banerjee's chapter, "Ethics and Human Evolution: A Perspective from Sri Aurobindo," elaborates Sri Aurobindo's ideas on ethics. Banerjee argues that Sri Aurobindo's writings on ethics have not received due attention. For Sri Aurobindo, ethics is a "sort of machinery for right action," in which the emphasis is on action. The focus on right or wrong of an action does not necessarily take a deeper view of the action. Ethics may not be an effective tool to judge higher consciousness and its action. Partho's chapter, "Integral Education: The Imperative for the Contemporary World," explores the concept of integral education and its various facets. True education, Partho argues, is not just training in professional skills, but also exploring one's hidden potentials without any conditions imposed. For this to happen, it is necessary to understand our old consciousness' mode of functioning, and its role in shaping individual and human society. An understanding of the operation of the human body and vital and mind would help us "build a better society by addressing the problems of the old and building new structures for the future." Some of the basic questions he addresses are: What would an integral education in today's world be? What would be its vision and its philosophy, its guiding principles? How would one practice it?

Part Four titled "Human Unity" draws upon Sri Aurobindo's ideas on human unity. While Sarani Ghosal Mondal adopts a poetic approach to the subject, comparing and contrasting Sri Aurobindo's ideas with select Western poets, I take an organizational approach and cast Sri Aurobindo's ideas on human unity into a broader international political spectrum. In her chapter, "Cosmic Consciousness: The Metaphor of Human Unity in Sri Aurobindo's Writings," Mondal primarily focuses on the poetry of Sri Aurobindo and examines how human unity forms a strong part of his ideas and visions. She examines how the ideas of freedom, equality, and brotherhood, what Sri Aurobindo calls supreme social trinity or three godheads of the soul, cannot be adequately realized through external machinery of force and pressure, but only through the application of soul-force, the force that actually does not use military force, but rather the inner force of the divine. She further explores the image of cosmic consciousness in Sri Aurobindo's writings and various phases in the development of this concept in his writings, and its significance to the realization of true human unity and harmony. In the chapter "Sri Aurobindo's Ideal of Human Unity and the Discourse on International Organizations and Global Governance," I focus on the relevance of Sri Aurobindo's ideas for the harmonious organization of international bodies, particularly the UN. Although global governance as an academic concept is nascent, it has long been a concern for states, and Sri Aurobindo in his writings, particularly in his book *The Ideal of Human Unity*, aptly focused on international organizations, and prospects of unity among states through a possible world federation. He examined the roles of international bodies such as the League of Nations and the UN and argued that though they were established to address international problems, they were not as effective as desired. They were more governed by ego, national-ego, which led to the clash of national interests.

Part Five titled "Vision of India" examines Sri Aurobindo's vision of India and its contemporary relevance. While Aryadeep S. Acharya concentrates on *Auroville*, a global township in India built on Sri Aurobindo's vision, Michel Danino addresses some of the problems afflicting India in the light of Sri Aurobindo. Acharya in his chapter, "The Force behind the Indian Renaissance and the Crucial Significance of Auroville's Emergence," focuses on Auroville Universal Township in India as a manifestation of the vision of Sri Aurobindo. He examines the factors that shaped the life and work of Sri Aurobindo and explores how Auroville constitutes a visible, material, social climax of their lifelong experiments. He expresses optimism that Auroville can pave the way for India's renaissance with an impact on world civilization. In his chapter "Sri Aurobindo's Vision of India's Rebirth," Danino focuses on Sri Aurobindo's vision of India by extensively drawing on the Indian philosopher's writings in early decades of the twentieth century. In the course of numerous speeches, articles, talks, and writings, Danino argues, Sri Aurobindo laid out a program for India to "rejuvenate the mighty outworn body of the ancient Mother." Is his vision merely idealistic or mystic? Or does it offer solutions to the "numerous and difficult problems that face this country or will very soon face it"? He explores answers to these questions in the light of Sri Aurobindo.

Notes

1 The Complete Works of Sri Aurobindo are compiled over a period of time. In the in-text reference, the publication year of the work is given.
2 It would be necessary to emphasize here that Sri Aurobindo's concept of spirit is different from the Western philosophical concept of spirit. For example, in the case of Hegel, who used the concepts like spirit, mind, real, rational, almost interchangeably, spirit is rational and it moves in a dialectic fashion. He famously asserted, "real is rational and rational is real." In the case of Sri Aurobindo, spirit is a divine spark, a divine element, in every unit including the human individual, of the universe; though evolution of the spirit varies in degrees in these myriad units. For a comparative perspective of the philosophies of Sri Aurobindo and Hegel, see Mahapatra (2007) and Maitra (1968).
3 Sri Aurobindo argues in his *The Synthesis of Yoga*, "Fullness, clear purity and gladness, equality, capacity for possession and enjoyment (purnata, prasannata, samata, bhoga-samarthya) are the fourfold perfection of the psychic prana" (CWSA 1999, vols. 23 and 24, 735).
4 On the eve of India's independence, Sri Aurobindo had sent a message to be read out by All India Radio, Tiruchirappalli (in the Indian state of Tamil Nadu). In his message, he had elaborated his five dreams. It is available at http://www.sriaurobindosaction.org/Dreams.htm (Accessed June 30, 2017).
5 According to Ayer, "For we shall maintain that no statement which refers to a 'reality' transcending the limits of all possible sense experience can possibly have any literal significance; from which it must follow that the labours of those who have striven to describe such a reality have all been devoted to the production of nonsense" (Ayer 1990, 14).
6 In the same chapter he defines and elaborates the concept of sense mind, "In a sense all our experience is psychological since even what we receive by the senses, has no

meaning or value to us till it is translated into the terms of the sense-mind, the Manas of Indian philosophical terminology. Manas, say our philosophers, is the sixth sense. But we may even say that it is the only sense and that the others, vision, hearing, touch, smell, taste are merely specialisations of the sense-mind which, although it normally uses the sense-organs for the basis of its experience, yet exceeds them and is capable of a direct experience proper to its own inherent action" (CWSA 2005, vols. 21 and 22, 68).

7   Sri Aurobindo further agued, "these (granting privileged positions to the victorious powers) were concessions to a sense of realism and the necessity of recognising the actual condition of things and the results of the second great war and could not perhaps have been avoided, but they have done more to create trouble, hamper the action and diminish the success of the new institution than anything else in its make-up or the way of action forced upon it by the world situation or the difficulties of a combined working inherent in its very structure" (CWSA 1997, vol. 25, 582–583).

References

Ayer, A. J. 1990. *Language, Truth and Logic*. London: Penguin Books.

The Complete Works of Sri Aurobindo (CWSA). Multiple Years, mentioned in the text. Pondicherry: Sri Aurobindo Ashram. They are available at https://www.sriaurobindoashram.org/sriaurobindo/writings.php

Guyer, Paul and Wood, A. W. 1998. "Introduction." In Kant, Immanuel. Guyer, Paul and Wood, A. W., eds. Critique of Pure Reason. Cambridge: Cambridge University Press, 1–73.

Mahapatra, D. A. 2007. "Political Philosophy of Hegel and Sri Aurobindo: A Comparison." *Indian Journal of Political Science* 68, 3: 483–496.

Maitra, S. K. 1968. *The Meeting of the East and the West in Sri Aurobindo's Philosophy*. Pondicherry: Sri Aurobindo Ashram.

Maslow, A. H. 1943. "A Theory of Human Motivation." *Psychological Review* 50: 370–396.

McDermott, Robert. 1987. "Introduction: Vision of a Transformed World." In McDermott, Robert, ed. The Essential Aurobindo. Great Barrington, MA: Lindisfarne Press, 13–38.

Orton, Martha S. G. 2008. *The Quest for Knowledge and Mastery: A Comparative Study of Motivation in the Light of Sri Aurobindo*. Pondicherry: SACAR Trust.

Parsons, W. B. 1999. *The Enigma of the Oceanic Feeling: Revisioning the Psychoanalytic Theory of Mysticism*. New York: Oxford University Press.

Part One

Philosophy, History, and the Global Age

1

Mapping Sri Aurobindo's Metaphysics of Consciousness onto Western Philosophies of Mind

Richard Grego

As a political activist, poet, mystic, religious visionary, and interpreter of Hindu philosophy, Sri Aurobindo is widely recognized by Western scholars as a preeminent voice in the twentieth-century neo-Vedanta movement. Brainard Prince (2017) has noted that, among his neo-Vedanta colleagues and contemporaries like Tagore, Radhakrishnan, and Gandhi, Sri Aurobindo is the only one who was raised entirely in the West and educated almost exclusively in the Western classics during his formative years. Although known primarily as an interpreter of the Advaita Vedanta tradition, Sri Aurobindo was also a global thinker whose ideas encompassed the entire breadth of human aspiration and thought. Though often sporadic (with the exception of some more detailed comparative studies involving classical Western metaphysics, cosmology, and philosophy of mind, as in *Heraclitus*, 1968), there are significant references to Western philosophy, psychology, and theology throughout his work.

Nonetheless, Sri Aurobindo's thought has received relatively little attention from Western philosophers—particularly from Western philosophers of mind and consciousness. Although he is one of Advaita Vedanta's most prominent interlocutors for the field of consciousness studies in the West, and his ideas have garnered much consideration in disciplines like comparative psychology (Dalal 1989, 1992 and Miovic 2004, for example), his thought remains largely unexamined in Western philosophy of mind. This chapter therefore attempts to map Sri Aurobindo's conception of consciousness onto the general schema and legacy of Western philosophies of mind. While the scope of such a survey is necessarily broad and—in the space provided here—somewhat cursory, using it as a kind of conceptual yardstick against which to measure the depth and breadth of Sri Aurobindo's ideas can still be helpful in important ways. First, it helps to situate Sri Aurobindo's conceptualization of mind and consciousness within the context of the Advaita Vedanta tradition generally. Second, it provides some valuable critical insight into the nature and history of Western philosophy of mind from a comparative cross-cultural perspective. Third, it illustrates how Western metaphysics and philosophies of mind might benefit from comparison with the interpretation of Advaita Vedanta that informs Sri Aurobindo's thinking.

This chapter contends that, because they are underwritten by a physicalist ontology and scientific bias, many of the most prominent contemporary Western theories of mind appear relatively superficial and simplistic when measured against Sri Aurobindo's conceptual framework. Advocates of these Western theories might argue that this is because Sri Aurobindo makes untenable claims about the nature of conscious. However, such arguments are themselves untenable because they are predicated on reductive and unfounded views about the nature of mind, metaphysics, and knowledge. In fact, Sri Aurobindo's conception of conscious is at least as epistemically coherent and metaphysically legitimate as any Western theory, and Western philosophy might therefore benefit from a serious examination of Sri Aurobindo's Advaita Vedanta–based hierarchy of consciousness, which provides an inclusive paradigm within which to understand Western conceptions of consciousness in a more expansive way.

The Advaitic Context of Consciousness in Sri Aurobindo's Integral Philosophy

In order to appreciate these comparisons however, it is necessary to first situate Sri Aurobindo's concept of consciousness within the context of the Advaita Vedanta metaphysical tradition that informs it. Again, although the range of Sri Aurobindo's thought is holistic and encompasses ideas from a wealth of Hindu philosophies, including the Visistadvaita, Sankya-Yoga, Tantra, and Vaisnava traditions, his metaphysics and philosophy of mind are perhaps best understood within the general parameters of an Advaita Vedanta framework—albeit as an innovation on this legacy. Ram-Prasad (2013, 220) explains:

> Advaita Vedanta holds that consciousness can be understood in three ways.... There is 'Brahman', which is.... consciousness as the universal and singular basis for all reality and from which reality is no different. Then there is 'Atman', which is the general name for Brahman in consciousness as the ground of every individuated being. Finally, there is the 'jiva', which, through ego, is the empirical consciousness of every individuated being.

The sustaining ground (as well as the transcendent telos) of Sri Aurobindo's worldview is the all-encompassing and all-pervasive Brahman as conceived by Advaita Vedanta. Often simply described by Sri Aurobindo in experiential terms as "satchitananda" (the Vedanta term for "Being-Consciousness-Bliss" which denotes the experience of Brahman and Atman), or sometimes in more abstract terms like "the Absolute," Brahman is the

> source of all determinations: its indeterminability is the natural, the necessary condition both of its infinity of being and its infinity of power of being; it can be infinitely all things because it is nothing in particular and exceeds any definable

totality. It is this essential indeterminability of the Absolute that translates itself into our consciousness through the fundamental negating positives of our spiritual experience.

(Sri Aurobindo 2005, 331)

The reference made to consciousness here is significant because for Sri Aurobindo, Brahman (or satchitananda or the Absolute) is the all-encompassing creative source and sustaining ground of existence, and manifests all existence through consciousness. In his definitive study of consciousness in the Advaita tradition, Timalsina also describes Brahman in terms of conscious awareness, saying "Pure Consciousness, identified as Brahman, is understood as the true nature of immediately experienced awareness itself" (2009, xvi), although Brahman, while encompassing and transcending all possibility and impossibility, is ultimately beyond any description. Nonetheless, consciousness in the sense described by Timalsina is perhaps the most authentic description possible for Brahman insofar as it can ever be comprehensible. Atman, which is Brahman expressed via human consciousness, is described further by Elliot Deustche as "that pure, undifferentiated, self-shining consciousness, timeless, spaceless and unthinkable, that is not different from Brahman and that underlies the individual human person" (1969, 48). "Jiva consciousness" is Brahman and Atman expressed through human cognition as a self-aware ego wherein, in Puligandla's words, "the individual empirical self, is Atman seen in ignorance" (1969, 244), while "Maya," or the entire universe of Brahman's diverse forms, is aptly depicted by Radhakrishnan as "Brahman seen in ignorance" (1969, 155).

For Sri Aurobindo, each of these states represents a stage in the progressive "involution" of Brahman as it projects itself through lower levels of consciousness, which are dimensions of its own devolving self-forgetfulness as it diverges into its multifarious forms. Brahman, which exists as a state of pure potentiality and awareness, expresses its potentials via consciousness in the forms of Atman, Jiva, and Maya. This process creates the variety of forms which are finite aspects of Brahman and then generates the illusion that these forms are separate from one another and their creative source. Ignorance (avidya) and suffering (dukka) are a consequence of Brahman's finite forms—including individual minds—identifying or being identified with this illusion and not realizing fully what they are. The entire panorama of existence then is the cosmic play of Brahman (lila) in the form of Maya—the creative self-forgetfulness of Infinite Brahman, expressed in and through the multifarious variety of its own finite forms. However this same process, being a self-generated creation of Brahman, invariably also leads back to its creative source. The means by which Brahman has forgotten itself via its forms (lila) is also the means by which it recalls itself. Since all is Brahman, the same cosmic play leading Maya away from Brahman also leads it back to Brahman—or, more accurately, brings about the realization that nothing was or could be separate from Brahman to begin with. This process of "involution" from Brahman to its many forms, and "evolution" from these forms back to Brahman, is the movement of cosmic destiny which is Brahman itself. It involves and evolves through the medium of consciousness, which is not only the substratum of existence in general but also the foundation of human experience and mind.

Thus, human consciousness is an expression of the larger universal consciousness from which it emanates, so its capacity for self-realization and identification with the universe is essentially limitless. Sri Aurobindo's ontological categories of mental development reflect this limitless capacity. He identifies stages of conscious existence whereby human conscious is conceived as both originating from Brahman and returning to this ultimate source and sustenance of its own being. "Supermind" is that level of conscious being which represents Brahman in its most clear and authentic form. It is the closest to Brahman that consciousness, still retaining any sense of differentiation from its source, can be: "Supermind is the vast self-extension of the Brahman that contains and develops. By the Idea it develops the triune principle of existence, consciousness, and bliss out of their indivisible unity. It differentiates them, but it does not divide" (Sri Aurobindo 2005, 137). This level of consciousness knows and experiences existence entirely, from the vantage point of Brahman. The "Overmind" is a step down, so to speak, from Supermind. In this state, consciousness fully understands and experiences its deep connection to Brahman in all its forms, but remains limited to understanding itself AS one of these forms. Sri Aurobindo (2005, 985) explains:

> Thought, for the most part, no longer seems to originate individually in the in the body or the person but manifests itself from above.... All inner individual sight or intelligence of things is now a revelation or illumination of what is seen or comprehended, but the source of revelation is in one's separate self and in universal knowledge.

S.K. Maitra, commenting on Sri Aurobindo's hierarchy of consciousness, describes Overmind as the link between Supermind and lower manifestations of mental experience. "Where the mind sees irreconcilable differences," he writes, "the Overmind intelligence perceives coexistent correlatives" (1965, 28). Beneath these more expansive levels of consciousness are lesser, but still enlightened, dimensions of mind which are more familiar to most people—although at higher levels and still rarely experienced. "Intuition," for instance, is a state of mind just below Overmind in which flashes of insight establish connections between the individual Jiva's personal awareness and the transpersonal awareness of Atman. This, says Sri Aurobindo (2005, 981), is

> when the consciousness of the subject meets with the consciousness of the object, penetrates it and sees, feels or vibrates with the truth of what it contacts.... Or when consciousness.... Looks into itself and feels directly and intimately the truth or truths that are there or so contacts the hidden forces that are behind appearances.... Or again, when consciousness meets the Supreme Reality or the spiritual reality of things and has a contractual union with it.

These higher or more expansive potentials of conscious life are necessarily extra-rational, since this mode of insight is necessary for the experience of undifferentiated levels of awareness. "Illumined Mind," just below "intuition," is the stage at which this kind of extra-rational, intersubjective insight becomes possible. At this stage, the Jiva's conscious awareness, which was previously delimited by its localized epistemic vantage point, becomes capable of intuitively, empathetically experiencing reality from other vantage points. This marks an important step in the growth of awareness toward the state of Supermind and Brahman's self-realization. Similarly, the state of "Higher Mind," just beneath "Illumined Mind," also facilitates this expansion of more localized and diminished forms of conscious existence to more expansive ones. In the state of Higher Mind, Jiva consciousness, though lacking the intuitive capabilities of Illumined Mind, begins to become aware of other possible modes of experience and of the legitimacy of conscious perspectives beyond its own localized and restrictively rational one (Sri Aurobindo 2005, 971–985).

Finally, the lowest levels of consciousness from rudimentary "Mind," which is limited to rational-analytical modes of comprehension and consequently to a piecemeal and fragmented perception of reality which sees the world as a mere collection of separate entities, to "life," which is simplistically sentient and perceives only discreet physical objects in the world, to "Matter," which consists of semi or pre-conscious entities, are all mental states that range from the most fundamentally aware to the essentially unconscious. They are also, however, the states of consciousness that most people are restricted to for most or all of their lives. Sri Aurobindo states that the "Mind is an instrument of analysis and synthesis, but not of essential knowledge. Its function is...measurement or delimitation of the whole, and again to analyze the whole into its parts, which it regards as separate objects" (Sri Aurobindo 2005, 135). And as limited in its purview as Mind is, its lower manifestations in "Life" and "Matter" are even more narrowly limited to the most rudimentary forms of sentience—or to complete unconsciousness.

The precipitous descent of consciousness from Brahman and Supermind to Maya and Matter in the creative play of lila through involution is only half of Brahman's cosmic self-expression, however. Just as important—and with respect to the human condition, perhaps more important—is its progressive ascent from Matter back to Supermind through evolution. This movement represents the recovery of Brahman's complete self-awareness and the full development of human potential. Just as Brahman's infinite potentialities drive it toward expression in its finite forms, the potentiality that inspires this creation invariably leads these forms back to their formless infinite source. The laws of physics and probability inherent in Matter organize it in ways that lead to Life and Mind. The rational capacities of Mind raise the prospect of other minds and alternate worldviews, which invite the realization of Higher Mind, and Higher Mind's deepening awareness of these views evokes their intuitive apprehension by Illumined Mind. The ability to empathize with other perspectives in the state of Illumined Mind necessitates the cultivation of Intuition. And the capacity for intersubjective intuition leads to the realization of Overmind and Supermind, through which Brahman is revealed and in which it is expressed.

Advaita Vedanta Consciousness, Dualism, Idealism, and Physicalism

The numinous tenor and vaulting spirituality of Sri Aurobindo's Advaita Vedanta would therefore seem to present a very stark contrast to the general trend of contemporary

Western metaphysics and philosophy of mind. The scientific, rationalistic, instrumentalist assumptions that underwrite late modern and current Western naturalism appear irreconcilable with the basic tenets of Sri Aurobindo's worldview. However, within the larger trajectory of Western cultural history, the kind of "monistic idealism" (unified, transcendent, and supra-physical reality), characteristic of Sri Aurobindo's philosophy, has often played a prominent role in shaping conceptions of mind and consciousness.

In fact, for most of Western cultural history (from the Classical era until the modern scientific revolution), this kind of idealism was predominant, and only relatively recently has reductive naturalism become the authoritative voice in philosophical discourse. If the history of Western philosophy, as Alfred North Whitehead famously commented, consists largely of footnotes to Plato, then it would stand to reason that Western philosophy of mind in the classical and medieval eras (in closer proximity to Plato's ideas) would, like his, tend to be more idealistically oriented than in modern times. Indeed, the Platonic and neo-Platonic worldviews—in which insensate material reality is an ontologically diminished incarnation of its more ontologically authentic, immaterial, and conscious source—recall the kind of idealism found in Sri Aurobindo's Advaita Vedanta. Sri Aurobindo describes both this similarity and its influence on his own thought in *Heraclitus* and elsewhere.

There is a well-established legacy of scholarship in comparative philosophy and religion on the similarities between south Asian and pre-modern European thought which suggests the possibility of direct cross-cultural influence. In *Eastern Religions and Western Thought*, for instance, Radhakrishnan examines the interchange between ancient Greek and Indian philosophers via Persian trade and conquest, and later via the direct medium of Alexander's empire and its successor kingdoms. Through this cross-cultural influence, a legacy of seminal thinkers from Pythagoras and Plato to Proclus and Plotinus held beliefs about the soul that reflect the kind of monism, idealism, trans-personalism, and extra-rational epistemology that Sri Aurobindo locates in Vedanta thought. In addition, Vedanta influences on Greek and Middle-Eastern religious and spiritual traditions like Orphism and Gnosticism, which then exerted a significant influence on Western religions from Zoroastrianism (and its successors like Manicheanism, Mithraism, Mandeanism, and Yazidism), to post-exile Judaism, Christianity (from the historical Jesus to St. Augustine), and Islam, are also evident in these same ways. Originating with the Orphic and Gnostic sources that inspired them, successive affirmations of monism and idealism in the "boundless" of Anaximander, "nature" for Pythagoras, "Being" for Parmenides, "the Good" of Plato, and "the One" of Plotinus established the historical foundation for a conception of God in Christian theology which was, like Brahman, the transcendent, immaterial, all-encompassing, author of reality. "Whether or not we accept the hypothesis of direct influence from India on Greece through the medium of Persia," Radhakrishnan (1941, 115–141) states, "a student of Orphic or Pythagorean thought cannot fail to see that the similarities between these and Indian religion are so close as to warrant regarding them as expressions of the same way of life." And citing the Upanishadic verse affirming the basic unity of existence, "the unity in all diversities...the self as the Universal soul," Bimal Krishna Matilal also claims that monism and idealism in "the thought of the Upanishads influenced not only Buddhism.... but also the Neo-Platonics, Christian mystics, and even Persian Sufis" (1994, 280). And, of course, there is a prominent legacy of neo-Platonic scholarship—in the work of thinkers from Emile Brehier (1958) to Roman Ciapalo (2002) and Paulos Gregorios (2002)—that acknowledges strong affinities between Vedanta philosophies and classical-medieval thought in the West.

However, with the onset of modernity in the West—inaugurating the scientific revolution, the Enlightenment, and the industrial revolution—came a new intellectual paradigm that radically reconfigured the classical and medieval worldview, along with its monistic/idealistic inclinations. The hegemony of rationalism in intellectual discourse, empirical-instrumentalist modes of inquiry, the "mechanized" depiction and "disenchantment" of the natural world, and the rise of secular learning, all engendered a need and desire for a new epistemic and ontological paradigm. Despite their pre-modern intellectual origins, modern Western philosophy and science repudiated the metaphysical assumptions that had sustained ancient-medieval cosmology. Erected on a new foundation of Newtonian-Galilean science, Cartesian metaphysics, and Hobbesian materialistic psychology, the Enlightenment paradigm essentially separated and excluded non-material consciousness from reality and, despite Descartes's mental/physical dualism (or perhaps because of it), made the possibility of any non-physical consciousness increasingly untenable. In his *History of the Concept of Mind*, MacDonald explains (2003, 356):

> In the first half of the seventeenth century, the Cartesian—Galilean understanding of the mathematical order of the natural world and the mechanical laws that govern change and motion would definitely overthrow the fundamental principles of a dynamic, spiritual nature. The model of a world-machine would supplant the model of a world-spirit....[which was] Channeled into side-roads, away from the main highway of European philosophical speculation about the nature and functions of the human soul and mind.

Indeed, it is no exaggeration to claim, along with Richard Rorty and Martin/Baressi, that what we in the West currently call "the mind" is an invention of seventeenth-century metaphysics (Rorty 1979; Martin/Baressi 2006). At the dawn of the Enlightenment, Descartes's "Cogito Ergo Sum" ("I think therefore, I am") laid the foundations for modern physics, psychology, and philosophical movements from logical positivism to behaviorism. By simply establishing the distinction between "thinking substance" and "extended or corporeal substance"—"It is certain that this I [that is to say my soul, by which I am what I am] is entirely and absolutely distinct from my body, and can exist without it" (Descartes 2006[1641], 416)—Cartesian dualism created a rift between the mental and the physical, and between the subject and the object, so complete that even its detractors have had to implicitly work through it in order to overcome it. By accepting that the respective Cartesian categories of "mental" (subjective, self-aware, first-person, and private) and "physical" (objective, non-conscious, third-person, and public) are radically distinct from one another and exhaust all possible states of existence, and then establishing physical science as the paradigmatic arbiter of competing knowledge-claims within the modern epistemic purview, Enlightenment thinkers laid the foundation for the hegemony of physicalism in contemporary philosophy of mind.

Thus, any assessment of current Western philosophies of mind in comparison with Sri Aurobindo's theory of consciousness should probably start with Cartesian Dualism—also known as "substance dualism." As described above, "mind-body dualism," or substance dualism, is the claim that there are two kinds of substances: mental and physical. Mental substance is the kind of conscious experience—consisting of thoughts, feelings, sensations, and self-awareness—that is found in human and animal minds. Physical substance is the kind of material that is measurable and describable in terms of the physical sciences. Though obviously connected in important ways to the physical world, consciousness is something completely different from the physical, and is not subject to physical laws. This concept of consciousness allows for the legitimacy of both the physical sciences and a non-physical self or soul, as well as concomitant mental dynamics like free will, moral responsibility, privacy, and immortality, which continue to exert a powerful influence on current institutions like law, government, and religion, even if contemporary Western philosophy has largely disowned Cartesian dualism (albeit with some notable exceptions: figures like Richard Swinburne 1997; E.J. Lowe 2000; and Alvin Plantinga 2011, for instance). This conception of mind and body is also the largely unacknowledged "folk-psychological" ontology of popular culture in the West—which assumes Cartesian mind-body distinctions in its art, media, pop-psychology, and common parlance.

Dualism of this kind (there are, technically, others, like non-reductive or "property dualism," as well as "epiphenomenalism" and "emergentism"—closely related to "physicalism" as defined below) has some significant similarities with Sri Aurobindo's Advaita Vedanta. Sri Aurobindo's philosophy certainly acknowledges both the mental and physical dimensions of existence as Western Cartesian dualism defines them. In fact, Sri Aurobindo's "Matter," "Life," and, perhaps, purely cognitive elements of "Mind" are roughly equivalent to the "body" of mind-body dualism, and have much the same characteristics. In both philosophies, these categories include what would generally be called material or "physical" and would be amenable to classification and measurement by the physical sciences. Similarly, Sri Aurobindo's levels of "Mind" through "Supermind," including and beyond the higher functions of "Mind," are analogous to the "mind" of mind-body dualism, whose qualities include most of what Sri Aurobindo considers higher dimensions of conscious experience.

However, mind-body dualism also differs in even more fundamental ways with Sri Aurobindo's theory. Dualism of any kind, which suggests that reality is in any way ultimately divided rather than one, cannot be reconciled with Advaita Vedanta from Sankara to Sri Aurobindo—whose very name ("Advaita") means "non-dual," and whose conception of Brahman precludes the possibility of assigning radically distinct metaphysical categories to either minds or bodies. Moreover, any dualism that entails the exclusion of consciousness from the physical world or the physical body from the human mind fails to recognize, in Sri Aurobindo's view, the integral conjunction of both in human experience. Sri Aurobindo often referred to his philosophy as "Purna Advaita Vedanta" ("integral nondual Vedanta"), reflecting its essential holism. The differentiated categories of "mental" and "physical," Sri Aurobindo contends, are intellectually and practically useful terms, but only as "sub-headings" of a single, larger reality. Brahman encompasses but transcends both. Disembodied minds and mindless substances can be conceived as abstract, partial concepts about the nature of reality, but do not correspond to the complete, vital experience of reality in its most authentic form. Mind-body dualism is therefore a stage in the conceptualization of human life and consciousness that more holistic conceptions are destined to eclipse.

Like Sri Aurobindo, current Western philosophy of mind has largely rejected Mind-Body dualism, albeit for much different reasons. After establishing these two Cartesian categories, it essentially diverged into two separate paths and—mediated by developments in the physical, behavioral, and social sciences—this separation still dominates contemporary Western conceptions of consciousness and the physical world. From Cartesian dualism, philosophy of mind seems to go pretty much in either one of the two diametrically opposed ways: Idealism or Neutral Monism on one hand, or varieties of physicalism-scientism on the other (including some quasi-dualist/quasi-physicalist schools of thought like "extended cognition," varieties of "panpsychism," integrated information theory, and hylomorphism, which are relatively recent and not yet widely established). However, the pervasive intellectual influence and authority of the physical sciences in recent Western cultural history have established physicalism's overwhelming predominance in current philosophy of mind and consciousness studies.

There have, of course, been significant undercurrents of dissent from the physicalist-scientific paradigm during the modern era. "Idealism," defined by Stephan Priest as the theory that "Only mind exists" and that "unless there were minds, so-called physical objects could not exist" (1991, 65), has exerted a persistent influence in Western culture since the scientific revolution—albeit as a minority report. It is also the Western theory closest to Sri Aurobindo's in tone and substance. Nineteenth-century romanticism and varieties of twentieth-century post-structuralism in literature and the arts, vitalism and panpsychism in biology, humanism and Jungian psychoanalysis in psychology, phenomenology and existentialism in the social sciences and philosophy, and varieties of nationalism, anarchism, socialism, and environmentalism in many social-political movements, all emerged in opposition to the hegemony of the scientific-physicalist Enlightenment paradigm, and were sympathetic to the idealist ethos. For this reason, various schools of nineteenth-century idealism have much in common with Advaita Vedanta's general tenets. German idealism from Fichte, Schelling, and Hegel to Schopenhauer, British idealism via Berkley/Bradley, and American philosophies from Emerson's transcendentalism through Royce's pragmatism, all at least to some extent share Advaita Vedanta's vision of a transcendent and unified ground of existence, its elimination of subject-object dualism, and its conception of consciousness as the source of this metaphysical unity. Many of these thinkers openly acknowledged the influence of Advaita Vedanta metaphysics on their own: Schopenhauer's concept of "will" and Emerson's "oversoul" being two prominent examples of Advaita Vedanta–inspired conceptions of a unified conscious intelligence encompassing the diversity of material reality (Riepe 1969; Cross 2013). The Idealism of Fichte and Schelling—inspired by Kant and anticipating Hegel—are described by Martin and Baressi (2006, 186) in terms that clearly recall Sankara and Sri Aurobindo:

God is everything and undivided. The world, which is illusory and merely appears to consist of separate objects, is produced by God's thought.... human knowledge is thus a distorted picture of infinite, undivided, and pure activity. The point of human life.... is to see through the distortions and realize complete spiritual freedom.

Hegel is perhaps the prominent exemplar of modern Idealism in the West, and his theory of mind has probably been compared to Sri Aurobindo's more than any other modern thinker. In *The Phenomenology of Spirit* ([1807]1977) and *Philosophy of Mind* ([1830]1971), Hegel advanced a theory of consciousness and metaphysics that, for scholars of comparative philosophy, is closely analogous to that of Sri Aurobindo. Commentators like Ram Shankar Misra have noted parallels between Hegel's all-encompassing Absolute Spirit, seeking through the dialectical process to overcome its own self-alienation, and Sri Aurobindo's Brahman, attempting to overcome its self-forgetfulness through self-realization via cosmic evolution (1998). Others, like Steven Odin and V. P. Varma, have compared the holism of Hegel's worldview, in which the transcendent Absolute mind is inextricably immersed in the physical world through which it becomes manifest, with Sri Aurobindo's involution of formless Brahman in the forms of matter, mind, and spirit (Odin 1981; Varma 1955). Hegel also traces the stages of mental evolution from "perception" all the way up the consciousness continuum through a series of levels to its culmination as "absolute knowing" in a way that is much like Sri Aurobindo's concept of spiritual evolution from "Matter" to "Supermind."

However, significant differences remain between their respective concepts of consciousness and its role in shaping reality. Odin concludes, for instance, that while both thinkers conceive of the Absolute in dynamic, rather than static, terms, Hegel's "dialectic" is a more mechanistic and deterministic "deduced product of dialectical logic" than is Sri Aurobindo's more fluid and intuitive notion of "evolution." Brahman's anti-foundationalist ontological and epistemic status—transcending any category of predication—also differentiates it from the rational intelligibility of Hegel's Absolute Spirit as "a totalistic system of dialectical reason" (Odin 1981, 179–180).

An even better conceptual fit between Sri Aurobindo and Western modes of consciousness in this regard might involve a more recent umbrella theory that has earned the term "Neutral Monism." Similar in many respects to idealism, and traceable to philosophers like Spinoza ([1676]1977), William James ([1904] 1977), and Bertrand Russell ([1921]1970) (and possibly supported by the kind of quasi-idealistic-mentalistic extrapolations from quantum physics in the work of contemporary scientists like Roger Penrose, Stuart Hameroff, Henry Stapp, and Donald Hoffmann, which unfortunately cannot be examined in the space provided here), the various theories that fall into the category "neutral monism" maintain that both physical reality and personal, localized consciousness derive from some transcendent, single, ultimate source that is not itself reducible to either subjectively "mental" or objectively "physical" terms. This source in some ways seems analogous to Vedanta's "Brahman." Unfortunately, however, it is usually interpreted in terms that tend to be functional rather than substantive in nature and has therefore been somewhat vaguely defined by its advocates.

Spinoza's pantheistic conception of "God" as the basic substrate of existence seems too coextensive with physical nature to align well with Sri Aurobindo's Brahman. William James's idea of "pure experience" as fundamental reality tends to sound rather mentalistic, despite his desire to repudiate simplistic subjective mentalism. Russell's concept of foundational "sensibilia" underlying both mental and physical sense-data is even more vaguely defined and sounds vaguely physical, although he wanted to refute simplistic physicalism. Thus, as Jawarski observes, "the repeated failures of neutral monists to provide informative descriptions of neutral entities gives us some reason to doubt that neutral entities really exist" (2011, 262), and neutral monism therefore lacks both the firmly idealistic inclinations and the kind of rigor and detail that Sri Aurobindo's hierarchy of consciousness provides.

Again, since the advent of the scientific revolution and the Enlightenment, "Materialism" or "Physicalism" has been by far the most prominent and influential theory of mind in the Western intellectual milieu, shaping the purview of philosophy, the social and behavioral sciences, the physical sciences, and popular culture. Papineau defines Physicalism as simply "the doctrine that everything, including prima facie non-physical stuff, is physical" (2000, 174). Jawarski (2011, 68) adds, "Physicalism claims that everything is physical; everything can exhaustively be described and explained by physics." Jawarski's definition is important because it establishes a necessary connection between physicalism and "Scientism" (the belief that everything that exists is, in principle, reducible to exhaustive description by the physical sciences). Indeed, the philosophical credibility of physicalism is derived directly from, and circumscribed by, the perceived intellectual authority of the physical sciences in Western culture.

For philosophy of mind, the important aspect of physicalism is that it denies the existence of any dimension of consciousness that is non-physical in this scientistic sense. In terms of Cartesian mind-body dualism, while Idealism wants to deny the reality of the body, physicalism wants to deny the reality of mind. There are many ways in which physicalists attempt to reduce the mental to the physical. "Eliminativism" is the theory that there simply is no such thing as consciousness, and is the basis for Patricia Churchland's well-known "neuro-philosophy," which reduces consciousness to neurologically explicable brain functions (similar, in a way, to psychological behaviorism, which reduces mental events to physical behavior) (2013). "Identity Theory" developed by thinkers like JJ Smart (1961) and David Armstrong (1993) amounts to much the same thing as eliminativism, claiming that every psychological event is explicable via a corresponding scientifically describable physical brain event. "Non-reductive physicalism" which, in various forms, is becoming increasingly popular claims that all events are physical, but can be legitimately described in pseudo-mentalistic ways for practical purposes and communication (Beckermann 2009, 172-195). "Epi-phenomenalism" claims that some form of mental substance—irreducible to physical substance—exists, but only as a byproduct of physical events in the brain (Walter 2009, 75-94).

While the current popularity of physicalism has inspired a great deal of subtle and nuanced variety in physicalist philosophies of mind, they all share a common incompatibility with Sri Aurobindo's theory of consciousness and its central place in his worldview. Sri Aurobindo certainly affirms the reality of both physics and the physical world. His concepts of Matter, Life, and aspects of Mind are, in large part, physical in the sense understood by contemporary physicalists. However, the notion that consciousness is somehow unreal, that it can be reduced to brain states, that the entire hierarchy of Higher Mind through Supermind can be collapsed into the physical operations of Matter and Life, or that Brahman is a meaningless concept, is diametrically opposed to everything he asserts.

Implications for Comparative Conceptions of Mind and Consciousness

Thus, even this relatively brief comparative survey highlights some important contrasts between Sri Aurobindo's theory of consciousness and Western philosophy of mind. There is a clear historical trajectory in Western philosophy from idealism to physicalism, which was never the case in the South Asian cultural legacy that engendered Sri Aurobindo's worldview. In Western philosophy of mind, the status of consciousness declined from its Platonic position as the transcendent source of reality in classical-medieval metaphysics, to becoming an inconsequential byproduct of brain-chemistry in contemporary neuro-science. The legacy of Western metaphysics can be conceived, in fact, as an inversion of the neo-Platonic paradigm: from mind—consciousness in the ancient world being the foundational source of a relatively less-real physical world, to the contemporary milieu in which the physical world is the foundational source of relatively less-real conscious experience. This Western physicalist ethos has since been transmitted to South Asian civilization via colonialism, and poses a stark contrast to the Vedanta worldview on which Sri Aurobindo's philosophy is predicated. Frazier remarks that "modern universities in Calcutta and Delhi.... would eventually give answers to cosmological questions with the language of modern physics rather than of Hindu philosophy.... This was one of the ways in which conquering Europe colonized the landscape of thought as well as the geographical terrain of the subcontinent" (2017, 187). Physicalism is, therefore, also a culturally imperialistic ideology that presents the most salient and forceful contemporary cultural-intellectual challenge to Sri Aurobindo's metaphysics and philosophy of integral consciousness. Stephen Phillips (2013) emphasizes this in his assessment of Sri Aurobindo's moral psychology:

> Regarding the truth of Aurobindo's worldview, my sense is that his advocacy of a mystic life would be well-founded only if his neo-Vedantic metaphysics is at least roughly right.... Contemporary psychology is dominated by a materialist paradigm. The inwardness of Yoga as well as its power for health and happiness are perhaps rallying points for the anti-materialist... clearly a metaphysics centered on consciousness will be at odds with all the prominent versions of scientific materialism. One should read Aurobindo against this backdrop of 'paradigm conflict'. So let us end with the remark that, if materialism is right, Aurobindo is wrong, and conversely.

In his survey of comparative Western-Asian psychology, Miovic (2004, 51) also states:

> Western science currently eschews such Aurobindo's teleological thinking and views the increasing neural complexity seen in the evolutionary tree as merely an epiphenomenon of random genetic mutation and selective pressure. Aurobindo notes, however, that this Western interpretation of the data rests upon the unproven assumptions of materialism, which he questions.

In fact, from Sri Aurobindo's perspective, contemporary Western concepts of mind seem relatively superficial, reductive, and small in comparison with both pre-modern Western theories of consciousness and Sri Aurobindo's own interpretation of Advaita Vedanta's metaphysics. Western physicalism is superficial because it only addresses the most simplistic levels of conscious phenomena and experience (namely Matter, Life, and the physical-cognitive elements of Mind) while ignoring its deeper dimensions. Physicalism is reductive because it attempts to explain the deeper dimensions of consciousness (Highermind, Supermind, and Brahman) purely in terms of its more superficial dimensions, and then deny these deeper dimensions any substantive ontological status. Physicalism is small because the purview of conscious potentials that it encompasses is very limited—and this is also why so many psychologically and spiritually expansive transpersonal and extra-physical experiences are often dismissed or stigmatized as "delusional," "dissociative," or just "superstitious," by current Western psychology and neuroscience, which is circumscribed by physicalist assumptions.

Physicalists respond to Sri Aurobindo's views by stating that they are untenable and that thinkers like Sri Aurobindo are making unsupportable and unjustifiable claims. There is no evidential or empirical basis, they state, for positing entities or phenomena, like an immaterial or "super-natural" mind or Brahman, beyond physical reality as described by the physical sciences. There is no scientific evidence for the states of consciousness or reality that Sri Aurobindo describes, and making these claims without scientific proof—or at least strong evidence—to support them is intellectually irresponsible. Further, the kind of evidence that Sri Aurobindo does rely upon—such as testimonial reports, subjective experiences of those who have experienced these levels of consciousness, intuition, and Vedanta philosophy—is unfalsifiable, unverifiable, and unrepeatable through controlled scientific testing. There is also a substantial body of scientific evidence drawing direct correlations between physical brain events and mental states, indicating that the former occur prior to, and therefore directly cause, the latter (hence, the legacy of the famous Libet experiment and its successors, 2002, 551–564) and/or that mental states simply ARE nothing more than brain states. Moreover, it would be impossible for the kind of supra-physical dimensions of consciousness that Sri Aurobindo posits to affect the physical world, because such effects would violate foundational laws and principles of physical science like the law of conservation of energy, the principle of causal closure, the principle of Occam's razor, and the causal overdetermination of physical events (Pereboom 2002; Kim 2007; Dennett 2017).

However, Sri Aurobindo could respond that these physicalist objections are, themselves, predicated on assumptions which are incoherent and untenable: like scientism, scientific realism, and physicalism itself—none of which, because they are metaphysical rather than physical or scientific claims, can be established by the physical sciences. Scientism (which is the claim that all reality is reducible to what can be discovered and/or described by the physical sciences) cannot be proven via the physical sciences. Scientism is a metaphysical claim rather than a scientifically testable thesis about the physical world, and therefore contradicts itself. Scientific realism is the contention that scientific concepts correspond to an objectively theory-independent reality, but this contention is itself a theory not demonstrable in an objectively theory-independent way. It claims that the success of science establishes the veridicality of science but, in circular fashion, uses the scientific method and empirical observations as evidence of its own success. Physicalism defines physical reality as that which science describes, but it then defines science as that which describes physical reality, so the logic of physicalism is also inherently circular and question-begging. Further, criticisms of science's epistemic foundations—from Hume's skeptical critique of causality and induction ([1748] 2006) to Hemple's Dilemma (1980) and Larry Lauden's "pessimistic meta-induction" (1981)— cast considerable doubt on science's pretensions to a unique kind of objectivity, veridicality, and consistency in first place, let alone the ability of science to explain or explain-away a phenomenon as mysterious (at least from a scientific-physicalist vantage point) as consciousness. Thus, far from being an objectively established arbiter of epistemic veracity between the competing claims of physicalism and Advaita Vedanta, science is arguably just another "subjective" system of thought.

Further, standards for evidence in any thought system are arguably ALL subjective in this fundamental sense, as Western thinkers from Sextus Empiricus ([c.100BCE?] 2000) to Kurt Gödel (2005) have, in various ways, demonstrated. Every thought system—science included—is invariably predicated on assumptions that cannot be proven within the system that they justify, and there is no definitive method (as Thomas Kuhn famously argued in *The Structure of Scientific Revolutions*, 1962) for objectively determining the relative veracity of competing paradigms. Interestingly, Jonathan Edelmann (2012, 637) makes a similar observation in his *Hindu Theology and Biology*:

> There is a long tradition of Western philosophical literature about the 'theory-ladenness' of all perception—we construct reality by the theoretical framework that we have been educated into..... Hindu intellectual traditions have their own rigorous discussion of what constitutes a reliable instrument of knowledge (pramana).... their own epistemological standards and criteria, and it is these standards one might use in judging the sciences, rather than merely using scientific epistemological standards to judge Hinduism.

So within his own paradigm, Sri Aurobindo does offer sound evidence for his claims and unless, as physicalists contend, the only kind of evidence that we can accept as objectively valid is scientific evidence (which, as we have seen, is an illegitimate claim) then there is no reason to believe that Sri Aurobindo's evidence is somehow objectively invalid in comparison. Surely, Sri Aurobindo asserts, there are modes of testimonial evidence and "first-person" types of knowledge (like Intuition as he understands it) that yield insights regarding the nature of consciousness, and many of these are beyond the epistemic ability of Western science or physicalism to countenance. He writes:

> Materialism indeed insists that, whatever the extension of consciousness, it is a material phenomenon inseparable from our physical organs and not their utiliser but their result. This orthodox contention, however, is no longer able to hold the field against the tide of increasing knowledge. Its explanations are becoming more and more inadequate and strained. It is becoming always clearer that not only does the capacity of our total consciousness far exceed that of our organs, the senses, the nerves, the brain, but that even for our ordinary thought and consciousness these organs are only their habitual instruments and not their generators... Our physical organism no more causes or explains thought and consciousness than the construction of an engine causes or explains the motive-power of steam or electricity. The force is anterior, not the physical instrument. (Sri Aurobindo 2005, 970)

Also, as contemporary philosophers like Thomas Nagel (2012), Lawrence Bonjour (2010), and Richard Swinburne (1997, 2013) and scientists like Jeffrey Schwartz (2002), Mario Beauregard (2008), and Rupert Sheldrake (2012) have pointed out, the inability of either contemporary science or Western physicalist philosophies of mind to coherently explain the most fundamental and undeniable aspects of conscious experience such as qualia, intentionality, self-awareness, value creation, unity of comprehension, memory, rationality in physicalist terms, or to provide any feasible scientific theory for these phenomena, makes the claim by physicalist philosophers to provide a "better" paradigm than Sri Aurobindo very dubious. Indeed, there are no current neuro-scientific theories (or evidence to support such theories) to account for consciousness at all, and it appears entirely possible that such an account would be impossible even in principle. Further, there is ample empirical evidence from the cognitive and neuro-sciences, according to recent researchers like Edward Kelly and Donald Hoffmann, to indicate that a model of the mind-body relation like that proposed by Sri Aurobindo, in which the body and physical world function as a "transmitter" or a "user interface" for mental energy and information, rather than as its cause, is much more effective than physicalist ones. The "transmitter" model provides a much better explanation of mental phenomena, like memory, binding/conscious unity, intentionality, and, indeed, consciousness itself, than any physicalist model is capable of accommodating (Kelly 2007, 2015; Hoffmann, 2008). And of course, several well-known and widely accepted interpretations of the "measurement problem" in quantum physics suggest that consciousness is, in some essential sense, integral to manifesting the physical universe itself (Henry 2006).

Conclusion

David Chalmers (2000) has argued that Western philosophy is currently focused mainly on what he refers to as the "easy problems" of consciousness (those addressed by the physical sciences, physicalist philosophy of mind, and Sri Aurobindo's concepts of Matter, Life, and Mind), and that it has failed to confront what he refers to as the "hard problems" of consciousness (such as those addressed by Sri Aurobindo's concepts of Higher Mind-Supermind). Consequently, Chalmers claims, philosophy of mind and scientific cosmology need to begin exploring the reality of consciousness as a basic ontological element of existence. Sri Aurobindo says precisely this about the limitations of a physicalist conception of consciousness: "since the universality of Matter can no longer be held as giving any sufficient explanation of the existence of Mind, and indeed Matter itself can no longer be explained by Matter alone.... we are thrown back from this easy and obvious solution to other hypothesis" (2005, 743). Sri Aurobindo's Advaita Vedanta theory of integral consciousness therefore poses a challenge to Western philosophy of mind (whose historical trajectory from idealism to physicalism represents an "easy path" which only engages superficial levels of reality), and he urges Western philosophy, psychology, and science to begin exploring a "harder" but more rewarding venue that confronts the deeper capacities of human potentials and existence.

References

Annas, J., and Barnes, J. 2000. *Sextus Empiricus: Outlines of Scepticism*. Cambridge: Cambridge University Press.

Armstrong, D. M. 1993. *A Materialist Theory of the Mind*. New York: Routledge.

Beauregard, Mario. 2008. *The Spiritual Brain: A Neuroscientist's Case for the Existence of the Soul*. New York: HarperCollins.

Beckermann, Ansgar. 2009. "What Is Property of Physicalism?." In Beckermann, Ansgar, McLaughlin, Brian P. and Walter, Sven, eds. *Oxford Handbook for Philosophy of Mind*. Oxford: Clarendon Press, 152-172.

Brehier, Emile. 1958. *The Philosophy of Plotinus*. Chicago: Chicago University Press.

Bonjour, Lawrence. 2010. "Against Materialism." In Koons, R. ed. *The Waning of Materialism*. Oxford: Oxford University Press, 3-24.

Chalmers, David. 2000. "Facing Up to the Hard Problem of Consciousness." In Shearer, Jonathan ed. *Explaining Consciousness: The Hard Problem*. Cambridge: MIT Press, 9-31.

Churchland, Patricia. 1986. *Neurophilosophy*. Boston: MIT Press.

Ciapolo, Roman. 2002. "The Oriental Influence on Plotinus' Thought." In Gregorios, Paulos Mar ed. *Neo-Platonism and Indian Thought*. New York: SUNY Press, 71-82.

Cross, Stephan. 2013. *Schopenhauer's Encounter with Indian Thought: Representation and Will and Their Indian Parallels*. Honolulu: University of Hawaii Press.

Dalal, A. S. 1971. *The Philosophy of Mind*. Translated by William Wallace. Oxford: Oxford University Press.

Dalal, A. S. 1989. "Sri Aurobindo and Modern Psychology." *Journal of South Asian Literature* 24, 1: 154-167.

Dalal, A. S. 1992. *Psychology, Mental Health, and Yoga: Essays on Sri Aurobindo's Psychological Thought; Implications of Yoga for Mental Health*. Pondicherry: Sri Aurobindo Ashram Trust.
Dennett, Daniel. 2017. *From Bach to Bacteria and Back: The Evolution of Minds*. New York: W. W. Norton.
Descartes, Rene. 2001. *Meditations on First Philosophy*. New York: Pearson Longman.
Descartes, Rene. 2006. "Meditations on the First Philosophy." In Thomson, G. and Kolak, D. eds. *Longman Standard History of Philosophy*. New York: Routledge, 416.
Deutsche, Eliot. 1969. *Advaita Vedanta: A Philosophical Reconstruction*. Hawaii: Hawaii University Press.
Edelmann, Jonathan. 2012. "The Role of Hindu Theology in the Religion and Science Dialogue." *Zygon: Journal of Science and Religion* 40, 3: 624–642.
Frazier, Jessica. 2017. *Hindu Worldviews: Theories of Self, Ritual and Reality*. London: Bloomsbury.
Goldstein, Rebecca. 2005. *Incompleteness: The Proof and Paradox of Kurt Godel*. New York: W. W. Norton.
Gregorios, Paulos. 2002. "Does Geography Condition Philosophy? On Going beyond the Oriental-Occidental Distinction." In Gregorios, Paulos Mar ed. *Neo-Platonism and Indian Thought*. New York: SUNY Press, 13–30.
Guthrie, W. K. C. 1970. *The Sophists*. Cambridge: Cambridge University Press.
Hegel, F. W. 1977. *The Phenomenology of Spirit*. Translated by Arthor Miller. Oxford: Oxford University Press.
Hempel, Carl. 1980. "Comments on Goodman's *Ways of Worldmaking*." *Synthese* 45: 193–199.
Henry, Richard Conn. 2006. "The Mental Universe." *Nature* 436, 7: 29.
Hoffmann, Donald. 2008. "Conscious Realism and the Mind-Body Problem." *Mind and Matter* 6, 1: 87–121.
Hume, David. 2006. "An Enquiry Concerning Human Understanding" and "A Treatise on Human Nature." In Thomson, G. and Kolak, D. eds. *Longman Standard History of Philosophy*. New York: Routledge, 602–635.
James, William. 1977. *The Meaning of Truth*. Amherst: Prometheus Books.
Jaworski, William. 2011. *Philosophy of Mind*. Malden: Wiley-Blackwell.
Kelly, Edward. 2007. *Irreducible Mind: Toward a Psychology for the 21st Century*. New York: Rowman and Littlefield.
Kelly, Edward. 2015. *Beyond Physicalism: Toward Reconciliation of Science and Spirituality*. New York: Rowman and Littlefield.
Kim Jagwon. 2007. *Physicalism or Something Near Enough*. Princeton: Princeton University Press.
Kuhn, Thomas. 1962. *The Structure of Scientific Revolutions*. Chicago: Chicago University Press.
Laudan, Larry. 1981. "A Confutation of Convergent Realism," *Philosophy of Science* 48, 1: 19–49.
Libet, Benjamin. 2002. "Do We Have Free Will?" In Kane, Robert ed. *Oxford Handbook of Free Will*. Oxford: Oxford University Press, 551–564.
Lowe, E. J. 2000. *An Introduction to the Philosophy of Mind*. Cambridge: Cambridge University Press.
MacDonald, Paul. 2003. *History of the Concept of Mind*. London: Ashgate.
Maitra, S. K. 1965. *The Philosophy of Sri Aurobindo*. Pondicherry: Sri Aurobindo Ashram.
Martin, Raymond and Barresi, John. 2006. *Rise and Fall of Soul and Self: An Intellectual History of Personal Identity*. New York: Columbia University Press.

Matilal, Bimal Krishna. 1994. "The Perception of Self in Indian Tradition." In Ames, Roger ed. *Self as a Person in Asian Theory and Practice*. Albany: SUNY Press, 171–197.
Miovic, Michael. 2004. "An Introduction to Spiritual Psychology: Overview of the Literature, East and West." *Harvard Review of Psychiatry* 12: 105–115.
Misra, Ram Shankar. 1998. *Integral Advaitism of Sri Aurobindo*. New Delhi: Motilal Banarsidass.
Nagel, Thomas. 2012. *Mind and Cosmos: Why the Neo-Darwinian Conception of Nature Is Almost Certainly False*. Oxford: Oxford University Press.
Odin, Steven. 1981. "Sri Aurobindo and Hegel on the Involution-Evolution of Absolute Spirit." *Philosophy East and West* 31, 2: 179–191.
Papineau, David. 2000. "The Rise of Physicalism." In Wolff, Jonathan ed. *The Proper Ambition of Science*. London: Routledge, 174–208.
Pereboom, Derek. 2002. "Living without Free Will: The Case for Hard Incompatibilism." In Kane, Robert, ed. *The Oxford Handbook of Free Will*. Oxford: Oxford University Press, 477–488.
Phillips, Stephen. 2013. "Ethical Skepticism in the Philosophy of Sri Aurobindo." In Heehs, Peter ed. *Situating Sri Aurobindo*. Oxford: Oxford University Press, 3–20.
Plantinga, Alvin. 2011. *Where the Conflict Really Lies: Science, Religion, and Naturalism*. Oxford: Oxford University Press.
Priest, Stephan. 1991. *Theories of the Mind*. Boston: Houghton Mifflin Company.
Prince, Brainard. 2017. *The Integral Philosophy of Sri Aurobindo: Hermeneutics and the Study of Religion*. London: Routledge.
Puligandla, Ramakrishna. 2010. Indian *Philosophy*. New Delhi: Printworld.
Radhakrishnan, Sarvepalli. 1941. *Eastern Religions and Western Thought*. Cambridge: Cambridge University Press.
Radhakrishnan, Sarvepalli. 2008. *Basic Writings*. Mumbai: Jaico Publishing.
Ram-Prasad, Chakravarti. 2013. "Situating the Elusive Self of Advaita Vedanta." In Siderits, M., Thompson, E. and Zahavi, D., eds. *Self, No Self? Perspectives from Analytical, Phenomenological, and Indian Traditions*. Oxford: Oxford University Press, 217–238.
Riepe, Dale. 1969. "Emerson and Indian Thought." *Journal of the History of Ideas* 28, 1: 39–54.
Rorty, Richard. 1979. *Philosophy and the Mirror of Nature*. Princeton: Princeton University Press.
Russell, Bertrand. 1970. *An Outline of Philosophy*. London: Routledge.
Schwartz, Jeffrey, and Begley, Sharon. 2002. *Mind & The Brain: Neuroplasticity and the Power of Mental Force*. New York: Regan Books.
Sheldrake, Rupert. 2012. *Science Set Free*. New York: Deepak Chopra Books.
Smart, J. J. 1961. "Free Will, Praise and Blame." *Mind* 70, 279: 291–306.
Spinoza, Benedictus. 1977. *Ethics*. Translated by A. Boyle. London: Houghton Mifflin.
Sri Aurobindo. 1968. *Heraclitus*. Pondicherry: Sri Aurobindo Ashram.
Sri Aurobindo. 2005. *The Life Divine*. Pondicherry: Sri Aurobindo Ashram.
Swinburne, Richard. 1997. *The Evolution of the Soul*. Oxford: Oxford University Press.
Swinburne, Richard. 2013. *Mind, Brain, and Free Will*. Oxford: Oxford University Press.
Timalsina, Sthaneshwar. 2009. *Consciousness in Indian Philosophy: The Advaita Doctrine of 'Awareness Only'*. London: Routledge.
Varma, Vishwanath Prasad. 1955. "East and West in Aurobindo's Political Philosophy." *Philosophy East and West* 5, 3: 235–244.
Walter, Sven. 2009. "Epi-phenomenalism." In McLaughlin, Brian ed. *Oxford Companion to the Philosophy of Mind*. Oxford: Oxford University Press.

2

Sri Aurobindo, Enlightenment, and the Bengal Renaissance: A Discourse on Evolution of Consciousness

Debashish Banerji

The philosopher Martin Heidegger and others following in his wake have seen our age, the "modern age," as one which is characterized by a peculiarly technical mode of being with the post-Renaissance phenomenon of the Enlightenment as its founding event (Heidegger 1977). The Enlightenment can be seen as providing the idea-forces, leading to consequences in the life-world, that we know today as Modernity. In a consideration of Modernity, as it pertains to India, it is necessary to turn to the Enlightenment and isolate its master ideas in order to see how they have impacted our times and the responses they were met with in Calcutta, the earliest "modern" city of India from the nineteenth century, moving into the turn of the twentieth century. In particular, in this chapter, I will examine the contributions of Sri Aurobindo to an Indian response to post-Enlightenment modernity and how his critique illuminates some of the fundamental problems and phenomena of our times and moves toward possible solutions.

Enlightenment

In this transnational transaction of early modernity, its encounter with India, it may be useful to begin with the very ambiguous nature of the term "Enlightenment." A favorite Orientalist trope, which remains with us in our conversational reference, is the use of the term to describe the spiritual attainment of yoga—we speak for example of "the Buddha's Enlightenment" to translate a category in the philosophical and psychological history of India, Buddha's Nirvana.[1] In the intellectual history of the West, when we use the term Enlightenment, it also comes with vast hazy overtones and undertones. For one, it invokes a shift that we may think of as a revolution in the location of knowledge. It represents a turning from a transcendental orientation toward knowledge, in which it is accessible only through mediators—churches, priests, power structures. In pre-Enlightenment Europe, knowledge is authorized by religious institutions. The

Enlightenment turns away from this by affirming a domain of knowledge which is accessible and common to all humanity. With this arises the intuition of a common humanity, what we may call Humanism. Thus Enlightenment thinkers looked for the essence of human knowledge in the least common denominators that all human beings could agree upon. They situated this foundation in the material evidence of the senses and the power of reason to analyze this evidence and arrive at understanding.

This line of understanding went further to ask about the scope and the limits of human knowledge. Particularly in its early deist phase, this line of thinking posited Reason as a divine power, determining the manifestation of the world and mediating between it and the human being.[2] We can know the world because the world is rational and because we are also rational. In effect, this represents a change in the location of truth from the Transcendence of God to the immanence of Reason in the world and in human beings. This rational focus thus inaugurated a new way of knowing, which is also a new way of being.

The Enlightenment from this point of view based itself on the faith of human ability to arrive at a totality of knowledge using the reason. If we understand this basis of the Enlightenment, we can see the central place occupied by the Knowledge Academy in it. This transnational and global structure of the modern academy is intimately interwoven so as to arrive at a totality of world knowledge. This is what may be called the nomos of modern education—the development of a systemic rational omniscience. This international enterprise of knowledge generation is the hidden engine to which modern humanity is yoked. This places demands of standardization on the human understanding of knowledge, its methodology and its boundaries. Without questioning these boundaries, we share this knowledge; we consider it "academic" in our ability to cross-reference each work of knowledge, in the evolution of knowledge thus conceived. We have thus been inducted as a "humanity" into a worldwide enterprise which begins with the Enlightenment.

Just as we find ourselves in an age and a world which we hardly question, an age whose historicity escapes us and a world whose rationality we assume, so we take this knowledge enterprise for granted. To be literate is to be a "knowledge worker" at the center of a global modernity. Thus, whether we are conscious or not, to be literate is to be yoked to the engine of world knowledge, to the enterprise of seeking for the rational omniscience of the Enlightenment, the knowledge which will grant us totality of understanding of the world and ourselves. This yoking has led to certain interesting results. To grasp the scope of these results it is necessary to understand the two sides of this knowledge enterprise.

Knowledge and Power

One aspect of this knowledge enterprise is knowledge of the world as we receive it through our senses, in its most material sense. This is the domain of science, primarily what are known as the hard sciences or physical sciences, the knowledge of the world as object. But also, and perhaps more centrally if less overtly, this includes the knowledge of the subject, that is, knowledge of ourselves as human beings. This seeking for a knowledge of the subject opens up the field of what we call the human sciences. The human sciences constitute our attempts at arriving at a definition of the Human. Thus they open up a normative vista which defines us as subjects. In our modern world this characterizes our mode of being, in a way different from the being of people in pre-modern times, in that we have a normative sense of the human which is different from that of earlier times.

This sense of being has a negative and a positive side. On the one hand, it implies a crystallization, a reduction of identity. Human beings today are increasingly understood in predictable molds, behaviorally, socially, culturally. On the other, we have developed a more universal sense of the human; an intuition of the human. Today a human being can immediately recognize the humanity of another human, irrespective of his/her culture, nationality, race, gender, or history. This is also a legacy of the Enlightenment. Perhaps at the center of the Enlightenment is this new international humanism.

If the domain of Science is the "pure" side of the knowledge enterprise of modernity, there is also another side we need to acknowledge. As an obverse of the "pure" Sciences, this is what may be called the "applied" Sciences. But if the obverse of "purity" is "application," the traces of its converse, "impurity," are not absent in its implications. Contemporary philosophers, drawing their heritage from Nietzsche have posited this other side as the primary side, that latent under the guise of the noble enterprise of "pure" knowledge lies the more ignoble motive of application, the enterprise of power.[3] Knowledge leads to Power, and perhaps, Power drives the engine of Knowledge. Knowledge lends itself to the designs of power, exploitation, possession, and enjoyment. One may question whether indeed it is always the case that the Will to Power hides under every Will to Knowledge. But at the least we can assert that the desire-being of man has its own understanding of the Enlightenment and very quickly aligns the mental enterprise of Knowledge to its own designs of Power.

The voyages of discovery became the means of colonization. Very quickly, even in the domains of its origin, the discoveries of Science lent themselves to the applications of Technology, mass production, forced consumption, the operations of power, and the creation of new desires in people so that they may consume what has been produced in excess. Along with the Knowledge Academy and the international definition of the human, this spawned that other peculiarly modern reality, the global World Market, as the field for the play of Power as capital and its accumulation.

Colonialism and the Bengal Renaissance

In India, this mercantile expansionism sought its fortunes and made its firm settlement with the founding of the modern city of Calcutta in the eighteenth century. But such a founding was impossible without extensive close interactions with Bengalis and the consequent class of Bengali middlemen that arose came to constitute what was called the *bhadralok* or native gentry, a new strata of Bengalis educated in the English language and the ways of occidental civilization. From the late eighteenth century, this *bhadralok* class began to develop an internal reality of its own through a culture which engaged in a rethinking of what it meant to be

Bengali and Indian and a critical assimilation of Western modernity. The politics of the *bhadralok* arose from their knowledge that they were necessary not only to the mercantile designs of the colonizers but to their civilizational ambition, as native informants in the institutional nexus of Knowledge and Power with which the Enlightenment proceeded in its world expansion (see Cohn 1996). This constituted the hybrid agency of the Bengali middleman, his resistance, and selective assimilation of the ways of colonialism and modernity. From the late eighteenth century, one sees a many-sided critical engagement of this kind with modernity among the *bhadralok* class of Calcutta.

Many scholars have analyzed this as a cultural engagement with colonial domination and an initiation of the process of nationalism. But the rethinking that began in the eighteenth century and ran through the nineteenth went much deeper than the stirrings of political independence, opposing colonialism with a predictable nationalism. This rethinking is better seen as a critique of post-Enlightenment modernity. This is what constitutes the post-colonial potential of the Bengal Renaissance, its continuing legacy. If we investigate this aspect of the Bengal Renaissance today, two hundred years from its inception, we rediscover its fertility. It is for us to re-open the pages of that chapter and probe its answers, answers and approaches that may be better adapted to our times than when they were given.

The Bengal Renaissance has been seen as a complex movement that has both revivalist and reformist tendencies in it (Bose and Jalal 1997). Of these, the reformist tendencies arose in alignment with the forces of modernity. An important strand of the Bengal Renaissance welcomed modernity as something to embrace, except for the oppressive aspects of colonialism. Many of these thinkers felt that colonialism was a blessing because it brought the gifts of an "enlightened civilization" to India. According to them, the oppressive aspects of colonialism were in contradiction to the enlightened principles espoused by the colonizers, and they could be contested on the grounds of these principles. This was the position of those who became politically known as the Moderates. The Moderates sought to appeal to the conscience of the colonizer, to change the conditions of inequality and oppression wherever they were seen to be practiced. A variant strain was constituted by those who embraced modernity conditionally, and rejected colonialism. Both these strains could be called reformist. On the other side of the drive to reform were the revivalist forces. These were conservative elements that felt threatened by change and by what were understood to be "foreign" elements. The tendency here was to revive past forms of culture and religion so as to resist the forces of modernity.

Interestingly, if we study the major figures of the Bengal Renaissance, we see that most of them demonstrated a mixture of these reformist and revivalist tendencies in a close braiding. In this kind of internal dialog, the reformative tendency was applied not merely to one's own culture but became a critical force which challenged colonialism and the contradictions of modernity and the revivalist tendency was not merely a call to repeat ancient forms and customs but a new birth or renaissance engaged with modernity. Here, I would like to isolate some forms of response which I consider to be central to modernity, seen as a derivative of the Enlightenment, in terms of these two tendencies of reform and revival.

Humanism

The first of these comes in response to the spirit of Humanism which is intrinsic to the Enlightenment. The Enlightenment ideal is based on an understanding of all human beings as equal possessors of Reason, seen as the ultimate principle which pervades the Universe. I would say this is the most powerful contributing factor that reformist tendencies open up in Bengal of that time, that is, the acknowledgment of the fact that all human beings are equal. This profound wave of thought, sentiment, and idealism enters as a strain into the Bengal Renaissance at a very early stage. It is present in most of its thinkers and has a variety of repercussions. One of these is the idea that whatever has created inequalities among human beings, such as class, gender, and caste hierarchies, should be eradicated. The Young Bengal movement of Henry Vivian Derozio (1809–1831) is a prime example of this reformist tendency. This movement espoused free thought and rejected the existing social and religious norms of Hindu orthodoxy.

Another approach to the same perceived inequalities is a rethinking of cultural behaviors and customs so as to make them egalitarian. This was the revivalist or, more properly, renascent idea, which often worked through etymology and genealogy to demonstrate the historical bases of cultural transformations leading to forces of division for the play of power. These thinkers pointed to nuggets of truth within traditional norms which could be re-established within the normative frame of modernity. A good example of this kind of thinking is provided by Swami Vivekananda (1863–1902) who reinterpreted caste through Vedanta, writing about it in terms of the professional division of society and individual soul capacity outside of hereditary or hierarchical definitions. Sri Aurobindo (1872–1950) entered into and furthered this discourse. He provided an interpretation of caste which went beyond professional necessity to an analysis of the soul, substantiating a theory of the soul as a form of becoming or evolution, resting on four lines of manifestation of the powers of the Divine Shakti, the four Mother Powers of wisdom, strength, exchange, and service (Sri Aurobindo 1999, 740–751). This reinterpretation of the idea of caste while rejecting hereditary and hierarchical notions brings to the front a mystical idea resting on traditional sources such as the Veda, Gita, and Tantra, re-interpreted in terms of the dignity of all human work and the discovery of the dynamic psychological proclivities of individual expression.

The importance of this move lies in its revision of the bases of Enlightenment humanism. It demonstrates a transformative ideal that, while accepting the modern premise of human equality, displaces its rational bias to accommodate the spiritual history of India. In his later writings, such as *The Human Cycle*, written in Pondicherry in the second decade of the twentieth century, Sri Aurobindo continued to engage Enlightenment humanism in this revisionary manner, demonstrating the ideal of humanism to be realizable only through the spiritual experience of the soul of humanity in all human beings (Sri Aurobindo 1997a, 564–570).

Rationality

As we have seen, Rationality is the watchword of the Enlightenment, its very foundation. In his displacements, Sri Aurobindo did not reject rationality but exploited its uncertainties to indicate ways to the experience of greater clarities. In this kind of strategy, Sri Aurobindo is neither the first nor the only thinker. Indeed, we find that most of the principal thinkers of the Bengal Renaissance strongly embrace rationality. This is an important revisionary factor because the Enlightenment was, in fact, largely a reaction against the irrationalism of religion in Europe; and in the colonized domain of India, a purely revivalist impulse could very well have asserted a spirit of pre-modern religion that rejected reason, but we rarely see this drive in Bengal.

The Enlightenment came as a reaction to what have been called the Dark Ages of superstition and religion in Europe. Hence a gulf was dug deep between the modern age based on Reason and the pre-modern world which was irrational. During the Bengal Renaissance an attempt was made to close that gulf, so that rationality and spirituality could walk hand in hand. From the late eighteenth century, whether we consider Ram Mohan Roy (1774–1833) or Debendranath Tagore (1817–1905), the founders of the Hindu-reformist Brahmo movement, or whether we look at Vivekananda, or later Rabindranath Tagore (1861–1941) or Sri Aurobindo, we find in all of them an attempt to build a bridge between rationality and the life of the spirit. Once more, in this, these thinkers were not creating in a vacuum, but rekindling the rich intellectual discursive Indian tradition of *darshana* (yoga philosophy), *bhashya*(commentary), and *vitarka* (debate), now translated into a hybrid engagement with an occidental philosophical discourse.

The Transrational

Sri Aurobindo's contribution here too is profound because he draws close attention to the transition between reason and what transcends it. He demonstrated the limits of Reason, why the Enlightenment was blighted by principled internal conflict, and impotence in the achievement of its own goals of knowledge. Like Immanuel Kant, who used the tools of logic to demonstrate the limits of Reason, Sri Aurobindo engaged the discourses of philosophy and psychology to work out the properties and office of Reason. He then indicated the transition from the power of rationality to the power of a spiritual rationality, a supra-rationality, through the mediation of a trans-rationality, cultivated systematically and called by him "intuitive mind." In this, he critiqued the mainstream Enlightenment notion of a static rational definition of the human by translating the premises of Indian yoga and echoing Nietzsche at the same time—"Man is a transitional being" (Sri Aurobindo 1972, 91).

This transitionality opens up a posthuman possibility, seen by Sri Aurobindo as the transformation of human Reason to an individualized cosmic Mind and what he calls Supermind. Thus, Sri Aurobindo, in his engagements with the discursive grounds of the Enlightenment, posited the conditions of their fulfillment through the further evolution of consciousness through the mind to its supramental origin. But this discourse found its voice in Sri Aurobindo due to the ground prepared by earlier thinkers of the Bengal Renaissance. The Bengal Renaissance provided the rich soil in which Sri Aurobindo formulated an alternative fulfillment to the Enlightenment. Although we have largely swept aside (or under) this discourse, a contemporary postmodernist critique of the Enlightenment makes its consideration possible and urgent.

This aspect of the Bengal Renaissance seemed to get attenuated and finally disappear from the 1920s. As the movement of cultural critique gave way to the political imperative of independence, the gap between the rational and the irrational on which the Enlightenment was premised re-asserted itself through a division into a political left and a right—socialism or religious orthodoxy, the first fashioned in the molds of an occidental humanism and the second after politicized indigenous religions. Reform and revival parted ways and reverted to a more simplistic antagonism.

Social Concern

But the Bengal Renaissance has other lessons to teach us. Along with the ideas of the power of rationality and the equality of human beings, as a corollary of these, comes concern with the emancipation of downtrodden people, women, subjugated classes and castes. This social concern also becomes an important and ubiquitous undercurrent of the Bengal Renaissance. We have already touched on some of these concerns in considering humanism and the caste system. But this concern finds more active manifestations, in which a revisionary transformation of Hinduism is mobilized to the benefit of social welfare. We find here personalities such as Swami Vivekananda, with his social service programs, introducing ideas on the emancipation of the downtrodden in terms of Hindu spiritual practice—the service of God, *Narayana*, in humans—*Naranarayana*. Bankim Chandra Chattopadhyay (1838–1894) is another important early figure of the Bengal Renaissance who couched an impulse toward social and political betterment in terms of a revisionary social spirituality.

Hinduism

In all these engagements with the prerogatives of the Enlightenment, whether in the concern with rationality, the equality of human beings, social service or other normative vectors of modernity, we find the Bengal Renaissance responding with an attempt at articulation which preserves the cultural history of varieties of Indian spirituality. Here I would agree with recent thinkers such as Wilhelm Halbfass that in all these instances of engagement, what results is a transformed Indian discourse (Halbfass 1988). This discourse of what has often been called Neo-Vedanta is castigated as a derived Orientalism by some contemporary critics, but I see this as a productive force whose discursive energy has found a place within modernity's voice as an alternative modernity or a postmodernity and whose potential is hardly spent. In these engagements the Bengal Renaissance takes a resistant and transformative stand on post-Enlightenment modernity. If one agrees with Nietzsche, that the modern age begins with the death of God, we may propose an alternative discourse arising from Bengal of the late eighteenth to early twentieth centuries, in which modernity is premised in a new birth of God. Such a birth is no more one of a God who stands at the head of religions, claiming a fascist right on all humanity, but a God who awaits each human being as the ever-extending horizon of his/her own self-exceeding, a God more akin to Nietzsche's Overman.

Indeed, if such an ideal could be said to stand at the head of the contemporary critique of modernity in the words of Nietzsche, a concern with its praxis meets us in the voices of the Bengal Renaissance. We encounter this from an early stage, in lineages such as Ram Mohan Roy, Debendranath and Rabindranath Tagore, or Sri Ramakrishna (1836–1886), Vivekananda and his collaborators, or with isolated personalities who assimilate what exists or create new ideas, such as Bankim Chandra Chatterjee or Sri Aurobindo. In all these voices, the ideal of a spiritual reconstitution of individual and social life is powerfully present as an alternative form of living modernity. It seeks to express itself not outside of the modern but within the modern and not outside of life but as a transformed definition of life. Each of these figures represents a powerful social force through which a spiritual practice expressed itself in its own way. Sri Aurobindo's contribution to this core concern of the Bengal Renaissance is perhaps the most profound, in that he heralds a new age of spiritual experimentation and development which treats all life as yoga.

It is important to note that this articulation straddles two discourses—reformist and revivalist, modernist and traditionalist—and is revisionary to both. We have touched on its contribution to the discourse of modernity, but this also implied a large-scale redefinition of what we call Hinduism. This is not clearly perceived, since there has been the rise of Hindu nationalism in India since the 1980s and many contemporary commentators have attributed the origins of Hindutva to the Bengal Renaissance. This is far from the truth. As an interrelated discourse, what the Bengal Renaissance introduced is a creative ongoing redefinition of Hinduism. This is because they inflected the burgeoning history of Indic spirituality in terms of modernist concerns. As I have mentioned, this discourse is largely conscious of the fascist implications of a God who claims unity through division. Its locus is therefore stretched from the start between the horns of universalism and plurality. In Sri Ramakrishna, for example, we find a mystic who could embrace any discipline or sectarian formulation of spirituality and arrive at an ecstatic spiritual realization from it, without the need to hierarchize or structure into a metaphysics. In Vivekananda, it is true that the urge toward metaphysics moved toward the formulation of a universalist *Advaita Vedanta*, but this is powerfully tempered with the message of individual freedom in seeking and spiritual practice. Again, in the Brahmo lineage, we find this braiding of universalism and pluralism. We find Ram Mohan Roy dialoguing throughout his adult life with Christians and Muslims, attempting to demonstrate the convergences of all spiritual approaches in a Vedantic monotheism, a grappling with plurality so as to bring it under a universalist frame. We find a much subtler approach to the same dialog between universalism and pluralism with Rabindranath Tagore, and so on even with a number of lesser-known figures.

Krishna and Kali

The two most powerful and popular cultural histories of spiritual practice in Bengal are Vaishanavism, the cult of Krishna; and Shaktism, the cult of Kali. Naturally, these two approaches inflect the writings of the Bengal Renaissance strongly, but in new and revised ways. Of course, the case of Sri Ramakrishna, who attained to the spiritual realizations of both Vaishnavism and Shakta Tantra, is well known. But, these two sectarian practices make their way into several other major figures of the time as reflected in the writings of Bankim Chandra and Sri Aurobindo, for example. If we look at the origins of Sri Aurobindo's yoga in his diaries, now published as the *Record of Yoga*, we find the central place both Krishna and Kali have in it (Sri Aurobindo 2001, 23); and decades later, we find him state in a correspondence that the two names Krishna and Kali arising together during the practice of his yoga provide a powerful sign toward the transformation of consciousness. Thus, it is this ability of taking localized practices and relating them to each other in syntheses, or making them universal that constitutes a highly creative contribution of the Bengal Renaissance and Sri Aurobindo's work constitutes a central part of this.

Universality and Plurality

Indeed, it is this dialog between universalism and plurality which is initiated in the Bengal Renaissance, something fraught with difficulty. It is much easier to define a national identity around a single ideology and a privileged history. This is what Hindutva attempts to do to the rich and complex history of Indic spiritual practice. The Bengal Renaissance, on the other hand, was largely creative and progressive in seeing this long cultural discourse as a living and mutating one, something lending itself to innovation in different contexts and demanding ongoing adaptations in the present. This redefinition of Hinduism was one which made it evolutionary, not something which embraced only a specific ideology but one which engaged with all histories of spiritual practice, making up the fabric of its unfinished body. This, indeed, is how Sri Aurobindo presented his definition of *Sanatan Dharma* in the famous Uttarpara speech (1909) (Sri Aurobindo 1983).

Sri Aurobindo saw clearly that the difficulty of defining a national identity in terms of religious ideology went back to the limitations of the mind. The mind divides reality in terms of binaries. Thus, we can dwell on unity and we can dwell on infinity, but the mind cannot hold these radically different realities at the same time. But the Brahman is both one and infinite. Hence we see that though Universalism seems to be an all-inclusive idea, what this implies to the mind is problematic, because true universality, or more properly integrality, is not within the power of human reason to grasp. In the contemporary academic discipline of religious studies, this problem is very clearly acknowledged through the use of the term "inclusivism" (Halbfass 1995, 245-246). As against "exclusivism," which refers to religions establishing their identity by denying relevance to other religions, or dubbing them as satanic, "inclusivism" proceeds by subordinating other religions under itself, a kind of ideological totalitarianism. The ideological construct of Hinduism, under mental compulsion to define itself in terms of a national identity, introduces this difficulty into modern India.

Thus "inclusivist" religious ideologies appropriate to themselves the right over all other religions. This can be seen as a peculiar problem of a universalism forced to define itself in terms of a mental taxonomy, which is one of the world organizing features of post-Enlightenment modernity. The hegemonic construct of Advaita Vedanta lends itself eminently to this ordering paradigm. In terms of the Bengal Renaissance, although it is true that Vivekananda privileged such an Advaita Vedanta as a "national" definition of Hinduism, as mentioned earlier, there was enough richness and complexity in his approach to spirituality to render this construct dialectical. However, it was in time conflated and identified with his teachings and normalized by later nationalistic philosophers and teachers such as Sarvepalli Radhakrishnan (1888–1975) or Swami Chinmayananda (1916–1993). The problem with this definition is its erasure of the irreducible difference between spiritual experiences. There is something that escapes every formula in any approach. Just as human beings are distinct—although we may intuit the common humanity in every human being, each individual is unique—so each name, relationship, and experience of the Divine has its irreducible reality, a unique form of the Supreme. This mentally irreconcilable plurality forms part of the mystic richness of the spiritual approach initiated in the Bengal Renaissance, and given a philosophical and psychological formulation by Sri Aurobindo.

Further contemplation may bring us closer to the solution proposed by Sri Aurobindo. This contemplation can come to us from the Gita's *Viswarupa Darshan*. In the chapter XI of the Gita, Arjuna asks to see Sri Krishna in his original form, undisguised by the Ignorance. Sri Krishna says to Arjuna that this vision is beyond human capacity but he will grant it to Arjuna by giving him "divine eyes" to see. He then provides Arjuna with a new sight and bestows on him the *Viswarupa Darshan*. In this darshan, Arjuna sees the ultimately paradoxical image. He sees something which is formless and infinite—a mass of radiance extended on all sides without beginning, middle, or end—and simultaneously he sees all possible beings—past, present, and future present in this Being, being born acting and dying. Such a co-existence of unity and infinity or of formlessness and all possibilities of form or of a static eternity and a dynamic perpetuity is bewildering beyond measure to the mental consciousness of Arjuna and he entreats Krishna to revert to his "universal" form, all-encompassing with four hands.

Of course, an "inclusivism" can easily be derived from this description and this too has happened, a theistic inclusivism, which subsumes all possible experiences under the rubric of Avatar Krishna. But what Sri Aurobindo sees in this kind of image is a post-humanist possibility. What Arjuna has been granted with the *Viswarupa* is not so much a proclamation regarding the *avatara*, as the possibility of an experience which surpasses the limitations of the mental consciousness and heralds the evolution of the overmental or supramental species. The Gita being a book of yoga, it is clear that such an evolutionary possibility is pointed to as an eventual outcome of human praxis.

Sri Aurobindo provides a philosophical basis for this form of experience in his written works such as *The Life Divine* and *The Synthesis of Yoga*. In a chapter in *The Life Divine* on "The Triple Status of the Supermind," he develops the form of supramental experience as a co-existence of transcendental, universal, and individual being-experiences (Sri Aurobindo 2005, 152–160). Similarly, in the last chapter of *The Synthesis of Yoga*, titled "Towards the Supramental Time Vision," he discusses both the psychology and philosophy of supramental time experience, dealing with the question of the co-existence of eternity and temporality within the same experience (Sri Aurobindo 1999, 885–904). Here he discusses how the supramental existence, operating in time and outside it, can maintain its reality as a becoming as well as a knowing of all possibility. This is achieved through degrees of self-concealment, or rather, co-existing modalities of self-access within the same being. At once, there is all revelation in eternity and the immanence of this knowledge working out as creative skill in time. This range of coincident consciousness is natural to supermind and is possible through the development of human consciousness extending beyond its mental limits. A transition to such a realization is mediated by an expansion of human capacity in terms of an infinite openness to God experience, allowing pluralism to prepare the ground for the supramental experience in which all possibilities of the divine may co-exist. Such a solution is not merely a repetition of the assertions of the past of Indian spirituality, but a pointer to a post-humanist future.

Body without Organs

In this post-humanist orientation, the work of Sri Aurobindo converges with the thoughts of certain postmodern seers. We may consider, for example, Gilles Deleuze (1925–1995). Deleuze pushed the boundaries of thinking about the experience of radical plurality. He concluded that such an experience could be found only beyond reason and beyond present "natural" human ability, but it is within our aspiration as an expansion of capacity. To Deleuze, the capacity for infinite variety of experience constituted "the earth" as a universal Body-without-Organs (BwO) (Deleuze and Guattari 1987, 40). This "ground" would be open to all experience, yet it would be one in its infinite expansiveness and productive creativity (the full earth). Though such a condition of experience would be beyond present human comprehension, it is latent as immanent possibility of evolution and one could prepare for it by increasing the body's capacity for experience. According to this, any experience, met with by the body's expanded capacity, would be an experience of bliss, belonging to a scale of intensities. This praxis of preparation comes close to Sri Aurobindo's experiments in the *Record of Yoga* where he attempts to turn all experiences into delight through the transformation of the body's capacity. It is through transformative preparations of this kind that we can develop the capacity to experience a consciousness which is supramental. According to Sri Aurobindo, the structures for this do not exist in human beings at present, but this does not mean that the definition of the human is bound within existing structures. At the same time, without aspiration, experiment, and practice/preparation, they will not appear, as if by miracle. Sri Aurobindo, in his essay on the *Viswarupa Darshan*, points out though it is through a kind of "miracle" that Arjuna is granted the supramental vision by Krishna, such a "miracle" is overpowering for Arjuna. Hence, a much longer preparation of yogic practice is necessary to bring humanity to the expansion of capacity necessary for this evolutionary transition to a consciousness beyond the mind, which resolves unity and plurality, without compromising either (Sri Aurobindo 1997b, 393–395).

Nation

So far, in our consideration of the transformations in Humanism, Rationality, or Religion, we have skirted around the category of the Nation. The Nation forms a central concern in any consideration of the Bengal Renaissance; indeed, the Bengal

Renaissance has often been seen mainly as a form of cultural nationalism. Here too, we find the discourse opened up by the thinkers of this period, though preparing the ground for nationalism, also providing interesting critiques highlighting its problematic nature. In contemporary postcolonial thinking, several of these problems have been articulated with clarity. This is not to under-rate the need of a subjugated people to rise as a collective and assert their own right to exist. The central problem associated with such collective movements is the problem of identity politics—in what name is collective unity to be orchestrated? Any collective unity becomes a contested domain in which a number of interests vie to lay claim to the ideological definition of the group. "Nation" in this sense, to use Benedict Anderson's term, is an "imagined community," a reified category made up of selections and suppressions (Anderson 2006). Such an identity builds its reality through the creation of a subjective sense of belonging, something achieved by the use of culture. Thus, the Bengal Renaissance, as a cultural movement consolidating a subjective consciousness in the face of political and cultural subjugation, can be seen pre-eminently in these nationalistic terms.

We discover that from an early period this cultural nationalism sought to focus attention on the unified territory and history of India as a substantialized agent, Mother India or *Bharat Mata*. Among the earliest articulations of this sentiment is Bankim Chandra Chatterjee's *Ananda Math* (1882), in which a band of revolutionary *sannyasis* take arms against injustice in the name of the nation seen as the Divine Mother. *Ananda Math* also introduced the song of adoration to this Mother, *Bande Mataram*. This image of the nation (along with Bankim's song) became very popular in Bengal during the early twentieth century, by dint of its spread through political propaganda and cultural dissemination. Sri Aurobindo was among those of the later generations of the Bengal Renaissance who were deeply influenced by Bankim's vision and actively promoted a form of nationalism in which Indians were asked to perceive the nation as the living form of the Divine Mother. He and his revolutionary collaborators published their rousing articles in a journal by the name of *Bande Mataram*. Songs addressing the Divine Mother, adapted from the rich tradition of Bengali Kali and Durga worship, carrying obvious nationalist overtones appeared in large numbers, including in the songs of Rabindranath Tagore and Kazi Nazrul Islam (1899–1976). Abanindranath Tagore (1871–1951) painted a poster of Bharat Mata which was used in a political rally. The practice of Durga Puja (worship of the warrior Mother) in public, particularly in Calcutta, was introduced as a quasi-nationalist call to arms as well as a celebration of collective identity, a practice which continues to this day. All this has caused some contemporary critics to see this aspect of the cultural nationalism of the Bengal Renaissance to be Hindu dominated and fascist in potential.

However, as Sugata Bose has pointed out, the image of Bharat Mata translated hazily between regional (*Banga Mata*) and national (*Bharat Mata*) realities in this early phase of Indian nationalism. As a regional Bengali movement, it drew on sources of popular sentiment which had developed a long history of syncretic devotional practice transcending sectarian or religious boundaries (Bose 1999, 68). Testimony to this fact is also borne by the large number of national songs addressed to the Divine Mother written by Kazi Nazrul Islam, a Bengali Muslim, who is today considered the national poet of Bangladesh; as well as by the large corpus of songs using Divine Mother imagery which were revived in the later movement for political independence of Bangladesh from Pakistan (1971).

Moreover, in a large number of its personalities, the problems associated with a fascistic nationalism were well understood and critiqued. Gayatri Spivak has used the term "strategic essentialism" to speak of the possibility of subjugated individuals coming together to contest classes or other large-scale group identities which oppress them (Spivak 1988). Whereas a simplistic essentialism implies an ahistorical set of characteristics and "ideologemes" which are said to define a nation, a "strategic essentialism" implies the dynamic consciousness of the political use and constructed nature of such characteristics, accepted by a group for its self-definition as a means to consolidate identity. "Strategic essentialism" implies the continuous presence of self-critique within the identity construct, a consciousness toward the undoing of hegemonic essentialisms which suppress minority voices and push toward the erasure of individual and local agencies and histories. As the name itself suggests, the Bengal Renaissance, as an early movement of cultural nationalism, was largely conscious of shifting between the prerogatives of regional and national culture. Along with this was the larger awareness of a civilizational critique, which might be called trans-national and/or international. This awareness of shifting boundaries and negotiations between micro and macro communities, or lived and imagined communities of various cultural characteristics, pervaded the discourse of the Bengal Renaissance, allowing for a greater cosmopolitanism in individual creative agency. The plural space of early urban Calcutta allowed for a rich mix of transactions and translations relating to regionalism, nationalism, pan-Asianism, and international Orientalism, opening up networks of affiliation and fraternity which allowed for a dynamic complexity in the construction of national subjectivity.

The category of "nation" is also a peculiarly modern form with its basis in the Enlightenment and its incipient ideology of arriving at a single unified description of the cosmos, what in today's terms is called a TOE (Theory-of-Everything). This is why the German philosopher Martin Heidegger (1889-1976) has referred to our age as the "Age of the World Picture" (Heidegger 1977, 115-154). Such an epistemological drive proceeds by creating classifications which tend to become more and more inclusive and normalize themselves as absolute. With the will-to-power which drives this knowledge-enterprise, the world-making endeavor of the Enlightenment may be well captured in the contemporary image of an omni-database, a kind of universal arrangement of data, in which all nameable entities are put in their slots along with their definable properties so that they can be manipulated at will. Such an image leads to Heidegger's designation of "standing reserve" as a characteristic feature of modern ontology—a drive to translate all things into static manipulable "resources" (Heidegger 1977, 115-154). This idea of putting in place, of classifying according to an absolute scheme, is profoundly problematic due to the fact that any "universal" perspective represents a contest of power to claim itself as truth.

Once more we return to the problem of universalism and pluralism. We may even say that there can be many possible universalisms. But the Enlightenment is premised on a single absolute universalism, the System. Thus, the notion of systematicity is intrinsic to the Enlightenment. These underlying epistemological ideas characterize modern understanding. A major discipline in the contemporary academy is Systems Theory. This discipline has been loosely classed as an inter-disciplinary or trans-disciplinary discipline, but it may be more properly addressed as an omni-disciplinary discipline. Behind it is the late twentieth-century idea of modular assemblage, the development of a coherent model for the universe by creating seamless interfaces across the boundaries that separate the specialized disciplines that bring us our knowledge of the world (object) and the human (subject)—the disciplines of physics, chemistry, biology, psychology, sociology, and the other humanistic disciplines. If we bring them all together, we will find the links and create one picture of the universe. This is the ambition of Systems Theory.

Geopolitics of Domination

This systematicity is present not only in the knowledge enterprise of modernity but also in its drive for power. The geopolitics of domination is a systematicity related to the creation of a unified political and economic world order. A world order implies something at the center and other things at various distances from the center, leading to its peripheries, so that they can be granted different degrees of agency and dominated to different degrees. This world ordering imagination finds its convenient handles in the idea of "nations." To arrive at such changeless and absolute classifications of people sharing territory and history, it becomes necessary to think of them in reified terms outside their lived experiences as individuals. Individuals with a collective history share a living sense of togetherness. Individual "Indians," for example, carry their own living sense of a cultural history of togetherness. They share symbols, practices, local histories. This constitutes their living social reality as a population, but if an absolute reality is to be sought for a people over-riding individual reality of social memory and lived experience, this can be orchestrated in two ways. One is to posit an ahistorical essence of the nation, something transcending any conglomeration of people and their histories. That is the "nation soul." The second is a political and administrative structure imposed on the people. That is what we call the "nation state." Thus, it is between the "nation soul" and the "nation state" that the Enlightenment project effectuates itself in its integration of nations.

Nation Soul

Like several other categories we have considered, which arose as a result of the cultural engagement between indigenous spiritual histories and modernity in the Bengal Renaissance, the idea of a nation soul took its hybrid form as a national reality. Though today, there is an attempt to claim an archaic origin of this idea within Indian history, it was not present in its theorized form prior to the modern period. Certainly, there are references to a quasi-national consciousness, going back to the Vedas, as in the Hymn to the Divine Word, *Vak*, where the Goddess is identified as *rashtri*, the Nation-Mother; or in the Puranic idea of the subcontinent united by the distributed limbs of Sati after her self-immolation—but these are sporadic and nascent ideas. The properly theorized idea of "nation soul" in modern times makes its appearance in late eighteenth-century

Germany. It is voiced in the writings of a philosopher named Johann Herder (1744–1803) and soon, through Herder's contemporary, G.W.F. Hegel (1770–1831). Hegel takes Herder's idea and makes it the cornerstone of his *Philosophy of History* which is a theory of evolution consonant with the ideology of the Enlightenment (Hegel 1956). One could argue, in fact, that Hegel's *Philosophy of History* provides the best philosophical description for the teleology of the Enlightenment. In Hegel's scheme, it is Reason (he calls this Consciousness) which is God, latent in matter. Matter has laws but these laws are not self-conscious; they are expressed unconsciously. But it is immanent as Time in the cosmos, the Subject of Time or Time-Spirit, *Zeitgeist*. This makes Matter evolve in time through the struggle and reconciliation of opposites (dialectics) creating forms that have increasingly greater power of consciousness, leading to the human being, who has rational choice. For Hegel, the human being is the pinnacle of this evolution of Reason. As we know, according to the Enlightenment idea (and the Renaissance which preceded it), Man, as possessor of Reason, is the measure of all things. Hegel's Philosophy of History then proceeds to trace the further evolution of Reason through human collectivities, the nation-souls.

Those who know of the evolutionary philosophy of Sri Aurobindo can see how close and yet how subtly different Hegel's idea is from that of Sri Aurobindo. At the start of this discussion, I spoke of the changes in epochs being guided by what Hegel calls the *Zeitgeist*, the Time-Spirit, as translated by Sri Aurobindo. According to Hegel, the change of an age is related to specific expressions of Rationality. Reason proceeds through dialectical experiments in different milieus, the nation souls, bringing to the social surface certain contradictions which are subconscious within it. But once a contradiction is solved in a certain set of people, according to Hegel's philosophy, the Time-Spirit leaves this "nation" and proceeds to another milieu to work out further possibilities. Each nation is thus chosen to express a stage in the evolution of Reason and remains forever stuck in that stage after it has served its purpose. For Hegel, India and China expressed two of the most primitive conditions in this history of the *Zeitgeist*, because they represented solutions to problems which arose prior to the appearance of political self-consciousness. They were thus doomed to remain as static preserves of essentialized identity. On the other hand, the same *Zeitgeist* advanced finally to Europe of the eighteenth century, where it achieved the fullness of its expression. Hegel's idea encompasses what he calls "the end of History," a term that made its reappearance recently in the writings of Francis Fukuyama (1952-), who argued in his book *The End of History and the Last Man* that the global universalization of the political form of liberal democracy and the world market constitute the finality of history as an experimental process seeking perfection and stabilization (Fukuyama 1992).

There are many others who have echoed this sense of culmination of Enlightenment teleology in our times, as a fulfillment of Georg Hegel's prophecy of the power of Rationality articulating itself in its fullness in a collective Godhood of Omniscience, Omnipotence, and Omnipresence. Unless we extend Hegel to see post-rational aporetic engagements of the *Zeitgeist*, such as those between Law and Love, or Freedom and Love or at its height, Absolutism and Pluralism, this Rational Godhood is a flat ideal, which cannot con(s)t(r)ain the radical plurality of all things in the cosmos, including (and especially) the human. Only a supramental possibility can achieve this. This was

Nietzsche's philosophic intuition. This is *l'avenir* of Derrida, the Body w/o Organs of Deleuze, the Golden Embryo, Hiranyagarbha. This is the extension of and departure from Hegel, which forms the lineage of Sri Aurobindo. Any deeper genealogical perusal of Hegel's ideas takes us back surely to the Eurocentric roots of the Enlightenment, its manifesting dream of a neo-colonial global world order and geopolitics of domination.

Sri Aurobindo and Hegel

We may note the root of the difference between Hegel's Metaphysics and Sri Aurobindo's idea of evolution as stated in *The Life Divine*. Although a similar process of the Involution-Evolution of Consciousness forms the basis of Sri Aurobindo's theory, Consciousness does not equate to Rationality in Sri Aurobindo's case, nor does it eschew Reason. As mentioned earlier, the hybrid form of this Metaphysics straddles two discourses, that of Western speculative Metaphysics and of the Indian *darshana-yoga* tradition, which invites subjective verification through the praxis of yoga. This dependence on praxis renders Sri Aurobindo's evolutionary theory closer to Nietzsche's project of self-transcendence or Simondon's micropolitics of individuation.

With Sri Aurobindo, we may speak of a new tradition of visionary or intuitive philosophy. The aim of this is the invention of realities philosophically. In the key of Deleuze/Bergson's intuition as method, his philosophy (and its genre) can be characterized as reality as method, or method as reality. This is another way of affirming the Gita's dictum, *yogahkarmasukaushalam*, yoga is skill in works. The method consists in reaching out with as many of one's faculties are willing, for the philosophical intuition of the Divine Being/Existence. By philosophical intuition of the Divine is meant the meditation on the idea "What is the perfect state of reality, given the Manifest, the Memory and the Dream?" This meditation yields a trail of parallel phylae of investigation, experimentation, and experience, mixing/relating/transducing to move toward increasingly more integrated experiences (vision, personal/universal Symbol[4] relations, endurance of plurality). Sri Aurobindo's praxis led him to a pantheistic process theory, involving evolving agency, leading to divine reality. According to this, even prior to the human with its location a "reversal of consciousness" and agency in relation to nature, the steps of the evolution are not continuous and determinable but having discontinuities and processes involving agency. Finally, the source of Consciousness in the evolution reveals itself to be the Supermind, individualized in each unique integral center, with its transcendental freedom from cosmic conditions and ability to transform them, as discussed above. In this cosmic evolution, souls (including individual and collective souls, such as nation soul) have a part to play, but none of these are static. We will consider this in some more detail below.

Nation Soul and the Western Dream

Thus it is in Germany of the eighteenth/nineteenth century that we find the beginnings of the theory of "nation soul," serving the ordering impulse of the Enlightenment. Such a nation soul is static. This idea of the nation soul migrates rapidly to the rest of Europe and often takes a dangerous form when it associates itself with colonialism and racism. As we know, Germany itself was hugely infected by racist essentialisms, leading ultimately to Nazism and the Second World War. The idea of nation soul, a subjective essence for the German nation, developed a strong resonance in its thought. It is present before Hegel in philosophers like Kant and continues after him in personalities such as Nietzsche and Heidegger. This is why Nietzsche was heralded as the source of Nazi ideology, though this was far from the truth. Nietzsche did not support racism, but the notion of a superior subjective essence was strong in German culture. An acknowledgment of this fact with its promises and dangers is what we find in Sri Aurobindo's powerful and seminal chapter "True and False Subjectivism" in *The Human Cycle* (Sri Aurobindo 1997a, 44–54). This chapter is primarily aimed at Germany but it also addresses the general idea of the nation soul for the future so as to distinguish the salutary possibility from the peril that nations may avoid falling into such a trap. The idea of the nation soul lends itself to the purposes of nationalism and makes its entry into the Bengal Renaissance at this time. This idea is not fully theorized in other thinkers of the Bengal Renaissance but is present as the being of cultural identity, independent of the norms of the colonizer; and the dispensing of the destiny of the Indian people—what Rabindranath Tagore called *Bharata Bhagya Vidhata* in his song *Jana Gana Mana*, later the National Anthem of independent India. We have also noted earlier the equation of this nation soul with the image of Mother India. We find a continuation of the matristic and spiritual ideas of this image and its form of address in the yogic praxis and teaching of Sri Aurobindo. Thus, Sri Aurobindo does not reject the idea of the nation soul but theorizes it so as to introduce a variant response to the Eurocentric discourse. The reality given by him to the nation soul is not that of a simplistic ahistorical essence. This is something to be noted, since the idea of "India" as an eternal Hindu nation has made its appearance in today's world in circles of religious nationalism, staking its claim of identity on the nation soul.

The nation soul for Sri Aurobindo is a being of becoming. It is a plural province of qualities, cultural histories with a specific matrix of reality-problems which develops individuality at a point in history. Individuality implies independence from any, many, or all constituents; an impersonal person of a set of reality-problems, hence qualitatively unique; yet an identity in a mutually transformative relation with each of its constituents. In Sri Aurobindo's yoga philosophy, there are two aspects to the nation soul, just as there are two aspects to the human soul—a psychic[5] entity and a psychic being. The psychic entity is an unformed matrix or reservoir of divine energy in relation to which, through historical processes, a psychic being and psychic personality get formed. This then evolves increasingly greater personhood. The relationship between psychic being and phenomenal nature determines the historical processes.

As we saw with the cosmopolitanism of the Bengal Renaissance, collective entities are not restricted to nations. So, too, in Sri Aurobindo's idea of a cosmic evolution, the collective soul is not restricted to nations, and includes sub-national and supra-national conscious agencies. Thus, one may speak of a pan-Asian soul, the soul of Asia or a regional soul, the soul of Bengal. These souls develop a cultural orientation over time. But this orientation is not static, it is in a process of continuous becoming. As a historical discourse, each collective soul develops a fuzzy qualitative specificity and also a perspective drift toward the universal. Each such perspective develops through its interactions with other perspectives and is part of a global evolution toward a radically plural international culture and realized supramental-spiritual oneness (Sri Aurobindo 1997a, 35–54).

As in the process of reconciling universalism and pluralism through praxis of individual consciousness, such a collective process ultimately rests on human agency if its trajectory is not to be derailed either through hegemonic universalisms (such as the "world-picture" of the Enlightenment) or through anarchic chaos (as in rabid contested particularisms). A modern commentator, Benjamin Barber, has characterized this dangerous polarization as the contemporary scenario of *Jihad vs. McWorld* (Barber 1995). Sri Aurobindo's thought was prescient of this danger and holds out instead a solution which privileges cultural histories in confederated relations of affect (Sri Aurobindo 1997a, 533–578). To understand this collective process in terms of spiritual praxis is a contribution of Sri Aurobindo to the journey of the expansion of consciousness in the world.

Conclusion

One of the more subtle contributions of the Bengal Renaissance was its critique and alternative formulations of the social dimension of modernity. A village sociality was largely self-governing in small-scale communities whose members interacted in the flow of a life in which the boundaries between work and play, public and private, were porous. The modern colonial city was organized and administered instead under the imperative of colonial governmentality, through taxonomic grids for productivity, utility, differentiation, and control.

The construction of the native subject through these practices was contested by a variety of strategies devised during the Bengal Renaissance. These ranged from creative mistranslations of both native and colonial terms so as to elude or satirize the classificatory intent of modernity, a thriving vernacular literature normalizing a new communitarian modernity, native architectural practices in which the home and the street were not strictly demarcated so as to allow porous interactions, alternative descriptions of the city in terms of neighborhoods utilizing a quasi-rural functionality, social practices such as *adda* (see, for example, Chattopadhyay 2006). At a more clearly articulated level of this discourse, the yoking of colonial and modern subjects to the post-Enlightenment imperative of knowledge and capital production was contested by a model of sociality built around human self-exploration and expression in loose forms of communitarian life.

Two of the thinkers who took this discourse furthest were Rabindranath Tagore and Sri Aurobindo. They both saw that, given the ubiquitous worldwide sweep of modernity, such an alternative destining could only be secure in islands dedicated to subjective exploration where the expansion of the inner life would provide a selective filter for the assimilation and reconstitution of modernity. In this, they both rethought the pre-modern form of the *ashrama*, ideating communitarian habit of continuous learning and spiritual growth, in engagement with the forces of the world. Tagore's ashrama of universal man-making, *Visva-Bharati*, at Shantiniketan and Sri Aurobindo's Ashram, Pondicherry and Auroville, may be seen as the materialized topoi of these creative social ideas. To what extent these strategies and experiments have been successful in their intent in the long run is questionable, but the compromised realities of these social forms today cannot be seen as lack of insight of their founders, since continuous subjective engagement, critique, and furtherance by living milieus would be needed to keep them alive, something dependent on succeeding generations.

In summing up, we find that the Bengal Renaissance initiated a wide and deep engagement with post-Enlightenment ideology, both in its more immediate expression as colonialism and in the global teleology of modernity. Within this discourse, we find the contribution of Sri Aurobindo as one which provided a penetrating critique and profound alternatives. These alternatives were not isolated solutions tangential to modernity or anachronistic regressions to the pre-modern. By demonstrating the limits of the Enlightenment idea and the creative adaptation of both new and pre-modern ideas toward overcoming these limits, the Bengal Renaissance opened up ways toward alternative modernities, and Sri Aurobindo's solutions in this context may be seen as not merely critiques but fulfillments of the ideals of the Enlightenment.

Notes

1   This use may be credited in large part to Max Muller (1823–1900) who used the term "enlightenment" to translate both "moksha" and "nirvana" in his extensive translations of early Indian texts.
2   Deism as a guiding philosophy of the Enlightenment gained prominence following the scientific descriptions of laws governing cosmic phenomena by Isaac Newton (1642–1727).
3   The idea is implicit in some of Nietzsche's work (1997, 2009). It has been adapted powerfully by Michel Foucault (1982, 1994).
4   Note that all symbols are plural images; Symbol is plurality itself.
5   Sri Aurobindo's use of "psychic" refers to the Greek use as "soul." It assumes a pantheistic world (actually panentheistic world) of "god-particles," qualitatively and in potency, different in each entity that exists, whether in material form or in virtual form. At the human level, it would be the "innermost being/person." In the pre-Christian Greek use, this was more being than person. The Christian mythos foregrounded the human soul as divine person.

References

Anderson, Benedict. 2006. *Imagined Communities*. London and New York: Verso.
Barber, Benjamin. 1995. *Jihad vs. McWorld: How Globalism and Tribalism Are Reshaping the World*. New York: Random House.
Bose, Sugata. 1999. "Nation as Mother: Representations and Contestations of 'India' in Bengali Literature and Culture." In Bose, Sugata and Jalal, Ayesha, eds. *Nationalism,*

Democracy and Development: State and Politics in India. New Delhi: Oxford University Press.
Bose, Sugata and Jalal, Ayesha. 1997. *Modern South Asia: History, Culture, Political Economy*. New Delhi: Oxford University Press.
Chattopadhyay, Swati. 2006. *Representing Calcutta: Modernity, Nationalism and the Colonial Uncanny*. Oxford and New York: Routledge.
Cohn, Bernard S. 1996. *Colonialism and Its Forms of Knowledge: The British in India*. Princeton, NJ: Princeton University Press.
Deleuze, Gilles and Guattari, Felix. 1987. *A Thousand Plateaus*. Translated by Brian Massumi. Minneapolis: University of Minnesota Press.
Foucault, Michel. 1982. *The Archaeology of Knowledge: And the Discourse on Language*. New York: Vintage.
Foucault, Michel. 1994. *The Order of the Things: The Archaeology of the Human Sciences*. New York: Vintage.
Fukuyama, Francis. 1992. *The End of History and the Last Man*. New York: Avon.
Halbfass, Wilhelm. 1988. *India and Europe: An Essay in Understanding*. Albany: SUNY Press.
Halbfass, Wilhelm. 1995. *Philology and Confrontation: Paul Hacker on Traditional and Modern Vedanta*. New York: SUNY Press.
Hegel, G. W. F. 1956. *Philosophy of History*. Translated by J. Sibree. London: Dover.
Heidegger, Martin. 1977. *The Question Concerning Technology and Other Essays*. Translated by William Levitt. New York: Harper Torchbooks.
Nietzsche, Friedrich. 1997. *Beyond Good and Evil*. New York: Dover.
Nietzsche, Friedrich. 2009. *On the Genealogy of Morals*. Oxford: Oxford University Press.
Spivak, Gayatri C. 1988. "Subaltern Studies: Deconstructing Historiography." In Guha, Ranajit and Spivak, Gayatri C. eds. *Selected Subaltern Studies*. Oxford: Oxford University Press.
Sri Aurobindo. 1972. *The Hour of God*. Pondicherry: Sri Aurobindo Ashram.
Sri Aurobindo. 1983. *Sanatan Dharma: Uttarpara Speech*. Pondicherry: Sri Aurobindo Ashram.
Sri Aurobindo. 1997a. *The Human Cycle, The Ideal of Human Unity, War and Self-Determination*. Pondicherry: Sri Aurobindo Ashram.
Sri Aurobindo. 1997b. *Essays on the Gita*. Pondicherry: Sri Aurobindo Ashram.
Sri Aurobindo. 1999. *The Synthesis of Yoga*. Pondicherry: Sri Aurobindo Ashram.
Sri Aurobindo. 2001. *The Record of Yoga I*. Pondicherry: Sri Aurobindo Ashram.
Sri Aurobindo. 2005. *The Life Divine*. Pondicherry: Sri Aurobindo Ashram.

3

Sri Aurobindo's Invalidation of the Aryan Invasion Theory and the Contemporary Western Archeological Evidence

Kundan Singh

Sri Aurobindo bid farewell to the Indian freedom struggle in 1910; however, he remained involved with issues pertaining to yogic matters as well as to all literature that misrepresented the history, philosophy, and culture of India. His *Foundations of Indian Culture* later renamed as *Renaissance in India and Other Essays* still remains a classic in an effort to explain the foundations of Indian culture through a yogic cosmology, which has been the bedrock of Indian ways of being since antiquity. Sri Aurobindo produced most of his literature between the years 1914 and 1920. By then, the idea of the invasion of the Aryans from the northwestern frontiers of India had already been put in place. Sri Aurobindo's contestation and refutation of this idea could be found in *The Secret of the Veda* and the *Hymns to the Mystic Fire*. However, before we address his argumentations and refutations, it may be worthwhile to locate the journey as to how this idea of Aryan Invasion came about.

Genesis of the Aryan Invasion Theory

With the following famous words, William Jones in 1792 outlined the connection between Sanskrit and European languages, and thus the creation of common ancestry between Indians and Europeans took root:

> The Sanskrit language, whatever may be its antiquity, is of a wonderful structure; more perfect than the Greek, more copious than the Latin, and more exquisitely refined than either, yet bearing to both of them a stronger affinity, both in the roots of the verbs and in the forms of grammar, than could possibly have been produced by accident; so strong, indeed, that no philologer could examine them all three, without believing them to have sprung from common source which, perhaps, no longer exists: there is a similar reason, though not quite so forcible, for supposing

that both the Gothick and the Celtick, though blended with a very different idiom, had the same origin with the Sanskrit, and the old Persian may be added to the same family.

(Cited in Bryant 2001, 15–16)

The common ancestry theory was not born with Jones as Bryant (2001) demonstrates. Such conjectures were prevalent even before him. Scholars such as Pere Coeurdoux, in as early as 1768, had contended that Sanskrit, as the language of the Brahmins, came to India from Caucasia. There were others such as Nathaniel Halhed and James Parsons, physician and fellow of the Royal Society and of the Society of the antiquities, who in the year 1776 had already drawn a connection between Indian and European languages. It was the reputation and stature of William Jones, who was a judge in the Supreme Court in Bengal, which engraved this idea in stone.[1]

In the initial years of common Indo-European ancestry, India was the cradle of the civilization. Thinkers such as Voltaire, Sonnerat, Schelling, and Schlegel argued that the epicenter of civilization was India, and that Europe owed its cultural and philosophical origins to India. Monboddo (1774), Halhed, Schlegel, and Kennedy (1828) believed that Greek and Latin were derived from Sanskrit. The mother tongue of all the Indo-European languages was Sanskrit. This theory however did not remain static. With the political ascendency of Europe over India, the mother-tongue theory began to fade into oblivion. One of the first people to challenge it was Frantz Bopp, who felt that there was an "original" tongue out of which Sanskrit as well as European languages was derived, although Sanskrit was able to preserve its originality better than others. The original tongue was termed the Proto-Indo-European language to which Sanskrit became one of the daughters, albeit the eldest of them all. For the people being represented, the terms Indo-German, Indo-European, and Aryan began to be used since the beginning of the nineteenth century (Bryant 2001).

With the decline of the status of Sanskrit as the original mother tongue of all European languages, India as the mother-region of all Indo-Europeans began to recede. In 1842, Fredrick Schlegel's brother, A. W. von Schlegel, contested that instead of migration happening from India to Europe, there existed some central region from which people went in different directions to Europe and India. Benfey, consequently, contended that since Southern India consisted of a "tribal" population (and hence by implication inferior given the prominent discourse of the times), it had to be subjugated by the invading "superior" Aryans from the North. Muir (1860), torturing the Sanskrit texts, claimed the gradual advance of Aryans from Northwest of India to East as well as South. The Aryan Invasion Theory (AIT) was thus born. Post the 1857 first war of Indian independence against the British, as the British established their political suzerainty over most parts of India, neither India remained the home of the Aryans nor Sanskrit regarded as the mother tongue of the European languages. Chakrabarti (1976, 66–67) writes, "With the Raj firmly established, it was time to begin to visualize the history and cultural process of India as a series of invasions and foreign rules."

Given that the colonizers and missionaries more often than not have been in cahoots with one another for the subjugation of people and culture, both the parties seized the opportunity and began driving the AIT hard. A common ancestry of the Hindus and Europeans was an idea that had made most of the missionaries and colonizers uncomfortable. Missionaries such as Alexander Duff and William Hastie and colonizers such as James Mill opposed the idea tooth and nail, and were more inclined to emphasize the differences between Indians and Europeans than the similarities. Disparaging Indians—their culture, civilization, traditions, and religion—was the master note of their utterances instead of focusing on convergences or similarities. With the "discovery" by the Madras school of Orientalists that southern Indian languages and Sanskrit did not come from a common root (Bryant 2001), the aforementioned notion of "Aryans" invading the "Indians" began to gain further credibility. Vedas were further tortured to show white and fair "Aryans," coming through the northwest, in conflict with the dark-skinned and flat-nosed "Dravidians" aka the original natives of the Indian subcontinent. The corollary to all this, as Trautmann (1982) shows, was that the European Aryans brought civilization and Sanskrit to India. The conclusion fitted extremely well with the "civilizing mission" notion of the Europeans: just as the Aryans of the past brought civilization, language, and culture to the Indians of yore, the colonizers and missionaries were bringing a second wave of civilization to the inter-mixed and corrupted (hence by default inferior) Indians. The AIT served many different political ends—of missionaries, colonialists, and "native" Indians (for details, see Bryant 2001).

The movement of the Aryan homeland from India to "somewhere in Asia" to Europe also happened in successive stages. It was assisted through German philology. The Germans had found themselves lagging in becoming a colonial power as some other European nations such as England, France, Spain, Holland, and Portugal had done, and they were desperately looking for sources that could bolster their national identity and ego. Sanskrit and India came in extremely handy for such objectives. If the Germans could show that they were the original Indo-Europeans, who were the cause of various European nations and India in history, their national pride would be stamped beyond question. This was at the basis of their quest for the pure Indo-German race. The Indo-Germans could consequently not have a homeland in Asia. Therefore, the homeland of the Indo Germans/Indo Europeans/Aryans had to be changed first and had to be moved to Europe.

And indeed the process began. Robert G. Latham in 1862 proposed a European homeland for the Indo-Europeans. In 1878, the German philologist L. Geiger contended that Indo-Europeans were blond and blue-eyed people, and that these traits had become diluted and darkened in those places where there had been a foreign admixture of genes (Bryant 2001). Since the contention served the European sense of superiority, in no time it began to gather steam and get regurgitated. Finding evidence for unadulterated blond, fair, and blue-eyed Indo-European in the areas of Germany, Austria, Switzerland, and Belgium was easy. And thus, this area became the original homeland of the Indo-Europeans. The rise of Nazism was exclusively related to this appropriation; although one must say that in the quest for the original homeland of Indo-Europeans, scholars have virtually pointed to almost every part of Europe (Bryant 2001).

In this melee, there emerged the German Indologist Max Muller, who had been hired by the East India Company for the translation of the Sanskrit texts in its possession. He arbitrarily attributed the date of the Rig Veda to around 1200 BCE. The arbitrariness of the dating was criticized by his contemporaries, to which he responded in 1890:

> I have repeatedly dwelt on the merely hypothetical character of the dates, which I have ventured to assign to first periods of Vedic literature. All I have claimed for them has been that they are minimum dates, and that the literary productions of each period, which still exist or which formerly existed could hardly be accounted for within shorter limits of time than those suggested.
>
> (Cited in Lal 2005, 51)

He explains further:

> If now we ask as to how we can fix the dates of these periods, it is quite clear that we cannot hope to fix a *terminum a qua*. Whether the Vedic hymns were composed [in] 1000 or 2000 or 3000 BC, no power on earth will ever determine.
>
> (Cited in Lal 2005, 51)

Consequently, the coming of Aryans to India in 1500 BCE was determined—a date which gets regurgitated in all mainstream academic literature on India and Hinduism (for instance, Flood 1996). Before we address Sri Aurobindo's response to the Aryan Invasion of India, the following are three points that emerge from the above:

1. The issue of Aryans and India has not been static. Over a period of time, the spectrum has encompassed from India being the cradle of the Aryan civilization to being invaded by fair, blond, and blue-eyed Aryans who had their homeland in Europe.
2. It has changed with the changing fortunes of India. That the "Aryans" invaded India from the northwestern frontier was a theory developed during the times when suzerainty of the British over India was almost complete.
3. The Aryan Invasion Theory is not divorced from—on the contrary contiguous with—the imperialistic designs of the colonialists and the evangelical zeal of the missionaries. Depending upon the political and missionary expediencies, the Aryan Invasion Theory was used by various parties involved.

Sri Aurobindo and the Aryan Invasion Theory

As mentioned earlier, by the time Sri Aurobindo began writing, the European presence in India from being traders to rulers had already spanned a period of at least 300 years, if we take the establishment of the East India Company in 1600 as the beginning point. However, if we take into account the writings of the Spanish as well as the Italian travelers in the Vijayanagara Empire, there was an ongoing contact between India and Europe for at least five hundred years. Bias and disparagement of the Indians and Hindus have been common features of the European contact with India: Heathens was a very common name used for the Hindus by the Italians and Spanish even when visiting the rich Vijayanagara empire for trade (Filliozat 1997). When Europe's political ascendency happened over India, it was time for the Europeans to institutionalize the ongoing and deep-seated biases and prejudices. The targeting of the Vedas, the most sacred texts of the Hindus, became a logical concomitant.

Toward the end of the nineteenth century, the Vedas came to be described as a collection of mumbo-jumbo, which were irrational utterances of primitive people, who engaged in nature worship through unconnected incantations. Representing the *purva-paksha* of the perspective that Sri Aurobindo undertakes to refute in the *Secret of the Veda*, he writes (1998, 4):

> The separate lines can be given, whether naturally or by force of conjecture, a good sense or a sense that hangs together; the diction that results, if garish in style, if loaded with otiose and decorative epithets, if developing extraordinarily little of meaning in an amazing mass of gaudy figure and verbiage, can be made to run into intelligible sentences; but when we come to read the hymns as a whole we seem to be in the presence of men who, unlike the early writers of other races, were incapable of coherent and natural expression or of connected thought. Except in the briefer and simpler hymns, the language tends to be either obscure or artificial; the thoughts are either unconnected or have to be forced and beaten by the interpreter into a whole. The scholar in dealing with his text is obliged to substitute for interpretation a process almost of fabrication.

Sri Aurobindo then goes on to explain the Vedas from within. He holds that the Vedas operate at two levels: one for the ordinary and the other for the initiated. The ordinary engage in the external symbols, such as sun, moon, fire, *soma* but the initiated understand, know, and work with the psycho-spiritual representation behind the external symbols.

> One of the leading principles of the mystics was the sacredness and secrecy of self-knowledge and the true knowledge of the Gods. This wisdom was, they thought, unfit, perhaps even dangerous to the ordinary human mind or in any case liable to perversion and misuse and loss of virtue if revealed to vulgar and unpurified spirits. Hence they favoured the existence of an outer worship, effective but imperfect, for the profane, an inner discipline for the initiate, and clothed their language in words and images which had, equally, a spiritual sense for the elect, a concrete sense for the mass of ordinary worshippers. The Vedic hymns were conceived and constructed on this principle. Their formulas and ceremonies are, overtly, the details of an outward ritual devised for the Pantheistic Nature-Worship which was then the common religion, covertly the sacred words, the effective symbols of a spiritual experience and knowledge and a psychological discipline of self-culture which were then the highest achievement of the human race.
>
> (Sri Aurobindo 1998, 8)

Thus, the externalities of the Vedas contain within them deeper and greater psycho-spiritual truths. Sri Aurobindo through his mystical pursuits was able to gain access to those spiritual truths. The *Secret of the Veda* as the name suggests is a text to reveal the psycho-spiritual truths behind the various externalities and symbols used in the Vedas. Not only are the symbols in the Vedas couched in symbolisms and mysteries, the Vedas themselves reveal a journey of a Rishi through the spiritual realms to gain truth and knowledge, represented in the symbolism of light—any scholar who does not see the Vedas through the yogic or spiritual paradigm will make a mess of it in terms of its interpretations. Whether the dominant materialistic-positivistic-secular paradigm (which has gained an upper hand in European consciousness Enlightenment onwards) gives legitimacy to the yogic paradigm is a matter of politics of knowledge production and its commitment to the perpetuation of its worldview at the expense of other valid worldviews; the fact of the matter is that the yogic paradigm of knowledge pursuit has its own cosmology and methodology of knowing the truths of our existence (Singh 2014). Consequently, the Vedas are records of experiences leading from human to divine in which many internal and external battles have to be waged over the powers of ignorance and evil (represented by darkness) to gain knowledge, truth, and immortality (represented by light and sun). That the European scholars had profoundly misunderstood the Vedas through their translations, given that they worked within the parameters of the materialistic-positivistic-secular paradigm that was further poisoned by imperialistic designs in knowledge production, was a fact not lost on Sri Aurobindo. He contends (1998, 24):

> The ancient Scripture was delivered over to a scholarship laborious, bold in speculation, ingenious in its flights of fancy, conscientious according to its own lights, but ill-fitted to understand the method of the old mystic poets; for it was void of any sympathy with that ancient temperament, unprovided with any clue in its own intellectual or spiritual environment to the ideas hidden in the Vedic figures and parables. The result has been of a double character, on the one side the beginnings of a more minute, thorough and careful as well as a freer handling of the problems of Vedic interpretation, on the other hand a final exaggeration of its apparent material sense and the complete obscuration of its true and inner secret.

The Vedic scholarship which Europe had built, in Sri Aurobindo's assessment, despite its stated laboriousness and rigor was a series of speculations, conjectures, half-truths, and falsities. He writes (1998, 24):

> By ingenious deductions from the comparative method applied to philology, mythology and history, by large amplifications of the existing data with the aid of ingenious speculation, by unification of the scattered indications available it has built up a complete theory of Vedic mythology, Vedic history, Vedic civilisation which fascinates by its detail and thoroughness and conceals by its apparent sureness of method the fact that this imposing edifice has been founded, for the most part, on the sands of conjecture.

Despite the claims of Comparative Philology, which since its beginning has claimed the status of science in order to get legitimacy and prestige in academia and the ear of the masses, Sri Aurobindo had serious concerns about the truths of its endeavors. Its conjectural nature to him was more than evident, and despite the claims of scientific status, the methods applied and the hasty conclusions reached made him dismissive of its truth contentions. He did not think that Comparative Philology held the standards applied to natural sciences, and consequently was distorting the truth contained in the Vedas.

> Modern Philology.... failed to create a Science of Language and we are still compelled to apply to it the apologetic description given by a great philologist after some decades of earnest labour when he was obliged to speak of his favourite pursuits as "our petty conjectural sciences." But a conjectural Science is no Science at all. Therefore the followers of more exact and scrupulous forms of knowledge refuse that name altogether to Comparative Philology and deny even the possibility of a linguistic science.... We have to recognise in fact that European scholarship in its dealings with the Veda has derived an excessive prestige from its association in the popular mind with the march of European Science. The truth is that there is an enormous gulf between the patient, scrupulous and exact physical sciences and these other brilliant, but immature branches of learning upon which Vedic scholarship relies. Those are careful of their foundation, slow to generalise, solid in their conclusions; these are compelled to build upon scanty data large and sweeping theories and supply the deficiency of sure indications by an excess of conjecture and hypothesis. They are full of brilliant beginnings, but can come to no secure conclusion. They are the first rough scaffolding for a Science, but they are not as yet Sciences (Sri Aurobindo 1998, 29–30).

One of the profound conjectures, erected on the platform of falsity and European supremacy, Sri Aurobindo opines, is the coming of the Aryans to India from the northwestern frontiers. He was familiar with the idea that the Vedas had been tortured to extract from them the substantiation of the AIT and that they contained no mention of the Aryan invasion of India. The Aryan/Dasyu divide on which the AIT is pegged is not racial; rather it is cultural. The battles that are depicted in the Vedas are battles between light and darkness, ignorance and Truth, culture and degeneration, nobility and savagery in terms of psycho-spiritual constitution. They are not between races and between invaders and aborigines. This is completely understandable in that the term "Arya" since antiquity has meant sophisticated and noble in the Indian context. Gaining enlightenment, the Noble Truths that the Buddha preached are "Arya" Truths—a term that he himself used. And given his tirade against the "ritualism" of the Vedas, and given that the Vedas are considered the texts of the Aryans, if the Arya/Dasyu divide were true, the Buddha would have never used the term "Arya" for naming his teachings. Sri Aurobindo enunciates (1998, 26):

> But the indications in the Veda on which this theory of a recent Aryan invasion is built, are very scanty in quantity and uncertain in their significance. There is no actual mention of any such invasion. The distinction between Aryan and un-Aryan on which so much has been built, seems on the mass of the evidence

to indicate a cultural rather than a racial difference. The language of the hymns clearly points to a particular worship or spiritual culture as the distinguishing sign of the Aryan,—a worship of Light and of the powers of Light and a self-discipline based on the culture of the "Truth" and the aspiration to Immortality,—Ritam and Amritam. There is no reliable indication of any racial difference.... There is nothing in the Veda, as there is nothing in the present ethnological features of the country to prove that this descent took place near to the time of the Vedic hymns or was the slow penetration of a small body of fair-skinned barbarians into a civilised Dravidian peninsula.

And as I have mentioned earlier, there was a great deal that was made of the Aryan nose to distinguish it from the Dravidian nose-less, and the Vedas were used to substantiate the speculation to turn it into theory. According to Sri Aurobindo (1998, 26, footnote):

It is urged that the Dasyus are described as black of skin and noseless in opposition to the fair and high-nosed Aryans. But the former distinction is certainly applied to the Ayan Gods and the Dasa Powers in the sense of light and darkness, and the word *anasah.* does not mean noseless. Even if it did, it would be wholly inapplicable to the Dravidian races; for the southern nose can give as good an account of itself as any "Aryan" proboscis in the North.

With the above contentions, he moves to explain the secrets of various symbols present in the Vedas through his writings in the *Secret of the Veda* and *Hymns to the Mystic Fire*.

Indus Civilization and Contemporary Discourse on Archeology

Truth has its own ways of springing surprises. The established and dominant narrative by the beginning of the century was that India knew no civilization before the coming of the Aryans. This was to change when in 1924, the Director General of the Archeological Survey of India, Sir John Marshall (through the excavations initiated by R.D. Bannerji and Daya Ram Sahni, respectively), announced the discovery of two ancient Bronze Age Civilization cities—Mohenjodaro and Harappa—of what he called as the Indus Civilization (also known as Harappan civilization in the current discourse) as both the cities were situated in the river valley of Indus. The subsequent decade-long excavations (excavations continued even later) revealed that the cities of the Indus civilization were massive and extremely well planned. They are marvels of urban engineering for the times in which they were built. They had roads intersecting at right angles with carefully laid out drainage and covered sewerage system. Mohenjodaro made use of baked bricks, which was quite unheard of in other Bronze Age civilizations. The houses of the inhabitants were well planned, many of them at least two storied. They also had brick-lined wells, bathing facilities, privies, and drainage connected to the city's main sewerage system, suggesting that town planning and cleanliness were of utmost importance to the Harappans (Possehl 2002).

Their economy was quite complex, with various craftspeople, metalworkers, seal cutters, architects, and engineers living in the city. The Harappans were wealthy people who traded as far away as with Mesopotamia, Sumer, and Egypt. The technological sophistication of the Harappan people can also be seen in the making of metal alloys such as bronze, square seals, high-quality faience, high-quality ceramics especially stoneware, and jewelry—in the cutting, polishing, etching, and drilling of long carnelian beads. The metalworkers worked with copper, tin, arsenic, lead, silver, gold, and electrum. They also built small ships, which could sail as far away as 4,000 miles to distant lands. The Harappan way of life was not possible without an in-depth knowledge of urban engineering, Chemistry, and navigation (Possehl 2002).

The discovery of Mohenjodaro and Harappa struck at the very root of the then prevalent discourse that the Aryans came to India in 1500 BCE and consequently established civilization. One would think that with such massive evidence, the AIT would suffer a fatal jolt. However, the ideas of European superiority and supremacy prevailed, and throwing all academic integrity to the wind the new evidence was reinterpreted. The Aryans still came as invaders. This time instead of defeating the civilization-less original inhabitants of India—the "Dravidians"—they defeated the civilized Dravidians and pushed them to the southernmost corners of the Indian subcontinent. The Vedic and Puranic texts again came in handy for the desired outcomes. In 1944 when the Second World War was coming to a close, a Brigadier General of the British Army serving in the North African front, Robert Eric Mortimer "Rick" Wheeler, was made the Director General of the Archeological Survey of India. Shortly after, he made a trip to Harappa which was in excavation at that point in time, and within a couple of hours of being at the site, he concluded that the mound at Harappa was a citadel—constructed to fend against the invading Aryans:

> The Aryan Invasion of the Land of Seven Rivers, the Punjab and its environs, constantly assumes the form of an onslaught upon the walled cities of the aborigines. For these cities the term used in the *Rigveda* is *pur*, meaning a "rampart," "fort" or "stronghold." ... Indra, the Aryan War god, is *puramdara*, "fort-destroyer." He shatters "ninety forts" for his Aryan protégé Divodasa.... Where are—or were—these citadels? It has in the past been supposed that they were mythical, or were merely "places of refuge against attack, ramparts of hardened earth with palisades and a ditch." The recent excavation of Harappa may be thought to have changed the picture. Here we have a highly evolved civilization of essentially non-Aryan type, now known to have employed massive fortifications, and known also to have dominated the river-system of north-western India at a time not distant from the likely period of the earlier Aryan invasions of that region. What destroyed this firmly settled civilization? Climatic, economic, political deterioration may have weakened it, but its ultimate extinction is more likely to have been completed by deliberate and large-scale destruction. It may be no mere chance that at a late period of Mohenjo-daro men, women and children appear to have been massacred there. On circumstantial evidence, Indra stands accused.
>
> (Wheeler 1947, 82)

Wheeler's contentions have not held the test of time. Excavations at Harappa and Mohenjodaro and the rest of the 1,050 sites of the Indus Civilization (till date approximately 1,052 sites of the civilization) have been either identified or excavated (Possehl 2002), which many scholars would rather prefer to call as Indus-Saraswati Civilization. This is because of the finding of over 500 sites on the currently dried-up riverbed of a mighty ancient river, Saraswati, which is called Ghaggar in India and Hakra in Pakistan that flowed from the Himalayas to the Arabian Sea (Possehl 2002). Tectonic movements around the beginning of the second millennium BCE made a part of the river go paleochannel and another meet the river Yamuna, which was not as big then as it is today (Agarwal and Sood 1982). Satellite images have proved the existence of this river in the past, and even today all over India there are Brahmin communities which name their *jati* by the name of the river Saraswati—they call themselves Saaraswat Brahmins, or Brahmins who lived by the banks of Saraswati at one point in time. Gregory Possehl (2002), who was engaged in archeological research on Indus Civilization in both India and Pakistan for close to four decades, holds that the Indus Civilization began around 7000 BCE and entered its mature phase, called the Mature Harappan phase, between 2500 BCE and 1900 BCE in which its numerous cities flourished. These cities had declined much before the mythical invasion of the mythical Aryans. Mohenjodaro along with many other cities in Sindh, Baluchistan, and Cholistan came to an abrupt end around 1900 BCE, and as far as the other cities are concerned, there is either a progressive decline or a relocation of the civilization eastwards toward the Indo-Gangetic plain in the Late Harappan period (depending upon the region, the time span of this phase is either 1900 BCE–1300 BCE or 1900 BCE–1000 BCE). Possehl (2002, 237) writes:

> There was an abandonment, or severe depopulation, of a number of important Indus settlements including Channu-daro, Kot Diji, Balakot, Allahdino, Kulli, Mehi, Nindowari, Nausharo, Kalibangan, Ropar, Surkotada, Dholavira, Desalpur, and Lothal. There was also a disruption in the Indus Economy. The production of a wide range of special materials, many of which seem to be have been luxury items, was curtailed.... [However] there was an increase in the number of settlements in the Punjab, Haryana, western Uttar Pradesh, and northern Rajasthan. The Harappans in Gujarat remained remarkably stable.

Jonathan Kenoyer (2005, 23), who has conducted excavations and research in both Mohenjodaro and Harappa, having worked in western and central India, substantiates:

> One of the most important developments is the emergence of new peripheral centers in the Gangetic region concomitant with the eclipse of urban centers in the old core of the Indus Valley. This suggests that the Late Harappan period is not so much of a decline in the Indus Valley, but rather of social, economic, and political reorganization on a larger scale that includes both the Indus and Gangetic regions as well as the adjacent Malwa Plateau.

Jim Shaffer, another archeologist who has conducted extensive fieldwork in Neolithic and Bronze Age Civilization sites in both India and Pakistan—holding the drying of the river Saraswati as the cause—along with Diane Lichtenstein, contends (2005, 85–86, italics original):

> Beginning in the late third millennium BC and continuing throughout the second millennium BC, many, *but not all*, Indus Valley settlements, including urban centers, were abandoned as a cultural response to the environmental "crisis."... Even within the Indus Valley, the cultural response of abandoning habitation sites varied. In Cholistan, along the Ghaggar-Hakra River, it was a dramatic response of abandonment. Yet all areas were affected in the Indus Valley. While the quality of the survey data is regionally variable, it is sufficient to show a gradual and significant population shift from the Indus Valley eastward into the eastern Punjab and Gujarat, beginning in the late third millennium BC and continuing throughout the second millennium BC.

Focusing exclusively on Harappa, Kenoyer (2005, 23–26, italics mine) states:

> [Recent excavations at Harappa] indicate that the Late Harappan occupation at the site was much more widespread than originally thought.... Baked brick architecture was constructed with both newly made bricks as well as reused bricks from earlier structures. During the Late Harappan period there is evidence of over-crowding and encroachment rather than abandonment and decline (Kenoyer 1991).... *There is no concrete evidence for the appearance of a new biological population* (Kennedy 1992, 1995). This suggests that the changes and discontinuities reflect a transformation of the local population rather than the appearance of new people and the eradication of the Harappan inhabitants.

We have mentioned earlier that the faience industry and bead making—an aspect of the lapidary industry—were quite developed in the Mature Phase of the Harappan civilization. Kenoyer notes that the making of stone beads became less common in the Late Harappan period and was substituted with glass beads. The production of glass beads in the Punjab continues all the way up to Painted Gray Ware Period (1400 BCE to 1000 BCE) and later till Northern Black Polished Ware Period, showing continuity between the Late Harappan period and the Early History. He writes: "Between 1700 and 800 BC, glass production developed into a common industry and became quite widespread throughout the northern subcontinent" (Kenoyer 2005, 37). In effect, if we take the evidence of the beads and faience industry into account, there is a continuity coming to the current times. The state of Gujarat, which is the southernmost area of the Harappan civilization, still has the city of Surat as one of the leading centers of the world even today in terms of the lapidary industry. The city is the biggest center in the world for the cutting and polishing of diamonds and gems.

What about the Citadel theory of Wheeler, standing on which he gave archeological evidence to the Aryan Invasion Theory? Possehl (2002) contends that the elevated mound was not a citadel—on the contrary, it was an elevated area, fortified with retaining walls to hold the mud used for its construction, on which buildings of significance such as the Great Bath (taking the example of Mohenjodaro), Warehouse, and other large buildings could be built; it was some sort of an ancient Indian acropolis. If it were meant for defensive purposes, then the western side of the Mohenjodaro mound would not have been open to the Indus plains.

In the excavations at Mohenjodaro, there were some human remains that were found—a total of forty-two skeletons, interned in rather a hasty manner at different places within the city; no cemetery as yet has been found there. At one site which is called the "HR Area Tragedy" site—located in the HR-B Area, Block 2, House V, Room 74—a total of fourteen skeletons (thirteen adult males and females and one child) were found. Wheeler (1959, 113-114) immediately connected this to the invasion of the Aryans:

> That final blow has often enough been described. It is represented by groups of skeletons—men, women and children, some bearing axes or sword-cuts—which have been found lying on the topmost level in the sprawled or contorted positions in which they fell. They had been left there by raiders who had no further use for the city which they had stormed. In that moment Mohenjo-daro was dead.

Dales (1964) and Kennedy (1982, 1984, 1994) have refuted the contentions. Kennedy (1984, 429), who investigated the skeletons, holds that though there was trauma on skeleton 10, the death did not seem to have occurred from the trauma because "the cut is not fresh and its margins are characterized by considerable bone absorption." Or even if the death had been caused by the wound, the wound must have been caused anywhere between thirty to seventy days earlier. Therefore despite that there were skeletons found in one room, all but one did not have mortal wounds. Although the skeletons suggest a hasty internment, there is no conclusive evidence to suggest that the people were put to death by any invading army. There are other three "massacre" sites where clusters of skeletons have been found. However all of them belong to a period (late Harappan Period) when civilization at Mohenjodaro had already come to an end. Possehl (2002, 164-165) concludes:

> Some experts on ancient Indian history have faith in the preposition that these deaths were cause [sic] by invading Aryans. There are, however, many problems with this theory, not the least of which is chronological: While there may have been speakers of one or more Indo-European languages in the Greater Indus region earlier, there is a gap of centuries between the abandonment of Mohenjo-daro at about 1900 B.C. and the documentation found in the Rgveda, which probably dates to circa 1000 B.C. Also note that the Rgveda is a not a text documenting the invasion and conquest of the Subcontinent, but speaks of the feuding among the Aryans as well as with the indigenous peoples. Sindh is a peripheral area in the Vedic literature: The center of this world was the Punjab. It is therefore noteworthy that there is no evidence for massacre at Harappa or any of the other Indus settlements in the geographical area described most prominently in the Vedas.

Kenoyer (2005, 44) seconds: "One of the most important results of the current work at Harappa is that there continues to be no support for the earlier interpretations of Vedic-Aryan invasions and the destruction of Harappan settlements." The Aryan Invasion Theory thus stands refuted. But just like the earlier situation where the emergence of the ruins of the massive cities of Harappa and Mohenjodaro did not refute the Aryan Invasion Theory but rather was appropriated to continue the narrative, the profound refutation of the AIT has morphed into a new theory: the Aryan Migration Theory (AMT). The AMT now contends that the European Aryans may not have come as invading armies but they still came as wandering pastoralists. The idea of European Aryans was racist and imperialistic right from the very beginning and it remains racist and imperialistic today in whatever guise we may experience it—within its scholarly facade, it continues to deny India its history and the cultural, philosophical, spiritual, artistic, architectural, scientific, and technological accomplishments of its ancestors. What is most surprising is that the same archeologists who refute the AIT promote the AMT on either weak or no evidence, even when they have to contradict themselves. For instance, Kenoyer (2005, 45) writes, "At the opposite end of the spectrum is the misconception that the Indus people as a whole represent the communities referred to in the Vedic literature." This is despite the fact of his own contentions as quoted above: "During the Late Harappan period there is evidence of overcrowding and encroachment rather than abandonment and decline.... *There is no concrete evidence for the appearance of a new biological population*" (2005, 23–26, italics mine). The non-appearance of a new biological population in Late Harappa should have been sufficient to contest the AMT theory. Kenoyer (2005, 46) however takes a contrary route:

> According to many scholars, the chronological framework for the final phases of the Harappan and the Late Harappan occupation at Harappa does correspond broadly with the time frame for the Rg Vedic period. Therefore, it is not improbable that some communities referred to in the Vedas were passing through or living in the regions controlled by Harappa during both the Harappan (Period 3C 2250–1900 BC) and the Late Harappan times (1900–1700 or 1300 BC).

This is also despite reporting the similarities in burial practices mentioned in the Vedas and found in the late Harappan period:

> The Rg Veda refers to several types of burial, including earth burials and cremation. It is clear from the careful reading the excavation reports of Vats that there is no evidence for cremation at Harappa, but there are earth burials in Stratum II of Cemetery H. In later texts dating to c.800 BC, there are detailed instructions on how to collect bones that have been either buried or exposed for a specified length of time and place them in a pot with a lid that is then buried in a pit.... Pot burials from the later Stratum I in Cemetery H could reflect an earlier example of this type of secondary or fractional burial. However, the limited nature of the data makes it impossible to make any conclusive statements about the presence or absence of Vedic communities at Harappa.
>
> (Kenoyer 2005, 45)

With the above data, Kenoyer could have taken the position that perhaps both the dating of the Vedas and the coming of the Aryans into India are profound myths created to bolster and enhance the European supremacy over the native Indians of the Indian subcontinent. He did not do so and instead perpetuated the AMT.

What has happened now is that the time of the coming of the Aryans has been moved by a few centuries. The possibility that the Harappan civilization was an indigenous creation of Indian Aryans is yet to be acceded to by most Western archeologists. Gregory Possehl (2002), who as we have seen earlier, has comprehensively refuted the AIT. However, he too does not find the idea fantastical in that wandering pastoralists could create a massive civilization which made India the jewel in the crown of the British empire—after having achieved a golden age in the early centuries of the first millennium CE—but not indigenous people who already were massive city builders with a highly advanced civilization for its times, who would disappear without a trace or leave a little trace. Mere wandering herdsmen, because they simply were European, could become harbingers of a profound ancient Indian civilization, the full scope of achievements of which in the current times is yet to be fully traced and unfolded:

> I believe from linguistic evidence that the homeland of the Indo-European peoples was somewhere in the temperate forest regions of Eurasia, so they came to the subcontinent from somewhere else. When the speakers of an Indo-European language(s) first came to the Subcontinent is not known. They first appear in the Near East just after 2000 B.C., but this is from linguistic evidence and they could have been there much before this, as would be the case for the Subcontinent.... No one knows for sure when the Indo-Europeans who spoke Vedic Sanskrit came to the Subcontinent, or how they got there. Speakers of other Indo-European languages were in the Near East early in the second millennium, and this may approximate the date of the Aryans into the Subcontinent. *But there is no evidence for an invasion, and most contemporary scholars who deal with this issue think more in terms of the movement that characterizes cattle pastoralists because of their need for pastureland, than military conquest.* Moreover, the Aryans may have come to the Punjab over a long period of time (a matter of centuries), not in a great rush, as an invasion would suggest.
>
> (Possehl 2002, 249, italics mine)

And they came so comprehensively that in no part of the world did they leave any trace of their language, culture, philosophy, etc., other than the Indian Subcontinent. Forget about evidence refuting the AMT, this theory militates against common sense. Given that Possehl earlier attests to the movement of Indus Civilization eastward after 1900 BCE, how does he explain the migration and the eclipsing of its fabulous urban centers? Comical as it may sound, Possehl holds that the Indus Civilization was so good that it failed. Its failure was not because of "flood, avulsion, drought, trade, disease, locusts, invasion, or any other of a myriad of 'natural' or 'outside' forces" but because of a "sociocultural flaw" (2002, 244). It was a social system that achieved great heights because of "social harmony in human relationships and with the environment (2002, 244)." He states that it was too good for its own good. Citing Heesterman

(1985), he feels that if a society does not have inner conflict, it cannot last for long because it is the inner conflict which allows the inhabitants to be in a "constant state of negotiating, resolving, dealing with maladaptation or lack of harmony in their lives" (Possehl 2002, 244) and because Indus Civilization built a system based on social harmony among and with one another, which included the environment, it collapsed under its own weight—it was too good for its own survival. The above position of Possehl is completely conjectural—as conjectural as the AMT. It is true there seems to be an absence of big temples and palaces within the Mature Harappan Civilization, quite unlike Mesopotamia and Egypt, but creating a comprehensive idea of an entire social system based on the lack of these artifacts is nothing but conjectural projection. Possehl is creating the radical "other" of the Egyptian and Mesopotamian civilizations in the Harappan Civilization, and basing his theory on it. He writes (2002, 148),

> One of the more interesting observations about the Indus Civilization is that no temples have been found. Nor is there much to be said of monumental architecture with a religious function or monumental architecture of any kind. The temples and pyramids of Dynastic Egypt and the ziggurats of Mesopotamia have no parallel in the Indus Valley.

He contends further that it is not that religion was not there in the civilization; it certainly was as is evident from structures like the Great Bath in Mohenjodaro and various figurines that have been found. And the capacity to build monumental structures—the engineering and the work force—was there too and yet no such structures were built. Similarly there are no palaces present either, much in contrast to the Egyptians and Mesopotamians: "Another contrast between Egypt and Mesopotamia and the Indus Civilization is the absence of palaces, the large abode of the heads of government and their powerful associates charged with managing the fortunes of the political apparatus" (2002, 148). The fact is that nothing conclusive is known about the social organization of the Harappans. Creating a social system completely in contrast to the Mesopotamians and Egyptians, based on the lack of similarity of structures found in the remains of the Mesopotamian and Egyptian Civilizations, is nothing but a sleight of hand—a pure work of fantasy and projection.

Then what really happened to most of the prominent cities of the Indus Civilization? The answer lies in the drying up of Saraswati. There is a correspondence between the time that Saraswati dried up and the abandonment or the decline (as the case may be) of the Harappan cities. Schaffer and Lichtenstein (2005, 84, italics original) write:

> In the early second millennium BC, there was the capture of the Ghaggar-Hakra (or Saraswati) river system (then a focal point of human occupation) by adjacent rivers, with subsequent diversion of these waters eastwards (Shaffer 1981, 1982, 1986, 1993; Mughal 1990, 1997; Shaffer and Lichtenstein 1995, 1999). At the same time, there was an increasing tectonic activity in Sindh and elsewhere. Combined, these geological changes meant *major* changes in the hydrology patterns of the region (Flam 1981, 1993). These natural geological processes had significant consequences for the food producing cultural groups throughout the greater Indus Valley area.

Further, they not only categorically refute the Aryan Invasion Theory but also are incisive about all attempts to twist data to show Western influences on the rise of prehistoric civilization in India. In their assessment, the most current archeological records show a remarkable continuity within the Indian subcontinent:

> The modern archeological record for South Asia indicates a history of significant cultural continuity; an interpretation at variance with earlier eighteenth through twentieth-century scholarly views of South Asian cultural discontinuity and South Asian cultural dependence on western cultural influences.
>
> (Schaffer and Lichtenstein 2005, 93)

They are cognizant of the initiatives of various European nations to bolster their national identity and ego through the appropriation of the Aryan identity and Sanskrit—undertaken in the colonial era but not yet been abandoned:

> The scholarly paradigm of the eighteenth and nineteenth centuries in conflating language, culture, race, and population movements has continued, with historical linguistic scholars still assiduously attempting to reconstruct a proto-Indo-European language, and attempting to link that language to a specific "homeland," in order to define population migration away from the seminal geographic base. Suggestions for such a proto-Indo-European homeland range from Siberia to more recent efforts to tracing the homeland to Anatolia (Renfrew 1987) and the Ukraine (Gamkrelidze and Ivanov 1985a, b; Gimbutas 1985; Mallory 1989; Allchin 1995), and these efforts now incorporate human genetic studies (Cavalli-Sforza et al. 1994) to verify the linguistic chronologies
>
> (Schaffer and Lichtenstein 2005, 93).

Their reasoned view backed by the analysis of massive amounts of data gathered from various archeological sites and spread all over the Indian subcontinent is that there is neither Western influence in the creation and shaping of the Harappan Civilization nor discontinuities in cultural records of the prehistoric Indian Subcontinent.

> The current archeological and paleoanthropological data simply do not support these centuries old interpretative paradigms suggesting western, intrusive, cultural influence as responsible for the supposed major discontinuities in the South Asian cultural prehistoric record (Shaffer and Lichtenstein 1999; Kennedy 2000; Lamberg-Karlovsky 2002).... It is currently possible to discern cultural continuities linking specific prehistoric social entities in South Asia into one cultural tradition (Shaffer and Lichtenstein 1989, 1995, 1999; Shaffer 1992, 1993). This is *not to* propose social isolation *nor* deny any outside cultural influence. Outside cultural influence did affect South Asian cultural development in later, especially historic, periods, but an identifiable cultural tradition has continued, an Indo-Gangetic Cultural Tradition (Shaffer 1993; Shaffer and Lichtenstein 1995, 1999) linking social entities over a period of time from the development of food production in the seventh millennium BC to present
>
> (Schaffer and Lichtenstein 2005, 93, italics original).

The above by Shaffer and Lichtenstein is conclusive and is in line with the colossal archeological data, which have been gathered over time. It also is in contradiction to the contentions of Possehl and Kenoyer, who despite the presence of such data perpetuate the AMT following linguistics and philology, which continue to remain non-science despite their bellowing claims to be science—had they been science, the "Aryan homeland" would not have spanned and continue to span the different parts of Europe and most parts of Asia (minus India). Sri Aurobindo's stand on the AIT and concerns that he had regarding Comparative Philology continue to get validated. It is time that modern academia backs off from perpetuating a colonial myth—either the AIT or the AMT—that continue to get mentioned in textbooks all the way from school to college to university level. This theory is deeply and profoundly embedded in the racial superiority of Europeans or people with European lineage over the inferiority of Indians: it is quite explicit in the ways in which it was crafted. Evidence after evidence keeps emerging but Western academia, which controls the academic discourse in practically all parts of the world, keeps appropriating it and keeps shifting the goalpost. If it is not the AIT then it is the AMT; if it is not the AMT, then it will be something else.

Conclusion

Distortion of history has been a mega project of the colonizers. The anticolonial writers were sophisticated enough to understand it. Although the postcolonial writers have built their legacy on the backs of the anticolonial writers, the distortion in history has not been such a serious undertaking among them, particularly when it comes to India. Eradicating the civilizational contributions of non-European people to humanity was the master-note on which the colonizers' representation of colonized cultures and nations played. By distorting history, the colonial project destroyed the identity of the colonized. Destruction of identity led to the destruction of their faith in themselves and hence to the resistance to the colonial rule. Whether it was Africa or it was India, the project was the same. Writing an introduction to Aimé Césaire's *Discourses on Colonialism*, Robin D. G. Kelly (2000, 22) writes:

> An entire generation of "enlightened" European scholars worked hard to wipe out the cultural and intellectual contributions of Egypt and Nubia from European history, to whiten the West in order to maintain the purity of the "European" race. They also stripped all of Africa of any semblance of "civilization," using the printed page to eradicate their history and thus reduce a whole continent and its progeny to little more than beasts of burden or brutish heathens.

By removing the "civilization" from the colonized, the European colonizers could turn the colonized "other" into primitive, which would then further and justify their civilizing mission. Kelly (2000, 9), commenting on Césaire, elucidates:

> Césaire reveals, over and over again, that the colonizers' sense of superiority, their sense of mission as the world's civilizers, depends on turning the Other into a barbarian. The Africans, the Indians, the Asians cannot posses civilization

or culture equal to that of the imperialists, or the latter have no purpose, no justification for the exploitation and domination of the rest of the world. The colonial encounter, in other words, requires a reinvention of the colonized, the deliberate destruction of the past-what Césaire calls "thingification."

The Aryan Invasion Theory, or its politically correct sibling the Aryan Migration Theory, is intimately tied with the above project. The invasion theory was tied directly to colonialism and the migration theory is tied to the racial superiority of the European people. The invasion or the migration theory strips the Indians of the agency to conceive, foster, nurture, and perpetuate a civilization. It is about denying the indigenous Indian population the creative, intellectual, and rational capacity to engender a civilization. The direct colonial rule may have ended but the paradigm running the colonial enterprise that it is only the European people or people with European lineage who are capable of establishing civilizations is solidly intact when we take the AIT or AMT into consideration.

It is this "othering," this turning of the Indian civilization, its culture, its history, its contribution to humanity into the primitive "other," that Sri Aurobindo systematically refuted in *Foundations of Indian Culture*, which has been renamed and reprinted as *Renaissance in India with a Defence of Indian Culture*. The demonization of the Indian civilization, its "greatest achievements, philosophy, religion, poetry, painting, sculpture, Upanishads, Mahabharata, Ramayana" (Sri Aurobindo 1959, 3), was so intense in the colonial times that Sri Aurobindo begins the *Foundations* with a basic question "Is India Civilized?" and then goes to write three chapters on the issue. However, refutation is not the central theme of his writings. The fulcrum on which his writings revolve is to basically explain the Indian culture and civilization from within—from the perspective of its own cosmology, paradigm, and worldview which is different from the cosmology that the Western world predominantly follows. Within the process, he also offers the critique of rationalism and positivism—two dominant notes of the Western civilization—pointing to the idea that the foundations of Indian culture essentially come from a paradigm, which transcends and integrates mind and senses: the faculty, the exclusive emphasis on which, give rise to the philosophies of rationalism and positivism, respectively. Given that these two philosophies are in opposition to the spiritual worldview, the Western civilization during the colonial period felt compelled to attack the Indian civilization, the foundation of which is essentially spiritual. He however points out that both the Western culture, with its emphasis on rationalism and positivism, and the Indian culture with its emphasis on spirituality are necessary for the completeness of the human race, and that the spiritual worldview does transcend and integrate reason and science as was the case in ancient India, which did not eschew either mathematics, science, or philosophy in the quest for spirituality.

Note

1 This section of the paper is largely inspired by the research work of Edwin Bryant (2001). Adequate attention has been paid to give credit to his ideas.

References

Agarwal, D. P., and R. K. Sood. 1982. "Ecological Factors and Harappan Civilization." In Possehl, Gregory L. ed. *Harappan Civilization: A Contemporary Perspective*. Delhi: Oxford and IBH Publishing Company, 223–231.

Allchin, F. R. 1995. *The Archaeology of Early Historic South Asia: The Emergence of Cities and States*. Cambridge: Cambridge University Press.

Bryant, Edwin. 2001. *The Quest for the Origins of Vedic Culture: The Indo-Aryan Migration Debate*. New York: Oxford University Press.

Bryant, Edwin. F., and Patton, Laurie L., eds. 2005. *The Indo-Aryan Controversy: Evidence and Inference in Indian History*. New York: Routledge.

Cavalli-Sforza, L., Menozzi, P. and Piazza, A. 1994. *The History and Geography of Human Genes*. Princeton: Princeton University Press.

Chakrabarti, D. K. 1976. "India and the Druids." *Antiquity* 197, 66–67.

Dales, G. F. 1964. "The Mythical Massacre at Mohenjo-daro." *Expedition* 6, 3: 36–43.

Filliozat, V., ed. 1997. *Vijayanagar as Seen by Domingos Paes and Fernao Nuniz (16th Century Portuguese Chroniclers and Others)*. New Delhi: National Book Trust.

Flam, L. 1981. *The Paleogeography and Prehistoric Settlement Patterns in Sindh, Pakistan (ca. 4000–2000 B.C.)*. PhD diss., South Asia Regional Studies, University of Pennsylvania.

Flam, L. 1993. "Fluvial Geomorphology of the Lower Indus Basin (Sindh, Pakistan) and the Indus Civilization." In Schroder, J. F. ed. *Himalaya to the Sea*. New York: Routledge, 265–326.

Flood, Gavin. 1996. *An Introduction to Hinduism*. Cambridge: Cambridge University Press.

Gamkrelidze, T., and Ivanov, V. V. 1985a. "The Ancient Near East and the Indo-European Question: Temporal and Territorial Characteristics of Proto-Indo-European Based on Linguistic and Historical-Cultural Data." *Journal of Indo-European Studies* 13: 3–48.

Gamkrelidze, T., and Ivanov, V. V. 1985b. "The Migration of Tribes Speaking the Indo-European Dialects from Their Original Homeland in the Near East to Their Historical Habitations in Eurasia." *Journal of Indo-European Studies* 13: 49–91.

Gimbutas, M. 1985. "Primary and Secondary Homeland of the Indo-Europeans." *Journal of Indo-European Studies* 13: 185–202.

Heesterman, J. C. 1985. *The Inner Conflict of Tradition*. Chicago: University of Chicago Press.

Kelly, Robin D. G. 2000. "Poetics of Anticolonialism." In Césaire, Aimé. *Discourse on Colonialism*. Translated by Joan Pinkham. New York: Monthly Review Press, 7–28.

Kennedy, K. A. R. 1982. "Skulls, Aryans and Flowing Drains: The Interface of Archeology and Skeletal Biology in the Study of the Harappan Civilization." In Possehl, Gregory L. ed. *Harappan Civilization: A Contemporary Perspective*. Delhi: Oxford and IBH Publishing Company, 289–295.

Kennedy, K. A. R. 1984. "Trauma and Disease in Ancient Harappans." In Lal, B. B. and Gupta, S. P. eds. *Frontiers of the Indus Civilization*. Delhi: Books and Books, 425–436.

Kennedy, K. A. R. 1992. "Biological Anthropology of Human Skeletons from Harappa: 1928–1988," *Eastern Anthropologist* 45, 1–2: 55–86.

Kennedy, K. A. R. 1994. "Identification of Sacrificial and Massacre Victims in Archeological Sites: The Skeletal Evidence." *Man and Environment* 19, 1–2: 247–251.

Kennedy, K. A. R. 1995. "Have the Aryans Been Identified in the Prehistoric Skeletal Record from South Asia? Biological Anthropology and Concepts of Ancient Races."

In Erdosy, G. ed. *The Indo-Aryans of Ancient South Asia: Language, Material Culture and Ethnicity*, Berlin: Walter de Gruyter, 32–66.

Kennedy, K. A. R. 2000. *God-Apes and Fossil Men: Paleoanthropology in South Asia*. Ann Arbor: University of Michigan Press.

Kennedy, V. 1828. *Researches into the Origin and Affinity of the Principal Languages of India*. London: Longman.

Kenoyer, J. M. 1991. "Urban Process in the Indus Tradition: A Preliminary Model from Harappa." In Meadow, R. H. ed. *Harappa Excavations 1986–1990*, Madison, WI: Prehistory Press, 29–60.

Kenoyer, J. M. 2005. "Culture Change During the Late Harappan Period at Harappa: New Insights on Vedic Aryan Issues." In Bryant, Edwin F. and Patton, Laurie L. eds. *The Indo-Aryan Controversy: Evidence and Inference in Indian History*. New York: Routledge, 21–49.

Lal, B. B. 2005. "Aryan Invasion of India: Perpetuation of a Myth." In Bryant, Edwin F. and Patton, Laurie L. eds. *The Indo-Aryan Controversy: Evidence and Inference in Indian History*. New York: Routledge, 50–74.

Lamberg-Karlovsky, C. C. 2002. "Archeology and Language: The Indo-Iranians." *Current Anthropology* 43: 63–88.

Mallory, J. P. 1989. *In Search of the Indo-Europeans: Language, Archeology, and Myth*. London: Thames and Hudson.

Monboddo, J. B. 1774. *Of the Origins and Progress of Language*. Edinburgh: Balfour.

Mughal, R. M. 1990. "Harappan Settlement Systems and Patterns in the Greater Indus Valley." *Pakistan Archeology* 25: 1–72.

Mughal, R. M. 1997. *Ancient Cholistan: Archaeology and Architecture*. Karachi, Pakistan: Ferozsons (Pvt.) Ltd.

Muir, J. 1860. *Original Sanskrit Texts*. London: Trüber.

Possehl, G. L. 2002. *The Indus Civilization: A Contemporary Perspective*. Boulder, CO: AltaMira Press.

Renfrew, C. 1987. *Archeology and Language. The Puzzle of Indo-European Origin*. New York: Cambridge University Press.

Shaffer, J. G. 1981. "The Protohistoric Period in the Eastern Punjab: A Preliminary Assessment." In Dani, A. H. ed. *Indus Civilization: New Perspectives*. Islamabad: Quaid-I-Azam University, 65–101.

Shaffer, J. G. 1982. "Harappan Culture: A Reconsideration." In Possehl, Gregory L. ed. *Harappan Civilization: A Contemporary Perspective*. Delhi: Oxford and IBH Publishing Company, 41–50.

Shaffer, J. G. 1986. "Cultural Development in the Eastern Punjab." In Jacobson, J. ed. *Studies in the Archeology of India and Pakistan*. Delhi: Oxford and IBH Publishing Company, 74–90.

Shaffer, J. G. 1992. "Indus Valley, Baluchistan, and the Helmand Traditions: Neolithic through Bronze Age." In Ehrich, R. W. ed. *Chronologies in Old World Archaeology: Vols. I & II*. Chicago: University of Chicago Press, 441–464.

Shaffer, J. G. 1993. "Reurbanization: The Eastern Punjab and Beyond." In Spodek, H. and Srinivasan, D. M. eds. *Meaning in South Asia: The Shaping of Cities from Prehistoric to Precolonial Times*. Washington, DC: National Gallery of Art, 53–67.

Shaffer, Jim. G., and Lichtenstein, Diane A. 1989. "Ethnicity and Change in the Indus Valley Cultural Tradition." In Kenoyer, J. M. ed. *Old Problems and New Perspectives in the Archeology of South Asia*. Madison: University of Wisconsin, Wisconsin Archeological Reports, 117–126.

Shaffer, Jim. G., and Lichtenstein, Diane A. 1995. "The Concepts of Cultural Tradition and Paleoethnicity in South Asian Archaeology." In Erdosy, G. ed. *The Indo-Aryans of Ancient South Asia: Language, Material Culture and Ethnicity*. Berlin: Walter de Gruyter, 126–154.

Shaffer, Jim. G., and Lichtenstein, Diane A. 1999. "Migration, Philology and South Asian Archeology." In Bronkhurst, J. and Deshpande, M. M. eds. *Aryan and Non-Aryan in South Asia: Evidence, Interpretation and Ideology*. Cambridge, MA: Department of Sanskrit and Indian Studies, Harvard University, 239–260.

Shaffer, Jim. G., and Lichtenstein, Diane A. 2005. "South Asian Archeology and the Myth of Indo-Aryan Invasions." In Bryant, Edwin F. and Patton, Laurie L. eds. *The Indo-Aryan Controversy: Evidence and Inference in Indian History*. New York: Routledge, 75–104.

Singh, K. 2014. "Beyond Mind: The Future of Psychology as a Science." In Cornellisen, R. M. M., Misra, G. and Varma, S. eds. *Foundations and Applications of Indian Psychology*. Delhi: Pearson, 40–52.

Sri Aurobindo. 1959. *The Foundations of Indian Culture*. Pondicherry: Sri Aurobindo Ashram.

Sri Aurobindo. 1998. *The Secret of the Veda*. Pondicherry: Sri Aurobindo Ashram.

Trautmann, T. R. 1982. "Elephants and the Mauryas." In Muckerjee, S. ed. *India: History and Thought*. Calcutta: Subernarekha, 245–281.

Wheeler, M. 1959. *Early India and Pakistan: To Ashoka*. New York: Frederick A. Praeger.

Wheeler, R. E. M. 1947. "Harappa 1946: The Defences and Cemetery R-37." *Ancient India* 3, 58–130.

4

A Philosophy for the Global Age

Richard Hartz

We live at a time of epochal change. The rush of change is exhilarating for some, threatening for others; but all have to live with it and try to make sense of it. Much of this change can be ascribed to globalization. But globalization means different things to different people. Surprisingly, this word which is so familiar and controversial today only started to catch on in the 1980s. A few years later, as one sociologist noted, it had "come from nowhere to be almost everywhere" (Giddens 2003, 7).

Whatever exactly it may be, globalization is with us whether we like it or not. Efforts to explain what it is, how it affects us, and where it is going have produced a large and growing literature drawing on economics, sociology, political science, anthropology, history, geography, psychology, and other fields. One discipline that has so far been underrepresented in this discussion is philosophy.[1] But without the critical insights of philosophy, the deepest implications of the global processes that are transforming our lives are likely to remain unexplored. The experts may be giving us brilliant answers, but failing to ask the most important questions.

Another limitation of globalization theory has been the predominant Eurocentrism it shares with most branches of current scholarship. Non-Western scholars have contributed to global studies, but mostly within Western intellectual and institutional frameworks.[2] Although Western as well as non-Western scholars have tried to avoid Eurocentrism, radically distinctive alternatives to Western perspectives have not often received serious consideration. But as the *Stanford Encyclopedia of Philosophy* points out in its article on globalization:

> At a minimum, globalization suggests that academic philosophers in the rich countries of the West should pay closer attention to the neglected voices and intellectual traditions of peoples with whom our fate is intertwined in ever more intimate ways.
>
> (Scheuerman 2014)[3]

Sri Aurobindo and Globalization

Clearly there is a need for a more global approach to understanding globalization. As a step in this direction, I propose to look at the writings of a thinker who lived before the term "globalization" had been coined, yet whose ideas are strikingly relevant to the challenges we face today. Aurobindo Ghose (1872–1950), usually referred to as Sri Aurobindo, is generally recognized as an important and original philosopher as well as a major political and spiritual figure of modern India. But his philosophy is not just a system of metaphysics, nor is it confined to the traditional preoccupations of Indian thought. His writings were specifically addressed to a worldwide audience and can be interpreted as an attempt to work out a philosophy for the global age.

Writing in English, Sri Aurobindo published most of his works in their original form in the second decade of the twentieth century in a monthly philosophical review with a modest but widely distributed readership on at least three continents. He made a point of distinguishing this journal from the type of publication that serves "as the mouthpiece of a sect, school or already organised way of thinking." Its stated object was "to feel out for the thought of the future, to help in shaping its foundations and to link it to the best and most vital thought of the past" (Sri Aurobindo 1998a, 103).

The future to whose thought Sri Aurobindo hoped to contribute was not that of any existing civilization. His Indianness asserted itself in his attempts to find inspiration for a global future in the ancient traditions of India. But this endeavor was subordinated to his overall futuristic orientation. His background had equipped him to be a breaker of traditional limitations and cultural barriers. Educated in England, after his return to India in his early twenties he underwent a conscious process of indigenization. His thought thus reflected what psychologists now call a bicultural or hybrid identity (Arnett 2002, 778). By the early twentieth century this was not unusual. But what is of interest in his case is the way in which it enabled him to integrate Western and Eastern worldviews in a balanced philosophical synthesis.

In his vision of the future, Sri Aurobindo looked beyond the Western-dominated world of the imperialistic age he lived in; but it was not only the demise of colonialism and the resurgence of the non-Western world that he foresaw. Long before decolonization, he was preoccupied with the growth of human unity at a level transcending political and cultural divisions. Writing a hundred years ago, he observed:

> The peoples of the world already possess a loose and chaotic unity of life in which none can any longer lead an isolated, independent and self-dependent existence. Each feels in its culture, political tendencies and economic existence the influence and repercussion of events and movements in other parts of the world. Each already feels subtly or directly its separate life overshadowed by the life of the whole.
> (Sri Aurobindo 1997c, 476; quoted from a chapter first published in 1917)

Here and elsewhere, we find Sri Aurobindo describing globalization decades before the word entered the dictionaries. No doubt he was not the only one to do so. References to certain features of globalization, such as the overcoming of distance by technology, can be traced in literature, philosophy, and social commentary as far back as the early nineteenth century. But Sri Aurobindo's account of the increasing interconnectedness of human life shows, for his time, a remarkably prescient awareness of the all-pervasive and multidimensional nature of this phenomenon.

In *The Ideal of Human Unity*, he focused on problems and possibilities associated with what we would now call political globalization. Aspects of this had been the subject of optimistic speculations at least from the time of Tennyson's lines on "the Parliament of man, the Federation of the world" (2007, 59) in a poem published as early as 1842. Sri Aurobindo's book, however, is as much a warning of the dangers of a centralized and homogenized world-state as it is an exploration of idealistic prospects of human unity in diversity. Its primary purpose is to determine the necessary conditions under which a global political union could come about without loss of individual and regional freedom, keeping the human race "intact in the roots of its vitality, richly diverse in its oneness" (Sri Aurobindo 1997c, 284).

Sri Aurobindo was also concerned about the consequences of economic globalization, as it is called today. He was critical of unregulated capitalism and appreciated the motives of socialism in "its will to get rid of this great parasitical excrescence of unbridled competition, this giant obstacle to any decent ideal or practice of human living" (1997c, 200). At the same time, he understood the positive role of economic forces in bringing humanity together. Moreover, his endorsement of the aims of socialism was qualified by a recognition of the pitfalls of collectivism. More than anything else, he insisted on the value of individual liberty as the key to all true progress.

The story of globalization properly begins with the gradual growth of interrelations among peoples since the dawn of history. But what we usually have in mind when we speak of globalization is largely an outcome of the European expansionism of the last few centuries. This relentless expansion, at once creative and destructive, has been driven by the dynamics of capitalism but enabled by advances in science and technology. At the heart of it all has been the idea of progress as the Western mind has understood it.

Progress has been a central theme of the modern age, if not its defining feature. Sri Aurobindo fully acknowledged the value of much that has been achieved in its name. The problem, he pointed out, is that modern society has been unable to discover the aim of this progress, "unless the aim is always more knowledge, more equipment, convenience and comfort, more enjoyment, a greater and still greater complexity of the social economy, a more and more cumbrously opulent life" (1997c, 224). But this only means more and more of the same or similar things on a larger and larger scale, with a frenetically accelerated movement and an increasingly mind-boggling complexity. Sri Aurobindo questioned whether this is the kind of progress humanity needs. But it seems to be all that modernity has to offer.

Modernity and the Globe

Continual expansion, development, and outward progress have produced the runaway world described around the turn of this century by the sociologist Anthony Giddens (2003). This is what has come to be called globalization, taking its name from the globe. Yet its relation to our planet is problematic. The expansionism of modernity and its corollary, globalization, have reached the point where they encounter the globe itself, with its finite space and resources and its fragile ecosystems, as an unwelcome obstacle to perpetual growth.

The geographer David Harvey (2010, 27–30) highlights the basic problem facing global capitalism when he writes:

> The current consensus among economists...is that a 'healthy' capitalist economy...expands at 3 per cent per annum. Grow less than that and the economy is deemed sluggish. Get below 1 per cent and the language of recession and crisis erupts.... When capitalism was made up of activity within a fifty-mile radius around Manchester and Birmingham in England and a few other hotspots in 1750, then seemingly endless capital accumulation at a compound rate of 3 per cent posed no big problem...Three per cent growth for ever is running into serious constraints. There are environmental constraints, market constraints, profitability constraints, spatial constraints.

If the apparently unstoppable march of globalization is on collision course with the finiteness of the globe, what is to be done? The magnitude of the crisis and the unprecedented challenges it poses demand that humanity collectively marshal all its resources to meet it. Pragmatic solutions may not be enough, if they do not go to the roots of the problem.

Such a turning point in history calls for the kind of rethinking of fundamental assumptions that have usually been the province of philosophy. But the philosophical traditions of the past, by themselves, also seem inadequate to the newness of the situation. Too much has changed. What seems required is something like the emerging approach of global philosophy, involving creative interaction among traditions (Connolly 2015, 193). The East-West synthesis found in Sri Aurobindo's philosophical writings early in the last century already foreshadowed this type of contemporary philosophizing.

It might be difficult to convince many of today's globalists of the importance of philosophy or the need for more cross-cultural engagement in order to grasp and solve the urgent problems of the contemporary world. This is partly because globalization is still propelled by the momentum of Western expansion set in motion around the end of the European Middle Ages. This headlong momentum has left most members of modern societies with relatively little time or inclination for calm reflection. But it is becoming obvious that this expansionist globalization cannot continue for much longer without a drastic reorientation or a serious reconsideration of where it is heading. When it falters, what then?

The Global Age

A starting point for seeking an answer has been suggested by the sociologist Martin Albrow in a thought-provoking book on the "global age." Albrow distinguishes globalization, which has been a manifestation of the dynamics of modernity, from the Global Age, his name for what comes *after* the Modern Age. He prefers "global" to "postmodern" for the latter purpose because the postmodern is defined in relation to the modern, of which it tends to become only a phase; it "has never escaped modernity" (Albrow 1996, 1). The concept of postmodernity fails to capture the epochal nature of the change that is occurring and gives no clue to its essential characteristics. "When we invoke the Global Age," Albrow explains, we "move from seeing globalization as yet another stage of modernity, an '-ization' which is a culmination of changes arising out of modernity, to seeing it as the preparation for the global becoming part of life and globality becoming a constitutive factor in potentially any sector, sphere, or institution" (Albrow 1996, 107).

This analysis provides a useful framework for appreciating the contemporary relevance of Sri Aurobindo's thought, especially if we underline a point in Albrow's theory which he left undeveloped. In passing, he comments on the challenge that arose for the West when, in its expansion over the globe, it encountered "rival civilizations, such as India and China, which operated with different conceptual frames in totally different configurations." Without elaborating on the implications of this challenge to Western cultural hegemony, Albrow observes, "Exchange with those cultures is now a factor in the transformation which makes the Global Age. For they proved resilient and capable of resisting Western domination and their survival highlights the limits of modernity" (Albrow 1996, 35).

At the end of the Cold War, the political scientist Samuel Huntington drew pessimistic conclusions from similar observations of the resilience of non-Western civilizations. But the nightmare scenarios he imagined are not inevitable, as Huntington himself admitted (1997, 312–321). There is plenty of reason to believe that more peaceful and cooperative relations among culturally diverse peoples are equally possible. What is certain is that, as the earth shrinks, exchange and mutual understanding among different cultures have become more necessary than ever before.

Few would dispute the major roles that Asian civilizations have begun to play and are sure to play more and more as the world shaped by Western modernism recedes behind us and we venture into a future whose contours are hard to discern in advance. The rise of China and India in the twenty-first century has often been perceived mainly in economic and political terms; but the cultural and, potentially, even the spiritual dimensions of this phenomenon should not be underestimated. Under these circumstances there is no denying the relevance of an Indian thinker of the stature of Sri Aurobindo, not only to the people of his own country, but to the rest of the world. Not only do his writings penetrate to the heart of what India has achieved in the past and still represents in modern times, but he has explored what India's survival and revitalization could mean for her own future and the world's. Though he wrote early in the last century, he knew how globalization is changing everything. And he envisioned the future in terms that point toward the global age which is upon us.

A Speck amid the Stars

We cannot go back to the past and reverse globalization. The only viable course is to go forward and become more global. The West has globalized our world outwardly. Perhaps the East will show us how to globalize ourselves inwardly. The global age calls for a global consciousness. Sri Aurobindo did not use the word globalization, but he adopted "global" in his vocabulary and used it in two different ways. He associated "global thinking" with the plane of cosmic consciousness he called the Overmind (Sri Aurobindo 2011, 158). He also spoke of an evolving "global consciousness of the earth" (Sri Aurobindo 2012, 299). Both usages suggest that he would have emphasized the subjective dimension of what later came to be known as globalization. But his literal application of "global" to a terrestrial consciousness also reflects his focus on the material globe. To return again to the concept of the global age, we may note in this connection another passage where Albrow (1996, 83) explains the distinction between modern and global:

> Modern is above all a time reference, highlights innovation and obsolescence, sifts and rejects the useless old.... 'Global' is above all a space reference, the product of the location of the earth in space, a material celebration of the natural environment on which human beings depend, the evocation of the concrete wholeness or completeness of existence, embracing humanity rather than dividing it.

The globe is a constantly recurring image in Sri Aurobindo's poetry. It appears at regular intervals throughout his epic, *Savitri*, from the first page, where the earth is pictured wheeling "in the hollow gulfs" of space (Sri Aurobindo 1993, 1), to the last passage before the epilogue, where the heroine returns from higher worlds to "the whirling dance of earth" (Sri Aurobindo 1993, 711). The globe is described in the poem as "transient and frail" (Sri Aurobindo 1993, 330), "a small globe dotting infinity" (Sri Aurobindo 1993, 486), and "a little speck amid the stars" (Sri Aurobindo 1993, 511). Such phrases convey a vivid sense of the earth's finitude and vulnerability. Sri Aurobindo's sense of our relationship to the earth resembles in this respect an attitude that has become widespread only in the last few decades, since human beings acquired the means to see their home from outer space and, around the same time, began to feel the looming shadow of a planetary ecological crisis. Few during Sri Aurobindo's time saw such a crisis coming. But as early as 1912, he commented in his diary on "the struggle of machinery with Nature" (Sri Aurobindo 2001b, 80). Some years later he warned of "perturbations of the earth system that threaten to break up the mould of civilisation" (Sri Aurobindo 1997b, 269).

Modernity has brought us to the threshold of the global age, but it has done so by seeing our planet in terms of territory, resources, and populations to be conquered and exploited. This movement has exhausted its utility and reached the point where its continuation could be disastrous. As we cross the threshold into an interdependent world, we need to rethink our view of things, our values, and our relation to the globe we inhabit. Conquest and exploitation must be replaced by interchange and sustainability. In the terminology of Indian philosophy and psychology, the *guna* of *rajas* must be replaced by *sattva*; the restless drive of the kinetic mode of energy must yield to the mode of harmony and equilibrium. What must be avoided is a relapse into *tamas*, the mode of inertia and disintegration. At present, unfortunately, much of the rising mood of globaphobia seems to represent this kind of retrogression.

A Vision of Unity

Nativist, isolationist, and other rejectionist reactions to globalization are throwbacks to a less integrated world. They arise from difficulties in adapting to rapid change and exponentially increasing complexity. Understandable as these resistances may be, they are likely to be counterproductive as we move ahead into the global age. At the same time, everything associated with the past—even the distant past—cannot, merely for that reason, be dismissed as regressive.

Surprising as it may seem, some of the ancient scriptures of India have much to offer at this critical moment. Let us take, for example, a verse in the Isha Upanishad, a text that Sri Aurobindo often cites:

yas tu sarvāṇi bhūtāni ātmanyevānupaśyati,
sarvabhūteṣu cātmānaṁ tato na vijugupsate.

He translates this verse: "But he who sees everywhere the Self in all existences and all existences in the Self, shrinks not thereafter from aught" (Sri Aurobindo 2003, 7).

There could not be a better formula for the ideal psychological attitude in an age in which all human beings—in fact, all living creatures—are increasingly interconnected. No doubt this realization of inner unity with all, described so long ago in the Upanishads, comes at a stage of spiritual development which few may be capable of reaching even now. But as Sri Aurobindo explains in his commentary, the fullness of this self-realization is preceded by preliminary forms which are not inaccessible to ordinary people. They include "the attempt to understand or sympathise with others, the tendency of a widening love or compassion or fellow-feeling for others, the impulsion of work for the sake of others." To the degree that these things increase, there is realized "a pluralistic unity, the drawing together of similar units resulting in a collectivity or solidarity." A crucial consequence is that "by this vision, in proportion as it increases in intensity and completeness, there disappears from the individual mentality all *jugupsā*, that is to say, all repulsion, shrinking, dislike, fear, hatred and other perversions of feeling which arise from division and personal opposition to other beings" (Sri Aurobindo 2003, 35-36).

In the global age, the whole diversified mass of humanity is drawn into closer and closer contact and interdependence. There is no longer the protection once amply provided by geographical and other barriers which prevented interactions from exceeding manageable levels. The collective ability to cope with so much otherness has had relatively little time to develop. Dealing with it is, in a sense, the central challenge of our age. There are two ways to respond: a movement of contraction—the Sanskrit word *jugupsā* means literally the impulse to protect oneself—or a movement of widening. We can try to run away from all this otherness or fight it off, or else we can embrace it. A new awareness of the problem of "othering," as we now call it, is symptomatic of our times. But the Rishis in India long ago sought to get to the root of the same issue. The Brihadaranyaka Upanishad puts it like this: "Where there is duality, there other sees other, other hears, touches, thinks of, knows other." We take this to be normal and inevitable, but for the author of the Upanishad it is not: "All betrays him who sees all elsewhere than in the Self" (Sri Aurobindo 2005, 543).

A consciousness of oneness with all is the foundation of Sri Aurobindo's philosophy. This realization can be characterized as Vedantic, insofar as it is associated historically with that particular tradition. But nothing about the spiritual realization itself or its philosophical formulation limits its relevance to a single culture. In the early twentieth century, the Austrian physicist Erwin Schrödinger argued for the Vedantic idea of the Atman or universal Self on the basis of "the empirical fact that consciousness is never experienced in the plural, only in the singular" (Wilber 2001, 87). At a time when the world is being drawn together as never before, some kind of philosophical vision of unity would seem required to help us come to grips with the new reality. Such a vision can be arrived at from more than one starting point and formulated in various ways; Sri Aurobindo's integration of Vedanta with evolution does not exhaust the possibilities. His philosophy has been compared, for example, with the Christian-inspired evolutionary mysticism of his contemporary, the Jesuit priest and paleontologist Pierre Teilhard de Chardin. In this connection it is worth mentioning the influence of Teilhard's ideas on Marshall McLuhan, the media theorist who in the early 1960s coined the phrase "global village" (Wolfe 2004, 21–24). In this instance, philosophical or theological speculation ran ahead of the more cautious development of globalization theory.

Philosophy and Life

But the ongoing transition into the global age is not just a theoretical matter. Humanity seems to be stumbling into a new way of being with little understanding of what is happening. In the ancient world and in non-Western civilizations, philosophy tended to step in under such circumstances. In the Hellenistic age, an unsettled period similar in some ways to our own, the teaching of the Stoics—who called themselves "cosmopolitans"—had a strong appeal. Today most of us seem to be too caught up in the maelstrom of events to have much leisure for philosophy. Yet philosophy has never been more needed, if we are to make sense of the epochal shift from the modern to the global age.[4]

The prestige of the physical and social sciences now overshadows that of philosophy. But science cannot explain the meaning of it all. Something in human nature asks for a deeper understanding than what any analysis of the surfaces of things can give. A global renaissance of philosophy could be just over the horizon. The general level of mental ability brought about by modern education, combined with new opportunities for cross-cultural dialogue, has created conditions under which there could be a flowering of philosophical activity such as the world has never seen.

If philosophy is again to take a leading role in human life, however, it will have to break out of the narrow grooves in which academic philosophy has largely confined itself in recent times. The origins of the professional specialization of modern philosophy can be traced back to an aspect of ancient Greek thought which valued the speculative pursuit of theoretical knowledge for its own sake. Much of the Western philosophical tradition has differed in this respect from the main trend of philosophy throughout Asia. As Sri Aurobindo points out:

Philosophy has been pursued in Europe with great and noble intellectual results by the highest minds, but very much as a pursuit apart from life, a thing high and splendid, but ineffective. It is remarkable that while in India and China philosophy has seized hold on life, has had an enormous practical effect on the civilisation and got into the very bones of current thought and action, it has never at all succeeded in achieving this importance in Europe.

On the other hand, philosophy among the Greeks and Romans also had another side on which it developed in ways that did make a difference to life. Sri Aurobindo acknowledges this when he continues: "In the days of the Stoics and Epicureans it got a grip, but only among the highly cultured; at the present day, too, we have some renewed tendency of the kind." The influence of the thought of philosophers such as Friedrich Nietzsche, William James, and Henri Bergson is mentioned by Sri Aurobindo as evidence of the latter tendency in his own time (1997d, 112). Today one could point not only to a revival of the philosophical pragmatism pioneered over a hundred years ago by James and his fellow Americans Charles Sanders Peirce and John Dewey (see Talisse and Aikin 2011; Kitcher 2012; Lachs 2012), but to signs of interest in returning to something like the Greco-Roman practice of philosophy as a way of life (see Irvine 2009; Chase, Clark, and McGhee 2013). But these revivals have lacked so far the broad appeal of some movements based on Buddhist, Hindu, and other Eastern philosophies and disciplines.

Vedanta and the Modern World

The growing receptivity of many Westerners to Asian thought—reminiscent of the openness of ancient Romans to the "light from the East"—may be a harbinger of things to come. In the Roman Empire, the outcome was the official adoption of a Near Eastern religion and the eventual Christianization of Europe. Under the far more complex conditions that now exist, a similar spread or imposition of a single doctrine is hardly conceivable. Yet the large cultural divisions of humanity which have been called for simplicity the "West" and the "East" are bound to go on interacting more and more intimately, learning from each other in the process. Much of what the East has to contribute to this mutual enrichment is undoubtedly contained in its philosophies and the systems of practice often associated with them. But in their traditional forms, the relevance of these to the world we live in today cannot be taken for granted. Not only is it doubtful how much of authentic value can survive the hazards of cross-cultural transmission. Even within a single culture, time moves on and what the past has handed down to the present is not necessarily what is needed for our growth toward the future.

Sri Aurobindo devotes a good deal of space in his writings to disputing philosophical ideas that for centuries supported a growing ascetic tendency in Indian spirituality. He attributes these ideas especially to Buddhism and, in a later period, the Advaita Vedanta of Shankara. Critical as he is of central tenets of these systems, he does not deny the force of their reasoning, the spiritual experiences behind them, or their contributions to Indian civilization. Defending Buddhism against ill-informed disparagement, he writes:

> Buddhism was not solely a cloudy sublimation of Nirvana, nothingness, extinction and the tyrannous futility of Karma; it gave us a great and powerful discipline for the life of man on earth. The enormous positive effects it had on society and ethics and the creative impulse it imparted to art and thought and in a less degree to literature, are a sufficient proof of the strong vitality of its method. (1997d, 239)

All the same, Sri Aurobindo sought a more compelling foundation for a life-affirming spirituality than what any philosophy based on Buddha's insights into the unsatisfactoriness of existence can offer. Likewise he was unconvinced by Shankara's thesis that the world is ultimately an illusion (*māyā*); he rejected both the metaphysical arguments for it (2005, 428–498) and the finality of the spiritual realization that seems to justify it (2011, 239–262). But what concerned him most was the long-term impact of essentially pessimistic views of the world on India's collective development:

> The spirit of these two remarkable spiritual philosophies—for Shankara in the historical process of India's philosophical mind takes up, completes and replaces Buddha,—has weighed with a tremendous power on her thought, religion and general mentality: everywhere broods its mighty shadow, everywhere is the impress of the three great formulas, the chain of Karma, escape from the wheel of rebirth, Maya. (Sri Aurobindo 2005, 432)

The role of such ideas in determining the tone of a whole phase of civilization is a sign of the philosophical turn of the Indian temperament. The considerable social repercussions of Shankara's illusionism can be compared with the negligible consequences of George Berkeley's immaterialism, which in a different way also cast doubt on the reality of the apparent world. Samuel Johnson is said to have had no difficulty disproving Bishop Berkeley's theory to his own satisfaction by simply kicking a stone and asserting, "I refute it *thus*" (Boswell 2008, 248). In India, for better or worse, subtle thinking has been taken more seriously and has made a significant difference to people's lives.

A reconsideration of the philosophical underpinnings of Indian culture was therefore a matter not only of theoretical importance, but of practical urgency for Sri Aurobindo in the context of the anticolonial movement of national reawakening. He did not start from scratch, but looked for support in widely respected textual traditions. For this purpose he went back, as Swami Vivekananda and others had done, to the Upanishads.[5] But what he discovered in that large and diverse body of texts seemed at first sight to include "an emphasis…increasing steadily as time goes on into an over-emphasis, on the salvation of the individual, on his rejection of the lower cosmic life." This element, if present even in the early Upanishads, might appear to justify an otherworldly reading of Vedanta. In a commentary on the Kena Upanishad, Sri Aurobindo posed the question:

Well then may we ask, we the modern humanity more and more conscious of the inner warning of that which created us, be it Nature or God, that there is a work for the race, a divine purpose in its creation which exceeds the salvation of the individual soul, because the universal is as real or even more real than the individual, we who feel more and more, in the language of the Koran, that the Lord did not create heaven and earth in a jest, that Brahman did not begin dreaming this world-dream in a moment of aberration and delirium,—well may we ask whether this gospel of individual salvation is all the message even of this purer, earlier, more catholic Vedanta. If so, then Vedanta at its best is a gospel for the saint, the ascetic, the monk, the solitary, but it has not a message which the widening consciousness of the world can joyfully accept as the word for which it was waiting. (2001a, 95)

From Past Dawns to the Noons of the Future

Contrary to this life-negating interpretation, what Sri Aurobindo found in the Upanishads as a whole was a positive message for our times which he tried to reformulate in modern language, although he did not restrict himself to restating a vision that has come down to us from the past. In answer to the question raised above, a verse near the end of the Kena Upanishad suggested to him a clue to reconciling the highest spiritual realization with the fullest acceptance of life:

Taddha tad vanaṁ nāma tad vanam ityupāsitavyaṁ sa ya etad evaṁ vedābhi hainaṁ sarvāṇi bhūtāni saṁvāñchanti.

The name of That [*Brahman*] is "That Delight"; as That Delight one should follow after It. He who so knows That, towards him verily all existences yearn. (Sri Aurobindo 2001a, 11)

Here the Kena seems to speak of the *ānanda* or delight of being that sustains all things, an idea developed more fully in the Taittiriya Upanishad. Elaborating on the implications of this verse for a life-embracing spirituality, Sri Aurobindo comments:

The connection with the universe is preserved for the one reason which supremely justifies that connection; it must subsist not from the desire of personal earthly joy, as with those who are still bound, but for help to all creatures. Two then are the objects of the high-reaching soul, to attain the Supreme and to be for ever for the good of all the world,—even as Brahman Himself; whether here or elsewhere, does not essentially matter. Still where the struggle is thickest, there should be the hero of the spirit, that is surely the highest choice of the son of Immortality; the earth calls most, because it has most need of him, to the soul that has become one with the universe.

(Sri Aurobindo 2001a, 97–98)

The principal Upanishads represent a many-sided synthesis of the results of an early outburst of philosophical thinking and spiritual seeking which left its stamp on the subsequent course of Indian civilization. The Bhagavad Gita is a later synthesis of spiritual thought and experience, on which Sri Aurobindo also commented at length. But these texts were only his starting point. Near the end of the first chapter of *Essays on the Gita*, he briefly reviews several such "great syntheses in which Indian spirituality has been as rich as in its creation of the more intensive, exclusive movements of knowledge and religious realisation" (Sri Aurobindo 1997a, 8). He then looks ahead and suggests some of the conditions for an even wider synthesis capable of fulfilling the needs of a global age:

> We of the coming day stand at the head of a new age of development which must lead to such a new and larger synthesis. We are not called upon to be orthodox Vedantins of any of the three schools or Tantrics or to adhere to one of the theistic religions of the past or to entrench ourselves within the four corners of the teaching of the Gita. That would be to limit ourselves and to attempt to create our spiritual life out of the being, knowledge and nature of others, of the men of the past, instead of building it out of our own being and potentialities. We do not belong to the past dawns, but to the noons of the future. A mass of new material is flowing into us.... All this points to a new, a very rich, a very vast synthesis; a fresh and widely embracing harmonisation of our gains is both an intellectual and a spiritual necessity of the future.
>
> (Sri Aurobindo 1997a, 10)

The intellectual necessity of such an all-encompassing integration of knowledge led Sri Aurobindo not only to reformulate the theory and practice of Yoga and to write extensively on Indian thought, culture, and spirituality, but to make substantial original contributions to fields as diverse as metaphysics, aesthetics, philosophy of history, political philosophy, and social psychology. His overall approach to these subjects can be described as philosophical in a broad sense, but with an understanding that "philosophy ought not to be merely a lofty intellectual pastime or a play of dialectical subtlety or even a pursuit of metaphysical truth for its own sake, but a discovery by all right means of the basic truths of all-existence which ought then to become the guiding principles of our own existence" (1999, 383).

In an article looking back on the first four years of the monthly philosophical review in which he published many of his works, Sri Aurobindo rephrased the purpose with which the journal was launched:

> Our idea was the thinking out of a synthetic philosophy which might be a contribution to the thought of the new age that is coming upon us. We start from the idea that humanity is moving to a great change of its life which will even lead to a new life of the race,—in all countries where men think, there is now in various forms that idea and that hope,—and our aim has been to search for the spiritual, religious and other truth which can enlighten and guide the race in this movement and endeavour.
>
> (Sri Aurobindo 1998a, 105)

It is primarily from this standpoint of the needs of the human race as a whole at a critical juncture of its history that Sri Aurobindo offered his philosophical vision to the world. Writing early in the last century, he foresaw many of the problems we face today as the earth goes on shrinking and the barriers that once isolated human populations from each other continue to break down. He hoped that his ideas would play a role in shaping the thought of a more luminous and harmonious future. Relatively few of his contemporaries seem to have been entirely ready for what he had to offer. But since then, things have moved in many ways along lines that he anticipated. Perhaps the time has come when more and more people will take the trouble to delve into his writings. They are sure to be richly rewarded.

Notes

1. A branch of philosophy that has made a place for itself in the globalization literature is ethics, as in Appiah (2007) and Singer (2016). A more unusual example of the convergence of philosophy with globalization theory is Uggla's (2010) study of Ricoeur, hermeneutics, and globalization.
2. For a survey of scholarship in this field, see Coleman and Sajed (2013).
3. By linking philosophy and globalization studies in a way that implies their relevance to each other, the SEP entry takes a position that is still rather unusual in either field. But at least the notion that globalization theory might benefit from more attention to philosophical questions is unlikely to be controversial. The same cannot be said about proposals to shed the Eurocentrism of mainstream academic philosophy. For a lively discussion of this issue, see Van Norden (2017).
4. Encouragingly, some mainstream social and political commentators are beginning to express concern about the neglect of philosophy. In *The Great Questions of Tomorrow*, for example, David (professor of international relations and former CEO and editor of the FP Group which publishes *Foreign Policy* magazine) writes: "The trouble is that, on this rapidly shifting ground, we are literally acting before we have the time to think. We are enshrining into law or promulgating as regulation views that have profound impacts on the nature of our societies without benefit of public debate or, perhaps more troublingly, of the intervention of philosophical reflection" (Rothkopf 2017, 47).
5. In his exploration of India's ancient traditions Sri Aurobindo went back even further than the earliest Upanishads, to the Rig Veda. His groundbreaking scholarship on this subject (see Sri Aurobindo 1998b) has not received the attention it deserves; but it is beyond the scope of this article to introduce it.

References

Albrow, Martin. 1996. *The Global Age: State and Society Beyond Modernity*. Stanford, CA: Stanford University Press.

Appiah, Kwame Anthony. 2007. *Cosmopolitanism: Ethics in a World of Strangers*. New York: W. W. Norton.

Arnett, Jeffrey Jensen. 2002. "The Psychology of Globalization." *American Psychologist* 57, 10: 774–783.

Boswell, James. 2008. *The Life of Samuel Johnson*. London: Penguin Books.
Chase, Michael, Clark, Stephen R. L., and McGhee, Michael, eds. 2013. *Philosophy as a Way of Life: Ancients and Moderns: Essays in Honor of Pierre Hadot*. Chichester, West Sussex, UK: Wiley Blackwell.
Coleman, William D., and Sajed, Alina, eds. 2013. *Fifty Key Thinkers on Globalization*. New York: Routledge.
Connolly, Tim. 2015. *Doing Philosophy Comparatively*. London: Bloomsbury Academic.
Giddens, Anthony. 2003. *Runaway World: How Globalization Is Reshaping Our Lives*. New York: Routledge.
Harvey, David. 2010. *The Enigma of Capital and the Crises of Capitalism*. New York: Oxford University Press.
Huntington, Samuel P. 1997. *The Clash of Civilizations and the Remaking of World Order*. New York: Simon and Schuster.
Irvine, William B. 2009. *A Guide to the Good Life: The Ancient Art of Stoic Joy*. New York: Oxford University Press.
Kitcher, Philip. 2012. *Preludes to Pragmatism: Toward a Reconstruction of Philosophy*. New York: Oxford University Press.
Lachs, John. 2012. *Stoic Pragmatism*. Bloomington: Indiana University Press.
Rothkopf, David. 2017. *The Great Questions of Tomorrow*. New York: TED Books.
Scheuerman, William. 2014. "Globalization." In Zalta, Edward N. ed. *The Stanford Encyclopedia of Philosophy*. Available at: https://plato.stanford.edu/archives/sum2014/entries/globalization/ (Accessed June 15, 2018).
Singer, Peter. 2016. *One World Now: The Ethics of Globalization*. New Haven, CT: Yale University Press.
Sri Aurobindo. 1993. *Savitri: A Legend and a Symbol*. Pondicherry, India: Sri Aurobindo Ashram.
Sri Aurobindo. 1997a. *Essays on the Gita*. Pondicherry, India: Sri Aurobindo Ashram.
Sri Aurobindo. 1997b. *The Future Poetry, with On Quantitative Metre*. Pondicherry, India: Sri Aurobindo Ashram.
Sri Aurobindo. 1997c. *The Human Cycle, The Ideal of Human Unity, War and Self-Determination*. Pondicherry, India: Sri Aurobindo Ashram.
Sri Aurobindo. 1997d. *The Renaissance in India and Other Essays on Indian Culture*. Pondicherry, India: Sri Aurobindo Ashram.
Sri Aurobindo. 1998a. *Essays in Philosophy and Yoga*. Pondicherry, India: Sri Aurobindo Ashram.
Sri Aurobindo. 1998b. *The Secret of the Veda with Selected Hymns*. Pondicherry, India: Sri Aurobindo Ashram.
Sri Aurobindo. 1999. *The Synthesis of Yoga*. Pondicherry, India: Sri Aurobindo Ashram.
Sri Aurobindo. 2001a. *Kena and Other Upanishads*. Pondicherry, India: Sri Aurobindo Ashram.
Sri Aurobindo. 2001b. *Record of Yoga*. Pondicherry, India: Sri Aurobindo Ashram.
Sri Aurobindo. 2003. *Isha Upanishad*. Pondicherry, India: Sri Aurobindo Ashram.
Sri Aurobindo. 2005. *The Life Divine*. Pondicherry, India: Sri Aurobindo Ashram.
Sri Aurobindo. 2011. *Letters on Himself and the Ashram*. Pondicherry, India: Sri Aurobindo Ashram.
Sri Aurobindo. 2012. *Letters on Yoga—I*. Pondicherry, India: Sri Aurobindo Ashram.
Talisse, Robert B., and Aikin, Scott F., eds. 2011. *The Pragmatism Reader: From Peirce through the Present*. Princeton, NJ: Princeton University Press.

Tennyson, Alfred Lord. 2007. *Selected Poems*. London: Penguin Books.
Uggla, Bengt Kristensson. 2010. *Ricoeur, Hermeneutics, and Globalization*. London: Continuum.
Van Norden, Bryan W. 2017. *Taking Back Philosophy: A Multicultural Manifesto*. New York: Columbia University Press.
Wilber, Ken, ed. 2001. *Quantum Questions: Mystical Writings of the World's Great Physicists*. Boston: Shambhala.
Wolfe, Tom. 2004. "McLuhan's New World." *The Wilson Quarterly* 28, 2: 18–25.

Part Two

Yoga and Metaphysics

5

The Psychic Being: Our Opening to the Divine

Marshall Govindan

A clear understanding of Sri Aurobindo's use of the term *psychic being* is essential to the practitioner of Integral Yoga. It is found throughout his writings and is a distinguishing feature of his Yoga. As we shall see, it cannot be equated with the English words *soul* or *Self* or with the Indian terms *Atman*, *Jivatman*, or *Purusha*. Although the Psychic Being is present behind everyone's heart, it is almost always hidden, and its workings are mingled with the movements of the mind and the vital. Until it emerges in the foreground of the consciousness, individual efforts in Yogic *sadhana* (discipline) remain fitful and limited by these movements. The practice of Sri Aurobindo's Integral Yoga—summarized in the words aspiration, rejection, and surrender—progresses to the extent that the Psychic Being comes to the forefront of one's consciousness. This occurs in four stages.

What is the Psychic Being?

Sri Aurobindo often refers to it metaphorically as a "spark which comes from the Divine."

> The psychic is a spark come from the Divine which is there in all things and as the individual evolves it grows in him and manifests as the psychic being, the soul seeking always for the Divine and the Truth and answering to the Divine and the Truth whenever and wherever it meets it.
>
> (Sri Aurobindo 2012, 105)

But Sri Aurobindo justifies the need for this new term, as distinct from the English word *soul*.

> The word soul is very vaguely used in English—as it often refers to the whole non-physical consciousness including even the vital with all its desires and passions. That is why the word psychic being has to be used so as to distinguish this divine portion from the instrumental parts of the nature.
>
> (Sri Aurobindo 2012, 112)

As such, it is an emanation, like the soul emanating from the Lord in the monistic theism of Saiva Siddhantha's *Tirumandiram* and Kashmir Saivism. But the Psychic Being is also a key evolutionary concept within Sri Aurobindo's Integral Yoga (Ganapathy 2010, 2012, 439–471).

> The psychic part of us is something that comes direct from the Divine and is in touch with the Divine. In its origin it is the nucleus pregnant with divine possibilities that supports this lower triple manifestation of mind, life and body. There is this divine element in all living beings, but it stands hidden behind the ordinary consciousness, is not at first developed and, even when developed, is not always or often in the front; it expresses itself, so far as the imperfection of the instruments allows, by their means and under their limitations. It grows in the consciousness by Godward experience, gaining strength every time there is a higher movement in us, and, finally, by the accumulation of these deeper and higher movements there is developed a psychic individuality—that which we call usually the psychic being. It is always this psychic being that is the real, though often the secret cause of man's turning to the spiritual life and his greatest help in it. It is therefore that which we have to bring from behind to the front in the Yoga.
> (Sri Aurobindo 2012, 103)

Nor can the Psychic Being be equated with the Atman of Vedanta.

> There is a difference between the psychic and the self. The self is the Atman above which is one in all, remains always wide, free, pure, untouched by the action of life in its ignorance. Its nature is peace, freedom, light, wideness, Ananda. The psychic (*antaratma*) is the individual being which comes down into life and travels from birth to birth and feels the experiences and grows by them till it is able to join itself with the free Atman above. The psychic being is concealed in the depths behind the heart centre. The Self has no separate place—it is everywhere. Your self and the self of all beings is the same.
> (Sri Aurobindo 2012, 106)

But Sri Aurobindo also reminds us that, although the English term is new in his Yogic system, it has an ancient antecedent in the age-old term *hrdaye guhayam*, "the secret heart."

> The psychic being in the old systems was spoken of as the Purusha in the heart (the secret heart—*hrdaye guhayam*) which corresponds very well to what we define as the psychic being behind the heart centre. It was also this that went out from the body at death and persisted—which again corresponds to our teaching that it is this which goes out and returns, linking new life to former life. Also, we say that the psychic is the divine portion within us—so too the Purusha in the heart is described as *Ishwara* of the individual nature in some places.
> (Sri Aurobindo 2012, 112)

It is secret because it is veiled by surface movements of the inner being composed of the inner mental, inner vital, and inner physical. The Psychic Being expresses itself as best it can through these outer instruments, which are governed more by outer forces than by the inner influences of the psychic. As a soul instrument, the Divine within, its evolutionary influence on human nature is usually hidden. Its will is for the divinization of life and, because of its purity, its action transforms these inner instruments.

It may be perceived as a mystic light behind the heart center.

> It may be said of the psychic that it is that [the luminous part of our being], because the psychic is in touch with the Divine and a projection of the Divine into the lower nature. The psychic is deep within in the inner heart-centre behind the emotional being. From there it stretches upward to form the psychic mind and below to form the psychic vital and psychic physical, but usually one is aware of these only after the mind, vital and physical are subjected and put under the psychic influence.
>
> (Sri Aurobindo 2012, 122–123)

As one surrenders to the Divine, egoism—the habit of identifying with the movements of the mind, the vital, and the physical—is replaced by the Psychic Being. This surrender of the ego perspective is the result of the practice of the Integral Yoga, as we will see below.

> There is individuality in the psychic being but not egoism. Egoism goes when the individual unites himself with the Divine or is entirely surrendered to the Divine. It is the psychic inmost being that replaces the ego. It is through love and surrender to the Divine that the psychic being becomes strong and manifest, so that it can replace the ego.
>
> (Sri Aurobindo 1972, 124)

The Influence of the Psychic Being, a New Evolutionary Concept

Sri Aurobindo stated that the evolutionary task of humanity is more than just reaching a spiritual level of existence. A further objective is the radical and integral transformation of Nature. This will reveal itself as the luminous Consciousness-Force, the trinity of Sat, Chit, and Ananda, whose revelation has yet to be accomplished in humankind as the self-affirmation of the supramental. To this end, when we become aware of the Psychic Being within, it leads the sadhana, the practice by which *siddhi* (perfection) is attained.

We can say that the Psychic Being is the soul in nature, evolving through it, supporting it, and at times when there is an opening to its influence, guiding our person in the drama of life. Sri Aurobindo tells us that it is a new, evolutionary concept that has not been discussed in the older sacred literature, such as the *Bhagavad Gita*.

> The psychic being evolves, so it is not the immutable. The psychic being is especially the soul of the individual evolving in the manifestation the individual Prakriti and taking part in the evolution. It is that spark of the Divine Fire that grows behind the mind, vital and physical as the psychic being until it is able to transform the Prakriti of Ignorance into a Prakriti of Knowledge. These things are not in the *Gita*, but we cannot limit our knowledge by the points in the *Gita*.
>
> (Sri Aurobindo 2012, 114)

He further writes,

> The Psychic Being is the developing soul consciousness manifested for the created being as it evolves. At first, the soul is something essential behind the veil, not developed in front. In front, there is only the body, life, mind. In the evolution, the soul consciousness develops more and more in the created being until it is so developed that it can come entirely in front and govern mind, life, and body.
>
> (Sri Aurobindo 2012, 118–119)

There are clear indications of its influence on the inner being, inner mind, inner vital, and inner physical.

> These things, love, compassion, kindness, bhakti, Ananda are the nature of the psychic being, because the psychic being is formed from the Divine Consciousness, it is the divine part within you. But the lower parts are not yet accustomed to obey or value the influence and control of the psychic for in men the vital and physical are accustomed to act for themselves and do not care for what the soul wants. When they do care and obey the psychic, that is their conversion—they begin to put on themselves the psychic or divine nature.
>
> (Sri Aurobindo 2012, 122)

Unlike the Self, or Atman, which merely witnesses the movements of the mind, emotions, and the senses, the psychic being can exert its influence upon these movements. The parts of the mind, of the vital and the body which can be so influenced by the vital are referred to as the psychic-mental, the psychic-vital, the psychic-physical. This influence can be according to the personality or the degree of evolution of each person... small or large, weak or strong, covered up and inactive or prominent and in action.

(Sri Aurobindo 2012, 108)

These parts may follow their limited aims, natures, or tendencies, or they may accept the psychic's motives and aims with or without modification.

Aspiration, Rejection, and Surrender: The Method of Integral Yoga

Before discussing the development of the Psychic Being, we must first understand the practice of Integral Yoga. In the following section, I quote extensively from or refer to *The Practice of Integral Yoga* by the late J. K. Mukherjee, who was for many years director of the Sri Aurobindo International Centre of Education, and whom I interviewed in 2009. In the words of A. S. Dalal, who wrote its foreword, this work "is a comprehensive treatise on the effective practice of the Yoga of Integral Transformation as propounded by Sri Aurobindo and the Mother." It is the first summing-up of the method of their practice, based on their disparate writings and in light of Mukherjee's own experience of over fifty-five years.

On Aspiration

The Integral Yoga of Sri Aurobindo and the Mother can be summarized in these two statements:

> (1) a steadily mounting ardent aspiration from the side of the sadhaka, and (ii) from the Divine's side an answering Grace descending from above in response to the sadhaka's call." But what is this aspiration? How does it differ from desire? Sri Aurobindo defines aspiration as "a spiritual enthusiasm, the height and ardour of the soul's seeking...an upward movement of our consciousness through the psychic part of our being toward all that is good, pure and beautiful." The Mother describes it as "an inner enthusiasm towards the New, the Unknown, the Perfection...a yearning, a longing for the contact with the Divine Force, divine Harmony, divine Love...an inner flame, a need for the light...A luminous enthusiasm that seizes the whole being...a purifying Will, an ever- mounting drive.
>
> (Mukherjee 2003, 42–43)

How to develop aspiration? Mukherjee describes its six stages, which are summarized here. First, the development of aspiration begins with an intense dissatisfaction with the habitual ways of human nature. You may wake up one morning and suddenly realize that you are no longer willing to go on living unconsciously, ignorantly, in a state in which you do things without knowing why, feeling things without knowing why, living contradictory wills, living by habit, routine, reactions, understanding nothing. You are no longer satisfied with that. How individuals respond to this dissatisfaction varies. For most, it is the need to know; for others, it is the need to do what is required to find meaning.

Second, the aspirant seeks ardently to escape this hollow human existence by seeking Truth, Love, Peace, Joy, and Being. These are probably still very vague, but the seeker is driven to find release from the present state of nauseating imperfection.

Third, after some time, because of the aspirant's persistent insistence, Divine Grace responds with a temporary piercing of the veil of ignorance, and one experiences the spiritual dimension of life. One sees the Light, feels Divine Love, or experiences Divine Bliss, the Presence, or Truth, depending on one's capacity and orientation. It may vary from person to person, but everything else previously experienced in ordinary life pales in comparison.

Fourth, the opening may close, so one must be careful not to forget or doubt it, but rather keep it vibrant and constantly direct one's aspiration toward its re-emergence.

Fifth, the sadhak will find the attraction to the higher life gradually growing and the attachment to the former, lower life diminishing. Not only might this manifest inwardly in the mental and vital planes, but also outwardly toward friends, even work and pastimes. A new type of yearning and resolution fills the heart and mind, which may express itself as: "O Lord, I want you and you alone. I do not want anything or anyone else except through you and for you. I want to belong entirely to you and will never allow anything to claim my consciousness. I surrender my all to you. Not my will, but Thy will be done. I am yours alone."

In the sixth stage, the aspiration is so intense that words and prayers, vocal and mental, are no longer needed or even wanted. There is only the flame of spiritual fire rising steadily upward in the background of profound silence. An intense craving to belong to the Divine, to be united with It, and to serve It as a perfect instrument, envelopes the whole expanse of the sadhak's consciousness. It is a great thirst for Love and Truth, for transformation, for supreme perfection (Mukherjee 2003, 45–46).

On Rejection

While still controlled by lower human nature, the sadhak must make personal effort to progress. This personal effort comprises the three operations of aspiration, described above, as well as rejection and surrender. The Siddhas, and more recently Sri Aurobindo, have insisted that a Yoga sadhak must renounce all habitual movements of the lower nature. These include the mind's opinions, preferences, habits, constructions, and ideas; the vital nature's desires, demands, cravings, passions, selfishness, pride, arrogance, lust, greed, jealousy, envy, and hostility to the Truth; and the physical nature's stupidity, doubt, disbelief, obscurity, obstinacy, pettiness, laziness, sloth, and unwillingness to change.

The goal is the total divine transformation of man's whole being, consciousness, and nature. Every ego-centered impulse and movement arising in the consciousness that does not turn the sadhak toward the Divine is an obstacle in this path. The sadhana of one who aspires to practice Sri Aurobindo's Integral Yoga includes responding to the constantly troubling reactions to life's ceaseless stream of obstacles. Identifying and removing them make up the yogic sadhana of rejection. There are three classes of them and a different strategy to deal with each. The three classes of obstacles are those of the past, the present, and the future.

When the obstacle is a type that the sadhak has already conquered in the past but is now indulging out of laziness, the sadhak should:

> (i) nip it at its very moment of sprouting, like a piece of dust on one's sleeve; (ii) never brood on it; (iii) take as little notice of it as possible; and (iv) even if one happens to think of it, remain indifferent and unconcerned.
>
> (Mukherjee 2003, 55)

The second category of obstacles, those of the present, often appears in the sadhak's consciousness and can even overwhelm it at times. But with sincere effort, the sadhak will discover the power to keep part of the consciousness free from their influence. To deal with this type, the sadhak must have this attitude:

(i) to apply one's willpower to resist the impulsion; (ii) never to rationalize or legitimize its appearance, but rather to withdraw all inner consent from its manifestation; (iii) never to yield any ground, however limited in extent; (iv) to act as a heroic warrior against the dark tendencies on behalf of the upward-moving forces of light; (v) turn immediately to the Divine and pray constantly and fervently that these weaknesses and impulses of his or her nature be vanquished and removed.

(Mukherjee 2003, 55–56)

How to recognize the third category of obstacles within—the deeply hidden potential weaknesses? At their first appearance, almost all of the sadhak's being becomes abnormally disturbed and agitated. The obstacles' roots are so deep and extensive that the sadhak feels that they are an intrinsic and ineradicable part of his or her being, so much so that the sadhak is not at all persuaded of the basic undesirability of these weaknesses. With their appearance, the sadhak temporarily loses the lucidity of his consciousness, as if in a storm. Most of the sadhak's consciousness is still deeply infatuated with these surging weaknesses and blindly yearns to fulfill some strong desires by letting them manifest. It would be foolhardy to attempt to eradicate such a weakness unaided before one is sufficiently prepared. There is a real danger of suppression of its outer manifestation leading to an internal conflict with that major portion of the sadhak's nature that obstinately clings to the attachment. An explosion is inevitable, disrupting the balance of the being. So, the aspirant should avoid as far as possible these intractable difficulties and refuse to allow them to manifest at all.

Rather the approach should be:

(1) to hold the difficulty or weakness in front of one's consciousness, without becoming scared by it or identified with it, (2) to go assiduously in search of its root cause or source, (3) to try to discover what parts of one's nature are secretly nurturing a fascination for this particular weakness, and are thrown into a turmoil at its slightest beckoning... (4) always to maintain a spirit of calm, quiet detachment, throughout the above observation, even if some ugly corners of one's being are exposed... (5) the *sadhak* has to keep alive in his heart a very sincere aspiration for the eradication of the weakness in question, addressing an earnest prayer to the Divine Mother that through the active intervention of her Grace these deep-rooted and recondite weaknesses and attachments may give up their malignancy and become quite innocuous in nature so that they can be easily faced and overcome... Such a prayer and aspiration coupled with a thorough self-examination will progressively turn these intractable obstacles first into manageable obstacles of the second class, and finally into easily detachable ones of the past.

(Mukherjee 2003, 59–60)

On Surrender

Self-surrender to the Divine, at all times and in all circumstances, is the key to the sadhana of Integral Yoga as well as the Kriya Yoga of Patanjali, who said in Yoga sutra I.23, "*Ishvara-pranidhanad-va*," or "because of one's surrender to the Lord, one successfully achieves cognitive absorption" (Govindan 2012, 17).

The phrase "my God and my all" summarizes its heartfelt expression. The day that a sadhak surrenders to the Divine, the Divine itself intervenes in the life of the student and helps remove all difficulties and weaknesses, and brings joy into the consciousness with its Presence.

For this to occur:

> (1) the sadhak must feel the vanity of one's own self-potency; (2) he must believe with all his heart that there is Someone called Divine who really exists, loves him, and has the omnipotence to do anything according to Divine wisdom; (3) the sadhak must turn to the Divine alone as his sole and ultimate refuge.
>
> (Mukherjee 2003, 87)

In the surrendered state of consciousness, whatever one does or feels, all movements are made as an offering to the Supreme Being, in absolute trust, freeing oneself of responsibility for oneself, handing all of one's burdens to the Divine.

The sadhak's habitual consciousness and nature contain ample resistance and obstruction that works against this surrender. One must unreservedly abandon oneself to the sole guidance of the Divine. How to know if one has done so? Sri Aurobindo gives a detailed description of the inner mood of a truly surrendered sadhak.

> I want the Divine and nothing else. I want to give myself entirely to him and since my soul wants that, it cannot be but that I shall meet and realize him. I ask nothing but that and his action in me to bring me to him, his actions secret or open, veiled or manifest. I do not insist on my own time and way; let him do all in his own time and way; I shall believe in him, accept his will, aspire steadily for his light and presence and joy, go through all difficulties and delays, relying on him and never giving up ... All for him and myself for him. Whatever happens, I will keep to this aspiration and self-giving and go on in perfect reliance that it will be done.
>
> (Sri Aurobindo 1972, 587)

Consequently, it is the Divine itself that takes charge of the entire course of the sadhak's sadhana.

> All can be done by the Divine—the heart and the nature purified, the inner consciousness awakened, the veils removed—if one gives oneself to the Divine with trust and confidence and even if one cannot do so fully at once, yet the more one does so, the more the inner help and guidance come and the experience of the

Divine grows within. If the questioning mind becomes less active and humble and the will to surrender grows, this ought to be perfectly possible.

(Sri Aurobindo 1972, 586–588)

If the power of self-surrender is so potent, why does man fail to do it?

Why is it not done? One does not think of it, one forgets to do it, the old habits come back. And above all, behind, hidden somewhere in the inconscient or even in the subconscient, there is this insidious doubt that whispers in your ear ... and you are so silly, so silly, so obscure, so stupid that you listen and you begin to pay attention to yourself and everything is ruined.

(The Mother 2004, 257)

Does personal initiative then cease? No, the ordinary sadhak's consciousness and will are far from being united with the Divine's Consciousness and Will, as are a Siddha Yogi's. One continues to live in the separative ego-consciousness with all of its likes and dislikes. The essential principle to follow is to surrender the fruit or results of one's actions to the Divine; otherwise, one only acts for the ego's satisfaction. Sri Aurobindo describes the attitude one must maintain in all actions.

The Divine is my sole refuge; I trust in Him and rely on Him for everything and Him alone. I am utterly resigned to His Will. I will see to it that no obstacle on the way nor any dark mood of desperation, ever make me waver from my absolute reliance on the Divine.

(Mukherjee 2003, 93)

The sadhak, however, should not become complacent, feeling that effort is unnecessary or that the Divine will accomplish everything. This is made very clear.

But the supreme Grace will act only in the conditions of the Light and the Truth; it will not act in conditions laid upon it by the Falsehood and the Ignorance. For if it were to yield to the demands of the Falsehood it would defeat its own purpose.

(The Mother 1972, 1,3)

There are conditions for everything. If someone refuses to fulfill the conditions for Yoga, there is no use in appealing for Divine intervention.

(Nirodbaran 1983, 197)

An effective surrender does not necessarily ensure the sadhak against all future storms and stresses, but it does assure the absolute security of the sadhak's spiritual health even in the midst of life's tempests. The path is not guaranteed to be sunlit and scattered with rose petals. It has been guaranteed, however, that He will lead the surrendered sadhak to his cherished spiritual goal despite every possible misfortune in life. The surrendered sadhak also knows that misfortune and suffering are not in vain, but are sanctioned by the Divine for fulfilling a necessary spiritual purpose whose significance will be revealed in time. The surrendered sadhak knows and feels that the Divine is not far away or absent during his suffering, but sitting in the heart of his most acute difficulty, guiding the circumstances to lead the sadhak to union with the Divine. The surrendered sadhak also knows that every difficulty will bring great spiritual benefit if faced with courage, patience, and right attitude in a spirit of surrender. Finally, the surrendered sadhak knows that there is an underlying purpose leading to some future spiritual good. His mantra remains: "Let Thy Will be done always and everywhere" (Mukherjee 2003, 101).

Four Stages in the Opening of the Psychic Being

Having discussed Sri Aurobindo's descriptions of the Psychic Being in the first part of this chapter and the three elements of his Integral Yoga in the second part, we can now examine how these three elements, namely aspiration, rejection, and surrender, contribute to the opening of the Psychic Being in four progressive stages.

The First Stage

The Psychic Being remains behind the veil of the inner being and the movements of the mind and vital. The lower parts of our being do not care what the soul wants. They respond habitually to desires and emotions, the need for physical comfort, and small likes and dislikes. Only occasionally will the psychic's influence become apparent: when there is a turning toward the spiritual life, love and surrender to the Divine, a yearning for the ineffable, the True, the Good, and the Beautiful, and an experience of unconditional love, kindness, compassion, Ananda, bhakti.

The Second Stage

When the inner being, the mind, and the vital "do care and obey the psychic, that is their conversion—they begin to put on themselves the psychic or divine nature" (Mukherjee 2003, 112). As described above, aspiration develops in stages, and the Divine responds with grace. One turns inward and gradually loses interest in the old sources of external sensual attraction. The practice of aspiration, rejection, and surrender progressively opens the influence of the psychic being. More and more, one feels its power to overcome desire, anger, old bad habits, and other manifestations of the ego. One lets go of the past, ceasing to dwell on what has happened. One is intuitively guided to do the right thing, not because of a moral injunction, convention, or the expectations of family and peers, but because one knows inwardly what is true and good. One rejects what resists, what may cause harm, what is untrue or exaggerated. Unconditional love, kindness, ease, and bliss become one's state of being. But one might return to old patterns of thought and feeling. It is intermittently veiled by the movements of the inner being. One must continually strive to witness and not manifest deep-seated, habitual inner movements.

The Third Stage

The Psychic Being comes from behind the veil of the inner mind and vital to the foreground and remains there. It continuously directs the sadhana of aspiration, rejection, and surrender. It identifies what must be transformed, let go of, and purified. One feels continuously supported and guided. The Divine's Bliss and unconditional love color one's perceptions, even as karma delivers rotten tomatoes to one's doorstep. One abides as effulgent Self-awareness, the master of one's vehicles on the mental, vital, and physical planes. One discerns and lets go of the ego's manifestations in deeper layers of the inner being, including desire and fear. One feels like an instrument in the hands of the Divine, performing surgery, removing all that resists and expresses ignorance of one's Divinity. One becomes a co-creator. Miracles abound in daily life. One experiences life as ever-new joy.

In this stage, the allegiance of the mind, the vital, and even the physical to the ego is replaced by a new allegiance to the Divine within. One seeks perfection, *siddhi*. Perfection in a diseased body or in a neurotic mind is not perfection. With discerning wisdom, the psychic transforms these lower instruments so that they express the Will of the Divine. One develops an enthusiasm for the process of self-transformation. During this process, one discovers what has been hidden. One experiments with methods of transformation.

The Fourth Stage

At this advanced stage, the Psychic Being transforms the cellular and subconscious levels. From 1926 to 1940, Sri Aurobindo and the Mother experimented with fasting, sleep, food, laws of nature, and habits, testing their own bodies at the subconscient and cellular levels. It was a race against time, not unlike what the Siddhas described in their use of Kaya Kalpa herbs to prolong their lives long enough for the more subtle spiritual forces to complete the divinization. "Fundamentally," said the Mother, "the question is to know, in this race towards the transformation which of the two will reach first, the one who wants to transform the body in the image of the divine Truth or the old habit in the body of gradually decomposing" (Satprem 1975, 330).

The work proceeded at a level that Sri Aurobindo called "the cellular mind" ... "an obscure mind of the body, of the very cells, molecules, corpuscles" ... this body mind is a very tangible truth; owing to its obscurity and mechanical clinging to past movements and facile oblivion and rejection of the new, we find in it one of the chief obstacles to permeation by the supermind Force and the transformation of the functioning of the body. On the other hand, once effectively converted, it will be one of the most precious instruments of the stabilization of the supramental Light and Force in material Nature (Sri Aurobindo 1969, 346).

To prepare the cells, mental silence, vital peace, and cosmic consciousness were necessary to permit the physical and cellular consciousness to enlarge and universalize itself. But then it became apparent that "the body is everywhere," and that one could not transform anything without transforming everything.

> I have been digging deep and long
> Mid a horror of filth and mire
> A bed for the gold river's song
> A home for the deathless fire ...
> My gaping wounds are a thousand and one.
>
> (Sri Aurobindo 1952, 6)

Sri Aurobindo and the Mother found that complete transformation is not possible for the individual, unless there is a minimum number of people participating in the work of transformation. "To help humanity out," remarked Sri Aurobindo, "it was not enough for an individual, however great, to achieve an ultimate solution individually, (because) even when the Light is ready to descend it cannot come to stay till the lower plane is also ready to bear the pressure of the Descent" (Roy 1952, 251).

"If one wants to do the work singly," said the Mother,

> it is absolutely impossible to do it totally, because every physical being, however complete it be, even though it be of an altogether superior kind, even if it be made for an altogether special Work, is never but partial and limited. It represents only one truth, one law—and the full transformation cannot be realized through it alone, through a single body ... so that if one wants to have a general action, at least a minimum number of physical beings is necessary.
>
> (Satprem 1975, 390)

Sri Aurobindo and the Mother began the third phase of their work of transformation. During this phase, the orientation was toward a global transformation. "This Ashram has been created ... not for the renunciation of the world but as a centre and a field for the evolution of another kind and form of life" (Sri Aurobindo 1969, 823).

It was organized so as to be open to all types of activities of a creative nature, as well as all types of individuals, men, women, and children, of all social classes. Activity in the world was a primary means.

According to Sri Aurobindo,

> The spiritual life finds its most potent expression in the man who lives the ordinary life of men in the strength of Yoga ... It is by such a union of the inner life and the outer that mankind will eventually be lifted up and become mighty and divine.
>
> (Sri Aurobindo 1950, 10)

References

Ganapathy, T. N. et al. 2010. *Tirumandiram*. Eastman, Canada: Babaji's Kriya Yoga and Publications.

Ganapathy, T. N., and Anand, Geeta. 2012. "Monistic Theism in the Tirumandiram and Kashmir Saivism." In Govindan, Marshall ed. *The Yoga of Tirumular: Essays on the Tirumandiram*. Eastman, Canada: Babaji's Kriya Yoga and Publications, 439–471.

Govindan, Marshall. 2012. *Babaji and the 18 Siddha Kriya Yoga Tradition*, 9th ed. Eastman, Canada: Babaji's Kriya Yoga and Publications.

The Mother. 1972. *The Mother, with Letters on the Mother and Translations of Prayers and Meditations, Sri Aurobindo Birth Centenary Library, vol. 25*. Pondicherry: Sri Aurobindo Ashram.

The Mother. 2004. *Mother's Collected Works, vol. 3*. Pondicherry: Sri Aurobindo Ashram.

Mukherjee, J. K. 2003. *The Practice of the Integral Yoga*. Pondicherry: Sri Aurobindo Ashram.

Nirodbaran. 1983. *Correspondence with Sri Aurobindo, vol. 1*. Pondicherry: Sri Aurobindo Ashram.

Roy, Dilip K. 1952. *Sri Aurobindo Came to Me*. Pondicherry: Sri Aurobindo Ashram.

Satprem. 1975. *The Adventure of Consciousness*. Pondicherry: Sri Aurobindo Ashram.

Sri Aurobindo. 1950. *The Ideal of the Karmayogin*. Pondicherry: Sri Aurobindo Ashram.

Sri Aurobindo. 1952. *Last Poems 1938–40*. Pondicherry: Sri Aurobindo Ashram.

Sri Aurobindo. 1969. *On Yoga I, Tome I*. Pondicherry: Sri Aurobindo Ashram.

Sri Aurobindo. 1972. *Letters on Yoga, Centenary Edition*. Pondicherry: Sri Aurobindo Ashram.

Sri Aurobindo. 2012. *Letters on Yoga, Complete Works of Sri Aurobindo, vol. 28*. Pondicherry: Sri Aurobindo Ashram.

6

The Metaphysical Foundations of Sri Aurobindo's Vision of the Future of Humanity

V. Ananda Reddy

Sri Aurobindo wrote to a disciple on September 4, 1934:

> "And philosophy!" exclaimed Sri Aurobindo, "Let me tell you in confidence that I never, never was a philosopher—although I have written philosophy which is another story altogether. I knew precious little about philosophy before I did the yoga and came to Pondicherry—I was a poet and a politician, not a philosopher. How I managed to do it and why? First, because X proposed to me to co-operate in a philosophical review—and as my theory was that a Yogi ought to be able to turn his hand to anything I could not refuse... Secondly, because I had only to write down in the terms of the intellect all that I had observed and come to know in practising Yoga daily and the philosophy was there automatically. But that is not being a philosopher!"
>
> (Sri Aurobindo, Sri Aurobindo Birth Centenary Library, hereafter referred as SABCL 1972, vol. 26, 374)

Interestingly, after about six months, on April 1, 1935, he wrote to another disciple, "The 'latent philosopher' failed to come out at the first shot (when I was in Calcutta)—after some years of incubation it burst out like a volcano as soon as I started writing the Arya" (SABCL 1972, vol. 26, 226). Whatever may be the controversy over Sri Aurobindo being a philosopher or not, what is of importance to us is that Sri Aurobindo has given us "in the terms of the intellect" a cosmic plan, hitherto unknown, and an ideal for both individual and collective life, which promises to deliver mankind from its present evolutionary crisis into a future that is beyond the mental level—a future aglow with revealed divinity in matter.

What then is this luminous and at the same time transmuting vision and ideal of Sri Aurobindo? Every ideal, be it ethical, religious, or spiritual, depends for its permanence and for its breadth and depth of influence on its philosophical foundation, that is, on the approach it takes toward the Divine or the Eternal. For instance, the Greeks realized the Eternal in his aspect of Beauty and therefore they developed everything in their culture—art, music, justice, law, and ethics—with a sense of beauty that reflected in balance, proportion, and taste, avoiding excessiveness in any direction. So did the Romans. They took to the Force and Power aspect of the Eternal and accordingly they governed their life with a stern and orderly restraint. Thus, discipline became the bedrock of their mental, vital, and physical development and enjoyment. But both these civilizations could not uphold their ideals for long because both Beauty and Power are only attributes of the Eternal and there are other aspects of the Divine which the human soul seeks and which these two civilizations failed to provide.

The ancient Aryans of India based the ideals of their life on the vision of the Eternal as both Transcendental Self and the individual self. They raised the veil completely, as it were, and saw the Eternal in all things, and had the experience of Him in themselves and in all around them. It is because of such a broad-based vision of the Eternal that India could give itself a civilization, which satisfied in every way the human personality and fulfilled the longings of the human soul. This is also the secret of its lasting.

In spite of its lofty vision and its multifaceted realization of the Eternal, the Indian ideal has apparently failed to deliver the final goods. The blue vistas of the Eternal's consciousness and the oceanic Bliss of the Supreme were meant more for the individual than the collective. It has been always the individual who had access to the lofty idealism and the collective was left to bask in the light of the individual's spiritual glow or to remain caught up in the quagmire of ignorance and suffering. The religious teachers, the saints, the philosophers, and even the *vibhutis* have all shown a way out of this world, but no one has really "tread the dolorous way" and tried to "bring the heavens here" or to uplift the human race as such.

As a result, there is no true change in the individual's consciousness and nature. His physical is still animal in its habits and needs, and is constantly a victim of disease and suffering and death. His vital being is a battlefield of greed and lust of base instincts and all the dark subconscious passions. The sorrowful state of the threefold nexus of man's mind, life, and body remains unregenerated in spite of all the high, noble, and catholic ideals put forth through his evolutionary history. His inferior nature has gone unchanged and unchallenged over the eons, except for a cosmetic change brought about by his higher cultural and religious pursuits. A deep-rooted change, a reversal of his nature and his life can be brought about only by a force beyond his present capacities. Like Heracles who turned the river Alpheus to cleanse Augean stables, so too, a new golden river, the Supramental Force, has to be brought down which alone can cleanse and transform man's nature and body.

Foundation of Sri Aurobindo's Philosophy

Sri Aurobindo puts before us the uncompromising ideal of the total transformation of the individual and a divine perfection of human life. The highest and the most complete life that awaits man's destiny in a divinized earth is the work undertaken by Sri Aurobindo. The unregenerate mind, life, and body of the human individual are taken up, purified, heightened, and uplifted into their true mold on the supramental truth-consciousness level. Man is asked to raise himself to his true manhood by which alone can he become a perfect, integral, and complete being: his psychic becoming the vehicle of true and pure love, his mind reflecting infallible knowledge, his vital manifesting inner power and strength, and his body expressing a perfect divine beauty and harmony. What Sri Aurobindo posits is the perfect solution: to immortalize the body, to spiritualize the material, to divinize the human. This solution seems to be the only complete one to the age-long dichotomy between Matter and Spirit, between Divinity and Humanity, between Immortality and Mortality. No one till now has been able to reconcile and bring accordance to these apparently self-contradictory and mutually self-exclusive pairs, neither the Vedantins nor the Mayavadins, neither saints nor gurus, neither pundits nor scholars. The eternal opposites have met for the first time in Sri Aurobindo.

In order to understand Sri Aurobindo's philosophy, we must try to grasp the fundamental ideas of the Eternal and Real in which Sri Aurobindo bases his ideal of a divine life. For Sri Aurobindo, the truth and permanent value of any ideal depends "on the closeness of its fundamental idea to the ultimate truth of the Eternal" (SABCL 1972, vol. 27, 201).[3] Very characteristic of his approach, which is to go from the near to the far, from the intimate to the unknown, Sri Aurobindo takes up the present constitution of consciousness in man which expresses itself majorly through his mind, life, and body, and traces it to its transcendental source, the Absolute, the *Sachchidananda*. Starting from the multitudinous world, he tracks it back to a single transcendental existence, the One who is also the Many. Other great philosophers, thinkers, and spiritual teachers stopped short, as it were, at this stage, namely, tracing the origins of the cosmic creation to the transcendental Reality. And this tendency, obviously, left the doors wide open for the theories of Illusionism which propound that the world is a myth, unreal, and that the One, the Brahman alone is real, indivisible, eternal, infinite, and unknowable.

Sri Aurobindo is not interested in only tracing the multitudinous world into the One. Starting from the Supreme Reality, the *Sachchidananda*, he shows us its descent, its extension within itself as phenomena, as the manifestation. By describing the process of the Divine Descent, Sri Aurobindo shows that this creation is verily true and real. He puts it simply,

> If then the world is a dream or an illusion or a mistake, it is a dream originated and willed by the self in its totality and not only originated and willed, but supported and perpetually entertained. Moreover, it is a dream existing in a Reality and the stuff of which it is made is that Reality, for Brahman must be the material of the world as well as its base and continent. If the gold of which the vessel is made is real, how shall we suppose that the vessel itself is a mirage?
>
> (SABCL 1972, vol. 18, 32)

Sri Aurobindo is thus very close to the ancient seers in his experience and vision of the Supreme Reality and its manifestation. The central experience and thought of the principal Upanishads are found to be progressively developed and brought to a perfect culmination and synthesis in his own experience and philosophy. For example, the pregnant ideas of the gospel of eternal Bliss in *Taittiriya Upanishad* and the teachings of knowledge and self-surrender to the universal Brahman found in *Kena Upanishad* find their full sway in his book *The Synthesis of Yoga*. And, of course, the gospel of a

Divine life on earth of *Isha Upanishad* forms the kernel of *The Life Divine*. What then is this concept of the Supreme Reality, which has found one end of its golden rainbow in the ancient seers and the other end in Sri Aurobindo?

The Absolute or the Transcendent Reality is incomprehensible and unimaginable because it is timeless, spaceless, eternal, infinite, indivisible, and stable. It is unconditioned and therefore indescribable by human language, neither by its ultimate negation nor by its absolute affirmation; "It is neither this nor that." It is beyond manifestation, beyond Existence and Non-existence, beyond Being and Non-Being, because, it is unmanifest. It is therefore called as *Tat* or That as a figure of speech, but is not conditioned by the speech.

As the Absolute leans toward manifestation, the first step It takes is to formulate or render in Itself a luminous Shadow of its inconceivable Being which is variously called as Parabrahman, Brahman the Eternal, God, Creator, the Supreme Spirit, etc. The Upanishads describe Him, subjectively as *Sat Chit Ananda*, and, objectively as *Satyam, Jnanam, Anantam*. Sri Aurobindo prefers the first trilogy—*Sachchidananda*: Existence, Consciousness, Bliss. *Sat* is Pure Being, Absolute Existence. He is without cause or object of His Existence. He cannot change because He is unconditioned by Time, Space, and Causality. He is alone and alone is He in the One Existence. *Chit* is Pure Awareness, Absolute Consciousness of the *Sat*. *Chit* and *Sat* are inseparable because there is nothing beyond the *Sat*. Nor is it that *Chit* is consciousness of one part of *Sat* because *Sat* is without parts, one and simple. *Ananda* is Pure Ecstasy, Absolute Bliss. Just as Existence and Consciousness are inseparable, so Bliss is the link between *Sat* and *Chit*.

Looking at the objective expression of this Trinity we see that *Sat* being the Absolute Existence can alone be the only Reality, the Supreme Truth, *Satyam*—all other existences being partially or relatively real. Likewise, *Jnanam*—which is the direct knowledge without the use of any medium—is at its highest degree *Chit*, the Absolute Consciousness. Finally, *Anantam*, Endlessness is *Ananda*, because Bliss consists in the absence of Limitation. Sri Aurobindo adds to this ancient trilogy, a fourth aspect, that of *Tapas*, *Shakti* or Force. It is as inseparable from Consciousness or *Chit* as is the power of fire and fire. The ancient seers knew about this aspect of *Sachchidananda*, but they did not stress it. But, in the experience and vision of Sri Aurobindo it gets a unique importance because in his scheme of the manifestation it is the Force that brings into *Chit* or the Consciousness, which otherwise is a breeding trance of immobility, perfect equilibrium, and indivisibility, the first stirrings of division, of creation. So, in Sri Aurobindo, whenever we speak of *Sachchidananda* we mean not just *Sat*, *Chit*, and *Ananda* but *Sat*, *Chit-Tapas* or *Chit-Shakti*, and *Ananda*.

So, with the first stirrings, the first urge toward activity in the ineffable and inalienable equality of the bliss of self-identity of *Sachchidananda*, there began the process of Involution, or the Descent of the Divine Consciousness. Somewhere a breach began in that unbroken continuity of absolute Existence, and the divine afflatus of consciousness flung itself into matrices of creativity. This self-pressure to divide sent the consciousness rolling, as it were, right into its very opposite, the very Inconscience. The stable Unity turned itself into infinitesimal particles by its power of self-limitation.

But, in this becoming, or descent, there is a definite process, a law, for otherwise, "infinite consciousness, into infinite action can produce only infinite results". One possibility out of the infinite possibilities was selected, one truth of manifestation out of the infinite truths of creation was chosen, organized, harmonized at different levels and then marshalled and released into manifestation. This selective faculty, which commissioned the present manifestation, put forth by *Sachchidananda*, is what Sri Aurobindo names the Supermind or the Gnosis.

From the point of manifestation, Supermind is the first step of devolution. On this level, the One retains still the essential oneness in and through the Many. That is because the Many here are as seed-truths, as Real-Ideas and there is here no shadow of separateness but only a difference of modes carrying within themselves the essential unity and identity. The next step of devolution or descent is the Overmind. Here, the multiplicity becomes sharper, as it were, and there is a greater differentiation, isolation, and separation. This stress on individuation, on exclusiveness breaks the unity and oneness of the One and Many that exists on the level of Supermind. The identity of the two recedes to the background and the Many comes to the forefront. Here is the beginning of Ignorance, *Avidya*, as talked of by the seers of the Vedanta.

The jealousy self-centeredness of the Many on the Overmental level becomes "intolerant egoism and solipsism" in the next step of devolution, the Mind. The unity, the harmony of the higher levels turn into fragmentation, disharmony, conflict, and confusion—the very bottom of ignorance. The transparency and subtlety are lost on the level of Mind and there is instead the sense of rigidity and crudity. The global outlook of the Overmind becomes a narrow vision, a piecemeal understanding of things, passing through other intermediary levels, such as the Intuitive Mind. With the Illumined Mind and Higher Mind, the consciousness becomes, according to the hierarchy, more and more dull, dense, uncertain, slow, and disintegrated. The intensity, purity, force, and the synthetic unity of the higher levels diminish gradually until the consciousness reaches the level of Life. On the level of Life, the consciousness becomes fiercely selfish, dark, and dense. Passion, lust, hunger, desire, blind cravings seize the consciousness, making it impervious to the workings of higher forces or light. There is here a sense of throttling, asphyxiation of consciousness.

Still, the descent does not stop here; it goes further into Matter, where there is a total self-oblivion, a complete wiping off of the consciousness. The first movement of division has now become the last movement of fragmentation; the self-luminous consciousness has become obscure, dense, dark, and hard. The original One has subdivided itself into trillions of atoms where Existence becomes non-existence, where Consciousness turns into Inconscience, where Bliss plunges into Immunity. The Highest descends into the lowest and not until then does the play halt. The Devolution is complete in Matter, the very opposite of the Spirit, the "plunge of the Light into its own Shadow."

But this is an illusion only. Opposite is not a zero, devoid of consciousness. The Highest and the Lowest, the positive and the negative are only apparent opposites. They, in fact, complete and explain one another. For, Matter is but "Brahman made concrete in atomic division"; it is the form of the Formless. It gives a body and a name to the Bodiless and the indeterminate and unknowable Consciousness. Eternity has been caught in the moment and Infinity in the finite. The white ecstasy of the Absolute Bliss is now reflected in "a million-bodied beatitude." If Spirit is Involution on the Summit, out of which everything devolved toward the other pole of Matter, Matter too is Involution at the bottom, containing all the potentials and from where everything evolves upward toward the other pole or Spirit. Spirit and Matter are therefore the obverse and reverse modes of the same Reality. Spirit is consciousness, it is awake; Matter is unconsciousness, it is true, but it is not utter absence or annihilation of consciousness—it is involved-consciousness. By this exclusive and concentrated involvement in atomic forms, by this complete and absolute identification with the scattered units of matter, consciousness forgets itself. The force and intensity of its concentration on the atomic division make the consciousness of itself, a self-forgotten nescience.

A Theory of Evolution

As the bottom of the downward drive is reached, there goes up a "deep spiritual cry" from the Inconscient and then there is a direct intervention of the Supreme's Grace which swings back the descending movement, and the ascent begins, evolution starts (SABCL 1972, vol. 28, 2):

> An unshaped consciousness desired light
> And a blank prescience yearned towards distant change....
> Arrived from the other side of boundlessness
> An eye of deity pierced through dumb deeps; ...
> Intervening in a mindless universe,
> Its message crept through the reluctant hush
> Calling the adventure of consciousness and joy ...

Evolution is the inverse action of involution; it is the upward movement of the consciousness through the stages it had taken in the descent. Therefore, what was the last derivation in involution becomes the first one to appear in evolution; what was the first highest and the Original in involution will emerge in evolution as the last apocalypse.

This being the principle of evolution, two basic characters of this movement become obvious and unchallengeable: (a) only that which is involved in Matter can evolve, for otherwise there would not be an evolution but a random and haphazard creation of new things, arbitrarily willed or conceived by an inexplicable Force; (b) all that is involved in Matter is bound to evolve in the ascending order until the final unfolding when the Consciousness which had lost itself finds itself again "divinely self-conscious, free, infinite and immortal."

Matter is the launching point of evolution. This is the inconscient stage of evolution when there is only Matter, when the consciousness is dormant, dense, dark, and insentient (SABCL 1972, vol. 28, 1–2):

> Then something in the inscrutable darkness stirred;
> A nameless movement, an unthought Idea
> Insistent, dissatisfied, without an aim,
> Something that wished but knew not how to be,
> Teased the Inconscient to wake Ignorance.

This stirring, this teasing created a kind of tension in the womb of Matter which soon increased and swelled into a mighty churning and an upheaval. Those were the birth pangs, so to say, of something that was already embedded in Matter and was seeking to be delivered. When this secret yearning was intense, then the descent of the Life principle from above took place. Then Life appeared. Consciousness, which was, as though in a stupor and dormant now opened its eyes, and looked around. Bare earth wrapped itself in a green robe and decked itself in innumerable bright colors. Still, everything was too static and rooted to earth. The semi-consciousness of the plant-world strove to come still further up and after aeons of struggle and preparation, there came the animal world. Consciousness was more awake now, able to express itself more freely through movement and feelings and through a rudimentary mentality in the more evolved animals. It took millions of years for Life to influence and mold Matter in "its own mode and law of existence." Matter that was once just physicochemical entity had undergone a change, had become ready to receive a living organism, in the form of the animal. At the same time, Life prepared itself to receive the higher principle. When, through the millennia, it attained a certain complexity of form, a certain maturity, a kind of readiness and organization to become the vehicle of the psychic element of consciousness, then the Mind principle seized Life and the human individual appeared on the earth's evolutionary scene.

If we follow this evolutionary trend, we see that the human individual is not the final rung of evolution. He is only a stage of transition. Just as Nature worked out Life in Matter and Mind in Life, so too a human individual is only a living laboratory of Nature "in whom and with whose conscious cooperation" she will work out by the same method and process the next higher principle of Supermind. To an extent, Man's eternal aspiration for God, Light, Bliss, Freedom, and Immortality is "simply the imperative impulse by which Nature is seeking to evolve beyond Mind ...," says Sri Aurobindo. Beyond this "imperative impulse," the mental consciousness too has to be widened, deepened, purified, made supple and receptive before the supramental principle can descend. This process of Mind's preparation is taking place at the present through a kind of catharsis of human consciousness. Mind was a helper in the past, but now it is a bar. With the guiding lights of religion, occultism, and religious thought it did lead man on his destiny. But now it has brought man to the brink of self-destruction. Unless humanity opens itself to the higher principle beyond Mind, there is no hope for it.

The path of evolution is not, however, linear. It follows two main processes, sublimation and integration, which form the single movement of ascension. Sublimation means a purification and refinement of the lower, dense, and obscure consciousness. Integration is the process of the higher principle embracing the lower and infusing it with its own light and consciousness. For instance, Matter, which was once a dense obscure unconsciousness, went through a process of refinement in order to become the basis of Life in the form of fauna. The Life principle injected into Matter its own higher principle of a soul-element and made it ready to receive and to express the vital principle in the form of the animal. Vitalized Matter then became more plastic, spontaneous under the pressure of Mind. Life too has been purified of its crudities and it has become more refined, sensitive, and responds to the light of the Mind. We thus see that Matter is constantly ascending in its aspiration to express a greater consciousness and light. The present-day computer technology is a significant example of how the once obscure Matter has become luminous, sentient, and capable of accepting the demands of the Mind and forces beyond it.

Parallel to this ascending movement is the movement of descent, the coming down of the higher involutionary principles. No amount of churning or yearning, shuffling and reshuffling, struggle and aspiration from below is sufficient to establish the higher status. The higher status, or the plane, awaits for a sufficient preparation of the lower level before it can actualize itself. It is the manifestation of the higher that gives the lower aspiration and preparation a definite form and pattern. At a precise moment, the principle that is seeking to evolve and the principle that is awaiting to descend, they meet and consummate, and then alone is born the new level. After a certain degree of preparation and maturity of its womb, Matter had to await the seed of Life before it could burst forth into millions and millions of living forms and moving shapes. Similarly, no amount of permutation and combination of the Life elements could bring forth Mind. After it got sufficiently organized and ready enough to become the receptacle of the psychic element of consciousness, it had to await the conjunction of the Mind principle embedded in itself and the Mind principle from above, for the new mental consciousness to shape itself into man.

Likewise, man, the representative of the Mind principle, has been preparing himself, though mostly unconsciously, for a higher life. Sages and saints, poets and idealists, scientists and reformers have, through the ages, prepared the Mind to open itself to higher levels than itself, have purified life with the godward emotion, and made Matter receptive, plastic, and supple, responding readily to the deeper needs of Life and Mind. There has been, on the whole, a kind of preparation for a higher life. Yet, the malady of man has not been cured, for the powers and resources in his hand are insufficient to cure himself.

> [Man] has been striving through his lesser powers, through the grace of the lower gods since his advent upon earth to arrive at a reconstruction of his life and surroundings. That is why he has never attained the full measure of success. Indeed a period of success or progress was always followed by a decline and retrogression, a so-called golden age by an age of iron. As a matter of fact, today humanity finds itself terribly enclosed in a cage of iron, as it were. The earth has become too small for his soaring capacities and multitudinous necessities—he is already thinking of a place on the moon! That is only the sign and symbol of an inner impasse to which he has arrived. The anguish of the human soul has reached its acme: the problems, social, political, educational, moral it is facing have proved themselves to be insolvable. Yes, he has run into a *cul-de-sac*, where he is caught as in a death trap. No ordinary rational methods, halfway nostrums can deliver him any more. All the

outer doors and issues are now closed for him; the only way is to turn inward; there lies the open road to freedom and fulfillment. That is the way to transcendence and self-surpassing.

(Gupta, Collected Works of Nolini Kanta Gupta,
hereafter CWNG 1974, vol. 5, 11)

It is always the higher principle that fulfils the lower: Man must transcend into the superman. Mind must surpass into the Supermind. Nature herself is endeavoring to bring out and establish this New Consciousness, the Supramental consciousness, for this is her evolutionary goal and this is what man must consciously strive for. The only way out of the human morass lies in the direction of the supramentalization of human consciousness; all other ways will only lead him to his doom.

Fortunately, for us, both the evolutionary processes of ascent and descent have been accomplished. Although Nature and Man have been laboring for aeons to prepare themselves for the New Consciousness, it is the advent of the Divine, which has hastened this process of Mind's sublimation. Sri Aurobindo has not only brought down the Truth to be established as the next evolutionary step, the Supramental Truth, but has acted here below, struggled, and suffered to carry forward the terrestrial movement toward its fulfillment. On December 5, 1950, he sacrificed his body in order to bring the supramental into the earth-consciousness. Presuming that the New Race of the supramental consciousness has come, does it mean that is the end of the march of civilization? It is not so. According to Sri Aurobindo, it only means that with Supermind, creation has leaped from the domain of Ignorance to Knowledge and Light. Mortality, which has been the governing principle of the present life on earth, will be replaced by immortality. Thereafter, after crossing the borderland of Ignorance, a new creation starts and the evolutionary course will continue *ad infinitum*—from light to greater Light, because *Sachchidananda* is infinite and his self-revelation and manifestation are also infinite.

This then is the philosophical foundation, which supports our ideal of the total transformation, the divinization of man and spiritualization of matter. Sri Aurobindo charts the very creation of the universe and traces in a god-like gesture the spiritual evolution of earth from the very first dawn when evolution began, from "the hour before the Gods awake." He does so only to show us the inevitability of the coming of the New Race and to convince the human mind about the urgent need of it to submit to the ideal of integral transformation. Yet, this is only half the story. An ideal never belongs to the past; it looks always to the future. The past only serves as the foundation to a future that is more luminous, more promising, and more stupendous than anything since the beginning of evolution. Sri Aurobindo once again paints the glorious future in magnificent hues. His "vision and prophetic gleam" have in themselves the necessary Force, Consciousness, and Light to sustain mankind in its present gloomy period of transition.

Vision of a New Race

To know "the mystery of the journeying years" of the future, to try to understand what awaits our destiny is itself a help on the way of fulfilling our ideal. However faintly we may understand the Vision, we at least become humble, and the more consciously we surrender ourselves to this Vision and Force, the greater are our chances of collaboration in the ideal. February 29, 1956, was the day when the New World was born. The New Consciousness is amidst us, recasting, unobtrusively, the old consciousness. It is there, spreading in every walk of life—the political, the economic, the spiritual, the artistic, urging man to cast off old habits, old institutions, old values, old ways of thinking and beliefs—the old consciousness based on falsehood, hypocrisy, and ignorance. Quietly, the New World is gliding into the old one, replacing it inch-by-inch, minute-by-minute. New foundations are being laid, "not below, but above," in the inner being, the psychic being of man. The New Man will be therefore not a slave to his outer nature, limited and obscure, but a monarch of himself and all around him—*Swarat* and *Samrat*. Living in his soul-status, he will be in conscious harmony and communion with other individuals. There will thus be neither strife nor competition, neither rivals nor opponents, for all would be one in the cosmic soul and therefore radiating the Divine Will. His mind would be a channel of profound, creative, and true knowledge. His heart will overflow not with the base human egoistic emotions, but with a "wide and intense *rasa* that lies in the divine identity of souls." His body will be beautiful, transparent, and supple, "a tabernacle of God."

With the increase of such individuals, the social structure too will change and will become one that is based on cooperation, collaboration, and free expression of one's own *Swadharma*. It will be a kind of living in one self by living in all and vice versa. With an increase of such aggregates, there will be a change in the nations, for each one would increasingly find its own true soul. It would automatically result in a "supra-nation" or a federation of nations. The world would thus move toward one indivisible humanity, which will be the basis of the superhumanity (SABCL 1972, vol. 29, 711):

> Thus shall the earth open to divinity
> And common natures feel the wide uplift,
> Illumine common acts with the Spirit's ray
> And meet the deity in common things.
> Nature shall live to manifest secret God,
> The Spirit shall take up the human play,
> This earthly life become the life divine.

Considering the apparent state of human consciousness at present, this lofty ideal, this vision of "a mightier race shall inhabit the mortal's world" seems a far-off cry, something impossible and chimerical. Even if it is to take place, it may take place in a "far-flung futurity," millions of years from now.

To this skeptical view Sri Aurobindo answers,

> I have already spoken about the bad conditions of the world; the usual idea of the occultists about it is that the worse they are, the more probable is the coming of an intervention or a new revelation from above. The ordinary mind cannot know—it has either to believe or disbelieve or wait and see... As to whether the Divine seriously means something to happen I believe it is intended. I know with absolute

certitude that the supramental is a truth and that its advent is in the very nature of things inevitable. The question is as to the when and how. That also is decided and predestined from somewhere above; but it is here being fought out amid a rather grim clash of conflicting forces. For in the terrestrial world the predetermined result is hidden and what we see is a whirl of possibilities and forces attempting to achieve something with the destiny of it all concealed from the human eyes. This is, however, certain that a number of souls have been sent to see that it shall be now. That is the situation. My faith and will are for the now.

(SABCL 1972, vol. 26, 167)

In another letter, he writes,

But I have not been discouraged by what is happening, because I know and have experienced hundreds of times that beyond the blackest darkness there lies for one who is a divine instrument the light of God's victory. I have never had a strong and persistent will for anything to happen in the world—I am not speaking of personal things—which did not eventually happen even after delay, defeat or even disaster.

(SABCL 1972, vol. 26, 169)

Along with this sanction and will of Sri Aurobindo for the coming of the supramental race, what is required to lay the foundations of a new world is a few pioneers, an avant-garde, a selected group of aspirants. In any case, it is never intended that the entire human race will be taken up into the new consciousness. Just as Matter continues to exist, though changed and influenced to an extent, after the advent of Life and Mind, so too Life and Mind will continue to be and they will not be obliterated from the face of the earth. However, as the small nucleus of forerunners snowballs and becomes a larger collectivity, the effects of the New Consciousness will be felt on humanity in general:

This change might happen not only in a few, but extend and generalise itself in the race. This possibility, if fulfilled, would mean that the human dream of perfection, perfection of itself, of its purified and enlightened nature, of all its action and living would be no longer a dream but a truth that could be made real and humanity lifted out of the hold on it of inconscience and ignorance.

(SABCL 1972, vol. 16, 48)

When asked by a disciple, "What will be the effect of the Supermind on the earth?" the Mother replied, "I told you immediately that before the effects of the Supramental manifestation become visible and tangible, perceptible to everybody, perhaps thousands of years may go by" (The Mother, The Collected Works of The Mother in 1978, hereafter CWM 1978, vol. 8, 292). As the complete transformation of the earth-life and the full manifestation of the supramentalized beings are propositions of hundreds of years from now, Sri Aurobindo envisages an intermediary race which could act as the bridge between man and the supramental race. It is the race of superman. The superman, though born in the human way, would transform his consciousness sufficiently—that of the mind, life, and body—by connecting it with the higher spiritual principle of Supermind. However, even the level of supermen is not in the immediate reach of man. Before achieving that level, there would be several attempts, successful and unsuccessful, each forming a partial realization according to one's capacity and the degree of transformation. Such men who give themselves to the attempt will be the apprentice-supermen, and they will be the candidates for Superman. "All those who strive to overcome their ordinary nature," defines the Mother, "all those who try to realise materially the deeper experience which has brought them into contact with the divine Truth, all those who, instead of turning to the Beyond or the Highest, try to realise physically, externally—the change of consciousness they have realised within themselves—all are apprentice-supermen" (CWM 1978, vol. 11). Apart from those "number of souls" who "have been sent down to see that it [the Work] shall be now,"— what is asked of us is "to overcome the ordinary nature," to realize materially the deeper experience, and "the change of consciousness." In one word, a transformation, or to become an apprentice-superman.

The starting point of the integral transformation is aspiration, aspiration coupled with a will to realize it. According to the Mother (CWM 1978, vol. 12, 80):

> But in addition to aspiration there is an inner opening, a kind of receptivity, then one can enter into this transformed consciousness in a single stroke and maintain oneself there. This change of consciousness is abrupt, so to say; when it occurs, it occurs all of a sudden, although the preparation for it may have been long and slow... It is a complete and absolute change, a revolution of the basic poise; the movement is like turning a ball inside out. To the transformed consciousness everything appears not only new and different, but almost the reverse of what it seemed to the ordinary consciousness. In the ordinary consciousness you advance slowly, by successive experiences, from ignorance to a very distant and often doubtful knowledge. In the transformed consciousness your starting point is knowledge and you proceed from knowledge to knowledge. However, this is only a beginning; for the outer consciousness, the various planes and parts of the outer active being are transformed only slowly and gradually as a result of the inner transformation.

In other words, it is the awakening of the psychic being in the seeker, the sadhak. After a considerable time of incubation, that is, a deepening of the ordinary consciousness, there is a sudden contact with the divine Presence in the heart center. This contact, when stabilized, guides the sadhak at every moment telling him what's to be done and how it is to be done, for the psychic has the absolute knowledge of the truth behind appearances. A change or reversal of consciousness is of primary importance because,

> In the inner reality of things a change of consciousness was always a major fact, the evolution has always had a spiritual significance and the physical change was only instrumental; but this relation was concealed by the first abnormal balance of the two factors, the body of the external Inconscience, outweighing and obscuring in importance the spiritual element, the conscious being. But once the balance

is righted, it is no longer the change of the body that must precede the change of consciousness; the consciousness itself by its mutation will necessitate and operate whatever mutation is needed for the body.

(SABCL 1972, vol. 19, 843)

Thus, after the first change of consciousness or the awakening of the psychic being, if the sadhak makes his outer nature of body, life, and mind move in the light and guidance of his psychic, then the higher consciousness purifies and regenerates his ordinary human nature. "Finally, when the psychic being is in full self-possession and power, it can be the vehicle of the direct supramental consciousness—which will then be able to act freely and absolutely for the entire transformation of the external nature, its transfiguration into a perfect body of the Truth-consciousness—in a word, its divinisation" (CWNG 1974, vol. 3, 14). Thus, a psychicization, leading to a spiritualization and culminating in a supramentalization can alone fulfill the ideal of total transformation of which "a transformation of the body must be an indispensable part of it; without that no full divine life on earth is possible" (SABCL 1972, vol. 16, 43).

Ashram as a Laboratory

It is basically for the work of the transformation in the body that Sri Aurobindo Ashram was created by the Mother. Apart from being a symbolic center, it is a laboratory where "each one of you," says the Mother, "represents one of the difficulties which must be conquered for the transformation." The Ashram was essentially meant to build the body that is receptive to the Supramental's working. "The golden light must come into the feet," writes Nolini Kanta Gupta, while describing the nature of the Mother's work on earth,

> and that was the work she was doing here and it is for that that she created the Ashram. You all know the special emphasis she laid on physical education in order to prepare the body and senses to receive the golden light. She always said, physical education gives you the basis for the new consciousness, the new light, we must have a strong body, a beautiful body, a body that endures: for the new light is powerful, it is not merely light, it is the force, one must be able to bear it and carry out its commands.

(CWNG 1974, vol. 6, 6)

In truth, the great emphasis is on the physical transformation because, "It is only when the circle will be completed, when the two extremes will touch, when the highest will manifest on the most material that the experience will be truly decisive. It would seem that one never truly understands until one understands with one's body." Until the supramental is realized here, in the body, nothing is realized permanently. So, the new consciousness is working itself out in the body and not on the mental or vital levels, because they cannot support it. A new body alone can stand the pressure of the new consciousness. "Only the body can understand," says the Mother. And for it to understand means the capacity to be able to do, she explained. This capacity and understanding are contagious. That is why the Mother gave her own body for experimenting with the principles of physical transformation, which in their essence had been realized by Sri Aurobindo in his own body. She believed that "it is there the transformation must be achieved; it is on earth that you progress, it is on earth that you realise. It is in the body that the Victory is won." If this victory is won in one single glorious body, then it will be a victory for all men and Matter. "Once it is done (Sri Aurobindo has said this), once one body has done it, it has the capacity to pass it on to others," confirmed the Mother (CWM 1978, vol. 2, 100).

Once the Supramental Force hooks itself to a single body, then it will open itself around the cells of the body and refashion and remould its new body.

> The moment a body, which was of course formed by the old animal method, is capable of living this consciousness (the New Consciousness) naturally, and spontaneously, without effort, without going out of itself, it proves that this is not one single exceptional case but simply the forerunner of a realisation which, even if it is not altogether general, can at last be shared by a certain number of individuals who, besides, as soon as they share it, will lose perception of being separate individuals and become a living collectivity.
>
> (CWM 1978, vol. 9, 140)

The Mother's own body has been the "forerunner" of such a realization. She transformed it to the extent it could be done, leaving behind her New Body and her promise (SABCL 1972, vol. 29, 521):

> One day I shall return, His hands in mine,
> And thou shalt see the face of the Absolute,
> Then shall the holy marriage be achieved,
> Then shall the divine family be born.
> There shall be light and peace in all the worlds.

References

Gupta, Nolini Kanta. 1974. *The Collected Works of Nolini Kanta Gupta*. Pondicherry: Sri Aurobindo Centre for International Education.

The Mother. 1974. *The Collected Works of the Mother*. Pondicherry: Sri Aurobindo Ashram.

Sri Aurobindo. 1972. *Sri Aurobindo Birth Centenary Library*. Pondicherry: Sri Aurobindo Ashram.

7

The Power of Inherent Oneness

Martha Orton

Sri Aurobindo explains the Oneness of All and writes from this realization throughout his works. Oneness, the true unity of all, is central to his teaching. We see this throughout Sri Aurobindo's exposition of his vision in philosophical terms in *The Life Divine* as well as in *The Synthesis of Yoga* and his letters to disciples, where philosophical concepts and the practice of yoga combine. Sri Aurobindo explains that the goal of human existence is not only to unite with the Divine in Oneness, but moreover to realize the fullness of this union through the entire transformation of our being, and he also details for us the processes involved in attaining this goal. Sri Aurobindo describes the development of the individual within itself and also in relation to all that is beyond itself. Within the individual there is the unification of the disparate parts of the being around the central divine core, the psychic being. Reaching beyond, there is the realization of the cosmic consciousness, a great universalization of the being. Reaching further beyond, there is the realization of union with the Divine Itself, in the realization of Sachchidananda. In Sri Aurobindo's writing we read of Oneness realized as Brahman, Brahman as synchronous with Sachchidananda—seeing this as the basis of everything in the universe and beyond. This essay explores the manner in which Sri Aurobindo's vision of Oneness originates in his explanation of creation itself and also his perspective on the inherent Oneness and actual divinity of the manifestation. Sri Aurobindo's assertion of the inherent divinity of the manifest universe is the basis for much of his philosophy, including his conceptualization of the evolution of consciousness. In addition, the continuing relevance of Sri Aurobindo's vision of Oneness is explored with particular emphasis on the hope which this offers for the resolution of human conflict and apparent division.

A Theory of Creation

Virtually every belief system rests on a creation story. Sri Aurobindo explains the creation of the manifestation in terms which may seem considerably more abstract than most, since his description of the processes and stages of creation is less symbolic and metaphorical than it is metaphysical and spiritual in style of description. We can consider that Sri Aurobindo's creation story emerges through his explanations of the nature of reality. He begins with the Absolute, the Transcendent, Brahman—vast, infinite, eternal—without beginning or end. This is pure Being, the original Existence. There is nothing greater, vaster. This is infinite Existence Itself. Being infinite and illimitable, the Absolute has the capacity to do anything, be anything. It has its active, personal aspect, Saguna Brahman, as well as its silent, impersonal aspect, Nirguna Brahman. In its active aspect, Brahman chose to extend Itself into physical being, to express Itself in form as material creation. As Sachchidananda, sublime Existence-Consciousness-Bliss, the Divine moved to create all that is in extension of Himself. The power which Sri Aurobindo has identified as Supermind and described as the supreme Truth-Consciousness is the dynamic power of Sachchidananda, a power through which It expresses Itself. It is through this supramental power that Sachchidananda created the worlds, including our universe and our material world of forms. Sri Aurobindo writes: "God is Sachchidananda. He manifests Himself as infinite existence of which the essentiality is consciousness, of which again the essentiality is bliss, is self-delight. Delight cognising variety of itself, seeking its own variety, as it were becomes the universe" (Sri Aurobindo 2009a, 41–42).

In considering the concept of Oneness, we need to emphasize that in creating the physical universe, Sachchidananda extended Itself. The key word here is "Itself." The creation is an extension of the Divine. There was nothing other than the Divine, the Brahman, before the universe was created and, as Sri Aurobindo explains, since the manifestation was created out of Brahman, as an extension of Itself, the physical manifestation *is* Brahman. It is, in essence, quite simple to grasp, even though our observations of the world as it appears to us may lead to questioning this essential fact. Yet, while there is inherent Oneness, there is differentiation—both in the world of forms and in relation to its Divine Creator. In the process of creation, of extension into actual physical matter, a progressive distancing occurred resulting in an apparent separation from its origin, the full Divinity. There was no loss of inherent divine status or being, for the Divine cannot be diminished or eliminated. Sri Aurobindo describes this fact in a passage of profound beauty, a small portion of which reads: "This gold does not cease to be gold because it shapes itself into all kinds of ornaments and coins itself into many currencies and values" (Sri Aurobindo 2009b, 668). However, as Sri Aurobindo explains, the divinity of the manifestation became increasingly concealed as distance, and stages of separation, increased. Sri Aurobindo has wonderfully identified and described the stages of the Divine descent from Sachchidananda, Supermind, Overmind, Intuition, Illumined Mind, Higher Mind, down to Mind (our usual level of functioning), and further on through the vital and physical levels of being into the Subconscient and Inconscient. While indications of separation are apparent below the level of Overmind, the most complete sense of separation does not begin until we reach the level of Mind, for this is where ego is strong and active.

Sri Aurobindo associates the development of the ego with the fall into the Ignorance, this being defined as separation from the Divine, while knowledge, true knowledge, is the knowledge of spiritual realization leading to Oneness with the Divine. While much of Eastern thought has rightly denigrated the role of the ego in relation to spiritual development, Sri Aurobindo asserts that ego does have a valuable role to play in that it enables individuation. He also explains that individuation is necessary for the separation of forms which, in turn, enables the friction of life and development of the individual, all of which is inherent in humanity's growth and its participation in the evolution of consciousness.

The descent of consciousness into the manifestation proceeds down through levels below the mental level into the Subconscient and finally the full Inconscient. Sri Aurobindo considers the Subconscient to be between the level of mind and the Inconscient. We experience the Subconscient in sleep and, although the surface consciousness is not aware of the interaction, our waking consciousness interacts with it as well. (Also, behind, rather than below, the surface mind is the subliminal consciousness which actually relates to the Superconscient and higher levels of being, though doing so subliminally and without direct cognizance by the surface mind of thought. Sri Aurobindo's explanation of the powers of consciousness behind the surface, yet with higher capabilities than the intellect, is important to recognize, though it is not our purpose to explore this here.) We do need to address the term "Inconscient" further, especially since this term is not generally recognized beyond Aurobindonian circles. However, it is important to have an understanding of the Inconscient, since its presence implies something of the challenges we face in our evolution. This is the stage at which consciousness has actually forgotten itself. It is completely concealed. The important point to acknowledge, however, is that consciousness is indeed present. In addition, Sri Aurobindo explains that "the first emergence from the Inconscient is Matter" (Sri Aurobindo 2009b, 629), thereby asserting the consciousness of matter itself.

Let us look directly to Sri Aurobindo for further description and clarification of the Subconscient and Inconscient:

> The subconscient is universal as well as individual like all the other main parts of the nature. But there are different parts or planes of the subconscient. All upon earth is based on the Inconscient as it is called, though it is not really inconscient at all, but rather a complete "sub"-conscience, a suppressed or involved consciousness, in which there is everything but nothing is formulated or expressed. The subconscient lies in between this Inconscient and the conscious mind, life and body. It contains the potentiality of all the primitive reactions to life which struggle out to the surface from the dull and inert obscurity of Matter and form by a constant development a slowly evolving and self-formulating consciousness; it contains them not as ideas or perceptions or conscious reactions but as the fluid substance of these things.
>
> (Sri Aurobindo 2012, 225–226)

Separation from the Divine is at its most complete at the level of the Inconscience. Yet the Divine is there. The entire manifestation is the creation of the Divine in Its self-extension, so necessarily the Divine is present within it, even in matter, even in the Inconscience. This is what Sri Aurobindo describes as the involution of the Divine in the creation. While we may tend to focus on the concealment, and the Inconscience, and what this means for our own sense of distance from the Divine in our lives in the material world, we can conversely focus on the extraordinary fact of the Divine's actual presence within all matter, including our own bodies. We could say simply: He is in the rock, the tree, and even me. Consequently, we see that Sri Aurobindo extends this meaning of Brahman as far as imaginable by including the material world, asserting the innate divinity and Oneness of All. Sri Aurobindo offers a new and more comprehensive interpretation of the classic Vedic description of Brahman as "One without a second," which had led to the ascetic interpretation separating God from the material world. Instead, he states: "'One without a second', has not been read sufficiently in the light of that other formula equally imperative, 'All this is the Brahman'" (Sri Aurobindo 2009b, 28).

Inherent Evolutionary Potential

It is this very presence of the Divine in matter, in everything, that enables the evolution of consciousness. In fact, Sri Aurobindo tells us that this makes the evolution inevitable. The presence of the Divine in matter drives the evolution, and essentially is its motive power. Sri Aurobindo explains that what is involved is compelled to evolve, to express, and to reveal itself. Therefore, the divinity inherent in the Inconscience will eventually emerge and participate in fulfilling the purpose of the manifestation. The Inconscient will reveal its concealed consciousness which will make its way in an ascent through the levels of consciousness which Sri Aurobindo has identified and described in his conceptualization of the evolution of consciousness. In doing so, the process involves an ascent through all the stages of the original descent which occurred in the very creation itself. As Sri Aurobindo states, "The apparent Inconscience of the material universe holds in itself darkly all that is eternally self-revealed in the luminous Superconscient; to reveal it in Time is the slow and deliberate delight of Nature and the aim of her cycles" (Sri Aurobindo 2009b, 668). This extraordinary process of revelation Sri Aurobindo conceives as unfolding in the progression through a range of levels of consciousness. He asserts that these are not only levels of consciousness, but actual levels of being. In seeking to understand Sri Aurobindo's conceptualization of this progression, it is best to refer directly to his elaboration of these in *The Life Divine*. For the purposes of the present chapter, we give only brief, and necessarily inadequate, summaries here, beginning with the higher mind, the first stage above the intellect.

Higher Mind

Sri Aurobindo describes higher mind as the "first decisive step out of our human intelligence, our normal mentality" (Sri Aurobindo 2009b, 974) and explains that it is a purer, more spontaneous, and truer form of thought and not dependent on information received and processed by the physical senses and the powers of reason and synthesis. Instead, higher mind consists of "a unitarian sense of being with a powerful multiple dynamisation capable of the formation of a multitude of aspects of knowledge, ways of action, forms and significances of becoming, of all of which there is a spontaneous inherent knowledge"(Sri Aurobindo 2009b, 974). Sri Aurobindo explains that it has a dynamic power through its will in addition to being a higher way of knowing. The action of higher mind works to purify the entire being through the truth which it brings and changes the mind, will, heart, body, and life of the individual into higher and truer forms of themselves.

Illumined Mind

Illumined mind is the first level of mind which goes beyond thought. Sri Aurobindo describes this as consisting of a direct vision brought about by the light of the spirit. At the level of illumined mind, perception, conceptualization, and the translation of this knowledge into language does not occur. Illumined mind seizes on the truth of things more directly through inner vision and perceives them more truly and fully than thought is capable of doing. In describing illumined mind as a force and a mind of spiritual light, Sri Aurobindo helps us understand that illumined mind consists of a significant departure from thought and the more familiar workings of the mind, and that it also has a dynamic, transforming effect, bringing the being closer to the Divine and to the union and transformation.

Intuition

Both higher mind and illumined mind have Intuition as their source, receiving their knowledge from this higher level and then translating it into thought and vision. Intuition comes significantly closer to the fullest and truest knowledge, the original knowledge by identity in which there is no separation and the knower and the known are one. Sri Aurobindo describes this: "Intuition is a power of consciousness nearer and more intimate to the original knowledge by identity; for it is always something that leaps out direct from a concealed identity" (Sri Aurobindo 2009b, 981). The power of intuition enables consciousness to experience direct and instantaneous truth, giving a more intimate and complete knowledge and consisting of a perception of the truth of things which goes beyond conception or sight.

Overmind and Cosmic Consciousness

Overmind is seen as associated with the cosmic consciousness, since it is usually necessary to have experienced the universalization of the cosmic consciousness, before ascending into the Overmind and receiving this higher level of consciousness fully into the being. The vast horizontal movement of the cosmic consciousness brings a great widening and expansion of the consciousness and is essentially the universalization of the being. Feeling completely One with all, those who have the experience of the cosmic consciousness come to know the true meaning of Oneness. Once this experience has become a stable and settled realization within the being, one's life is forever changed. The realization of unity with the universe and all its manifestations and aspects brings a sense of rebirth and an entirely new view of oneself and the world. Ego is transcended and the individual is liberated into the truth of one's being. Sri Aurobindo explains that this universality of consciousness is needed in order to accommodate the dynamism of the Overmind and its action. He writes:

> When the overmind descends, the predominance of the centralising ego-sense is entirely subordinated, lost in largeness of being and finally abolished; a wide cosmic perception and feeling of a boundless universal self and movement replaces it: many motions that were formerly ego-centric may still continue, but they occur as currents or ripples in the cosmic wideness. Thought, for the most part, no longer seems to originate individually in the body or the person but manifests from above or comes in upon the cosmic mind-waves: all inner individual sight or intelligence of things is now a revelation or illumination of what is seen or comprehended, but the source of the revelation is not in one's separate self but in the universal knowledge.... In this boundless largeness, not only the separate ego but all sense of individuality, even of a subordinated or instrumental individuality, may entirely disappear; the cosmic existence, the cosmic consciousness, the cosmic delight, the play of cosmic forces are alone left.
>
> (Sri Aurobindo 2009b, 985)

In the Overmind consciousness, the realization of Oneness is a liberation and a joy, infusing life with new capacity and meaning, as the individual lives more fully in the reality of Brahman.

The Supramental

The full realization of Oneness comes at the level of the Supermind. It is our understanding that Sri Aurobindo discovered intimations of this higher level in his study of the Vedas, and that he was actually the first to identify and describe the supramental consciousness. Sri Aurobindo explains that, while the Overmind has great transforming effects, only the power of the supramental force can effect complete liberation from the Inconscience. Necessarily, the realization of the supramental consciousness is far beyond the conception of the mind, and it is also, as Sri Aurobindo observes, very much beyond the power of words to describe. In his description of gnosis, Sri Aurobindo offers a sense of the power and beauty of the Supermind. In describing gnosis, which he relates to the term "Vijnana" of the Upanishads, Sri Aurobindo writes: "The gnosis, the Vijnana, is not only this concentrated consciousness of the infinite Essence; it is also and at the same time an infinite knowledge of the myriad play of the Infinite" (Sri Aurobindo 2009d, 477).

In the supramental consciousness, the individual lives in the truth and power of the Divine consciousness, having become an individual expression of its vast multiplicity in Oneness and conscious of its universality and transcendence. The entire being is transformed, including the individual's capacities and efficacy in life. Nevertheless, there is no sense of individual power, since the individual consciousness has become universal and transcendental. Sri Aurobindo describes the results of the supramental realization for the individual:

His own life and the world life would be to him like a perfect work of art; it would be as if the creation of a cosmic and spontaneous genius infallible in its working out of a multitudinous order. The gnostic individual would be in the world and of the world, but would also exceed it in his consciousness and live in his self of transcendence above it; he would be universal but free in the universe, individual but not limited by a separative individuality. The true Person is not an isolated entity, his individuality is universal; for he individualises the universe: it is at the same time divinely emergent in a spiritual air of transcendental infinity, like a high cloud-surpassing summit; for he individualises the divine Transcendence.

(Sri Aurobindo 2009b, 1007–1008)

Let us then draw back from considering the specific progression and reflect further on what is involved. The entire series of processes, levels, stages, which we seek to grasp in intellectual terms, Sri Aurobindo tells us is actually much more subtle and fluid than our mentality can conceive. We may experience our own individual evolution of consciousness in a way which cannot be identified as discrete stages. In fact, struggling to objectify these can be counterproductive for one's spiritual progress. For example, if we need to ask ourselves if we are yet free of ego, perhaps that implies that we are giving rein to ego by even asking the question!

Most important, these processes and stages all connect us to the Divine in a full and unbroken unity. The Divine Sachchidananda extended Himself through His dynamic supramental power and created all the universes, the worlds, and us. We are from Him. He is all that is. We are One. We are part of Him. He is within us. There is a vast unity within everything. Sri Aurobindo describes the cosmos as one with the Divine and not separate and less real than the Transcendent. The world and all in it are the Divine's creation, are one with the Divine as Itself. He unites the concepts of Brahman, the Self, the Transcendent Divine, the individual, and the world of phenomena and explains:

If Brahman alone exists, all these must be Brahman, and in Brahman-consciousness the division of these concepts must disappear in a reconciling self-vision; but we can arrive at their true unity only by passing beyond the intellectual Reason and finding out through spiritual experience where they meet and become one and what is the spiritual reality of their apparent divergence. In fact, in the Brahman-consciousness the divergences cannot exist, they must by our passage into it converge into unity; the divisions of the intellectual reason may correspond to a reality, but it must be then the reality of a manifold Oneness.

(Sri Aurobindo 2009b, 480)

If we have the belief in Oneness, based either on faith, on the logic of intellectual philosophical explanation, or a combination of both, we see the world differently. It does not have to appear as the conflicted and troubling place that it is described to be through the various news and media sources. Yes, all the violence and other heinous acts are occurring and they are real. Yes, these are terrible and must end. However, all this is happening within the One body of the Lord. Even all this is part of the divine Lila. As Sri Aurobindo writes: "Himself the play, Himself the player, Himself the playground" (Sri Aurobindo 2009b, 111). In response to the darkness and conflict which trouble us and appear to separate us from the Divine, we know that He has given us the opportunity to evolve and to return to Him through the evolution. As we know from Sri Aurobindo, that is not all. The Divine has also given us the opportunity to transform ourselves, to fully reveal His presence within us, to give this expression to the fullest extent in order that our innate divinity can completely transform our entire being. Furthermore, this is not to reach its culmination with individuals, but extend to our entire world, transforming it, filling it with the revealed Divine presence.

Experiencing Oneness

We can regard the creation of the many from the One as primarily a downward movement in a vertical direction and its converse, the evolution of consciousness and fulfillment of the purpose for which the material world was created, to be a vertical movement upward. As we grow in consciousness, we also participate in a horizontal movement, a universalization, which consists of the experiences and ultimately the realization of the cosmic consciousness. Experiencing the sense of unity with those around us, with the manifest beauty of the creation, and even with beings and worlds we cannot see or mentally conceive of, is a profound realization of the inherent Oneness in which we exist. This realization necessarily brings us closer to union with the Divine and, as Sri Aurobindo describes, does not necessarily follow any set order in the progression of consciousness. The individual may have many experiences of universalization and of union with the Divine before these experiences settle into complete realizations within the being. While intellectually we tend to separate such higher experience into categories defined by specific terms, the actual interplay of these and the progression of spiritual growth and realization are beyond our mental formulations. All of this extraordinary range and interplay of experience are possible because of the very nature of the divine reality in which we live.

Our conflicted individual being is just as much one in itself as it is with the manifestation, even though it can seem very divided within itself and also at times in opposition to itself. We are often aware of our internal conflicts and sometimes taken over, even overwhelmed, by them and their various warring factions. Our internal conflicts can be seen in terms of tension between our higher and lower natures. Addressing this in a much larger sense, Sri Aurobindo couches this conflict in terms of the tension between soul and nature, Purusha and Prakriti. This conceptualization reflects in a universal sense what occurs within the individual. In his wonderful way of resolving dualities, Sri Aurobindo does so by exploring the relation of the two and concluding that when Purusha becomes master of Prakriti, they exist as a harmonious unity. Purusha supports and sanctions the actions of Prakriti, and Prakriti takes direction and finds support from the Purusha.

So it is within the individual, when the various disparate aspects of being become centered around the soul, the psychic being. In his wonderful conceptualization of the planes and parts of being, Sri Aurobindo has far exceeded the conceptions of modern psychology and given us much more profound insights into who and what we are. Without elaborating on these, let us look briefly at the various elements of personality which may conflict with the soul and its own, true direction. These consist of the mental, vital, and physical aspects, each with its own ego and self-interests, as well as levels of degree. The surface mind is the mind of intellect, the thought mind, which Sri Aurobindo considers to be fraught with problems relating to its limited ability to attain true knowledge. The vital, emotional aspect of the individual is associated with cravings, desire, and self-interest. The physical aspect is, of course, the body with its needs, which then is also associated with the vital and its desires and wants. Apart from the deep inner motivation for spiritual development, the aspects of our outer nature are greatly influenced by various other factors: ego and its desire for expression in myriad ways, environmental forces, the collective consciousness, as well as aspects of personality expressed in the varying play of the modes of nature, the gunas of sattwa, rajas, and tamas.

When the individual comes in touch with the psychic being, there is a clear recognition of having encountered something compelling and undeniably important. This contact may happen readily within the experience of the individual due to past development. It may come through the stresses and crises of life, as the result of an inner cry and calling to the Divine. It may come through experiences of great beauty of the natural world or of music and the arts. In any case, the contact with the psychic being is a gift of Grace. This "spark of the Divine" (Sri Aurobindo 2009b, 238) in the individual being, once recognized, can be fostered and subsequently grown increasingly significant and powerful in one's life. It can also be suppressed by denying it and not following its dictates. However, it emerges again and, with each recognition, increases in strength and power within the being. Ultimately it can become the prime mover of the individual. It effectively organizes the disparate elements of being around itself in its role as the central core of the individual. Its influence infuses the mind, vital, and physical with its higher light. In unifying the various aspects of being around the soul, the psychic being facilitates the entire evolution of consciousness within the individual being. Consequently, the psychic being becomes master of the outer nature of the individual and puts all the complex and developed aspects of being to use in the overall evolution. Sri Aurobindo describes this sublime action:

> This is the first step of self-realisation, to enthrone the soul, the divine psychic individual in the place of the ego. The next step is to become aware of the eternal self in us unborn and one with the self of all beings. This self-realisation liberates and universalises; even if our action still proceeds in the dynamics of the Ignorance, it no longer binds or misleads because our inner being is seated in the light of self-knowledge. The third step is to know the Divine Being who is at once our supreme transcendent Self, the Cosmic Being, foundation of our universality, and the Divinity within of which our psychic being, the true evolving individual in our nature, is a portion, a spark, a flame growing into the eternal Fire from which it was lit and of which it is the witness ever living within us and the conscious instrument of its light and power and joy and beauty. Aware of the Divine as the Master of our being and action, we can learn to become channels of his Shakti, the Divine Puissance, and act according to her dictates or her rule of light and power within us.
> (Sri Aurobindo 2009b, 654)

Complete Oneness

Sri Aurobindo asserts the importance of the individual to the entire universal progression. For example, in writing of the individual and the universal in *The Life Divine*, Sri Aurobindo states:

> The liberation of the individual soul is therefore the keynote of the definitive divine action; it is the primary divine necessity and the pivot on which all else turns. It is the point of Light at which the intended complete self-manifestation in the Many begins to emerge. But the liberated soul extends its perception of unity horizontally as well as vertically. Its unity with the transcendent One is incomplete without its unity with the cosmic Many. And that lateral unity translates itself by a multiplication, a reproduction of its own liberated state at other points in the Multiplicity. The divine soul reproduces itself in similar liberated souls as the animal reproduces itself in similar bodies. Therefore, whenever even a single soul is liberated, there is a tendency to an extension and even to an outburst of the same divine self-consciousness in other individual souls of our terrestrial humanity and,—who knows?—perhaps even beyond the terrestrial consciousness. Where shall we fix the limit of that extension?
>
> (Sri Aurobindo 2009b, 45)

Oneness is a fact, with or without our recognition of it, with or without our conscious pursuit of the realization of the cosmic consciousness, with or without our conscious pursuit of union with the Divine. Yet, with our consciousness and active engagement in pursuing a spiritual path, we contribute, each in our own way, to the evolution of the whole. The action is like what happens when you throw a stone into a pool. A series of concentric rings goes out again and again from the spot where the stone fell into the water. The progress each of us makes has a similar effect. Since we are all One, all necessarily connected, of course this is so. Sri Aurobindo has written on collective yoga in specific contexts, but also described the overall functioning of collective consciousness. For example:

> For the initiation of the evolutionary emergence from the Inconscient works out by two forces, a secret cosmic consciousness and an individual consciousness manifest on the surface. The secret cosmic consciousness remains secret and subliminal to the surface individual; it organises itself on the surface by the creation of separate objects and beings. But while it organises the separate object and the body and mind of the individual being, it creates also collective powers of consciousness which are large subjective formations of cosmic Nature; but it does not provide for them an organised mind and body, it bases them on the group of individuals, develops for them a group mind, a changing yet continuous group body. It follows that only as the individuals become more and more conscious can the group-being also become more and more conscious; the growth of the individual is the indispensable means for the inner growth as distinguished from the outer force and expansion of the collective being. This indeed is the dual

importance of the individual that it is through him that the cosmic spirit organises its collective units and makes them self-expressive and progressive and through him that it raises Nature from the Inconscience to the Superconscience and exalts it to meet the Transcendent.

(Sri Aurobindo 2009b, 720)

This description gives us a clear and powerful sense of the role of the individual in the general spiritual advance of the human collectivity. Furthermore, it is a definite recognition of our connectedness. We can also reflect on the ways in which we have intimations of our Oneness in relation to others. For example, we empathize with others whom we know, and also even with the vicissitudes in the lives of strangers and fictional characters. Participating in group activities, such as singing in a chorus, gives a definite feeling of satisfaction, perhaps even a sense of greater completeness, because we are joining with others in the spirit of harmony, as well as creating a harmonious result. The various ways we seek to resolve conflict and live compatibly and in harmony with others can vividly reveal indications of Oneness. Sri Aurobindo explains that our drive to attain harmony in life is an essential component of human motivation. The pursuit of harmony is in its essence the drive to discover and manifest the reality of Oneness.[1] In describing the drive for harmony, Sri Aurobindo explains this as inherent and central to human experience, as well as having an evolutionary aspect:

For all problems of existence are essentially problems of harmony. They arise from the perception of an unsolved discord and the instinct of an undiscovered agreement or unity. To rest content with an unsolved discord is possible for the practical and more animal part of man, but impossible for his fully awakened mind, and usually even his practical parts only escape from the general necessity either by shutting out the problem or by accepting a rough, utilitarian and unillumined compromise. For essentially, all Nature seeks a harmony, life and matter in their own sphere as much as mind in the arrangement of its perceptions. The greater the apparent disorder of the materials offered or the apparent disparateness, even to irreconcilable opposition, of the elements that have to be utilised, the stronger is the spur, and it drives towards a more subtle and puissant order than can normally be the result of a less difficult endeavour.

(Sri Aurobindo 2009b, 4–5)

Our quest for harmony with others and with the world around us is acted out in many ways in our outer lives and, rising in consciousness, we can ultimately attain its fulfillment in the full realization of Oneness, as Sri Aurobindo describes: "We perceive the soul in all bodies to be this one Self or Sachchidananda multiplying itself in individual consciousness. We see also all minds, lives, bodies to be active formations of the same existence in the extended being of the Self" (Sri Aurobindo 2009a, 36).

In recognizing and acknowledging our innate sense of Oneness in simple ordinary ways, we can see more clearly how it plays a real part in our lives. This is true for the whole of humanity. We are happier and feel more in balance when we join in productive or enjoyable activities with others. Even if these appear superficial in nature, the meaning goes deeper. Each attempt at reconciling conflict, seeking harmony, feeling empathy, helping others in any way is an inherent expression of the Oneness of humanity with itself. Yet we know there is more. The feelings of peace or elevation we experience when centered in ourselves, whether in quiet meditation, or dynamically active in the world, reveal the presence of the Divine within us. This is our link to the Oneness above and around us. We are part of that and, as Sri Aurobindo explains, destined to manifest and express the Oneness of the Divine with the manifestation. Sri Aurobindo has envisioned that humanity will unite with the Divine and, in the fulfillment of this union, become transformed to reveal the inherent divinity of All. For we are one substance, created by the Divine from Himself. That being so, we can only be One with the Divine, One with each other, One with All. As Sri Aurobindo expresses so profoundly in *Savitri* (Sri Aurobindo 2009c, 61):

> His semblances he turns to real shapes
> And makes the symbol equal with the truth:
> He gives to his timeless thoughts a form in Time,
> He is the substance, he the self of things.

Conclusion

In accepting the innate Oneness of humanity and reflecting on this as a reality truer than our outward perception of separateness acknowledges, we can consider that the realization of Oneness through the evolution of consciousness holds the key to the end of human suffering. This can be considered as having two particular aspects, the first of which is humanity's sense of division, of separateness from each other, which pits individuals, societies, and nations against each other. At the individual level, transcending ego and universalizing consciousness through the realization of the cosmic consciousness, individuals necessarily recognize their commonalities with others, but also go even beyond this. They experience fully the realization of their Oneness with others. For the individual who has attained this realization, All is truly One and there can be no sense of division, no potential for interpersonal tension or conflict. Of course, this doesn't immediately address the general overall problem of interpersonal conflict, since we cannot expect everyone to progress in the evolution of consciousness at the same rate, or even for everyone to be receptive to it and consciously choose to participate. Although conscious will and openness to change accelerate the process, even without these change is inevitable. As Sri Aurobindo has explained, the inner truth of the being drives the evolution at the individual level and, consequently, innate Oneness and divinity will ultimately be expressed and fully manifested. Ultimately, we can hope for eventual transformation of the human race to higher levels of being. Each of us has the potential to participate in and contribute to the evolutionary process.

In addition, the problem of ego ranges far beyond that of individual human beings, since there are also collective egos built up through the collective consciousness of communities, societies, and nations. At its highest and most idealistic level, this can result in a sense of national pride in a country's attributes and values and, of course, at its lowest and most rigid level, it can lead to a sense of superiority and even aggression and incitement to conflict. In our present times, we can look at world events and wonder if humanity will ever be free of suffering from war. We can also look closer to home and wonder if we will ever be free of acts of cruelty committed by one person against another or, as sometimes occurs in current times, by one person against many. But looking back on human history and behavior, we can assess that such problems have been with us for centuries, though perhaps on a different scale, especially since the invention of modern weapons of war and assault. So, how can this all change for the better?

Sri Aurobindo explains to us that more than our usual superficial remedies are needed in order to make the world a truly better place and also that the solution has always been available to us from our very inception. True and lasting change can only come about by a change of consciousness. For it is through our consciousness that we live and act in the world, and the nature of our consciousness determines the nature of our actions. In realizing our Oneness, through the realization of the cosmic consciousness, we will find the innate truth of our unity and ultimately be able to achieve harmony. This will begin within our own individual selves and expand to become a true and enduring harmony between persons and, ultimately, between nations. The answer lies in the evolution of consciousness, which will reveal to us and establish, within us and the manifest world, the truth and reality of Oneness.

The other aspect of the realization of Oneness which can solve humanity's suffering is the elimination of our sense of separation from the Divine. This aspect of the realization occurs within the individual at a deeply personal level. It develops naturally and concurrently along with the realization of Oneness with all other beings, with particular individuals discovering unity sometimes more readily with the outer world, and sometimes more readily with the inner Divine. Naturally, these two possible movements are in essence one process since, as Sri Aurobindo explains, the Divine is inherently within the manifestation and the manifest universe is entirely within Him. This being the reality of existence, human consciousness, in its evolutionary drive, is compelled to discover and realize this truth. Until we achieve this, we will necessarily feel unfulfilled. It is the sense of separation from the Divine reality which is the core reason for the suffering and disquiet which we experience within ourselves. This is the source of our restlessness, dissatisfaction, sense of emptiness, and even depression. As individuals, we are incomplete without the discovery of the divine spark within ourselves. Once discovered, this spark, which Sri Aurobindo has conceptualized as the psychic being, leads the further development of the individual, giving one's life a fuller sense of meaning and purpose, culminating ultimately in full union with the Divine and transformation of the being. The union with the Divine, essentially rediscovering our true Self in our divine Origin, and manifesting this throughout our entire being, is the complete fulfillment of our being and our purpose on earth. In attaining this union Sri Aurobindo explains that we will do more than come full circle, because we will have used the friction and tension of life experiences to evolve in consciousness, doing so integrally through all the parts of our being, gradually coming to fully embody and express the divine essence with which we were originally created. It is this inherent drive for true Oneness that motivates us and will become our salvation.

Note

1 For a more complete discussion of this subject and how it relates to humanity's deep motivation toward union with the Divine in concert with the evolution of consciousness, the reader can refer to Orton (2008).

References

Orton, Martha. 2008. *The Quest for Knowledge and Mastery: A Comparative Study of Motivation in the Light of Sri Aurobindo*. Puducherry: Sri Aurobindo Centre for Advanced Research.
Sri Aurobindo. 2009a. *Isha Upanishad*. Pondicherry: Sri Aurobindo Ashram.
Sri Aurobindo. 2009b. *The Life Divine*. Pondicherry: Sri Aurobindo Ashram.
Sri Aurobindo. 2009c. *Savitri*. Pondicherry: Sri Aurobindo Ashram.
Sri Aurobindo. 2009d. *The Synthesis of Yoga*. Pondicherry: Sri Aurobindo Ashram.
Sri Aurobindo. 2012. *Letters on Yoga*. Pondicherry: Sri Aurobindo Ashram.

Part Three

Poetry, Ethics, and Education

8

Poetry at the Center of Human Knowledge

Goutam Ghosal

Disclaiming the title "philosopher," Sri Aurobindo always indicates and affirms that he is primarily a poet and a politician, meaning his exploration of the soul as a lone voyager to the peaks nobody has attained yet and also indicating the politics of an ideal nature, which stresses the future of man on this planet. This is interesting because he is a leading psychologist, sociologist, and a dreamer of a new map for the future, which will see a new creation on this polluted and plundered earth. What is the role of his poetry in those contexts? One may well ask.

Apart from his more than fifty thousand lines of epic, lyric, dramatic, and narrative poetry, his majestic prose edifices are often concealed poetry by virtue of their experiential nature. Poetry is the leader of our inward voyage, a sacred fire, which moves alongside our inner adventure, of which Sri Aurobindo speaks both in poetry and in prose, breaking the barrier often between the two forms. What kind of poetry does he write? The chapter examines Sri Aurobindo's poetry, and argues how his poetry is at the center of human knowledge and how it evokes spiritual pilgrimage and realization.

Sri Aurobindo's Poetry and Philosophy

Let us have a glimpse at some samples:

> Thy golden Light came down into my brain
> And the grey rooms of mind sun-touched became
> A bright reply to Wisdom's occult plane,
> A calm illumination and a flame.
> Thy golden Light came down into my throat,
> And all my speech is now a tune divine,
> A paean song of thee my single note;
> My words are drunk with the Immortal's wine.
> Thy golden Light came down into my heart
> Smiting my life with Thy eternity;

Now has it grown a temple where Thou art
And all its passions point towards only Thee.

Thy golden Light came down into my feet:
My earth is now thy playfield and thy seat. (The Complete Works of Sri Aurobindo or CWSA 2009, vol. 2, 605)

Or

There is a brighter ether than this blue
Pretence of an enveloping heavenly vault,
Royaler investiture than this massed assault
Of emerald rapture pearled with tears of dew.
Immortal spaces of cerulean hue
Are in our reach and fields without this fault
Of drab brown earth and streams that never halt
In their deep murmur which white flowers strew

Floating like stars upon a strip of sky.
This world behind is made of truer stuff
Than the manufactured tissue of earth's grace.
There we can walk and see the gods go by
And sip from Hebe's cup nectar enough
To make for us heavenly limbs and deathless face. (CWSA 2009, vol. 2, 158)

The first sonnet is pure revelation, showing a gradual descent of a light from above. The second and the third are also experiences, visions that are expressed either through thought-images or as pure revelations. But then, this is not the poetry that we usually know as poetry. It is neither an argument nor a nautch girl of fancy. For, Sri Aurobindo revives an ancient poetic code, which was known to the Vedic seers only in its essential purity.

> What would be the ideal spirit of poetry in an age of the increasingly intuitive mind: that is the question which arises from all that has gone before and to which we may attempt some kind of answer. I have spoken in the beginning of the Mantra as the highest and intensest revealing form of poetic thought and expression. What the Vedic poets meant by the Mantra was an inspired and revealed seeing and visioned thinking, attended by a realisation, to use the ponderous but necessary modern word, of some inmost truth of God and self and man and Nature and cosmos and life and thing and thought and experience and deed. It was a thinking that came on the wings of a great soul rhythm, chandas. For the seeing could not be separated from the hearing; it was one act. Nor could the living of the truth in oneself which we mean by realisation, be separated from either, for the presence of it in the soul and its possession of the mind must precede or accompany in the creator or human channel that expression of the inner sight and hearing which takes the shape of the luminous word.
>
> (Sri Aurobindo Birth Centenary Library or SABCL 1972, vol. 9, 199)

It is obvious through Sri Aurobindo's commentary that sight and listening are related in the poetry of incantation. Also, thinking or the thought-substance may have direct relation with the vision and then again he uses the unavoidable word "realization," which is the kernel of this inspired art. Sri Aurobindo continues the argument by further efforts at communication of what he has to say:

> The Mantra is born through the heart and shaped or massed by the thinking mind into a chariot of that godhead of the Eternal of whom the truth seen is a face or a form. And in the mind too of the fit outward hearer who listens to the word of the poet-seer, these three must come together, if our word is a real Mantra; the sight of the inmost truth must accompany the hearing, the possession of the inmost spirit of it by the mind and its coming home to the soul must accompany or follow immediately upon the rhythmic message of the Word and the mind's sight of the Truth. That may sound a rather mystic account of the matter, but substantially there could hardly be a more complete description of the birth and effect of the inspired and revealing word, and it might be applied, though usually on a more lowered scale than was intended by the Vedic Rishis, to all the highest outbursts of a really great poetry.
> (SABCL 1972, vol. 9, 199)

Rhythm is an extremely important factor for Sri Aurobindo, the thing which comes as a discovered vibration along with the substance and suffused with the substance. There is true rhythm for every mantric word or speech, be it apparent to the ear or hidden only for the soul's listening. The inspired word or arrangement or selection comes with that specific rhythm associated with the voyage of self-discovery. The rhythm is also part of man's ascension of consciousness. The poetry as a sacred fire has an automatic impact on evolving humanity. That is the value of the immaterial in changing the world:

> But poetry is the Mantra only when it is the voice of the inmost truth and is couched in the highest power of the very rhythm and speech of that truth. And the ancient poets of the Veda and Upanishads claimed to be uttering the Mantra because always it was this inmost and almost occult truth of things which they strove to see and hear and speak and because they believed themselves to be using or finding its innate soul rhythms and the sacrificial speech of it cast up by the divine Agni, the sacred Fire in the heart of man. The Mantra in other words is a direct and most heightened, an intensest and most divinely burdened rhythmic word which embodies an intuitive and revelatory inspiration and ensouls the mind with the sight and the presence of the very self, the inmost reality of things and with its truth and with the divine soul-forms of it, the Godheads which are born from the living Truth. Or, let us say, it is a supreme rhythmic language which seizes hold upon all that is finite and brings into each the light and voice of its own infinite.
> (SABCL 1972, vol. 9, 199–200)

Thus Sri Aurobindo is speaking of a revival in the field of poetry, which was in the past related to the ascension of man's consciousness. The Rishi of the past was either a poet-seer or a seer-poet, the two near identical phrases Sri Aurobindo uses to characterize those poets as Rishis. And then again, it will not just be a revival, but a dynamic revival of the incantatory verse, mantra, and a "rhythmic voyage of self-discovery." Why dynamic? The human consciousness is moving ahead all the time seeking to explore new things in the inner and higher provinces. Sri Aurobindo observes the future possibility of this new spirit:

> The note which has already begun and found many of its tones in Whitman and Carpenter and A. E. and Tagore will grow into a more full and near and intimate poetic knowledge and vision and feeling which will continue to embrace more and more, no longer only the more exceptional inner states and touches which are the domain of mystic poetry, but everything in our inner and outer existence until all life and experience has been brought within the mould of the spiritual sense and the spiritual interpretation. A poetry of this kind will be in a supreme way what all art should be, a thing of harmony and joy and illumination, a solution and release of the soul from its vital unrest and questioning and struggle, not by any ignoring of these things but by an uplifting into the strength of the self within and the light and air of its greater view where there is found not only the point of escape but the supporting calmness and power of a seated knowledge, mastery and deliverance.
>
> (SABCL 1972, vol. 9, 252)

Sri Aurobindo has a specific stress on his favorite trio, Whitman, Carpenter, and Tagore, but the Irish poets also come quite frequently in his frame of reference, especially when he speaks directly about the poetry of vision, prayer, revelation, magic, and incantation.

> In the greatest art and poetry there should be something of the calm of the impersonal basing and elevating the effort and struggle of the personality, something of the largeness of the universal releasing and harmonising the troubled concentrations of the individual existence, something of the sense of the transcendent raising the inferior, ignorant and uncertain powers of life towards a greater strength and light and Ananda. And when art and poetry can utter the fullest sense of these things, it is then that they will become the greatest fortifiers and builders of the soul of man and assure it in the grandeur of its own largest self and spirit. The poetry of Europe has been a voice intensely eager and moved but restless, troubled and without a sure base of happiness and repose, vibrating with the passion of life and avid of its joy and pleasure and beauty, but afflicted also by its unrest, grief, tragedy, discord, insufficiency, incertitude, capable only of its lesser harmonies, not of any great release and satisfaction. The art and poetry of the East have been the creation of a larger and quieter spirit, intensely responsive as in the far East to deeper psychic significances and finding there fine and subtle harmonies of the soul's experience or, as in India, expressing in spite of the ascetic creed of vanity and illusion much rather the greatness and power and satisfied activity of human thought and life and action and behind it

the communion of the soul with the Eternal. The poetry of the future reconciling all these strains, taking the highest as its keynote and interpreting the rest in its intensity and its largeness, will offer to the human mind a more complex aesthetic and spiritual satisfaction, express a more richly filled content of self-experience raised to a more persistent sight of things absolute and infinite and a more potent and all-comprehending release into the calm and delight of the spirit.

(SABCL 1972, vol. 9, 252-253)

He uses the comparative degree "more," because he believes a greater era of man's living is on the way. As man is not static in his consciousness, his poetry will also not be static in its search for deeper realizations in his self and above his head. If one observes carefully the Scriptures quoted at the top of every chapter in *The Life Divine* and then reads the following words, one has the feeling that this writer is not just repeating the Scriptures, is not offering us a summary. Rather, he takes them as a starting point to move ahead through his experiential knowledge. Man is not a full stop, not even a comma. He is a transitional creature in search of a new species in the making through him. This poetry had nothing to do with teaching, sermonizing, and philosophizing. The ancients just saw and sang about what they saw. It speaks of man's inward progress and upward movements. Poetry for Sri Aurobindo is vision, revelation, prayer, and incantation. Sight is the most essential of a true poet. Sri Aurobindo says:

Vision is the characteristic power of the poet, as is discriminative thought the essential gift of the philosopher and analytic observation the natural genius of the scientist. The Kavi (the Sanskrit word for poet) was in the idea of the ancients the seer and revealer of truth, and though we have wandered far enough from that ideal to demand from him only the pleasure of the ear and the amusement of the aesthetic faculty, still all great poetry instinctively preserves something of that higher turn of its own aim and significance. Poetry, in fact, being Art, must attempt to make us see, and since it is to the inner senses that it has to address itself,—for the ear is its only physical gate of entry and even there its real appeal is to an inner hearing,—and since its object is to make us live. In classical Sanskrit it is applied to any maker of verse or even of prose, but in the Vedic it meant the poet-seer who saw the Truth and found in a subtle truth-hearing the inspired word of his vision. Within ourselves what the poet has embodied in his verse, it is an inner sight which he opens in us, and this inner sight must have been intense in him before he can awaken it in us.

(SABCL 1972, vol. 9, 29)

In the above passage, Sri Aurobindo differentiates between the ancient meaning of the word poet and the meaning attributed to it later in the middle ages. He is also careful to distinguish between the function of the philosopher or logician and that of the poet. There is an obvious clash between the intellect and the vision, between argument and revelation. Sri Aurobindo further explains:

> Therefore the greatest poets have been always those who have had a large and powerful interpretative and intuitive vision of Nature and life and man and whose poetry has arisen out of that in a supreme revelatory utterance of it. Homer, Shakespeare, Dante, Valmiki, Kalidasa, however much they may differ in everything else, are at one in having this as the fundamental character of their greatness. Their supremacy does not lie essentially in a greater thought-power or a more lavish imagery or a more penetrating force of passion and emotion; these things they may have had, one being more gifted in one direction, another in others, but these other powers were aids to their poetic expression rather than its essence or its source. There is often more thought in a short essay of Bacon's than in a whole play of Shakespeare's, but not even a hundred cryptograms can make him the author of the dramas; for, as he showed when he tried to write poetry, the very nature of his thought-power and the characteristic way of expression of the born philosophic thinker hampered him in poetic expression. It was the constant outstreaming of form and thought and image from an abundant inner vision of life which made Shakespeare, whatever his other deficiencies, the sovereign dramatic poet. Sight is the essential poetic gift. The archetypal poet in a world of original ideas is, we may say, a Soul that sees in itself intimately this world and all the others and God and Nature and the life of beings and sets flowing from its centre a surge of creative rhythm and word images which become the expressive body of the vision.
>
> (SABCL 1972, vol. 9, 30)

What exactly is the function of the poet-seer or the seer-poet? Sri Aurobindo sees in the visional function of the poet a very special quality. It is special and largely different from the way the philosopher or the prophet sees. It is a kind of direct sight of the truth without the aid of the intellectual mind, which obstructs poetic sight. He observes:

> The poet-seer sees differently, thinks in another way, and voices himself in quite another manner than the philosopher or the prophet. The prophet announces the Truth as the word of God or his command, he is the giver of the message; the poet shows us Truth in its power of beauty, in its symbol or image, or reveals it to us in the workings of Nature or in the workings of life, and when he has done that, his whole work is done; he need not be its explicit spokesman. The philosopher's business is to discriminate Truth and put its parts and aspects into intellectual relation with each other; the poet's is to seize and embody aspects of Truth in their living relations, or rather,—for that is too philosophical a language,—to see her features and excited by the vision create in the beauty of her image.
>
> (SABCL 1972, vol. 9, 31–32)

This is how Sri Aurobindo critiques the misinterpretation of the true poetic form and its merger in later times with the philosophic form and substance. Although poetry is not exactly to be taken as a substitute for spiritual practice, it must be seen as an accompaniment to spiritual *sadhana* of the human being in search of a transformation of consciousness. Poetry records a concrete experience; it is not a sermon preached from the pulpit asking men and women to obey a moral law for the refinement of consciousness. The refinement of consciousness can be done directly by the poetic mode, the true poetic mode, which is now lost in the present times. What then is the function of a poet or a *Kavi*. Sri Aurobindo answers with a significant clarity in the following passage:

> The essential power of the poetic word is to make us see, not to make us think or feel; thought and feeling must arise out of the sight or be included in it, but sight is the primary consequence and power of poetic speech. For the poet has to make us live in the soul and in the inner mind and heart what is ordinarily lived in the outer mind and the senses, and for that he must first make us see by the soul, in its light and with its deeper vision, what we ordinarily see in a more limited and halting fashion by the senses and the intelligence. He is, as the ancients knew, a seer and not merely a maker of rhymes, not merely a jongleur, rhapsodist or troubadour, and not merely a thinker in lines and stanzas. He sees beyond the sight of the surface mind and finds the revealing word, not merely the adequate and effective, but the illumined and illuminating, the inspired and inevitable word, which compels us to see also. To arrive at that word is the whole endeavor of poetic style.
>
> (SABCL 1972, vol. 9, 24)

Sri Aurobindo's Theory of Poetry

Contrary to the popular view, the *Future Poetry* is not a complete document of Sri Aurobindo's theory of poetry, the poetry that he himself practiced since he began his yoga, and more particularly the poetry he wrote between 1930 and 1950. Along with the *Future Poetry*, one has to take the post-1926 letters to get a complete view of his poetics and poetry. Sri Aurobindo sought more revisions of the book, which he could not do, and because of his dissatisfaction about its perfection, the book remained unpublished during his life time. One suspects he had certain problems in articulation about what he had to say and that could have been the reason why twenty-four of the book's thirty-two chapters received some revision at one time or another. We get to see a clue to the overhead planes only once in the *Future Poetry*, that too very briefly toward the close of the book, where we find a lone reference to the "overmind" without much clarification of the highest plane of the human mind:

> It will be first and most a poetry of the intuitive reason, the intuitive senses, the intuitive delight soul in us, getting from this enhanced source of inspiration a more sovereign poetic enthusiasm and ecstasy, and then, it may even be, rise towards a still greater power of revelation nearer to the direct vision and word of the overmind from which all creative inspiration comes.
>
> (SABCL 1972, vol. 9, 207)

About the nature and function of the overmind relating to poetry, Sri Aurobindo does not say anything more beyond that in the *Future Poetry*. But then in his letters to Sethna we see elaborate commentaries on Overhead aesthetics centering round the ascending overhead or spiritual planes: the Higher Mind, the Illumined Mind, the Intuition, and the Overmind. Interestingly enough, Sri Aurobindo had been throwing sufficient light on these Overhead planes in *The Life Divine* in detail, offering a complete map of the consciousness tiers. Whereas, three years later in the *Future Poetry*, he seems to have been clueless about them. There are efforts to explain the Mantra in the *Future Poetry*, but we do not know as yet that the operating level is the highest peak of the mind, which influences either the style of a line or the theme or both. Therefore, much of Sri Aurobindo's theory of poetry remains unknown in the *Future Poetry*. Without reading the letters to Sethna, no comprehensive picture of mantric poetry, or inspired poetry from comparatively low planes, can be grasped by the readers. Seen from this angle, it will be a mistake to call the *Future Poetry* the total poetic manifesto of Sri Aurobindo. However, the *Future Poetry* should be there, the entire text especially the first four chapters and the last nine chapters, along with the letters, in our quest for the total poetics of Sri Aurobindo. In an unfinished chapter entitled "Mantra," which is now put in Appendix III, he made perhaps his last attempt to clarify the nature of mantra in the book. This time he was very close as he had been in the chapter "The Word and the Spirit" in the *Future Poetry*:

> The poet has to do much more than to offer a precise, a harmonious or a forcefully presented idea to the intelligence: he has to give a breath of life to the word and for that must find out and make full use of its potential power of living suggestion; he has to make it carry in it not only the intellectual notion but the emotion and the psychical sensation of the thing he would make present to us; he has to erect an image of its presence and appeal with which we can inwardly live as we live with the presence and appeal of the objects of the actual universe. As in the Vedic theory the Spirit was supposed to create the worlds by the Word, so the poet brings into being in himself and us by his creative word fragmentarily or largely, in isolated pieces or massed spaces an inner world of beings, objects and experiences. But all creation is a mystery in its secret of inmost process and it is only at best the most outward or mechanical part of it which admits analysis; the creative faculty of the poetic mind is no exception.
>
> (SABCL 1972, vol. 9, 269)

This is a total deconstruction of the technique of modern poetry with its stress on precision and force in favor of an exploration of the rhythmic word, which is the other name of mantra. The word must carry the suggestion of the Infinite, must be brimming with a living fire of Truth-consciousness, which rises in the heart of the seer-poet. Quite often the poet himself is unaware of what he is uttering, the divine *agni* gushing out of the fountainhead of the Spirit in him. Sri Aurobindo observes:

> The poet is a magician who hardly knows the secret of his own spell; even the part taken by the consciously critical or constructive mind is less intellectual

than intuitive; he creates by an afflatus of spiritual power of which his mind is the channel and instrument and the appreciation of it in himself and others comes not by an intellectual judgment but by a spiritual feeling. It is that which must tell him whether the word that comes is the true body of his vision or whether he has to seek or to wait for another that shall be felt as its adequate, its effective, its illuminative, its inspired or its inevitable utterance. The distinction that I am trying to draw here between the various powers of the always intuitive speech of poetry can therefore better be felt than critically stated, but at the same time certain indications may serve to make it more clearly sensed in its spirit with the sympathetic aid of the critical intelligence.

(SABCL 1972, vol. 9, 269–270)

Even this extremely forceful and living language is not able to tell all between 1917 and 1920, when he was serializing the *Future Poetry* in the *Arya*. Something is not here still, which appeared later in the post-1926 prose of lucidity and perception, that we see in the letters to Sethna. Sri Aurobindo became more relaxed as an exegete after 1926. The Mother's presence had a great impact upon the entire community and on Sri Aurobindo himself. It is not a wild imagination to believe that the Mother's influence was a significant factor behind the clarity of his post-1926 exegeses. It is natural to believe, considering the sweeping impact of the Mother on his disciples, that he developed a lot about expressive skill from the Mother's own French writings, which have a sublime clarity in the exposition of subtler things about the integral yoga. There is a marked transformation in his prose style in the '30s and his progressive lucidity reached a supreme height in *The Supramental Manifestations on Earth* (1947), his last major prose edifice. While writing the introduction to his *Overhead Poetry: Poems with Sri Aurobindo's Comments*, Sethna too drops his usual ornate and exhaustive rhetoric and opts for a straightforward style to explain the overhead aesthetics:

The Future Poetry would be written from those rarer levels whose voices have occasionally joined the utterances from the usual sources to make the profoundest moments of past poetry. The rarest of those levels give birth to overhead poetry: they are "planes" whose afflatus comes as if from an infinitude of conscious being above our brain-clamped mentality.

(Sethna 1972, i)

These explanations will be immensely beneficial in our efforts to tie up the scattered materials helping in our own practice of criticism of overhead aesthetics, the lines that come from the overhead planes, of which we have already mentioned earlier (1) the Higher mind, (2) the Illumined Mind, (3) the Intuition, and (4) the Overmind. In these highly illuminating letters, he unveils his hitherto unexplained wisdom for us, through Sethna, and teaches us how to locate the sources, beginning from the echo of the inmost self, the psychic poetry, and then going up from that gateway toward the overhead zones. He comments in detail about the wavering of the influences, as there is no consistent stamp of a particular plane on the entire poem. He speaks of how the planes operate directly or in fusion with other planes on a line or lines. All overhead poetry cannot be classified as mantra, as the most authentic types come either by the overmind influence or by the intervention of very lofty spiritual intuition, which is a plane just below the overmind. Much of the supermind stuff percolates down to the overmind. And that could be the reason behind Sri Aurobindo's statement in the *Future Poetry*, which takes us by surprise because of its direct reference to the Supermind.

> The voice of poetry comes from a region above as, a plane of our being above and beyond our personal intelligence, a supermind which sees things in their innermost and largest truth by a spiritual identity and with a lustrous effulgency and rapture and its native language is a revelatory, inspired, intuitive word limpid or subtly vibrant or densely packed with the glory of this ecstasy and lustre.
> (quoted in Sethna 1972, 264)

The most significant phrases, clauses, and sentences in these letters to Sethna may be underlined, and by repeated readings of these letters a perception has to be formed. Because this is not intellectual poetry, our intellectual judgments will fail to characterize such lines. A different kind of language habit will strengthen that perception. Sri Aurobindo frequently uses words and phrases such as "inevitability," "absolute inevitability," "supreme inevitability," "inevitable word," "revelation," "direct overmind transmission." Sri Aurobindo's letters cited in Sethna's *Overhead Poetry* offer us a finished image of Mantra and indicate why he was not willing to publish the *Future Poetry* as a book.

The overmind expresses a cosmic consciousness, even by its touch, as the full overmind inspiration rarely comes down upon human poetry. It may be a touch on the substance or the style of a line, which may or may not have any relation with mysticism or spirituality proper, or it may affect both the style and the substance in its more powerful touch. Sri Aurobindo also speaks of a "mental overmind" (quoted in Sethna 1972, 18) as contrasted with the overmind proper, which has some Gnostic light in it. There are at least four divisions of the overmind in his letters to Sethna: mental overmind, intuitive overmind, true overmind, and supramentalized overmind. Sri Aurobindo frankly admitted to Sethna that he was not in a position at that point of time to describe the workings of the "overmind Gnosis." Sri Aurobindo stresses the point of feeling and perception, because there is still a problem of objective correlative for the critic while dealing with lines that drop in from the overmind. There may be an inspired selection, an unusual bringing together of words, and obviously they come as discovery refusing to be intercepted by the intellectual mind. One cannot improve such lines.

Sri Aurobindo's yoga is Mother-centric; his best poetry, like *Savitri* and *Rose of God*, is also a revelation of his Mother-oriented yoga meant to change the consciousness of humanity. Without a change of consciousness, the world cannot change and human unity will remain elusive to the world. He chose the medium of his yogic poetry to send out his message to the aspiring world. It is about this poetry he writes, mostly to K. D. Sethna, in the post-1926 letters, which has to be taken along with the *Future Poetry* to get a complete view of his theory of poetry. Aurobindonian aesthetics proper and a hastily developed, but new, theory of poetry came as the fitting finale of a great series, as if to give the final shape to the Aurobindonian worldview that poetry remains the highest form of expression for imaging the evolving consciousness of mankind. Contrary to the practice in our English disciplinary departments, where the other major prose works of Sri Aurobindo are not consulted with the *Future Poetry* and the letters, I must say that his poetics can only be grasped thoroughly with reference to his total view of life. How is *The Life Divine* related to his art and poetry? Just a brief explanation from the *Future Poetry* will tell all:

> Poetry and art most of all our powers can help to bring this truth home to the mind of man with an illumining and catholic force, for while philosophy may lose itself in abstractions and religion turn to an intolerant otherworldliness and asceticism, poetry and art are born mediators between the material and the concrete, the spirit and life. This mediation between the truth of spirit and the truth of life will be one of the chief functions of the poetry of the future.
> (SABCL 1972, vol. 9, 205)

This is a key statement in "The Ideal Spirit of Poetry," a vital chapter in the *Future Poetry*. Sri Aurobindo is virtually discarding philosophy and religion on his way to the supreme work of hyphenating Matter and Spirit with the help of poetry. But what kind of poetry is his ideal pathfinder? What type of poetry will be in harmony with man's search for the Eternal?

> A divine Ananda, a delight interpretative, creative, revealing, formative,—one might almost say, an inverse reflection of the joy which the universal Soul felt in its great release of energy when it rang out into the rhythmic forms of the universe the spiritual truth, the large interpretative idea, the life, the power, the emotion of things packed into an original creative vision,—such spiritual joy is that which the soul of the poet feels and which, when he can conquer the human difficulties of his task, he succeeds in pouring also into all those who are prepared to receive it. This delight is not merely a godlike pastime; it is a great formative and illuminative power.
> (SABCL 1972, vol. 9, 10)

In these initial chapters of the *Future Poetry*, Sri Aurobindo was more inclined to explaining the ancient and classical Sanskrit aesthetics with his additional commentaries and that perhaps prevented him from an investigation into the sources of poetry. We have already checked that he could not exactly clarify the sources in the *Future Poetry*. He went on revising the book again and again, adding a chapter here, a passage there. And yet he was never satisfied. He firmly negated the idea of bringing it out in a book form during his life time (it only came out in book form in 1953 with the permission of Nolini Kanta Gupta). R. Y. Deshpande, a living encyclopedia of *Savitri*, had first indicated to me in a private conversation that Sri Aurobindo's power of expression had become much higher and clearer in his letters written after 1926. It is in the letters that he specifically tells us that mantra comes either directly from the Overmind or from a very high Intuition. The influence of these zones may operate on the theme or the style or on both simultaneously.

> The *mantra* as I have tried to describe it in *The Future Poetry* is a word of power and light that comes from the Overmind inspiration or from some very high plane of Intuition. Its characteristics are a language that conveys infinitely more than the mere surface sense of the words seems to indicate, a rhythm that means even more than the language and is born out of the Infinite and disappears into it, and the power to convey not merely the mental, vital or physical contents or indications or values of the thing uttered, but its significance and figure in some fundamental and original consciousness which is behind all these and greater.
>
> (Sethna 1972, 12)

This letter admits to his lack of expressive power in the *Future Poetry*. However, he is speaking with a more authoritative voice in such letters to K. D. Sethna.

Poetry at the Center of Knowledge

Sri Aurobindo draws our attention to the privilege of the poets to widen our universe, the advantage of expanding our consciousness toward Knowledge by Identity. Sisirkumar Ghose sums up the idea masterfully: "The possibility of a new and higher evolution of mankind, of which poetry is both an index and an instrument, is taken for granted" (Ghose 1969, 45). "Rose of God" is another statement of Sri Aurobindo's *Savitri* in a capsule form. As there are plenty of observations on *Savitri*, I would like to focus on this miraculous poem of incantation and revelation of the essence of man's evolutionary drive with the direct assistance of a mediating force, whom Sri Aurobindo calls the Mother.

> Rose of God, vermilion stain on the sapphires of heaven,
> Rose of Bliss, fire-sweet, seven-tinged with ecstasies seven!
> Leap up in our heart of humanhood, O miracle, O flame,
> Passion-flower of the Nameless, bud of the mystical Name.
>
> Rose of God, great wisdom-bloom on the summits of being,
> Rose of Light, immaculate core of the ultimate seeing!
> Live in the mind of our earthhood; O golden Mystery, flower,
> Sun on the head of the Timeless, guest of the marvellous Hour!
>
> Rose of God, damask force of Infinity, red icon of might,
> Rose of Power with thy diamond halo piercing the night!
> Ablaze in the will of the mortal, design the wonder of thy plan,
> Image of Immortality, outbreak of Godhead in man.
>
> Rose of God, smitten purple with the incarnate divine Desire,
> Rose of Life, crowded with petals, colour's lyre!

Transform the body of the mortal like a sweet and magical rhyme;
Bridge our earthhood and heavenhood, make deathless the children of Time.

Rose of God, like a blush of rapture on Eternity's face,
Rose of Love, ruby depth of all being, fire-passion of Grace!
Arise from the heart of the yearning that sobs in Nature's abyss:
Make earth the home of the Wonderful and life Beatitude's kiss.

(CWSA 2009, vol. 2, 564)

The poem is a miraculous extension and revelation of the ancient symbol so far half-opened in the history of the earth. It is densely Sanskritic in its symbolic texture and strange intonation and suggestively Aurobindonian in its oblique hint at the power and action of the Universal Mother on earth as an agent of the Supreme acting for the Supramental transformation of the earth. The directive verbs, Leap up, Live, Ablaze, Transform, and Arise, are not giving directions to the Rose of God, but appealing to Her earnestly to come down on earth, in human life. The phrase "seven-tinged with the ecstasies seven" stands for the joy of being in all the seven lokas, planes of existence, each rendering its tinge to the Rose of God—Bhu, Bhuvah, Svaha, Maha, Jana, Tapa, and Satyam: earth, water, enlightening speech, mighty, creative generation, intuition, and the Unchangeable Absolute. Bliss, Light, Power, Life, and Love are the five-fold harmonies. The climax comes with the Rose of Love. Iyengar sheds significant light in one sentence: "Bliss, Light, Power, Life, Love are the five essences that fuse as the integral perfection of God" (Iyengar 1985, 615). The "summits of being" indicate the gradations of the Supermind, which is not a single plane. Sri Aurobindo himself uses the phrase "the highest Supermind" in his great little book *The Mother*. Earth is referred to in every stanza in different names. In the fourth stanza, there comes the prayer for bridging earth and heaven. And the final prayer in a supreme incantatory verse is to invite the Force to occupy the Earth-Nature permanently. The Grace of the Rose opens the Psychic, the purusha antaratma. The emphasis on Earth lies at the core of Sri Aurobindo's integral spirituality. That is why the Epilogue in Savitri is entitled "*Return to Earth*."

Poetry or lines that come from the overmind are supremely revelatory and inevitable utterances. Such lines cannot be improved upon. These are *mantric* or incantatory lines, which are rare even in the world's greatest poetry. While such lines are more frequent in Sri Aurobindo's *Savitri*, in the sonnets too, there are lines like that, which go beyond all analysis. They come from the Infinite and disappear into the Infinite.

A momentless intensity pure and bare,
I stretch to an eternal everywhere.

(Sri Aurobindo 1980, 39)

I have looked, alive, upon the Eternal's face. (51)

I shall be merged in the Lonely and Unique
And wake into a sudden blaze of God,
The marvel and rapture of the Apocalypse. (29)

Sri Aurobindo explains in a letter to K. D. Sethna:

> The Overmind is essentially a spiritual power. Mind in it surpasses its ordinary self and rises and takes its stand on a spiritual foundation. It embraces beauty and sublimates it; it has an essential aesthesis which is not limited by rules and canons; it sees a universal and an eternal beauty while it takes up and transforms all that is limited and particular. It is besides concerned with things other than beauty or aesthetics. It is concerned especially with truth and knowledge or rather with a wisdom that exceeds what we call knowledge; its truth goes beyond truth of fact and truth of thought, even the higher thought which is the first spiritual range of the thinker. It has the truth of spiritual thought, spiritual feeling, spiritual sense and at its highest the truth that comes by the most intimate spiritual touch or by identity. Ultimately, truth and beauty come together and coincide, but in between there is a difference. Overmind in all its dealings puts truth first; it brings out the essential truth (and truths) in things and also its infinite possibilities; it brings out even the truth that lies behind falsehood and error; it brings out the truth of the Inconscient and the truth of the Superconscient and all that lies in between.
>
> (Sethna 1972, 50)

This plane is the borderline of the mind, as it is about to climb to the plane beyond the human mind, that is, the Supermind. That is why it catches a lot from the Supermind light and yet it is mind. The Supermind is not mind. Sri Aurobindo sheds more light on the Overmind and its link with the other comparatively low overhead planes in the following passage. What happens when it speaks through poetry? He answers:

> When it speaks through poetry, this remains its first essential quality; a limited aesthetical artistic aim is not its purpose. It can take up and uplift any or every style or at least put some stamp of itself upon it. More or less all that we have called overhead poetry has something of this character whether it be from the Overmind or simply intuitive, illumined or strong with the strength of the higher revealing Thought; even when it is not intrinsically overhead poetry, still some touch can come in. Even overhead poetry itself does not always deal in what is new or striking or strange; it can take up the obvious, the common, the bare and even the bald, the old, even that which without it would seem stale and hackneyed and raise it to greatness.
>
> (Sethna 1972, 50–51)

Sri Aurobindo's sonnets, most of them touch all the overhead planes starting from the Higher mind, the Illumined Mind, and the Intuition, and ranging up to the Overmind. As the Overmind is also the source of cosmic consciousness, it is easy to see how Sri Aurobindo's lines in the sonnets express that plane of mind, which is the gateway to the Supermind and the Satchidananda. Poetry may not be a substitute for Sadhana; but it affirms the highest spiritual realization as an accompaniment to spiritual practices. That is why Sri Aurobindo keeps poetry at the center of human knowledge, as the captain of our pilgrimage, the white fire of purification in our evolving consciousness.

References

Ghose, Sisirkumar. 1969. *The Poetry of Sri Aurobindo*. Calcutta: Chatsukone Private Limited.
Iyengar, K. R. Srinivasa. 1985. *Sri Aurobindo: A Biography and a History*. Pondicherry: Sri Aurobindo International Centre of Education.
Sethna, K. D. ed. 1972. *Overhead Poetry: Poems with Sri Aurobindo's Comments*. Pondicherry: Sri Aurobindo International Centre of Education.
Sri Aurobindo. 1972. *The Future Poetry, Sri Aurobindo Birth Centenary Library (SABCL)*, vol. 9. Pondicherry: Sri Aurobindo Ashram.
Sri Aurobindo. 1980. *Sonnets*. Pondicherry: Sri Aurobindo Ashram.
Sri Aurobindo. 2009. *The Complete Works of Sri Aurobindo. vol. 2*. Pondicherry: Sri Aurobindo Ashram.

9

Ethics and Human Evolution: A Perspective from Sri Aurobindo

Anurag Banerjee

The word "ethics" originated from the Latin word "ethicus" and the Greek word "ethikos," which means character or manners. The horizon of ethics may be further expanded to incorporate the concepts of right or wrong behavior or conduct. Therefore ethics can be defined as the science which speaks of morality, moral principles, and acceptable doctrines of conduct. It has been argued whether ethics could be termed as a science or an art, but the widely accepted opinion is that ethics is a science because it is a systematic knowledge of moral behavior and conduct. As ethics acts as a guide of action, it is termed as a "normative science." Ethics has been described by ancient philosophers as a set of moral principles which deals with values related to human conduct with respect to right or wrong actions. However, the actions of man have to be voluntary and not compelled in any way. Since the character of a person is expressed as per his actions or conduct, ethics can also be defined as the science of a man's character, which is expressed as right or wrong conduct of action. In other words, ethics primarily deals with what is right or wrong.

One might ponder: what are Sri Aurobindo's views on ethics? It is interesting to observe that he has written on ethics in many of his thought-provoking books but somehow his views have not received their due importance. In this chapter, an attempt has been made to present before the reader his views on ethics.

Sri Aurobindo has described ethics as a "sort of machinery of right action" (Sri Aurobindo 1999, 564). Action occupies the foremost importance because it is the means which facilitates the growth of the soul toward God. The quality of the soul is given more emphasis instead of the quality of action to be taken because it is from the former that "the action flows, upon its truth, fearlessness, purity, love, compassion, benevolence, absence of the will to hurt, and upon the actions as their outflowings" (Sri Aurobindo 1999, 564). The nature of man contains—along with a "passionate rajasic" and "downward-tending tamasic quality"—a "purer sattwic element" which deals with ethics. This "sattwic element" increases the divine nature (which can be materialized by realizing God as the "higher Self," "the guiding and uplifting Will," and the Master who is loved and served) of man and eradicates all demoniac elements in him. To quote the words of Sri Aurobindo: "To grow into the divine nature is the consummation of the ethical being" (Sri Aurobindo 1999, 565). Elsewhere he has remarked that ethics is the "standardising of the highest current social ideas of conduct" (Sri Aurobindo 1998a, 462). According to him, the "act" is of foremost importance while the manner of conducting the "right act" is the "whole question and the whole trouble" (Sri Aurobindo 1999, 564). Ethics, to him, is a means to develop the diviner self in the character of one's being and action which would act as a step of one's growth into "the nature of the Godhead" (Sri Aurobindo 1997a, 35).

Sri Aurobindo has further added that ethics deal exclusively with the desire-soul and the active exterior energetic part of man's being while its field is limited to character and action. Certain actions, desires, impetus, and tendencies are prohibited and inhibited by ethics, while qualities like chastity, compassion, charity, truthfulness, and love are inculcated in the act. Once the aforementioned activities are accomplished and a "base of virtue," "possession of a purified will," and "blameless habit of action" are assured, the work of ethics comes to an end (Sri Aurobindo 1999, 644).

According to Sri Aurobindo, ethics—along with science, art, philosophy, psychology as well as action, knowledge, and past of man—is the means by which one arrives at the knowledge of God's workings through life and Nature. Initially, one is occupied by the forms of Nature and workings of life but as he proceeds deeper and gets a thorough view and experience, he comes face-to-face with God by the virtue of the aforementioned subjects. Hence, ethics should observe that the law of good sought by it is, in fact, the law of God and it is dependent on the nature and being of the "Master of the law" (Sri Aurobindo 1999, 514).

Elsewhere Sri Aurobindo refers to the *Gita*, the holy scripture of the East, and remarks that the said sacred book—while recognizing the significance of ethics—strives to "fix the principle of action deeper in the centre of man's soul" and points out to the "government of our outward life by the divine self within" (Sri Aurobindo 1998a, 462). Ethics is considered a corrective measure. But Sri Aurobindo has pointed out that the "first laws of ethical conduct" succeed in checking the egoistic rule of life but do not overcome it. The ethical idea pushes itself forward into the opposite principle of altruism as a result of which there arises a "clearer perception of collective egoisms and their claim on the individual egoism" and "a quite uncertain and indefinable mixture, strife and balancing of egoistic and altruistic motive in our conduct" (Sri Aurobindo 1997b, 628).

In his *The Problem of Rebirth*, Sri Aurobindo has described justice as an "ethical notion" and elevated true ethics to the rank of Dharma which happens to be the "right fulfilment and working of the higher nature." As action is of immense importance in ethics, Sri Aurobindo has said that right action should possess right motive, be its own justification, and remain free from fear and greed. When a work is done for its very own sake, such an act makes the growing spirit a noble one. Therefore it is "truly ethical." However, a work done out of sheer fear or with the view of getting something in return can never be called ethical no matter how practical or useful it may appear. This is so because such an act degrades the soul of man. Man tends to return good for good and evil for evil but he is also capable of returning evil for good and good for evil. Sri Aurobindo has remarked that evil and good emerge from one another in the cosmic dispensation and there hardly exists any correspondence between vital and moral measures. Being a practical philosopher, Sri Aurobindo has pointed out that just as good deeds would increase the "sum and total power of good in the world" which, in turn, will cause a substantial increase in human bliss, evil deeds also would increase the sum total of suffering and sorrow on earth. Since good and evil are moral values and have a "clear right" to a moral return only, a moral order cannot be created by them. Hence man has to create a moral order within himself and that too for its own sake. Once it is created and it finds its right relation to other powers of life, one can hope to make it "count at its full value in the right ordering of man's vital existence" (Sri Aurobindo 1998a, 412).

Ethical Impulses, Instincts, and Activities

Sri Aurobindo has made an in-depth study of the origin of ethical impulses, instincts, and activities in his book *The Human Cycle*. Ethical impulses and instincts take birth in the infrarational and rise from the subconscient.[1] "They arise as an instinct of right, an instinct of obedience to an understood law, an instinct of self-giving in labour, an instinct of sacrifice and self-sacrifice, an instinct of love, of self-subordination and of solidarity with others" (Sri Aurobindo 1997b, 152). Reason attempts to analyze what man's impulses and instincts crave so that he may utilize his ethical impulses to transform instincts into ethical ideas and eventually put into order a system and multi-sided rule of ethical action. It also differentiates between egoistic, mundane, and selfish emotions and those approved by the ethical sense. Religion and spirituality also play a pivotal role in influencing one's impulses and activities because the laws of universal goodwill and universal compassion, loving and serving one's neighbor, were created by a religio-ethical sense. However, Sri Aurobindo has also pointed out that the law of works is a means which stops when its purpose is achieved. Hence, to become the highest plane of a secular system of moral and mental ethics, the humanitarian ideal should disengage itself by a "sort of secular refrigeration," eradicating the intensity of religious element in it. This is because the religio-ethical ideal cannot be a sufficient guide. Sri Aurobindo explains: "This is a compromise or compact of mutual concessions for mutual support between a religious urge which seeks to get a closer hold on earth by taking into itself the higher turns of ordinary human nature and an ethical urge which hopes to elevate itself out of its own mental hardness and dryness by some touch of a religious fervour" (Sri Aurobindo 1999, 152–153). That is why Sri Aurobindo has emphasized greatly on the law of works as it gets promoted into an object itself in the secular ideal and, thus, becomes a "sign of the moral perfection of the human being" (Sri Aurobindo 1999, 152).

Sri Aurobindo was frank enough to admit that the world where we live is not an ethical place. That is why he has criticized human efforts which strive to impose an ethical meaning into Nature and condemned such attempts as acts of "wilful and obstinate self-confusion." Since man is not enlightened enough to read himself, he forces his "limited habitual human self" into everything and judges from the standpoint he has arrived at on the basis of his own personal evolution without acquiring "real knowledge" and "complete sight." Man fails to realize that the law which governs material Nature is a co-ordination of fixed habits which has little knowledge of good and evil but is well aware of the forces that create, preserve, and destroy. According to Sri Aurobindo, true ethics starts with self-blame and self-condemnation. When one blames others without applying the same law to himself, his is not a true and ethical judgment but a mere application of the language ethics has evolved for man to have "an emotional impulse" or "recoil from or dislike of that" which hurts and displeases him. The aforesaid dislike or recoil has been termed as the primary origin of ethics by Sri Aurobindo, who has also remarked that it is itself not ethical. This is because man's approval and disapproval of things depend on what he likes and dislikes. As he craves self-expression, self-development, and "satisfaction of his progressing self," anything which hurts the aforementioned factors appears to him as evil, whereas things which help, raise, and ennoble the same factors earn his appreciation.

Sri Aurobindo has written in his magnum opus, *The Life Divine*, that ethics is a stage in evolution and that there exists an urge of Sachchidananda toward self-expression. The said urge is initially non-ethical; in the animal and intelligent animal, this urge is infra-ethical and anti-ethical because "it permits us to approve hurt done to others which we disapprove when done to ourselves" (Sri Aurobindo 2005, 104), respectively; the said urge is infra-ethical at the stage beneath us but in the future it is sure to arrive at the supra-ethical stage where there would be no need of ethics. Sri Aurobindo (2005, 104–105) explains:

> The ethical impulse and attitude, so all-important to humanity, is a means by which it struggles out of the lower harmony and universality based upon inconscience and broken up by Life into individual discords towards a higher harmony and universality based upon conscient oneness with all existences. Arriving at that goal, this means will no longer be necessary or even possible, since the qualities and oppositions on which it depends will naturally dissolve and disappear in the final reconciliation.
>
> If, then, the ethical standpoint applies only to a temporary though all-important passage from one universality to another, we cannot apply it to the total solution of the problem of the universe, but can only admit it as one element in that solution. To do otherwise is to run into the peril of falsifying all the facts of the universe, all the meaning of the evolution behind and beyond us in order to suit a temporary outlook and a half-evolved view of the utility of things. The world has three layers, infra-ethical, ethical and supra-ethical. We have to find that which is common to all; for only so can we resolve the problem.

There exists in Nature an "evolutionary intention" to fulfill itself. Man has adopted the method of selection and rejection to bring about the said fulfillment which, however, has taken the form of a religious sanction, a moral and social rule of life or an ethical ideal. But such empirical means do not arrive at the root of the problem because they lack the vision of the cause and origin of the problem they strive to solve. Moreover, good and evil are relative in nature, and the standards set by ethics are also relative and uncertain because one comes across a mixture of various viewpoints which constitute the "complex substance of morality." A mental control over man's vital and physical instincts and desires, his personal and social actions, and his dealing with others is indeed indispensable and a standard is created by morality, which guides man and helps to establish a "customary control." However, this control is never stamped by the mark of perfection for man continues to be what he has been since time immemorial, "a mixture of good and evil, sin and virtue, a mental ego with an imperfect command over his mental, vital and physical nature" (Sri Aurobindo 2005, 648). But the endeavor to select everything which is good and reject anything which is bad or evil is a deep ethical motive as it helps to reform man's being, reconstitute and reshape him into an "image of an ideal."

All systems of ethics should have an approval of validating their plans of action and an aim which would give man the impetus he requires to overcome or destroy his anti-ethical instincts. As man is not purely an ethical being, he possesses immoral and non-moral impulses which are stronger than his ethical tendencies. That is why practical ethics—irrespective of their nature being religious or non-religious—aims to check immoral impulses and "liberate, strengthen and train" non-moral ones. To materialize the aforementioned objective, a true knowledge of human nature and its psychology is required. This is because in case an ethical system is psychologically false, it fails to perceive human nature and reach man's highest and noblest instincts; it could be ineffective and might be detrimental for the moral growth of humanity. However, Sri Aurobindo points out that even a psychologically sound morality would not be able to dominate general consent in practice unless there is an approval behind it, which will be acceptable to reason and prejudices of mankind to necessitate obedience. With the help of this approval, ethics would be able to influence the thoughts and actions of the human race though the said influence would only be a "repressive and disciplinary influence." Therefore, ethics—to become a strong moral lever and active stimulus—should be able to establish an aim which would enroll powerful natural forces on the virtuous side or an ideal which would appeal to instincts "deep-seated and persistent in universal humanity."

Ethics, Morality, and the Dharma

Sri Aurobindo has not failed to observe that religion and ethics become hostile to each other when they are in a state of conflict with the vital instincts and dynamic life-power in man. For instance, instinct for pleasure would be met with the ideal of self-denial and absolute mortification; similarly, instincts for wealth and constant action would be met with austere poverty and inaction or passivity, respectively. That is why one feels the need of an ideal ethical law which has to be created based on Dharma. Since the concept of Dharma is essentially and predominantly moral, it holds up the moral law "for its own sake" and "in its own right" with the view of obtaining its acceptance and observance from man. One must remember that the initial movement of mind is not moral and only possesses a notion of "standard of action" which is justified by predominant customs and rules of life which, in turn, are found suitable and hence accepted because they are found to be beneficial for the attainment of power, success, victory, honor, and good fortune. One must also keep in mind that the ethical elements tend to predominate and monopolize the concept of Right created by man in religion. This happens because ethics is concerned with the actions of life and man's dealings with his vital being as well as his associates. This, Sri Aurobindo writes, becomes man's first preoccupation and his "most tangible difficulty" due to the pressure of the desires, instincts, and interests of his vital being, which come into conflict with the demand of higher moral law and the ideal of Right. Hence, Sri Aurobindo remarks: "Right ethical action comes therefore to seem to man at this state the one thing binding upon him among the many standards raised by the mind, the moral claim the one categorical imperative, the moral law the whole of his Dharma" (1998a, 403).

In the beginning, man's ethical conceptions and the direction, output, and "demand of return of" his ethical energy get mingled with the demands and conceptions of his vital being. Innumerable rules of action arising out of prevalent customs find place in human morality which receives essential approval of right from conventional and traditional practices (which, in fact, possess "very doubtful moral value") and superimposes on it the "true things of the ethical ideal." Ethics convinces man through the medium of religion that—to quote the words of Sri Aurobindo—"the moral law is imperative in itself, but also that it is very expedient for him personally to follow it, righteousness in the end the safest policy, virtue the best paymaster in the long run,—for this is a world of Law or a world ruled by a just and virtuous or at least virtue-loving God" (1998a, 403). Man is made to understand that a wicked individual would perish whereas a virtuous or righteous person would certainly prosper, for his good actions would cause good things to happen to him while bad actions would affect him adversely. Man is assured that an ethical law governs the world, ascertains the extent of his earthly fortunes, and promises a better life for him in Heaven or in the next birth. But Sri Aurobindo has admitted candidly that experience does not support the aforementioned supposition and that man does deceive himself but cannot do so all the time. Hence, he writes:

> It is these notions, this idea of the moral law, of righteousness and justice as a thing in itself imperative, but still needing to be enforced by bribe and menace on our human nature,—which would seem to show that at least for that nature they are not altogether imperative,—this insistence on reward and punishment because morality struggling with our first unregenerate being has to figure very largely as a mass of restraints and prohibitions and these cannot be enforced without some fact or appearance of it compelling or inducing outward sanction, this diplomatic compromise or effort at equivalence between the impersonal ethical and the personal egoistic demand, this marriage of convenience between right and vital utility, virtue and desire,—it is these accommodations that are embodied in the current notions of the law of Karma.
>
> (1998a, 404)

Sri Aurobindo writes that Indian thought and literature have been accused of spreading ethical obsession in every nook and corner so much so that the ethical note recurs everywhere. The concept of Dharma forms the very foundation of life. Hence, it occupies the most important position after the concept of the Infinite. Dharma has emphasized on almost every ethical idea and enforced the same by teaching, parables, formative instances, and injunction with truth, fidelity, chastity, self-sacrifice, forgiveness, compassion, and benevolence being its common themes which, in turn, form the very stuff of human life and the very essence of man's religion. Ethical teaching preached by Hinduism, Buddhism, and Jainism occupies the highest rank and possesses the strongest effective power so much so that it can never be considered inferior in theory and practice as compared to any other religion or system.

Ideal Ethical Law

Man is compelled to obey "most rigorously" collective or social rule of conduct demanded by law and tradition as such demands are rooted deep in his mind. However, he chooses not to follow the restrictions imposed upon him by tradition and law when he comes out of their conventional circle. Instead of following the law of truth, harmony, beauty, love, and mastery, man is forced to follow the obligation of self-control, righteousness, justice, and conduct. The first necessary preoccupation of man is the regulation of his desires, instincts, and external vital actions, and he is expected to find his poise and a settled, sanctioned order before he proceeds to tread in the direction of his inner being. The ideal mind of man brings the relative obligation into the superficial moral sense and the intuition of an inner and complete ethical imperative which tends to give ethics the most important place. It happens due to the fact that the priority of action causes man to apply his idealism to action as well as his relations with other beings. There exists, in the mind of man, moral, aesthetic, emotional, and dynamic instincts. While moral instinct is concerned with the attainment of good, aesthetic, emotional, and dynamic instincts as well as that instinct which craves knowledge, there is the developing reason which strives to bring about an evolution in the ethical direction. This is because love, beauty, truth, strength, and power are required for the accurate growth of mind and life just as justice, purity, and righteousness are needed for the fullness of action. Eventually, they become "no less than the ethical motive, no longer a seeking and necessity of this relative nature and importance, but a law and call to spiritual perfection, an inner and absolute divine imperative" (Sri Aurobindo 1998a, 421).

Sri Aurobindo, while analyzing the connection between good and evil and pleasure and pain, writes that ethical power does not always turn into a sort of related hedonistic result. According to him, love—which is a joy in itself—suffers as well whereas hatred—despite being a troubled and self-afflicting object—has its own gratifications and "perverse delight of itself." However, hatred leads to a greater extent of misery to man due to its denial and perversion, whereas love emerges victorious in its own nature as it originates in the universal Delight. While evil is a "missing" or "perversion of the Right and the Truth" which exposes man to false joy or suffering, true moral good moves toward the "supreme Right" or the "highest law of a highest Truth" of man's being which is the door of the spirit's bliss and its beatific nature.

Ethics and Karma

One might wonder: how does man's ethical good bring prosperity and bliss to him, whereas his ethical evil ushers in misfortune and suffering? Ideally, the ethical goodness in man translates itself into a good action and causes the emergence of material and mental delight in others. Similarly, ethical evil translates itself into an evil action and brings about suffering and misfortune. But man's action does have "the motion of recoil" for evil actions are often met with unfavorable results. Here comes the principle of Karma which is neither a "pure mechanism" nor a wholly mixed ethical-hedonistic order in its absolute importance because other forces of man's consciousness and being are involved in it. The ethical values of man depend on the approval of inferior hedonistic values, pain, and suffering as well as material, vital, and lower mental pleasure and appeal strongly to man's normal will and consciousness. But as man proceeds toward the greater heights of his being, the intensity of appeal loses all its force. Therefore such dependence can never be the final power or guiding norm of Karma. One must not forget that the law of Karma is neither an extension of the human concept of practical justice into forthcoming births nor a correction of the apparent injustice of life. In the law of Karma, there exists a universal Spirit which deals with man in the lower scale of values "only as a part of the transaction and as a concession to man's own present motives." The Spirit of existence acts as a growing godhead in humanity. This godhead gradually surpasses the dependence on the approvals of pleasure and pain, which govern the primary being of man. Sri Aurobindo has pointed out that both pain and pleasure act as Nature's advertisement and lure of things. Both should be avoided by man to reach a higher nature, and for that man should develop a nobler spiritual law of Karma and remain firm in his quest for Truth.

Sri Aurobindo has said that the Consciousness-Force of the Spirit manifests itself into several types of energies like inner activities of mind, life, desire, character, passion, impulse and pursuits of truth, knowledge, beauty, ethical good and evil, power, love, joy, delight, success, pleasure, fortune, health, strength, and individual or collective items. This complicated sum of manifold experiences and multisided actions of the Spirit in life can neither be put into various segments of the single duality of ethical evil and good nor be kept aside favoring a single principle. Therefore, ethics can neither be "the sole principle of determination of the working of Karma" nor be "the sole preoccupation of the cosmic Law" (2005, 841). As already discussed, the result of ethical good will be an increase in virtue and the bliss of ethical growth or development, whereas the outcome of ethical evil would result in a deeper immersion into the evil, an excess of which could lead to a serious and permanent spiritual damnation. Punishment was created to prevent man from committing harmful acts just as reward was created to encourage man to do and be good. But a genuine ethical being would not need reward or punishment to follow or shun the path of good and evil, respectively. Sri Aurobindo writes that sin brings with itself its own punishment, which leads to a fall from man's own law of nature, while virtue is looked upon as its own reward. At the same time, he expresses his doubt whether reward and punishment can be set up as a "general law of cosmic Nature" or "a law of the supreme Being" or "the supreme law of existence" (Sri Aurobindo 2005, 844). This is because it is unwise to impose narrow and insufficient standards of human ignorance on the larger but complicated operations of "cosmic Nature" or "on the action of the supreme Wisdom and supreme Good" (2005, 844) which draw or raise man toward itself with the help of a spiritual power which works slowly in man, not by a "law of temptation and compulsion on man's outer vital nature," but through his inner being. There exists in all dealings of Nature a lesson of relation as well as a lesson of experience. The action of the cosmic Energy is complex and identical forces may act differently according to human requirements, situations, and "intention of the cosmic Power in its action." The life of man is not just affected by its own energies but also by the energies of others as well as by universal Forces. Hence Sri Aurobindo writes: "All this vast interplay cannot be determined in its results solely by the one factor of an all-governing moral law and its exclusive attention to the merits and demerits, the sins and virtues of individual human beings. Nor can good fortune and evil fortune, pleasure and pain, happiness and misery and suffering be taken as if they existed merely as incentives and deterrents to the natural being in its choice of good and evil" (Sri Aurobindo 2005, 846).

The Root of Ethical Ideals

Sri Aurobindo has said that every ethical and religious ideal depends for its truth and permanence on its philosophical foundation, that is, on the proximity of its fundamental idea to the Eternal's ultimate truth, for, it is on the Eternal that anything that has phenomenal existence stands with reality being looked upon as a reflection in the mirror of the Eternal's existence. According to Sri Aurobindo, "if the ideal implies a reading of the Eternal which is only distantly true and confuses Him with His physical or psychical manifestations in this world, then it is a relatively false and impermanent ideal" (Sri Aurobindo 1972, 201).

In one of his lesser-known writings, Sri Aurobindo has made a minute analysis of the ideals of ethical values in the ancient Greek, Roman, Chinese, and Indian civilizations. According to his observation, in the eyes of the Greeks, ethics was a matter of proportion, balance, and taste which depended on the avoidance of both excessive virtue and vice. Their education was characterized by the inspiration of music and "graceful play" of intellect which resulted in excellent development of their personality; while justice was looked upon as a fine equilibrium between one's obligations to oneself and to others, decorum formed the basis of their public morality, "the sense of proportion the one law of restraint in their private ethics." However, he also pointed out that Greek ethical thought, which consisted of four gradations (*euprepēs, dikaion, agathon,* and *kalon*[2]) never went beyond the aesthetic stage of morality. Even in Aristotle's system of morality parts of conduct were classified not as per the Indian concept of virtue or sin but by a "purely aesthetic standard, the excess, defect and golden, in other words correct and beautiful, mean of qualities" (Sri Aurobindo 2003, 443). Ethics, for the Romans, was full of a "lofty strength and sternness" which could not last long due to the imperfection of the ideal on which it was based. The Chinese envisaged the Eternal not in the "manifested physical Universe" but in the "origination and arrangement out of the primal materials" from which it emerged and their ethics was governed by the concept of reverence for parents and senior members of the society who stood "in the place of parents." The Indians envisaged the Eternal as "the universal Transcendent Self of all things" who was omnipresent as a result of which the civilization of ancient India was multisided and integral and their intellectual as well as ethical ideals were "perfect and permanent" in comparison with those of other countries. Not only did they have a better sense of justice, nobler public decorum, and a sharper sense of ethical and social equilibrium as compared to the Greeks, but also had a higher spiritual ideal that "governed and overrode" customary ethics that were developed by other countries. Sri Aurobindo aptly remarks: "Humanity, pity, chivalry, unselfishness, philanthropy, love of and self-sacrifice for all living things, the sense of the divinity in man, the Christian virtues, the modern virtues were fully developed in India at a time when in all the rest of the world they were either non-existent or existent only in the most feeble beginnings. And they were developed because the Aryan Rishis had been able to discover the truth of the Eternal and give to the nation the vision of the Eternal in all things and the feeling of His presence in themselves and in all around them" (1972, 204). He has further added that the yogis of ancient India had rightly realized the dependence of "ethical ideals on the fundamental philosophy of the Eternal and Real." This explains why the Upanishads, the sacred scriptures of India, had prefaced it with the aspect of the Eternal Reality, while setting forth the ethical rules and ideals as well as the intellectual attitude toward life, because its value and truth depended on it. That is why, Sri Aurobindo has remarked, the Hindus attained the "highest idea and noblest practice of morality."

Sri Aurobindo (2003, 443–444) sums up his observation of the root of the ethical values in the following words:

> The progress of ethics in Europe has been largely a struggle between the Greek sense of aesthetic beauty and the Christian sense of a higher good marred on the one side by formalism, on the other by an unlovely asceticism. The association of the latter with virtue has largely driven the sense of beauty to the side of vice. The good must not be subordinated to the aesthetic sense, but it must be beautiful and delightful, or to that extent it ceases to be good. The object of existence is not the practice of virtue for its own sake but *ānanda*, delight, and progress consists not in rejecting beauty and delight, but in rising from the lower to the higher, the less complete to the more complete beauty and delight.

Insufficiency of Ethics

While discussing the demerits of ethics in his book, *The Synthesis of Yoga*, Sri Aurobindo writes that an ethical rule exercises a difficult and partial control over Nature but is powerless to transform her so that Nature may "move in a secure freedom fulfilling the intuitions that proceed from a divine self-knowledge" (Sri Aurobindo 1999, 136). He considers ethical solutions to be insufficient because their methods simply lay down certain limits and put a wall of "relative and very doubtful safety" around man. Such methods of self-protection could be necessary in yogic and ordinary life for a certain period. However, it would only be a "mark of a transition" in Yoga. As the sadhak of the integral yoga aims to attain a "fundamental transformation" and "wideness of spiritual life," one must search for a profound solution, "a surer supra-ethical dynamic principle." Sri Aurobindo calls the ordinary religious solution, which advocates being spiritual internally and ethical externally, a "compromise." According to him, the sadhak of the integral yoga aims not to bring about a compromise between life and the spirit but strives to spiritualize outer life and inward being. As ethics is a mental control and "the erring mind" can never be the "free and ever-luminous spirit," hence, it is not possible to accept the conviction which makes life the singular aim, accepts life's elements "fundamentally as they are," and invokes "a half-spiritual or pseudo-spiritual light to flush and embellish it." The attempt to bring about an unhappy union between the spiritual and the vital is also insufficient as such an attempt too is an unsafe and unsuccessful compromise which exists far away from the divine Truth. Therefore Sri Aurobindo (1999, 137) concludes: "These are all stumbling solutions of the fallible human mind groping for a transaction between the high spiritual summits and the lower pitch of the ordinary mind-motives and life-motives. Whatever partial truth may be hidden behind them, that truth can only be accepted when it has been raised to the spiritual level, tested in the supreme Truth-consciousness and extricated from the soil and error of the Ignorance."

The Ethical Being and Reason

Sri Aurobindo writes that the truest truth of practical life as well as its actual and highest practicality becomes easily clear in the ethical being of man. Although the rational man tries to diminish ethical life and ascertain its nature, law, and practical action by certain laws of reason, he would never succeed in his endeavor. The hedonistic theory looks upon ethics as a system of formulas, conduct emerging from social sense and a ruled direction arising out of social impulses and would, hence, try to regulate the actions of ethics by the said inadequate standard. But no success would ever come if one tries to regulate the principle and phenomena of ethics because the ethical being—which is a law to itself and traces its principle in its own eternal nature—would escape from all possible formulas. One must remember that the nature of the eternal being is not a "growth of evolving mind" in its essential character; it is, in fact, a light emanating from the ideal—a reflection of the Divine in man. Since ethics can never be a matter of calculation, Sri Aurobindo suggests that the ethical man should always stick to "his principle of good, his instinct for good, his vision of good, his intuition of good and to govern by that his conduct"(Sri Aurobindo 1999, 150). The ethical man might commit mistakes or stumble down but in spite of that he would be on his right path because he is faithful to the law of his nature which is the pursuit of good. His actions are not induced by inner pleasure but by the "call of his being, the necessity of an ideal, the figure of an absolute standard, a law of the Divine" (Sri Aurobindo 1999, 151). Hence Sri Aurobindo (1999, 151) remarks about him: "The ethical man is often called upon to reject and do battle with the social demand, to break, to move away from, to reverse the social standard. His relations with others and his relations with himself are both of them the occasions of his ethical growth; but that which determines his ethical being is his relations with God, the urge of the Divine upon him whether concealed in his nature or conscious in his higher self or inner genius. He obeys an inner ideal, not an outer standard; he answers to a divine law in his being, not to a social claim or a collective necessity. The ethical imperative comes not from around, but from within him and above him."

Ethics in Society and Practical Life

Sri Aurobindo writes that ethics is accepted by society as an influence and bond. Society would not prefer to make its life absolutely ethical; on the contrary, it would prefer to govern its life partly by ethical laws or else egoistic individuals would clash with one another to destroy their own aims. Sri Aurobindo draws a comparison with religion, which is permitted by society to have a fixed place (like temple and church) and certain events on holy days but it would never make life in its entirety a religion or a constant remembrance of God. To individuals of special type like holy men, artists, thinkers, and men of ethics, society does give special place and offers homage but for itself it follows its "own inherent principle of vital satisfaction, vital necessity and utility, vital efficiency" (Sri Aurobindo 1997b, 156). But Sri Aurobindo also observes that if a spiritualized society comes into existence, it would not establish a rule of action as its ethical aim but develop the divine nature in human beings.

Conclusion

Sri Aurobindo writes that even if man's conscience is a product of his own evolving nature and that if his conceptions of ethical law are mutable and dependent on his stage of evolution, there exists—at their very root—something constant which lies at the bottom of man's own nature as well as that of the world. Nature in the world and man is infra-ethical and infra-rational at its starting point just as it is supra-ethical and supra-rational at its zenith. However, there is something in the infra-ethical which becomes the ethical at the human level. The supra-ethical is a consummation of the ethical which can be reached by only those who have walked on the long ethical path. Beneath it lies that "secret of good in all things" which man approaches and attempts to deliver, although partially, through ethical instinct and idea whereas "the eternal Good" that surpasses man's partial and fragmentary ethical conceptions lies above it.

To conclude in the words of Sri Aurobindo (1998a, 382–383):

> This universe is not solely an ethical proposition, a problem of the antimony of the good and the evil; the Spirit of the universe can in no way be imagined as a rigid moralist concerned only with making all things obey the law of moral good, or a stream of tendency towards righteousness attempting, hitherto with only a

very poor success, to prevail and rule, or a stern Justicer rewarding and punishing creatures in a world that he has made or has suffered to be full of wickedness and suffering and evil. The universal Will has evidently many other and more supple modes than that, an infinity of interests, many other elements of its being to manifest, many lines to follow, many laws and purposes to pursue. The law of the world is not this alone that our good brings good to us and our evil brings evil, nor is its sufficient key the ethical-hedonistic rule that our moral good brings to us happiness and success and our moral evil brings to us sorrow and misfortune. There is a rule of right in the world, but it is the right of the truth of Nature and of the truth of the spirit, and that is a vast and various rule and takes many forms that have to be understood and accepted before we can reach either its highest or its integral principle.

Notes

1 There are certain terms used by Sri Aurobindo, which the reader may not be acquainted with. For his benefit, a brief description of such terms is produced here. By "infra," Sri Aurobindo denotes something which is below the rational or dimly rational. Similarly, "supra" means something which is beyond rational. The subconscient has been defined by Sri Aurobindo as an "automatic, obscure, incoherent, half-unconscious" region which lies beneath the waking physical consciousness. It is that submerged part of man's being where no "wakingly conscious and coherent thought, will or feeling or organized reaction" exists but it is capable of receiving, although obscurely, "the impressions of all things and stores them up in itself and from it too all sorts of stimuli, of persistent habitual movements, crudely repeated or disguised in strange forms can surge up into dream or into the waking nature. For if these impressions rise up most in dream in an incoherent and disorganized manner, they can also and do rise up into our waking consciousness as a mechanical repetition of old thoughts, old mental, vital and physical habits or an obscure stimulus to sensations, actions, emotions which do not originate in or from our conscious thought or will and are even often opposed to its perceptions, choice or dictates. In the subconscient there is an obscure mind full of obstinate sanskaras, impressions, associations, fixed notions, habitual reactions formed by our past, an obscure vital full of the seeds of habitual desires, sensations and nervous reactions, a most obscure material which governs much that has to do with the condition of the body. It is largely responsible for our illnesses; chronic or repeated illnesses are indeed mainly due to the subconscient and its obstinate memory and habit of repetition of whatever has impressed itself upon the body consciousness" (Sri Aurobindo 2014, 596). Elsewhere Sri Aurobindo writes that the subconscient includes the larger part of man's vital being, physical mind, and the secret body-consciousness. He also adds: "That part of us which we can strictly call subconscient because it is below the level of mind and conscious life, inferior and obscure, covers the purely physical and vital elements of our constitution of bodily being, unmentalised, unobserved by the mind, uncontrolled by it in their action. It can be held to include the dumb occult consciousness, dynamic but not sensed

by us, which operates in the cells and nerves and all the corporeal stuff and adjusts their life process and automatic responses. It covers also those lowest functionings of submerged sense-mind which are more operative in the animal and in plant life" (Sri Aurobindo 1998b, 151).

Sri Aurobindo writes that when man's consciousness is separated from other consciousnesses, it plunges into Ignorance and the last result of Ignorance is the "Inconscience," which is "an inverse reproduction of the supreme superconscience" and possesses the "same absoluteness of being and automatic action, but in a vast involved trance: it is being lost in itself, plunged in its own abyss of infinity." The Supreme is capable of manifesting in Itself something which is its opposite; these opposites include Darkness, Inertia, Disharmony, Disintegration, and Inconscience which are seen at the basis of material world and are broadly termed as the "Inconscient." He further adds a possibility of the Infinite Consciousness and its power of self-absorption can plunge into a state where self-awareness does exist but not as knowledge. "This self-absorption ... is again, no longer luminously but darkly, the state which we call the Inconscient; for the being of the Infinite is there though by its appearance of inconscience it seems to us rather to be an infinite non-being: a self-oblivious intrinsic consciousness and force are there in that apparent non-being, for by the energy of the Inconscient an ordered world is created; it is created in a trance of self-absorption, the force acting automatically and with an apparent blindness as in a trance, but still with the inevitability and power of truth of the Infinite" (Sri Aurobindo 1998b, 56).

2   The term *Euprepēs* means something which is apparently or outwardly attractive; *Dikaion* means that which is in accordance with law or justice; *Agathon* stands for the good which represents a combination of both the seemly and the just; and *Kalon* means that which is purely beautiful.

References

Sri Aurobindo. 1972. *Sri Aurobindo Birth Centenary Library, vol. 27*. Pondicherry: Sri Aurobindo Ashram.
Sri Aurobindo. 1997a. *Complete Works of Sri Aurobindo, vol. 20*. Pondicherry: Sri Aurobindo Ashram.
Sri Aurobindo. 1997b. *Complete Works of Sri Aurobindo, vol. 25*. Pondicherry: Sri Aurobindo Ashram.
Sri Aurobindo. 1998a. *Complete Works of Sri Aurobindo, vol. 13*. Pondicherry: Sri Aurobindo Ashram.
Sri Aurobindo. 1998b. *Glossary of Terms in Sri Aurobindo's Writings*. Pondicherry: Sri Aurobindo Ashram.
Sri Aurobindo. 1999. *The Synthesis of Yoga*. Pondicherry: Sri Aurobindo Ashram.
Sri Aurobindo. 2003. *Complete Works of Sri Aurobindo, vol. 1*. Pondicherry: Sri Aurobindo Ashram.
Sri Aurobindo. 2005. *The Life Divine*. Pondicherry: Sri Aurobindo Ashram.
Sri Aurobindo. 2014. *Letters on Yoga, vol. IV*. Pondicherry: Sri Aurobindo Ashram.

10

Integral Education: The Imperative for the Contemporary World

Partho

Much has happened over the last half a century. Individuals across the planet, in different languages, different guises, different expressions, are turning to their inner sources of knowledge and wisdom. There is a growing senselessness of division and fragmentation. We are witnessing, in almost every sphere of human activity, the birthing of a new world, driven by powerful evolutionary forces, which at this point in time are manifesting primarily through the combined agencies of communications and economy. The Internet has made possible a single global working system across geopolitical boundaries and time zones; and a rapidly growing global economy is ensuring that the whole planet balances out and shares its human and natural resources. The post-Industrial era, with its communications technology and global businesses, and the globalized knowledge-worker, has already passed into a neo-Industrial era where information technology is moving toward "technologies of consciousness," quantity-driven consumerist economies are transiting to quality-of-life economies, the knowledge-worker is changing to the wisdom-worker, compelled by sheer pace of change to bring the deeper wisdom to the fore, even in hard-core businesses and politics. The neo-Industrial era depends on a burgeoning global economy, where nations and societies must work toward common prosperity or sink together into common poverty. The very system ensures that no one nation or government overrides the interests of the other. Poverty, unemployment, wars, and even political repression are regarded as serious threats to global economic stability and therefore a nuisance and quickly to be outgrown.

In our present reality, we are all fragmented and dispersed, in varying degrees. One may regard oneself as an individual, a person, but the psychological fact is that very few of us attain what can be called true personhood—that is, the state of being completely

---

The chapter is adapted from my book *Integral Education: A Foundation for the Future* (2007). It is not governed by the copyright frames of the book.

integrated and wholly consistent, all things in place, all aligned, all organized. We are, on the contrary, quite disorganized, a complex of senses, feelings, thoughts, beliefs, ideas, needs, fears, hopes, frustrations, complexes, and appetites that refuse to hold together into any kind of a coherent structure. We are simply not centered. The fact of course is that incoherence, disharmony, conflict, and contradictions are not "natural." They are, in deeper truth, *antithetical* to consciousness.[1] The *initial* condition of human nature may be divided and dispersed only because no conscious work of assimilation or organization has been done on the individual nature. Integration is a function and an expression of a person's growing capacity to know and understand himself and give his being and life a conscious direction in the growing light of his self-understanding, and then learning to assimilate his life experiences around this understanding; it is this that aligns and organizes the being and one attains to the conditions of maturity and self-mastery. The more internally inconsistent a person, the more fragmented he will be.

In a deeper sense, however, we are all responsible; we are all creators and forerunners of our own future. What we are doing today is determining, in profound ways, what shall exist on this planet in the generations to come. And thus, the way we educate our young today will determine, in perhaps the most direct manner, the way life will be lived in the years to come, for it is our education that molds most significantly our beliefs and attitudes and culture. It is very simple: If we must create a new future, we must first create a new consciousness in our young. This means that the education for the future will have to be a *consciousness education*, an education nurturing the growth of consciousness in all aspects and parts of being. The central purpose of such an education would not be to repeat what others have done or are doing but to attempt something that may never have been attempted before on the planet—to create conditions for the emergence of a new way of being on earth. But we must bear in mind that this is not something that will lend itself too readily to our understanding or to our systems, for most of us are still too attached to old thought patterns and old knowledge to seriously consider the possibility, leave alone a necessity, of any fundamental transformation in the conditions of life and society. It is the deep-seated belief in most of us that things cannot change too radically or too universally that might actually be preventing any serious and sustained attempt at radically changing the way we are and live on earth.

This is the reason why we need an *education* that will help break the hold of such debilitating beliefs, for it is education more than any other means that can enable fundamental levels of learning and unlearning. But if we are to seriously attempt fundamental levels of unlearning and new-learning, of breaking out of our old consciousness and life molds, we will first need to understand, as clearly as we can, the nature of our old consciousness, the meaning of the old patterns and the forces that have shaped our destiny so far. Such an understanding will help us build a better society by addressing the problems of the old and building new structures for the future. What would an integral education in today's world be? What would be its vision and its philosophy, its guiding principles? How would one practice it? These are the questions that I have attempted to answer in this chapter by applying the Aurobindonian framework.

Integral Education

An integral education will be an education of the whole person. While most of the education practiced in our schools focus almost exclusively on the head, an integral and unitive education addresses the head, as well as the heart, the body, *and* the spirit. For the integral educator, the child is not a disembodied head or a heart, nor is she a headless or a heartless body: she is *integrally* the head, the heart, the senses, and the body, and more: she is too, in her wholeness, a soul and a cosmos. It is the spirit in the child which gives to her human uniqueness and strength and beauty, and it is this strength and beauty that integral education seeks to bring out in all aspects of the child's life and being; but evoking the spirit, though of central importance, is only one part of the integral process—the body itself with its hidden beauty and grace, the heart with its power of transforming love, and the mind with its power of understanding and receiving must be evoked too so that the children, as much as the teacher, find their integral truths in the very fields of their daily lives. The aim is not to walk half-conscious through the days of one's life, but to fully awake to the meaning and beauty in every moment, *to make of one's daily way,* as Sri Aurobindo once wrote, *a pilgrimage.*

To achieve this end, two things need to be done: first, the finding of the soul, the seat, and center of our psychological being within; and then the progressive integration of the being around the unifying core of the soul. In other words, the symphony we seek will be orchestrated by the soul within and not by the limited prowess of the mind or the still obscure lead of the heart. This implies clearly that the finding of the soul would be the pivot of the whole process. This would apply to both—the teacher and the child. The processes will of course differ: the means through which the teacher or the educator will come to the finding of the soul and the means through which the child would do so would be intrinsically different. For an entire understanding of the integral process, we will need to follow through with both. Let us keep in mind that without the teacher, the educator, embodying and living the principles of integral education, it will not be possible to educate the child integrally. This is really a fact of cardinal importance: to miss this obvious point would be to miss the whole thing! If we wish to bring up our young integrally, *first let us be prepared integrally.* It is for this reason that we shall first concentrate on the processes needed for the teacher of the integral system. By teacher we shall mean the adult involved in working with children within the system of integral education—the adult may be a teacher, educator, resource person, administrator, parent, or even friend.

Principles of Integral Education

An integral education will consist essentially of a threefold process: self-knowledge, awakening of the true center of one's being, and a consequent process of integration and harmony. The work of analyzing one's psychological movements and developing an accurate understanding of the parts of one's being, one's psychological dynamics, and the workings of one's personality will constitute the first movement of integral education and will be the sine qua non for the further movement of integration and harmonization. An important question here is how would this work of integration be accomplished? How would one observe oneself? How would one work on one's own psychological movements and processes? Most of the pedagogical tools used in conventional education—lectures, demonstrations, experimentation, study of text, personal research—are all directed to academic and intellectual training. But self-observation and self-awareness are essentially non-intellectual activities. It is here that integral education will have to return to the psychological tools of Yogic knowledge, used and validated through the ages by all those who made it their business to know and perfect themselves—the central formulation, *gnosce te ipsum*[2], echoed in mystic traditions across most of the world. These psychological tools with which the integral process can start are self-observation, introspection, and meditation. It must however be noted that self-observation, introspection, and meditation[3], however perfected, are tools only; the objective is to attain a progressive self-awareness and self-mastery.

However much we may speak of inner realties and self-knowledge, unless one actually gets into serious and sustained self-observation, there is no way one can come to know or understand oneself. Self-observation and systematic introspection are perhaps the only ways of peeling away the several layers of conditionings that constitute personality. A tangled mass of thoughts, ideas, beliefs, biases, emotions, desires, and fears constitute the normal human personality. Once the confusion and chaos are sorted out, organized, brought under a rule of order and harmony through introspective means, these same means would then take the learner toward an inner deepening and quietening of the consciousness. As a matter of fact, the integral process aims at developing, among other things, a lifelong habit of introspection in the learner, so that it gradually becomes impossible for the learner to do or say anything without a brief inward look. It is this psychological habit that prepares the ground for an eventual integration of the being while opening the conscious mind of the learner to the rich experiences of the inner worlds.

The training in self-observation thus becomes the first and most critical component of integral education. Most of the usual instructive and prescriptive components of conventional education would need to be consciously replaced by self-observation, introspection, and a growing self-understanding. This would have an important spin-off effect for integral education: the more one learns to observe oneself, to introspect and meditate, the more one gets liberated from the need for social approbation—whether of friends, teachers, or family. In proportion to this liberation, one gets individualized, autonomous, and self-directed—all very significant developments in the overall integral process.

Let us take a closer look at the threefold process of integral education:

1. Self-knowledge: A clear understanding of the many strands and influences of one's own being; a clear-sighted awareness of how one's own being and nature work.
2. Awakening the Principle of Harmonization: A necessary second movement in the process would consist of a progressive awakening of the deepest consciousness of unity and harmony within oneself, that which is independent of the external environment, independent of all external influences and conditionings and is

unique to oneself, that which can form the basis of a true individuality; such a consciousness would obviously be one's inmost soul-being, the psychic self, as that alone is one's most authentic and independent self.
3. Integration: Once the principle of harmony is established within oneself, and the individual has awakened to his true center of being, the process of unifying the various conflicting strands and movements of the being gathers momentum and power. Knots and tangles are then gradually resolved and one begins to attain a certain mastery of one's being, as one moves progressively toward a deepening and widening balance and harmony.

One can now readily see that if such an experience were to spread, it would be the single and most potent force moving humanity toward a radical human transformation. It is the psychic principle in human beings, which is the one sure motive force and inspiration for deeper human change. The problem and paradox of education are solved once education recognizes this principle of evolution and brings it into play in the dynamics of school systems and pedagogy. And it also restores to education its deeper truth in the scheme of human life—to be the means for the creative transformation and inner flowering of the individual and of society. For the individual teacher, it is this understanding that becomes the guiding light in his work with children, and indeed all humans. His practice of integral education will not be so much a teaching as it will be a transforming, not so much a theorizing or moralizing but always the direct touch and transmission. He will not merely be an educator, but a guru whose touch and influence would radically transform the child's nature and consciousness and enable her to reach her highest and deepest potential. This highest and deepest potential will not be an ethical or intellectual ideal but a practical movement toward the fullness and fruition of her own nature.

Educating the Vital

The education of the vital will involve three movements: a transformation of one's emotional nature; the sensitization, enrichment, and refinement of one's senses; and the transformation and progressive perfection of one's character. An integral vital education will seek a dual cumulative outcome of these three movements: a change in the quality of personal life leading to a change in the quality of collective and social life. The three movements are logically related. There is a direct relationship between the quality of one's senses and emotions. The more refined and the more beautiful one's perception and responses, the better and more positive, the more life-enhancing are one's emotions. As one's emotional nature evolves, one's character, one's very way of being changes, becoming increasingly beautiful, more sensitive, more in harmony within and without. In brief, this is the purpose of an integral vital education.

Vital education would start with the education of the emotions but will go beyond the emotions and encompass the whole gamut of man's life, his driving motives, his life force, the entire field of his manifest action. The vital may be regarded as the motor of human existence; even the highest intellectual flights humans take are powered by the vital fuel. Individual or social—all manifestation is driven by the vital. It is in the vital that our will and desires, likes and dislikes, ambitions and motivations are generated and so it is from the vital that we derive the inspiration and power to dream, to work, to realize. If the vital in us is weak and ineffectual, nothing can be accomplished in life—however noble or brilliant our ideal and ambitions might be. But if the vital is strong, balanced, disciplined, and focused, there is no achievement that is not possible for it. The vital is also the source of all relationships, with other humans, with the environment, with work, and with the world at large. All our attachments, as well as our aversions, our hopes, expectations, and our disappointments in this complex realm of relationships also arise from the vital substance in us.

It is thus easy to see the decisive importance of the vital in life and work. One would expect the education of the vital to dominate all curricula, yet it is perhaps one of the greatest ironies of our culture that such an education is either relegated to the periphery in some of our education systems or entirely neglected in most. It is a universal truth that human beings are driven and sustained more by emotions than by reason. It is also a fact that the majority of humans live predominantly in their vital beings and only occasionally in the mind; rarely ever in the psychic. Thus if any real change in the quality of human existence on earth is to be attempted, it is the substance of human emotions that must first be transformed. If human nature cannot be changed, then the whole purpose of education is lost. To get to a deeper understanding of the vital would then be necessary to see if any real and sustained education of the vital is at all possible—and if so, what directions such an education should take. Let us consider some important aspects of vital education.

First, let us understand that in spite of a tremendous evolution of the human intelligence, the vital has remained largely unintelligent. In spite of creating an impressive civilization and culture over millennia, the average human nature has remained uncultured, almost wild, held accountable by forced discipline, either of law or of religion. When we examine individual natures, we find that most people grow naturally in the body; some even grow in the mind—in rationality, in intelligence, in knowledge—but very few grow in the vital—emotionally, in sensibility, in compassion, and in sensitivity. As a matter of fact, if you were to observe emotional patterns of human behavior, you would be surprised to find that few so-called adults actually grow beyond their emotional adolescence: even at the age of forty or fifty, their emotional reactions and responses to life are that of a fifteen-year-old. The fear or anger or greed that you felt at the age of fifteen is almost exactly the same that you feel at the age of forty or fifty—the only difference being the way you *express* your anger or greed. There too, the expression is only more controlled—not in any way remarkably different in substance.

The vital mind possesses a still lower, or more primitive, stage where there is no intervention of the thinking mind at all. This part of the vital mind merely expresses the vital without *subjecting it to any play of intelligence* (Sri Aurobindo 2012, 178). The vital mind is of enormous significance to integral educators, and especially early childhood educators, because it is primarily through this that the vital passions, impulses, and desires invade the reasoning mind and either distort its workings or confuse it. It is also through this vital mind that the vital can very easily make the thinking and reasoning mind into an accomplice, willing or unwilling, and make it justify its own actions and reactions. The chief reason why it is so difficult for many of us to objectively assess the merits and demerits of our own actions is this particular tendency of the vital mind to cloud and distort the thinking mind. A clear awareness of the dynamics of the vital mind would thus be essential to any work on inner change and progress. The vital mind proper is not much interested in reasoning. It is limited by the vital predispositions, beliefs, and feeling of things and does not admit the validity of thought and reason too easily. It tends therefore to remain fixed in its ways and its so-called understanding. It is so difficult to work on human nature primarily because of the vital's settled resistance to change.

There are two ways the mind can be urged to break these set patterns and create newer ones: the first is by creating a counter-pattern, a contradiction of an earlier pattern repeated till it becomes a new pattern; this method has its drawback as it attempts to break pattern by re-patterning. The other way is the way of education—by training the mind from an early age not to get "attached" to patterns, to be able to create a "psychological" distance from the pattern itself, be aware of the pattern, its origins and its workings, and thus be able to *use* the pattern rather than be used by it. It would then also be possible to see the patterns that are still necessary and relevant and the ones that no longer serve any purpose. One could then make a reasoned choice to break and recreate certain patterns at will. It is the second way that concerns us here: To become aware of the mind and the mind's patterning, and to free the mind of the automatic psychological, emotional, and intellectual patterns and habits, leading on to a retraining of the mind. This would be critical to an effective education of the vital.

The education of the vital mind will consist of three components:

1. Refinement of the senses
2. Psychological maturity
3. Balance and equality

Simultaneously with these components, such an education will also need to bring about an intervention of a mind more intelligent and better trained than the vital mind—which, in most humans, would be the rational mind. But even then, it will not be completely effective because the rational mind itself has its own limitations and weaknesses; it must be remembered that the rational mind in most human beings is not wholly or purely rational, its so-called rationality is mixed with the vital strains and is fallible on its own grounds as much of its functioning and understanding depends on its sense-based cognition. Therefore, work on the senses would be a possible first step toward changing the quality of the vital mind. For the integral educator, the challenge would be to provide an educational environment where such a conscious work could be done on emotions, and especially so in the early years. The conscious training in emotional awareness would need to start relatively early in life. Young children can be trained to look at their own emotions as they occur and take responsibility for one's emotions. This will obviously be done without involving intellectual concepts—entirely through dialogue with the child, or through role play and drama. Dialogue, role play, and drama are all very effective tools in vital education. Emotional awareness, as I have said, is a first step but a very important first step. Once this step is taken, the rest of vital education becomes smooth flow—awareness leads naturally to control and mastery.

Physical Education

An integral physical education program would also need to actively incorporate certain significant vital aspects in physical education. Vital education, in fact, beyond a certain stage, becomes an inseparable part of physical education. This is most clearly seen in the domain of collective sports and activities. Collective sports, field events, and activities can lead to development of character, building up of the will, developing the qualities of courage and endurance, cultivating team spirit and leadership. Most of the qualities of team work and effective leadership that have such wide-ranging effects in adult life are actually developed in the sports field. A still deeper dimension of the vital aspect in physical education needs also to be considered: the relationship of the body with vital desire. This is another point that has not been considered too seriously by either medical experts or educationists, but has always been a matter of paramount interest to practitioners of traditional and Integral Yoga. Although desire is more specifically a vital-emotional issue, its effects are entirely physiological—both in indulgence and in deprivation. It is the body inevitably that pays the price for the vital's indulgences as well as its dissatisfactions and revolts. As we have seen, every reaction of the vital alters the chemistry of the body, and sometimes irreversibly. Whether one is aware of it or not—and for most people such awareness is difficult—every emotional reaction, every movement of desire or passion, every thought or memory of violence in the vital leaves a disturbance in the body in its wake. The vital may forget the movement or the reaction in a while, but the body remembers—the chemical imbalance remains in the physiological system and accumulates as stress. The stress is neurochemical and over a period of time, it turns to disease.

The final objective of physical education is to develop a physical culture that is free of weakness, indulgence, and lethargy; a physical culture that celebrates beauty, strength, and harmony, for these indeed are the bases of health. To attain such a physical culture, the body will need to practice austerity in matters of work and exercise, sleep and rest as well. Just as in food, here too the guiding principles are balance and moderation: Neither too much work and activity nor too much rest and sleep. In this area too, the child will need to be sensitive to the body's needs. Since every body has its own character, its needs will be different, and will change with age and circumstances—thus there is a need for sensitivity and awareness instead of rigid regimens. Work and activity are important for the body; an inactive body loses its vitality and health, whereas an active body remains in good health and actually prolongs its life. But a body too active, or feverishly active, under the pressure of vital ambition, wears out faster, and also loses its vitality and health. A sense of balance and awareness of one's body's capacities would then be indispensable to the practice of austerity in this aspect.

Developing Self-awareness

Developing self-awareness is the first real step toward vital education and transformation. Unless one is aware of the whole vital-emotional drama within oneself, unless one can take that first step of stepping back from the action of the drama, there is no way of beginning to act on the vital or change its quality. The process of developing self-awareness can begin any time. Young children can not only do it, they enjoy doing it—provided of course that the teacher makes it an interesting process. A small note of warning must be sounded here: adults by and large tend to make such processes into serious affairs. With children, it is *playfulness* that works. One of the most important points that one has to keep in mind before one begins work on awareness with children is that developing self-awareness has nothing to do with religion, or prescribed meditation, or finding the soul, or becoming quiet. All these terms—religion, meditation, soul—are mere concepts for children and entirely meaningless. Adults who cannot wait to push children into the so-called spiritual way of life and teach them meditation often end up turning the children against this beautiful process for the rest of their lives. Developing self-awareness is simply a way of tuning in to yourself—that really is all.

Most people live in a sea of noise emanating from a thousand and one sources—from ourselves, our past experiences, our imaginations, fears, and desires; from other people around us, from the world itself—and this noise is not just physical, for the most part it is a non-physical, psychological noise, a noise of vibrations. Living in this sea of noise is a continuous source of distraction, and it is the kind of distraction that saps our vital energies over a period of time. The only thing that keeps most of us from going stark mad in all that noise is our complete imperviousness to it. In a way, most of us are too coarse in our sensitivity to be consciously distracted by it. This is the reason why we do not know what is happening within and without us: we can neither figure ourselves nor others out. It is like trying to listen to a melody playing in the background while a cacophony rages all around us! These then would be the steps toward becoming conscious: first to sensitize ourselves to this sea of noise and distraction, then learn to tune in to the melodies—or cacophonies—playing inside us, and then, as we grow in our capacity to listen, start fine-tuning the inner instrument.

This is the fundamental point: the act of listening. We cannot listen; we have not been educated to listen; and so we do not educate our children to listen. The whole system of education that we have established is so preoccupied with talking, teaching, and performing that we have almost entirely lost the capacity to listen. Much of vital education would perhaps turn out to be a re-discovery of listening—listening to ourselves, listening to others, listening to Nature, listening to life itself; listening without a purpose or an objective; and listening with the whole of our being. Progressively, in the process of listening, one becomes clearer, more sensitive, more alive, and more conscious. It should also be clear by now that we are not recommending any "technique" of meditation. Becoming aware, conscious, mindful is not *necessarily* meditation. The children need only to watch, to observe, and to observe minutely and carefully. There is no technique here: one does not need techniques to watch and listen. This process will start with external observation, but will turn to inward observation as well. To facilitate this process naturally, children will need to be given enough time to be with themselves, simply being, not doing something or the other. This is yet another fundamental aspect of growing in the vital—children must have enough time and space to be with themselves. Our schools normally crowd the child's consciousness with activity, study, and interactions. All these are necessary no doubt, but if activity is not balanced with quietude, interactions and relationships are not balanced with aloneness, and study is not balanced with the brain's stillness and rest, then the whole process becomes useless and even counter-productive. The integral teacher must also note at this point that to facilitate the development of self-awareness and mindfulness in children, the teacher himself or herself will have to be living consciously. Once that is established in the teacher, there should be no need to "teach" meditation or mindfulness—the teacher will only need to be *engaged* with the children, to be able to follow their movements and processes, and through that enable them to become more increasingly conscious of themselves and of others!

We have seen the inherent difficulties of the vital nature and the possibilities of vital progress and change—but into what shall the vital change? What is the nature of a perfected vital? Toward what end shall integral vital education move? These are significant questions for the integral educator, for without a clear understanding of the ends, the means do not make complete sense. The ultimate objectives of an integral vital education would be enabling the human vital to attain to the fullest flowering of its seed powers. The vital possesses four such seed—or potential—powers and capacities: the capacity for perfect and complete experience of life and cosmos—no longer limited in its reach and possession; the capacity for perfect enjoyment—no longer limited by petty desires and frustrations, perpetually subject to misery and suffering; the capacity for perfect detachment and equality—no longer buffeted by fortune and circumstances; and the capacity for perfect universal oneness and love—no longer isolated and imprisoned by walls of ego and selfishness. These are of course ultimate aims and will need a prolonged and arduous education before even the first signs of accomplishment become visible. But however arduous the process may be, its fulfillment is possible.

Toward Integrity

Another very critical area of integral education would be the evolution of integrity—honesty and faithfulness to the truth of one's being. A persistent difficulty in almost all vital natures, and one that has always vitiated the collective life of humans, is the prevalence of falsehood, pretension, and hypocrisy in this matter. For a hundred different reasons, each more pious than the other, human beings sacrifice the truth and integrity of their being for convenience, or for apparent and false "harmony," or the need to avoid pain and suffering, or simply to be accepted and approved. If the aim of our education is to create true harmony and genuine selfhood, then our education will have to address this difficulty, for without resolving this knot, no other attainment will be secure or lasting.

The breeding of falsehood starts very early in childhood and stems from the School—through the insidious process of the adult imposing his expectations, moral constructs, and existential ambitions on the child. Consider the child: typically full of energy and enthusiasm for life and its experiences, completely open to whatever life brings, or takes away; bearing no one any grudge, entirely free of ill-will, worry, or ambition; totally absorbed in her own universe, playing with the world in total trust and confidence. And then consider the same child in school: being shown to her classroom, usually a closed room with not too comfortable chairs and desks; walls usually drab and lifeless or sometimes—if she is lucky—splashed with artificial colors and static pictures of animals or flowers and windows that look out on a promising, alluring but inaccessible world.

The purpose of integral education is to reverse this whole process and sow instead the seeds of truth, sincerity, and integrity on the grounds of a true selfhood and not breed falsehood, hypocrisy, pretension, discordance, rebellion, or frustration. This is a difficult objective to attain. Even in an integral education environment, there can be no certainty of sustaining the purity of the process as the child will always be subject to external social and cultural influences which would be outside the integral education environment. Integral education will need to carefully nurture the growing sense of selfhood so that it becomes rooted enough to resist contrary pulls and influences. The growing sense of the self would need to be firmly grounded in a growing psychic realization, for it is only psychic selfhood, the sense of self arising from an inner identification with the psychic center, which can ensure a truly secure and integrated selfhood. This growing sense of the psychic as the basis, and the real and inalienable center, of one's self constitutes a fundamental step toward developing selfhood.

Perfection of the Mind

The objectives of an integral mental education are twofold: first, to perfect the mind's functioning within its present powers and capacities, and second—though not in any strict sequential order—to awaken and develop powers and capacities the mind possesses only potentially to make it an effective instrument for the higher evolution. Thus, the education of the mind would have a practical and an evolutionary aspect, both equally important for an integral fulfillment of human life. The evolutionary aspect of mental education in fact will assume even more significance in the light of the fact that the mind has always been at the front of Nature's evolutionary drive. Consider the fact that Nature begins her tremendous evolutionary labor with Matter[4] in which she awakens Life, and then awakens the potential for Mind. These have been, in fact, the three primary terms of Nature's evolution. It is only with the emergence of Mind that Nature truly begins her higher evolution characterized by intelligence and self-consciousness; through Matter and Life, which includes the whole range of plant and animal life, Nature's manifestation was more or less of the same order—development determined by natural adaptation and survival; with the emergence of Mind, the *order* changes and becomes more of an increasingly conscious and self-willed process. Up until the emergence of Mind, evolution was driven by Nature's largely unconscious impulse, what some evolutionist thinkers have called Nature's Will; with Mind it was a change of order because Nature—hitherto unconscious in her evolutionary labor—suddenly woke up to her own design and became *conscious of her own purpose.*

A true mental education, which will prepare man for a higher life, has five principal phases:

1. Development of the power of concentration, the capacity of attention.
2. The development of the capacities of expansion, widening, complexity, and richness.

3. Organization of one's ideas around a central idea, a higher ideal or a supremely luminous idea that will serve as a guide in life.
4. Thought-control, rejection of undesirable thoughts, to become able to think only what one wants and when one wants.
5. Development of mental silence, perfect calm, and a more and more total receptivity to inspirations coming from the higher regions of the being.

Becoming an Integral Teacher

For the teacher of the integral process, it is necessary to intimately understand the way the vital, mind, and the body function in us, their intricacies, their inherent capacities and weaknesses, where and how they become dysfunctional. It evidently will not be enough to know all this intellectually, as one would study a psychological system, for the mind's understanding is always an incomplete thing; it is the whole being that has to understand—the body's processes will have to be understood in the body, physically; the vital's processes must be understood in the vital itself, without being stationed in the mind from where one can only understand the mind's projections of the vital; the mind itself will have to be understood in the very processes of the mind, and only then will the understanding be profound and lasting, and only then will the teacher have the true ability to guide similar processes in children.

Thus, the preparatory work for the teacher will be twofold: first, to plunge within to find one's soul, and to learn more and more to stand in the light of the soul; and, simultaneously, to observe and understand each part of the being, their disharmonies and discords, their secret and subtle longings, the obstinate points of resistance and equally the points of openness to a higher light; he will have to know, through personal experience, where the source of his strengths and weaknesses lies, be able to unerringly discern the origin of all the movements of his being, his most-hidden motivations. In other words, he will have to lay bare to the all-discerning gaze of his highest intelligence and sincerity in every fiber and strand of his being. It is only in that crystal clear light will he see and know the processes of transformation, the possibilities of change. And what he shall learn within, and every step that he will take there, will become for him the surest beacons along the way, for each thing that one does within oneself, each little conquest and change that one makes in one's nature adds that much more strength and clarity to the work one would do on children. The discovery of the psychic and the progressive harmonization of one's own being in the psychic light would be very important processes and steps on the way of the teacher's preparation, but these would be only first steps. Becoming an integral teacher is becoming a guide and a guru, to oneself and to all others who come into contact with oneself, which demands an absolute and lifelong commitment to learning, growing, and self-becoming.

Paradoxical it may sound, but the integral teacher will not teach. His work will be to facilitate and enable learning. His guiding belief is that education is a personal process and must be meaningful to the learner for it to be truly effective. From this belief stems the attitude that the child is not passive clay to be molded into any fancy shape by the teacher, but is a being growing in consciousness with a power of conscious choice in her learning and growth.

The School As It Is

Schools are the expression and reflection of the prevalent social and cultural paradigm of the age. The nature of education that a society or a nation provides to its young will depend largely on what it culturally perceives, and accepts, to be the driving aim and purpose of life. A society molded by the Industrial Age paradigm would logically regard the school as a means and tool for perpetuating the virtues and values of an Industrial-Consumerist society: stability, order, uniformity, conformity, and hard work. What we are referring to as conventional education has been shaped principally by the Industrial Age mindset and continues to do so. Let us take a brief look at this Industrial Age mindset and see how exactly it affects the nature of the modern School.

The Industrial Age mindset typically regards humans as tools to serve a vast socio-economic machinery; the individual is but a cog in the gigantic wheels of Industry and Society, and his usefulness is directly proportional to the degree that he serves the Machinery. Viewed from this perspective, the primary purpose of the individual is to become capable of serving the Machinery as efficiently as possible, and the whole purpose of life is to be productive in the social cause. The social Cause is of capital importance, and all individual variations must be subservient to the social Cause. It would also be very important to maintain the subservience to the System, and thus the individual would need to be indoctrinated with a value system that would perpetuate the System. The most important of these values would be stability and order, for without stability and order there could be no coherent way of life.

On the other hand, with a stable order, those designated to labor would labor; those assigned to supervise would supervise; those meant to train and educate would train and educate; goods would be produced efficiently; markets would operate efficiently; and wealth would circulate efficiently. In other words, society would be an efficiently running machine; and the human would be an appropriate component of this efficiently running machine. Any deviation from the established order would obviously threaten the whole system. If the individual serves the System well, he is rewarded; if he cannot or does not do so, he is dismissed as a failure and, overtly or subtly, penalized. This utilitarian thinking persists even today as a strong undercurrent in our modern systems and institutions, and greatly shapes corporate behavior.

The Industrial Age mindset with its dominant strain of pragmatic utilitarianism would then regard an efficient and stable order of things as the Ideal for the Age of the Machine, and the Machine itself would symbolize the power of technology to generate wealth, and therefore the good life for humanity. The Machine would also symbolize the liberation of human life from the tyrannies and uncertainties of Nature. Whereas Nature is completely unpredictable, technology is exactly predictable; whereas Nature seems to disregard human existence, technology serves only one purpose: to benefit human beings; whereas Nature is totally independent of human control, technology manifests the supreme power of human control; and most of all, technology promises to deliver Nature itself to human control. With so much promised, and so much at stake, it becomes imperative to maintain the System and the Ideal. And in all this, the School is obviously the most preferred instrument to perpetuate the scheme.

The School would thus perpetuate a value system most in consonance with the Ideal of the Machine Age: the values of uniformity, predictability, efficiency, order, and stability. In such a value system, conformity to the established order would be the preferred behavior, and all deviations from the norm would be discouraged. Individual variations would be of no importance and therefore marginalized, if at all tolerated. The stress would be on uniformity—of appearance, thought, behavior, and ambition. This is the guiding rationale of the schooling system spawned by the Industrial Age paradigm. Following this rationale, schools operate on a simple linear logic—that if all parameters were kept under control, and an effective learning program implemented, the school would succeed in producing, like an efficient assembly line in the factory, the desired product, in this case, the well-informed and well-trained school graduate who would unquestioningly join the industrial mainstream to fulfill his designated function.

It would be instructive to trace some of the principal characteristics of the modern school to the logic of the Machine Age mindset. For instance:

- The prevalence of a uniform and standardized curriculum and pedagogy to serve all learners equally—a logical outcome since the preferred ideal was uniformity and conformity to the established order. The existence of a standardized system and method for evaluation of all learners, who would be judged by the same standards, since the concept of individual variations was already marginalized.
- The disproportionate emphasis on the development of the intellect—in order to produce an ideal industrial-age efficiency, the whole school machinery is directed to one specific purpose: the most efficient use of the mind in assimilating the information and skills imparted by the school. Other faculties or skills were considered distractions, and therefore relegated to the backwaters of the educational process.
  The prevalent peculiarity of an education that addresses only the head and marginalizes the heart and the body. Even when the body is addressed, it is done so only to maintain optimal health in order to serve the social-industrial machinery efficiently, not to enable the body to develop any kind of beauty or strength or individuality. The emotions are, of course, things to be weeded out of the system by a hegemony of Reason.
- As a result, the emotions neither get weeded out nor are they enlightened by Reason, because Reason itself is flawed. It is too severely limited to serving the System for it to come to any kind of independent and full flowering. The System, on its insistence on perpetuating only the kind of intelligence that will neither question nor threaten its established order, ended up corrupting Intelligence itself.
  The all-prevalent belief that learning is limited to pedagogical structures: it happens only in classrooms and only when initiated by the experts; and its powerful corollary that learning is dependent on the authority of the teacher or the expert.

- The success or failure of the learner is assessed and judged by the teacher. The teacher, in sitting on judgment over the learner, reinforces the ultimate power of authority and hierarchy.

The Next School: From Teaching to Learning

So what is wrong with the school as it is? What most schools should do is teach—and that is what they do. *But what they teach most often does not mean anything to those who learn.* That is the first serious flaw in the system. Those who run such schools will need to understand that what is important to the adult does not have to be important for the child. For this one does not need to do courses in education, one only needs to connect with the child's real universe. Perhaps instead of reading child psychology text books, the teacher should be reading *The Little Prince* (Saint-Exupéry 2000).[5] The second serious flaw is this: *the school informs, it does not transform*. In the best of cases, it makes the child smart, efficient, and well informed, but it does not give her the capacity to be aware, to know the truth of her own being, and to understand the truth of the others with whom she shares this planet. In the more unfortunate cases, it teaches her to manipulate, exploit, and deceive. It breeds competition and conflict and isolates one from the other. Most teachers, as well as parents, seem to be in a tearing hurry to teach the many *important* things of the world to the child as early as possible. Most findings of scientists who have studied cognitive and affective development in children are conveniently forgotten in this unholy rush to teach! And so what happens is inevitable: the child gets buried under the Teaching and never learns to learn. That is the tragedy.

The pedagogical, academic system of education that most schools practice has a definite context and arises from a definite mindset. The teacher of the integral system must clearly understand this mindset so that in no form is it allowed to continue, even unconsciously. This mindset may be defined by two characteristic beliefs: that children are wild and uncivilized and therefore need to be trained and civilized by an educational process; and that the educational process needs to be supervised by capable adults as children, left to themselves, will never learn anything. In other words, it is *good* for children if they are *made* to learn in structured ways and through a predefined praxis. The integral approach to learning is practical and child-centered. It goes back to the basics of the human learning experience: human beings learn only what they *want to* learn; and they want to learn only what they really *need to* learn. This is the fundamental logic for learning, and the sequence deriving from it is thus obvious and deeply significant for those wishing to practice integral education:

1. Learning is entirely a function of necessity; one wants to learn only what one needs to learn. It is only when one is learning what one wants to learn that one is enjoying the process of learning, even if it is challenging or extremely exacting.
2. Necessity is internal and subjective; it cannot be imposed or prescribed; it is not necessary to have previous theoretical knowledge of what one needs; since needs

are spontaneously generated by real life and its continuous and multi-natured demands, they do not need to be artificially created or prescribed.
3. Learning is an intensely personal affair; it is an inner dialogue one has with life in all its varied aspects: environmental, personal, interpersonal, social, even ultimately cosmic; and it is through the varied dynamics of this dialogue that one grows as a human being through lifelong exploration, discovery, and understanding.
4. As learning is a lifelong, dynamic dialogue with life and the cosmos, it is necessarily omni-dimensional, omni-directional, and integral; it cannot involve only one part or function of our beings. If humans are as much physical as they are intellectual, as much emotional as they are physical, as much spiritual as they are emotional, as much social as they are individual; then it follows logically that learning will have to be omni-dimensional and integral: physical, emotional, intellectual, spiritual, social, and individual.

This is the logic of learning: all real learning experiences of life flow with this logic—and this applies equally to the adult as to the child. So long as this internal logic of learning is respected and education systems are built on and around it, there is no problem. Problems arise when this logic is violated or distorted, or even dismissed as impractical or utopian and replaced with a logic alien to the essential and real processes of learning.

Conclusion

The integral education model subsumes the pedagogical and goes beyond: it exceeds the fragmented epistemology of the knower and the known and points to a more synthetic epistemology where the knower does not stand apart from the object of knowledge but identifies with it, becomes one with it. If the dualistic epistemology of the knower studying the object of knowledge from the outside culminates in an essentially intellectual or sensory construct of the object of knowledge, then the synthetic epistemology where the knower identifies with the object of knowledge would culminate in a knowledge by identity, an internalized knowing of the object as it is, and the knowledge so gained would be a *real* knowledge and not an intellectual or sensory construct. Learning is a synthetic and unitive experience, not culminating in duality of perception and knowledge but in unity; not substituting knowledge of a thing by an intellectual or sensory construct, but exceeding constructs to arrive at a true knowledge and inner understanding, validated by personal experience. Integral education posits the synthetic epistemology but *does not reject* the dualistic epistemology either. It seeks to combine the elements of both. Knowledge by identity is one aspect; intellectual study and knowledge by construct is another; the experience of learning will have to integrate both to be entirely effective and complete.

The difference between learning and studying is therefore the difference in epistemologies, in ways of primary cognition. Most children love learning and are averse to studying because at very young ages, they are more open to identification, they exist at a pre-intellectual and strongly intuitive level and can synthesize experience more efficiently than analyze. As the innate intuitive capacities degenerate and the intellectual-sensory capacities get stronger—entirely because of cultural biases—the ability to identify and synthesize diminishes in proportion to the strengthening of the intellectual ability to study. In an integral education context, however, the objective is to develop the intuition and the capacity to synthesize as much as to develop the intellect and the capacity to analyze. One will need to balance the other. It is when the intellect is given an overriding importance in the educational process, and the intuitive, the emotional, and other aspects are almost completely neglected or relegated, that education leads to imbalance and disharmony in the individual and in society.

Once the teacher is well-grounded in the psychology and practices of integral learning, is well-grounded in his own being, is working as much toward his own integral change as toward becoming an effective integral teacher, is living increasingly in the light of the psychic in him, he is ready to start consciously working toward the creation of an integral school. He either would do this with a group of like-minded individuals or would seek to initiate the whole process on his own, depending on where he is, and in his inner condition of preparedness for the Work. To create an authentic environment for integral education, some of its fundamental assumptions will have to be honored. These assumptions may be summarized thus:

1. The integral-psychic[6] way of life cannot be taught: the soul has to be evoked, and drawn out; it cannot be socially fabricated through any instrumentality or means of education.
2. The evocation and drawing out of the deepest and highest potential of the child can be done only through the impact or effect of reality; this implies that if I want to draw out the highest excellence from my student, I will first have to draw out my own highest excellence and be able to live out of that excellence; it also implies that excellence and the psychic consciousness cannot be faked.
3. If an integral flowering is possible only though living example, then it follows that a school for integral growth will have to draw to itself adults who can, and are, living out of their own evolutionary drives, their own overriding need for growth, excellence, and consciousness.
4. If that has to happen, the school will have to create that extraordinary ambience, the special *vibration* that will draw such people to it; this is the principle of like attracting like.
5. Such an ambience or vibration can be created only if the school is an expression and manifestation of complete sincerity and total alignment to the goal and purpose of integral life and education. In other words, those who would be involved in creating an integral school will have to make it a labor of their deepest passion and vision.

Finally, the acid test of the effectivity of an integral school will be the extent to which integral principles can be lived by the child, as much as the teacher, in the dynamic everyday reality of life in the world. What one learns at school must finally be validated in the experiences of real life for the learning to have any real significance. The first steps of this integration of school and life are taken in the school itself, for life in the school must not be divorced from life in the world. If that happens, then the school is reduced to an ineffectual laboratory only and all that is learnt within that laboratory is regarded as mere theory. In an integral school, this must not happen. One of the central principles of integral education is the integration of life and learning. Any learning that cannot be applied to real life is useless. This implies that the integral school will have to implement its principles and values in all its aspects and functioning. There can be no question of anyone being treated any differently for any reason. If the school believes in personal choice and responsibility, for instance, then the space for personal choice will have to be given to everyone who is part of the school. This might sometimes, in some cases, be very difficult to enforce—but how to evolve a system where such difficulties can be honestly encountered and overcome is part of the work an integral school has to do, and on a daily basis.

Notes

1 It is interesting to note that while the entire universe, and all processes in it, moves inexorably toward dissipation and chaos, only consciousness moves toward increasing coherence and integration. It seems that life confronts us with a serious choice: either to move along the downward curve of the material universe toward chaos or to move consciously upward, through self- integration, toward cosmos.
2 It means, "Man, Know Thyself."
3 The reader must be warned here that there is no one definition of meditation. There could be as many ways of meditation as there would be meditators. I am using the word in this book in its widest sense—ranging from concentrating on an idea or a process to focusing of awareness to simply being aware without doing anything at all. The reader should not assume meditation to be limited only to practices prescribed by popular books and teachers on Yoga.
4 To be precise, the first cosmic Matter was more of an indeterminate state between Energy and Matter, neither matter nor energy, but a state fluctuating continuously between the two. We might call this, more accurately, the quantum state.
5 An utterly delightful little book that shows more of the child's universe than many learned text books put together.
6 I use the phrase "integral-psychic" to distinguish integral education based on the discovery and realization of the psychic from other theories and practices of holistic education which are considerably similar, in many of their aims and guiding principles, to integral education.

References

Partho. 2007. *Integral Education: A Foundation for the Future*. New Delhi: Sri Aurobindo Society.

Saint-Exupéry, Antoine de. 2000. *The Little Prince*. Translated by Richard Howard. San Diego, CA: Harcourt, Inc.

Sri Aurobindo. 2012. *Letters on Yoga I, The Complete Works of Sri Aurobindo vol. 28*. Pondicherry: Sri Aurobindo Ashram Press.

Part Four

Human Unity

11

Cosmic Consciousness: The Metaphor of Human Unity in Sri Aurobindo's Writings

Sarani Ghosal Mondal

Sri Aurobindo, the Yogi and the seer-poet from India, had a lifelong passion for human unity. He grew up in the late Victorian England, between 1879 and 1893, with a critical mind toward orthodox religion and dry rationality, but also with a perceptive feeling for the indwelling Supreme and its relation with the external world. In a wonderful one-liner found in his early notes in England, we find this perception: "Not to have ever heard the voice of God is man's idea of sanity" (Sri Aurobindo 1972, 71). In an unfinished dialogue entitled *The Harmony of Virtue*, Sri Aurobindo, the teenager, may be seen struggling to find out a clue to human harmony. There he criticizes the religious doctrines and the societal codes of morality and ethics. He tells Broome Wilson: "A code of morality built upon religion has no commerce with the demands of society or our personal sense of the right and just, but is the very law of God" (Sri Aurobindo 1972, 3–4). A little later, in the same essay, he says, "A limited God is not God at all" (Sri Aurobindo 1972, 5). He also highlights a crucial point that human beings are incapable of "balanced personality" (Sri Aurobindo 1972, 8). At a very young age, he had a faint perception of the fundamental problems of human harmony but he failed to express that. Much later, he wrote in *The Life Divine*, "All problems of existence are essentially the problems of harmony."

With this, I would like to explore the image of cosmic consciousness in Sri Aurobindo's writings and show how it helps humanity to attain harmony. Along with that, I would also like to analyze the evolution of Sri Aurobindo's vision of global harmony through different stages of his life.

It is very difficult to have a feeling of identification with the cosmos or cosmic consciousness overnight. It usually requires a long preparation. It may start with a feeling of nationalism, which gradually culminates into cosmic consciousness with the progressive realization of the essential principles of existence.

The Image of Nationalism in Sri Aurobindo's Writings

Sri Aurobindo was popularly known for his stance of aggressive nationalism during the Baroda phase (1893–1906), when he wrote ten articles, which were published in *Indu*

Prakash between June 26, 1893, and March 6, 1894. Here is an example of his sardonic writing taken from *New Lamps for Old-1* where he criticizes the National Congress:

> If the blind lead the blind, shall they not both fall into a ditch?...I shall stir the bile of those good people who are so enamoured of the British Constitution, that they cannot like anyone who is not a partisan. "What!" they will say, "you pretend to be a patriot yourself, and you set yourself with a light heart to attack a body of patriots.
>
> (Sri Aurobindo 1965, 9)

One can find the image of stormy political activism in the quoted passage. After that he left for Calcutta in 1906. Karan Singh is right when he says: "From the very first line he wrote upon political affairs in 1893, right up to his withdrawal from active politics in 1910, Sri Aurobindo was a trenchant critic of the Congress" (Singh 2000, 48). His political writings continued and in order to encourage the revolutionaries, he wrote profusely on nationalism in *Bande Mataram*, a newspaper founded by Bipin Chandra Pal in 1906. He became the editor of that newspaper responding to Pal's request in April 1906. Sri Aurobindo's articles created a stir among the English-speaking intelligentsia of contemporary Bengal. Although he believed in violence as a stage toward non-violence, he was for the present, taking the stance of non-cooperation and boycott. During that time, his art of combat was passive resistance, which Gandhi used later as a major weapon for "*Swaraj*." According to Sri Aurobindo, "the time needed an organised resistance against an existing form of government" (Sri Aurobindo 1965, 126), which could be done through "self-development" and "self-help" (Sri Aurobindo 1965, 121). If a nation becomes independent in every aspect, there is no need to look up to the aid of foreign power. He further explains that it is the most effective means compared to "armed revolt" (Sri Aurobindo 1965, 121). Here is a relevant passage from the treatise entitled "The Doctrine of Passive Resistance."

> Organised strength of the nation, gathering to a powerful central authority and guided by the principle of self-development and self-help, can wrest the control of our national life from the grip of an alien bureaucracy, and developing into a free popular Government.
>
> (Sri Aurobindo 1965, 132)

Like Gandhi, Sri Aurobindo propagates the doctrine of self-help. But he extends the metaphor of "self-help" to self-development. The freedom of a nation is contingent on both. We all know that Gandhi's objective was also to promote the doctrine of self-help for growth and sustainable development in the villages. He opted for collective empowerment through different self-help groups, which could remove deprivation and poverty for nation-building. Such an endeavor was especially meant to empower the marginalized in rural India. And the Gandhian self-help groups like Sarvodaya and others helped in inculcating group identity and activity. As a result, the villagers in India gained a certain degree of independence.

Colonization has two aspects: territorial and psychological. Both Gandhi and Sri Aurobindo believed that the doctrine of passive resistance could withstand the process of the colonization of the psyche of the Indian mass, which would finally lead to freedom. But one has to keep in mind the fact that Sri Aurobindo's objective was not limited to collective existence for socio-economic causes. His aspiration was human unity through love, harmony, and cosmic consciousness, which will be discussed in the subsequent sections.

In late 1907 or early 1908, Sri Aurobindo wrote "The Morality of Boycott." He could not revise it later as the manuscript had been seized by the police. This article is extremely important in the present context as here one may find the clue to the image of love and cosmic consciousness, the fundamental principles of his philosophy.

> Love is a sacred name, but it is easier to speak of love than to love. The love which drives out hate, is a divine quality of which one man in a thousand is capable... Love has a place in politics, but it is the love of one's country, for one's countrymen, for the glory, greatness and happiness of the race, the divine *ānanda* of self-immolation for one's fellows, the ecstasy of relieving their sufferings, the joy of seeing one's blood flow for country and freedom, the bliss of union in death with the fathers of the race. The feeling of almost physical delight in the touch of the mother-soil, of the winds that blow from Indian seas, of the rivers that stream from Indian hills, in the hearing of Indian speech, music, poetry, in the familiar sights, sounds, habits, dress, manners of our Indian life,... realisation of the Motherhood of God in the country, the vision of the Mother, the knowledge of the Mother, the perpetual contemplation, adoration and service of the Mother.... Between nation and nation there is justice, partiality, chivalry, duty, but not love. All love is either individual or for the self in the race or for the self in mankind. It may exist between individuals of different races, but the love of one race for another is a thing foreign to Nature.
>
> (Sri Aurobindo 1965, 361)

The country as Mother is an essential point in his idea of nationalism. The repetitive use of "Indian" puts a strong signature of his patriotic feelings. Purani, his earliest biographer, refers to the letters written to his wife, where he asserts that his country is not a piece of land. It is synonymous with the Mother. "I look upon my country as the Mother. I adore Her. I worship Her as the Mother" (Purani 1978, 81). The last sentence of the long passage cited above hints at racial disharmony. Humanity is yet to learn to love irrespective of races. His idea of "boycott" is associated with freedom and nationalism: the Indians have to admire everything of Indian origin. Every Indian has to be free from the hangover of Western influences. There lies the sentiment of boycott. In another article entitled "A Practicable Boycott," he insists on independence in industry and commerce (Purani 1978, 507). If a country is self-sufficient, there is no point of depending on foreign aids. This strong stance of nationalism continued till 1909 and the first part of 1910, when he edited almost simultaneously two journals: *Karmayogin* in English and *Dharma* in Bengali. This was the phase after his imprisonment. By the middle of 1909, one finds a quiet tone in his language of resistance. In "The Country and Nationalism," he writes that the foundation of nationalism is the country. Many mutually antagonistic races may live in a single country, if they can call their country "Mother." A feeling of love for fellow beings will originate if humanity believes in the fraternity. A feeling of Brotherhood within the country can unite a nation consisting of different races.

Thus, it may be seen that his quest for human unity moves within his own brand of Nationalism through his formative days in Baroda and the stormy phase of activism in Calcutta. The same ideas grow and deepen in his earlier and final days in Pondicherry. His idea of nationalism starts with a rhetoric of aggression in Calcutta, but within that aggressive metaphor, he developed a systematic theory as we see in the essays on passive resistance and boycott. His language acquires a comparatively milder tone in the later Calcutta phase, the post-prison period, when he clarifies better, but not with his full maturity, the aspect of divinity in his idea of nationalism. His country is his Mother and the citizens of the country should serve Her. He also explains there very clearly the link between his idea of nationalism and human unity. In "The Ideal of the Karmayogin," he says: "Our aim will therefore be to help in building up India for the sake of humanity—this is the spirit of the Nationalism which we profess and follow" (Sri Aurobindo 1965, 385). Despite Ashis Nandy's sarcastic criticism of Sri Aurobindo's ideology in *The Intimate Enemy* (2005), this is a metaphor of nationalism having a strong base of intuitive logic, more maturely developed in his later writings, especially in *The Ideal of Human Unity*. The clues are already there in "The Ideal of Karmayogin";

> The time has come when you must take the great step and rise out of a material existence into the higher, deeper and wider life towards which humanity moves. The problems which have troubled mankind can only be solved by conquering the kingdom within, not by harnessing the forces of Nature to the service of comfort and luxury, but by mastering the forces of the intellect and the spirit by vindicating the freedom of man within as well as without and by conquering from within external Nature. For that work the resurgence of Asia is necessary, therefore Asia rises. For that work the freedom and greatness of India are essential, therefore she claims her destined freedom and greatness, and it is to the interest of all humanity, not excluding England, that she should wholly establish her claim.
>
> (Sri Aurobindo 1965, 386)

This metaphor of human unity within the texture of Nationalism gradually culminates into a vast cosmic consciousness and oneness in the poetry and prose works composed during the Pondicherry phase. During the Calcutta period, his thought and action primarily corresponded to the need of the time. A strong criticism of the Indian national congress and an assertive stance on nationalism were required to rescue the congress from its policies of prayer and petition. At the same time, the congress did not have any touch with the proletariat. Many congress leaders later acknowledged that Sri Aurobindo's ideology had a great impact on the freedom struggle.

Cosmic Consciousness, Psychic Being, Ego, and Human Unity

Cosmic Consciousness

While talking about the Aurobindonian ideas of cosmic consciousness and human unity, we have to remember that Walt Whitman (1819–1892) had been one of the potent influences on Sri Aurobindo during his formative years. Whitman had left the fragrance of his "leaves" in the intellectual corridors of Cambridge, where Sri Aurobindo was studying in the late 1880s. One suspects his later fascination for Whitman had been rooted there in him as a student in Cambridge. Some of his early poems (1893–1910) show us the influence of the Whitmanesque cosmic consciousness on Sri Aurobindo, as we see in "Invitation" (Sri Aurobindo 2009, 201):

> I sport with solitude here in my regions,
> Of misadventure have made me a friend.
> Who would live largely? Who would live freely?
> Here to the wind-swept uplands ascend.
> I am the lord of tempest and mountain,
> I am the Spirit of freedom and pride.
> Stark must he be and a kinsman to danger
> Who shares my kingdom and walks at my side.

This "I" is an expansion of the individual "I" into a world-embracing cosmic consciousness, which both Whitman and Sri Aurobindo use as liberator from the self-centered world. An example from Walt Whitman's "Salut Au Monde" section of *Leaves of Grass* will shed light on the issue:

> My spirit has pass'd in compassion and determination around the whole earth,
> I have look'd for equals and lovers and found them ready for me in all lands,
> I think some divine rapport has equalized me with them ...
> What cities the light or warmth penetrates
> I penetrate those cities myself.
> All islands to which birds wing their way
> I wing my way myself.
>
> (Bradley and Blodgett 1973, 148)

The similarity is much too obvious. They are talking of merging with the cosmos. Sumita Roy in her book entitled *Consciousness and Creativity* quotes Richard Maurice Bucke's definition:

> Cosmic Consciousness is a consciousness of the cosmos that is life and order of the universe. Along with the consciousness of the cosmos there occurs an intellectual enlightenment or illumination which alone would place the individual on a new plane of existence—would make him almost a member of a new species. To this is

added a state of moral exaltation, an indescribable feeling of elevation, elation and joyousness, a quickening of the moral sense which is fully as striking and more important both to the individual and to the race than is the enhanced intellectual power. With these come, what may be called, a sense of immortality, consciousness of eternal life.

(Roy 1991, 30)

R. M. Bucke, in fact, was the first critic, who offered us a comprehensive account of this mystical state. Bucke's explanation of cosmic consciousness is slightly different from Sri Aurobindo's idea of cosmic consciousness as certain expressions in Bucke's explanation appear to be contradictory to Sri Aurobindo's views. Sri Aurobindo asserts that the enlightenment achieved is intuitive, not intellectual. Also, it has nothing to do with "moral exaltation" or "moral sense." We have to remember that cosmic consciousness should not be equated with moral or intellectual aspects. It is an intuitive realization. It involves widening of the consciousness through intuitive perception, which places the individual on "a new plane of existence." However, Bucke did come very close to the Aurobindonian idea. Sri Aurobindo's sonnet entitled "Cosmic Consciousness" (Sri Aurobindo 1980, 24) can be read as a definition of the concept:

> I have wrapped the wide world in my wider self
> And Time and Space my spirit's seeing are.
> I am the god and demon, ghost and elf,
> I am the wind's speed and the blazing star.
> All Nature is the nursling of my care,
> I am its struggle and the eternal rest;
> The world's joy thrilling runs through me, I bear
> The sorrow of millions in my lonely breast.
> I have learned a close identity with all,
> Yet am by nothing bound that I become;
> Carrying in me the universe's call
> I mount to my imperishable home.
> I pass beyond Time and life on measureless wings,
> Yet still am one with born and unborn things.

Walt Whitman had already anticipated the voice of this Indian seer-poet. The tonal similarity is unmistakable. They seem to have undergone similar kind of experiences. V. K. Chari explains cosmic consciousness as "the mystic's unifying vision, which obliterates distinctions" (Bradley and Blodgett 1973, 930). It is an all-embracing love or a feeling of identification with the world. The metaphor of cosmic consciousness, which comes only after the abolition of the ego that leads to a feeling of identification with the world, has been a key metaphor in Sri Aurobindo's early prose and poetry. This metaphor enlarges and becomes intensely evident in his later poetry, especially in the sonnets and *Savitri*. A more clarified exegesis of the experience appears in *The Ideals of Human Unity*, which will be discussed in a subsequent section.

Psychic Being and Ego

According to Sri Aurobindo, the psychic being is the source of this feeling of identification or cosmic unity. The Wikipedia defines the word "psychic" as faculties or phenomena that are apparently inexplicable by natural laws, especially involving telepathy or clairvoyance and it also relates to the soul or mind. A. S. Dalal, an anthologist of Sri Aurobindo's prose writings, tells us that it has been derived from a Greek root *psukhē* meaning soul (Dalal 2001, 344). It is the portion of the eternal present in all things of the universe. There is a significant reference to it in *Katha Upanishad*, where the soul has been described as the wise one. He cannot be slain, even when the body is slain. The Vedic seers had used the mystic sound *Om* to indicate Him (Hume 2014 [1930], 78). Sri Aurobindo further explains it in *Letters on Yoga*, calling it "the spark of the Divine... it grows and evolves in the form of the psychic being" (1970, 270). However, for Sri Aurobindo, there is a subtle difference between the psychic being and the soul. The soul is eternal, constant, and unchangeable. The psychic being is the spark of the divine-grows and evolves to the divine. The psychic being is called in Sanskrit the *Purusha* in the heart or the *Chaitya Purusha* (Sri Aurobindo 1970, 301).

> The psychic part of us is something that comes direct from the Divine and is in touch with the Divine... there is divine element in all living beings, but it stands hidden behind the ordinary consciousness, is not at first developed and, even when developed, is not always or often in the front... It grows in the consciousness by Godward experience, gaining strength every time there is a higher movement in us, and, finally, by the accumulation of these deeper and higher movements, there is developed a psychic individuality,— that which we call usually the psychic being.
>
> (Sri Aurobindo 1970, 288)

At another place in the same book, Sri Aurobindo opines that it is our true conscience, which has nothing to do with conventional conscience and morality. This is the essence of our being, which is pure sans any gross emotion. According to Sri Aurobindo, when one becomes aware of the presence of our innermost being or the *Chaitya Purusha*, one is a step forward to the Divine consciousness. Realization of the awakening of the psychic being makes one full of adoration, self-giving, compassion, and an all-embracing love. One then rejects the negative influence of our separatist ego. Kabir wrote in one of his dohas (translated by Rabindranath Tagore 1915, 51):

> So long as man clamours for the I and the Mine, his works are as naught:
> When all love of the *I* and the *Mine* is dead, then the work of the Lord is done.

This self-explanatory doha exactly expresses the conviction of Sri Aurobindo that our ego does not allow us to be liberated from the shackles of fame, ambition, pride, and aggression. We have to remember that the popular Freudian concept of Ego or I-sense defines ego as just a mediator between *id* and *super-ego*. It operates on reality principles. It controls the desires of *id* and coordinates with the morality principle of *super-ego* (McLeod 2007). Sri Aurobindo has gone a step ahead of Sigmund Freud and explained the characteristics of ego in a more detailed manner. According to the Indian philosopher, the sense of ego helps us till some point in our life as in an ordinary state of consciousness; the ego or I-consciousness makes one aware of his/her individuality and independent existence. It is a part of the core of our being. It is also an agent of our entire thought process as we say, "I think" or "I feel," which is our experience of existence. It may be justified by Rene Descartes's famous proposition, *cogito ergo sum* or "I think therefore I am." The sense of ego is synonymous with sense of self. Assagioli says: "Man's basic existential experience...is being a living self" (Assagioli 1987, 126). We may thus deduce that the sense of ego or self makes one aware of one's identity and helps one to establish that in the society. It is also distinctive from others. Therefore, it has a boundary. The individual ego separates one from the other due to one's individuality. Ken Wilber puts his argument in a frame of dichotomy as "self" versus "not-self" (Wilber 1979, 46). According to Wilber, the fundamental is the boundary between self and not-self. Every individual distinguishes himself from others who are not part of his self and that leads to separate existence. Ego also shapes up one's group identity as well as national identity. Therefore, the sense of ego has some positive influences till some point of our life. In the ordinary state of consciousness, we find that the sense of "I-ness" gradually moves toward certain impulses like possessiveness, attachment, a drive toward accumulation of more and jealousy. But then, humanity has to march forward beyond this ordinary sense of ego toward cosmic unity. Sri Aurobindo explains this forward march from ego to cosmic consciousness in *Letters on Yoga*.

> The cosmic consciousness is that in which the limits of ego, personal mind and the body disappear and one becomes aware of a cosmic vastness which is or filled by a cosmic spirit...It is not that the ego, the body, the personal mind disappear, but one feels them as only a small part of oneself. One begins to feel others too as part of oneself or varied repetitions of oneself. The same self-modified by Nature in other bodies. Or, at the least, as living in the larger universal self which is henceforth one's own greater reality.
>
> (Sri Aurobindo 1970, 315)

Sri Aurobindo is talking of merging in the cosmic vastness to experience the greater reality. Our self is a part of both the individual and the cosmic self. In order to experience this identification, one needs to have an awakened psychic being, which helps us to get rid of anger, jealousy, and desire. The realization of the presence of Chaitya Purusha has nothing to do with intellectual quest. It is intuitive realization, which can be attained by the power of aspiration, love, sacrifice, and surrender. All these refined emotions remove the veil of ignorance from our mundane state of consciousness. Sri Aurobindo describes this as "psychic transformation." However, this does not imply a total rejection of intellectual knowledge but a transformation of the intellect in the intuition. In other words, the higher consciousness does not negate the rational principle, but rather transcends it. D. H. Lawrence, in his essay entitled "Whitman," wrote:

At last the lower centers are conquered. At last the lowest plane is submitted to the highest. At last there is nothing more to conquer. At last all is one, all is love, even hate is love, even flesh is spirit ... it is man's accession into wholeness, his knowledge in full. Now he is united with everything into himself in a oneness ... Nothing is rejected. Because nothing opposes him. All adds up to one in him ... and this accumulative identity he calls One Identity.

(Bradley and Blodgett 1973, 845)

We may therefore conclude that Sri Aurobindo and D. H. Lawrence are of the opinion that the principles of our inner being are love, surrender, and cosmic unity. The moment one is capable of leaving behind the desires and the interest of individual self, one is free and becomes a part of the larger scheme of existence. This relates to the Aurobindonian ideal of human unity.

Aurobindonian Concept of Human Unity

In an essay entitled "The Religion of Humanity" (from *The Ideal of Human Unity*), Sri Aurobindo (567–568) writes:

That enemy, the enemy of all real religion, is human egoism, the egoism of the individual, the egoism of class and nation. These it could for a time soften, modify, force to curb their more arrogant, open and brutal expressions, oblige to adopt better institutions, but not to give place to the love of mankind, not to recognise a real unity between man and man.

The passage sheds light on the key problem of human unity: the egoistic impulse in humanity. Sri Aurobindo highlights the enemy and its manifold operations in the human consciousness, class consciousness, and national consciousness. Indeed, the influence of ego makes all the religions sectarian. According to Emile Durkheim, religion is a "unified system of beliefs and practices relative to sacred things, that is to say, things set apart and forbidden—beliefs and practices which unite in one single moral community called a Church, all those who adhere to them." Durkheim also opines that practice of religion is either a communal or a collective activity, which binds the people sharing the same faith and religious beliefs (Coser 1977, 136–139). That is beneficial to some extent in building the group cohesiveness or "class consciousness." People who come from the same religion assemble at one place for celebration, which strengthens the kinship and harmony culminating in a sense of group cohesiveness. One upholds the age-old beliefs and customs of a particular religion for future generations through the celebration of rituals. Discipline and ethical sense also originate from religion. Over all, each religion is unique because of its distinct beliefs, rituals, practices, and ceremonies as it generates the solidarity of collective consciousness but it is not fruitful in the long run for the larger context as then "it degenerates to competitive religion" (Parrinder 1962, 12). We have to remember that the vision of Sri Aurobindo is not limited to any class or nation. He looks beyond the national boundary in favor of global harmony by not rejecting the specialties of a nation. Variety is against the boredom of a mechanical unity.

According to Sri Aurobindo, love is the essential principle of life. It means an expansion, a deepening of consciousness, a widening of consciousness, and a heightening of consciousness and that is possible when humanity realizes the presence of the Psychic being deep within every person. He presents his theoretical argument in an inspired language in *The Ideal of Human Unity*. Inspiration and logic are fused in the chapter entitled "The Religion of Humanity."

> The fundamental idea is that mankind is the godhead to be worshipped and served by man and that the respect, the service, the progress of the human being and human life are the chief duty and the chief aim of the human spirit. No other idol, neither the nation, the State, the family nor anything else ought to take its place; they are only worthy of respect so far as they are images of the human spirit and enshrine its presence and aid its self-manifestation. But where the cult of these idols seeks to usurp the place of the spirit and makes demands inconsistent with its service, they should be put aside. No injunctions of old creeds, religious, political, social or cultural, are valid when they go against its claims. Science even, though it is one of the chief modern idols, must not be allowed to make claims contrary to its ethical temperament and aim, for science is only valuable in so far as it helps and serves by knowledge and progress the religion of humanity. War, capital punishment, the taking of human life, cruelty of all kinds whether committed by the individual, the State or society, not only physical cruelty, but moral cruelty, the degradation of any human being or any class of human beings under whatever specious plea or in whatever interest, the oppression and exploitation of man by man, of class by class, of nation by nation and all those habits of life and institutions of society of a similar kind which religion and ethics formerly tolerated or even favoured in practice, whatever they might do in their ideal rule or creed, are crimes against the religion of humanity, abominable to its ethical mind, forbidden by its primary tenets, to be fought against always, in no degree to be tolerated.
>
> (Sri Aurobindo 1962, 565)

This is the logical aspect of his ideology of human consciousness, as Sri Aurobindo raises a crucial issue in the chapter, the issue of the individual ego, group ego, and the national ego. When the ego is subdued, the man will be in a position to consider the importance of another man in our evolving nature.

> Man must be sacred to man regardless of all distinctions of race, creed, colour, nationality, status, political or social advancement. The body of man is to be respected, made immune from violence and outrage, fortified by science against disease and preventable death. The life of man is to be held sacred, preserved, strengthened, ennobled, uplifted. The heart of man is to be held sacred also, given scope, protected from violation, from suppression, from mechanisation, freed from belittling influences. The mind of man is to be released from all bonds, allowed freedom and range and opportunity, given all its means of self-training

and self-development and organised in the play of its powers for the service of humanity. And all this too is not to be held as an abstract or pious sentiment, but given full and practical recognition in the persons of men and nations and mankind. This, speaking largely, is the idea and spirit of the intellectual religion of humanity.

(Sri Aurobindo 1962, 565)

The same argument of human unity has also been expressed beautifully by Sri Aurobindo in his poems. One can find that there is a lasting shadow of Whitmanesque cosmic awareness in Sri Aurobindo's poetry almost till the end of his life in 1950, although the level of Sri Aurobindo's experience seems to be deeper as the Indian poet reaches a spiritual stage ahead of Whitman, the stage of *Knowledge by Identity* by crossing the phase of Whitmanesque cosmic consciousness. Here is the Whitmanesque tradition behind Sri Aurobindo's poetry.

> I seize the descending man and raise him with resistless will,
> O despairer, here is my neck,
> By God, you shall not go down! Hang your whole weight upon me.
> I dilate you with tremendous breath, I buoy you up,
> Every room of the house do I fill with an arm'd force.

(Bradley and Blodgett 1973, 74)

The vast cosmic identity grows and deepens in Sri Aurobindo's later sonnets and also in some other poems like "The Cosmic Man," which shows not only his identification with the world, but also the destruction of the animals and environment by Man, who endangers his own position by slaying the animals. In "The Cosmic Man," the poet casts his eyes across the world and finds no horizon. All the war-affected cities of the world wake up before his eyes: Tokyo, Paris, New York, Barcelona, and Canton. In his global vision, he sees in himself the same man who slays the beasts is also engaged in feeding the birds. The last line of the poem is Whitmanesque and also hints at a complete sense of identification with the distressed humanity.

> I bear the sorrow of millions in my lonely breast".

(Sri Aurobindo 2009, 603)

Sonnets found in Sri Aurobindo's manuscripts with dates ranging from 1934 to 1947 project an obvious shift from the prophet of nationalism to the lover of humanity. In the sonnet entitled "Cosmic Consciousness," we do not just see a subjective identification with all the creations of God, but a commitment to humanity, as we have seen in "The Cosmic Man."

> I have wrapped the wide world in my wider self
> And Time and Space my spirit's seeing are.
> I am the god and demon, ghost and elf,
> I am the wind's speed and the blazing star.

> ... I have learned a close identity with all, ...
> Carrying in me the universe's call
> I mount to my imperishable home.
>
> (Sri Aurobindo 1980, 24)

Here is a poet whose aim is not just a merger with the Eternal Spirit, but he deliberately wishes to carry with him the suffering earth in order to place it before the solar gaze of the Supreme in His imperishable home. As if he is a messenger of the soil, who is aspiring for the God-touch. The earth has to be changed by the light of Heaven. The call of the universe has to reach the cosmic ear. The poet is undertaking the labor for the sake of humanity. In "Life-Unity," he is projecting his concern for earth as well as realizing a unity with the Divine through small things of life.

> I housed within my heart the life of things,
> All hearts athrob in the world I felt as mine;
> I shared the joy that in creation sings
> And drank its sorrow like a poignant wine ...
> One love I shared in a million bosoms expressed.
> I am the beast man slays, the beast he saves
> I rose by them towards a supernal plane
> Of power and love and deathless ecstasies.
>
> (Sri Aurobindo 1980, 27)

Unified with the joy and sorrow of the material universe; unified with the anger, passion, and love of the world, he rises to the supernal plane of power, love, and immortal Ananda. As a pioneer of the tracks to human unity, he feels the troubling world fulfilled in himself. The "Epilogue" of *Savitri* is a clue to his real endeavor on the path to human unity. It speaks of the light coming down from above on the earth to change our erroneous earth-nature. Love descends on earth permanently to build Her eternal home.

> A playing-ground and dwelling-house of God
> Who hides himself in bird and beast and man
> Sweetly to find himself again by love,
> By oneness.
>
> (Sri Aurobindo 1951, 341)

It was not only the dream of Walt Whitman and Sri Aurobindo. Rabindranath Tagore also spoke of the same thing in *Religion of Man*. "However, whatever name our logic may give to the truth of human unity, the fact can never be ignored that we have our greatest delight when we realise ourselves in others, and this is the definition of love. This love gives us the testimony of the great whole, which is the complete and final truth of man" (Tagore 2012, 39). Sri Aurobindo's essay "The Religion of Humanity," which forms a key part of his exegesis on human unity, has been overlooked surprisingly in contrast with Tagore's book *The Religion of Man*, which came out more than a decade later. There is no effort as yet to take the two texts together to examine the essential similarity between them, although Tagore's book lacks the compact structure of Sri Aurobindo's essay, where the highlights have been strongly marked, highlights like the hitherto unseen phrase " the brotherhood of the soul" and the repeated stress on the liberation from the ego-sense. Tagore does speak about the need of the abolition of the ego, but that in his own discursive manner, which is characteristic of his English prose. Sri Aurobindo moves ahead systematically and presents a complete thesis on the progressive enlightenment of humanity invading all the layers of society from the higher elites down to the meanest individual, whom Whitman would have called "one leaf of grass." Chatterjee articulates this process in this way: "Existence is destined to reach a point when the whole will assimilate the good in all its constituted particulars ... towards this objective one needs to be sensitized spiritually to seek God on a higher plane" (Chatterjee 1994, 243).

Conclusion

Sri Aurobindo believes in a progressive transformation of the human ego, the class ego, and the national ego. He suggests a transcendence of the ego, a release into a new identity with all, an awakening into our true self, life, a growth into a new being, and that not by suppression but a transformation of the lower impulses, which continuously tend to drag us down to the provinces of strife and discord. He hopes for a fulfillment, not by mutilation of the lower members of the self but by an elevation of them into the higher principles of life leading to harmony between man and man.

Sri Aurobindo believes that man's "international existence is still primitive." Human beings do not even have the prescient knowledge of an extension of consciousness. We hardly care for our fellow human beings. Finally, it may be said following the arguments and revelations of Sri Aurobindo that human unity is destined in some era in the future, but that unity does not demand the abolition of the individual characteristics of a race or a nation. It will be something like a unity in diversity. Otherwise, the world will cease to be dynamic and it will be full of boredom without the spices of variety. Sri Aurobindo's vision of man as a necessary footbridge to the future implies the creation of a new species beyond man to be created out of man. An increasing number of better individuals is not an absurd dream as Nature cannot be satisfied with an imperfect creation and will always work toward a higher manifestation of consciousness.

The present humanity is handicapped by a strong desire-soul, an ego-sense, in both the individual and the larger units and all our strife is caused by this acute ego-sense, which refuses to leave us. Sri Aurobindo suggests a three-fold movement in our effort at liberation from the entanglement of the ego: a deepening of consciousness, a widening of consciousness, and a heightening of consciousness. The unification of this world can only be made possible by this massive expansion in the individuals. An increasing number of men and women must feel this sense of oneness, an identity with the fellow human beings. No change is possible without a change of consciousness. All the revolutions have failed because economic factors are not the only factors for human disharmony. Evolution, not revolution, is the way forward. Man can hasten this evolution by his own efforts. It is like ascending to a "higher awareness" (Chatterjee 1994, 249) or transcendence of the ordinary consciousness by virtue of our progressive realization of the godhead in man.

The yoga integrating all our separate parts of the being, which Sri Aurobindo prescribes for humanity, is a surrender of the lower nature to the higher principles and an intervention of the higher to purify the lower members of the being. Sri Aurobindo does not argue that the entire world will be transformed overnight. It is a slow process of growth into a new consciousness in certain advanced individuals who will be the leaders of the future society, a developed group of exceptional individuals without the ego-sense. For all disharmonies are due to the human ego, which has to go making room for a new metaphor of love.

References

Assagioli, Roberto. 1987. *The Act of Will*. New York: Penguin Books.
Chatterjee, Margaret. 1994. "Rabbi Abraham Isaac Kook and Sri Aurobindo: Towards a Comparison." In Goodman, Hananya ed. *Between Jerusalem and Benares: Comparative Studies in Judaism and Hinduism*. Albany: State University of New York Press, 243–266.
Coser, Lewis A. 1977. "The Sociology of Religion." In Coser, Lewis A. *Masters of Sociological Thought: Ideas in Historical and Social Context*. 2nd ed. Fort Worth: Harcourt Brace Jovanovich, Inc. Also available at http://media.pfeiffer.edu/lridener/DSS/Durkheim/DURKW3.HTML (Accessed August 14, 2018).
Dalal, A. S. 2001. *An Introduction to the Psychological Thought of Sri Aurobindo: A Greater Psychology*. Pondicherry: Sri Aurobindo Ashram.
Hume, Robert Ernest. 2014 [1930]. *The Thirteen Principal Upanishads*. Delhi: Vijay Goel.
Lawrence, D. H. 1973. "Whitman," In Bradley, Sculley and Blodgett, Harold eds. *Norton Critical Edition of Leaves of Grass*. New York: W. W. Norton, 842–850.
Mathai, M. P. 1999. "What Swaraj Meant to Gandhi?" Available at http://www.mkgandhi.org/articles/swaraj.htm (Accessed August 14, 2018).
McLeod, Saul. 2007. "Id, Ego and Superego." Available at https://www.simplypsychology.org/psyche.html (Accessed August 14, 2018).
Nandy, Ashis. 2005. "The Intimate Enemy." *Exiled at Home: At the Edge of Psychology, The Intimate Enemy, Creating a Nationality*. New Delhi: Oxford University Press, 87–100.
Parrinder, Geoffrey. 1962. *Comparative Religion*. London: George Allen & Unwin Ltd.
Purani, A. B. 1978. *The Life of Sri Aurobindo*. Pondicherry: Sri Aurobindo Ashram.
Roy, Sumita. 1991. *Cosmic Consciousness and Creativity: A Study of Sri Aurobindo, T.S. Eliot and Aldous Huxley*. New Delhi: Sterling.
Singh, Karan. 2000. *Prophet of Indian Nationalism*. Mumbai: Bharatiya Vidya Bhavan.
Sri Aurobindo. 1951. *Savitri*. Pondicherry: Sri Aurobindo Ashram.
Sri Aurobindo. 1962. *The Human Cycle, The Ideal of Human Unity, War and Self-Determination*. Pondicherry: Sri Aurobindo Ashram.
Sri Aurobindo. 1965. *On Nationalism*. Pondicherry: Sri Aurobindo Ashram.
Sri Aurobindo. 1970. *Letters on Yoga*, vol. 22. Pondicherry: Sri Aurobindo Ashram.
Sri Aurobindo. 1972. *Early Cultural Writings*. Pondicherry: Sri Aurobindo Ashram.
Sri Aurobindo. 1980. *Sonnet*. Pondicherry: Sri Aurobindo Ashram.

Sri Aurobindo. 2009. *The Complete Works of Sri Aurobindo, Vol-2 (Collected Poems)*, Pondicherry: Sri Aurobindo Ashram Publication Department.
Tagore, Rabindranath. 1915. *Songs of Kabir* (Introduction and assistance: Evelyn Underhill). London: Macmillan and Co.
Tagore, Rabindranath. 2012. *Religion of Man*. New Delhi: Niyogi Books.
Wilber, Ken. 1979. *No Boundary*. Boston and London: Shambhala.

12

Sri Aurobindo's Ideal of Human Unity and the Discourse on International Organizations and Global Governance

Debidatta Aurobinda Mahapatra

This chapter introduces Sri Aurobindo to international organization and global governance studies to make an argument that there is a linkage between global governance and human unity, and Sri Aurobindo's argument provides a useful linkage between the two. The debate on global governance has assumed increasing importance in the West, and the chapter argues that in this context the Ideal of Human Unity (IHU) as proposed by Sri Aurobindo is significant. It is interested in widening the scope of debates on global governance and argues how IHU is particularly relevant in the post–Cold War global order. It aims at reviving and contextualizing the debate on Sri Aurobindo's philosophy, and its usefulness for international organizations and global governance. The chapter attempts to introduce a philosophical dimension to global governance and human unity debate. International peace has become an abiding concern for international relations discipline, and this chapter, while bringing into focus the urgency of world unity, makes an attempt to introduce a new angle to global governance discourse. Various methods, approaches, and policies have been tested for international peace and security with varied consequences. Against such a background, the chapter aims to provide a hitherto under-researched Indian approach to draw attention toward non-Western cultures to enrich the discourse on global governance and human unity.

The chapter does not elaborate on the nature and scope of global governance as the main argument of the chapter does not necessitate such a study. The literature on global governance is impressive.[1] The chapter focuses on a least researched subject—Sri Aurobindo's ideas on the world and its evolution and their relevance to international organizations and global governance. It recognizes the differences between the terms of global governance and IHU; global governance can be considered a process—it is about "govern*ance* in the absence govern*ment*" (Ruggie 2010, xv). IHU can be considered a goal. Also, while most of the literature on global governance gives primary importance on formal mechanisms, IHU emphasizes on the transformation within individuals and within collectivities toward an enduring and peaceful global community. The discussion in the chapter follows this order. The first section elaborates

Sri Aurobindo's theory of evolution, and how his ideas about individual, state, nation, and IHU are linked. The second section elaborates his IHU, and its basic elements. The third section deals with international organizations, particularly the United Nations (UN), considered a primary vehicle of global governance, and how it reflects the IHU. The final section summarizes the main arguments.

A Theory of Evolution

Sri Aurobindo was born in British India in 1872. At the age of seven, he was sent to England for education and upbringing in Western culture. He completed his studies at King's College and returned to India in 1893 to join the service of the princely state of Baroda (Vadodara). In 1906, he joined the Indian freedom struggle and edited the weekly *Bande Mataram*, in which most of his ideas about nation and nationalism appeared. In 1910 he took voluntary retirement from active politics and relocated to Pondicherry (Puducherry), then a French colony in Indian Territory, to engage in yoga, philosophy, poetry, and mysticism. In Pondicherry he edited a philosophical magazine *Arya*, in which he exposed his philosophical ideas. His book *Ideal of Human Unity* first appeared in this magazine serially from September 1915 to July 1918, which was later compiled as a book in 1919. Sri Aurobindo made a final revision of the book in 1949 and included contemporary developments including the creation of the UN and his reflections on them. This chapter mainly draws from the book *The Human Cycle, the Ideal of Human Unity, and the War and Self- determination* (Sri Aurobindo, The Complete Works of Sri Aurobindo, hereafter CWSA, 1997, vol. 25).

That human evolution is continuous is one of the central arguments of Sri Aurobindo's philosophy. The evolutionary force, or what Sri Aurobindo refers to as Nature, is linked to individuals as well as groups of individuals and the whole human society. The developments in individual life or collective life are part of a formidable process determined by Nature, which does not stop at the level of mind and intellect, the highest evolution so far. Sri Aurobindo was influenced by the Greek philosopher Heraclitus's idea that things are in a perpetual flux, but he found in Heraclitus's philosophy the emphasis on being. According to him, "The idea of the One which is eternally becoming many and the many which is eternally becoming one... is the foundation of Heraclitus' philosophy" (Varma 1960–1961, 141). Although Heraclitus is regarded as the founder of the theory of perpetual change and flux, Sri Aurobindo identified the concept of being as a key element in the ideas of the Greek philosopher. He believed that there is a fundamental unity as the very basis of existence, and at the foundation of all things, and it is the Nature that moves to realize this unity. In the philosophy of Sri Aurobindo, the Vedantic philosophy, especially that of *advaitism* (which literally means non-dualism), is quite perceptible (Trivedi 1971, 137). There are also some parallels between his evolutionary ideas and those of the German philosopher Georg Wilhelm Friedrich Hegel. He believed, like Hegel, that Nature, which is self-contained and self-determining, is *causa sui* and unfolding itself. But while for Hegel the zenith of the movement of the spirit is the realization of state, Sri Aurobindo's Nature moves further to realize an essential unity of the human race.[2] For

Sri Aurobindo, in the evolutionary process, human society appeared in a later stage, the first stage being the physical world of matter and the second stage being life. The manifestation of consciousness is the highest manifestation so far. The human being is the basic unit of society. Uberoi argues that Sri Aurobindo's conception of ideal human unity does not limit the human potentials in a uniform structure. Rather, "the theory of evolution means... the development of many varieties of existence out of the original few, and without humanity in anyway losing the unity of its universe of discourse" (Uberoi 2002, 130). According to Minor, in Sri Aurobindo's philosophy the evolution of Nature in human being gradually develops "oneness with our fellowmen," which becomes "the leading principle of all our life, not merely a principle of co-operation but a deeper brotherhood, a real and an inner sense of unity and equality and a common life" (Minor 1979, 376).

Sri Aurobindo argued that human society has evolved throughout history and is destined to move toward a better organization of life. The state represents a stage in this evolution. Sri Aurobindo made a distinction between state and nation. The state imposes an organic unity of the aggregate people's political, social, and economic life through centralized administration. The state "has been most successful and efficient means of unification and has been best able to meet the various needs which the progressive aggregate life of societies has created for itself and is still creating" (CWSA 1997, vol. 25, 465). The idea of nation goes beyond the idea of state. While the state is an outward form, convenient machinery to enforce unity and uniformity, the nation is the living unity of the aspirations and powers of its peoples. The progression of human society does not end at the nation idea because there is an evolutionary urge toward the larger organization and this drive leads to the final establishment of the largest of all and the ultimate union of the world's people (CWSA 1997, vol. 25, 797). Here comes the intersection of his ideas with those of global governance, in which he emphasizes that it is a natural human tendency to strive toward human unity, beyond the confines of states. Sri Aurobindo, however, argued changes "through mechanical means, through social and political adjustments" would not lead to enduring unity of the human race (CWSA 1997, vol. 25, 281).

Sri Aurobindo's distinction between "national ego" and "nation-soul" is a significant contribution to the global governance debate. National ego implies a vague sense of group subjectivity that is reflected in national idiosyncrasies, habits, prejudices, and marked mental tendencies. Nation-soul embodies a deeper awareness of group subjectivity (Mohanty 1993, 142). While the national ego is a barrier toward larger unity of mankind, the nation-soul has in itself a tendency toward larger unity of mankind. National ego is an obstacle on the path of larger coordination among nation-states and nation-soul can be an aid in the process. Wherever there is a domination of national ego, national leaders tend to profess supremacy of their nation and the pace of evolution toward human unity falters. As far as there is national egoism, the strife among nation-states and means like war would remain. Sri Aurobindo traced the cause of the First World War and the imperialism of nineteenth and twentieth centuries to national ego (CWSA 1997, vol. 25, 390). This argument can be further extended to international organizations such as the UN, in which there is a clash between the concerns of international peace and security and interests of its powerful members.

The concept of national ego approximates the theory of realism in international politics in which the national interest is the core guiding principle. Sri Aurobindo argued it is crucial that national ego is replaced by nation-soul. Without this replacement or evolution, it will be difficult for the states to address global problems collectively.

The Indian philosopher developed the term "religion of humanity," which "means the growing realisation that...humanity is its highest present vehicle on earth, that the human race and the human being are the means by which it will progressively reveal itself here" (CWSA 1997, vol. 25, 577). It embodies three core values—liberty, equality, and fraternity or what he calls, applying a religious vocabulary, "supreme social trinity." These three supreme values, however, cannot develop and transform the world until the nation-states cultivate them in thinking and practice. This has not happened even though all these three values are proclaimed by most of the modern states. Sri Aurobindo argued, "The liberty that has been so loudly proclaimed as an essential of modern progress is an outward and mechanical and unreal liberty. The equality that has been so much sought after and battled for is equally an outward and mechanical and will turn out to be an unreal equality. Fraternity is not even claimed to be a practicable principle of the ordering of life and what is put forward as its substitute is the outward and mechanical principle of equal association or at best a comradeship of labor" (CWSA 1997, vol. 25, 762–763). These three principles, core to the very functioning of a democratic international order, cannot be reconciled unless states rise above egoism. He further argued that liberty and equality appear as contradictory principles but can be reconciled with the higher principle of fraternity. This reconciliation appears unworkable in the present scheme of things as it puts emphasis on a mere perfunctory order because fraternity in its present working means the mere formal coming together of nation-states or just some kind of ceremonial unity without a change in character and motives. The emphasis continues to be on the state and narrow national interest rather than on the globe and global interests. For human unity the first principle must be a "system of free and natural groupings which would leave no room for internal discord, mutual incompatibilities and repression and revolt as between race and race or people and people" (CWSA 1997, vol. 25, 429).

Ideal of Human Unity

Sri Aurobindo's idea of union might appear unconventional to dominant schools of IR (International Relations). For the realist school, states work in an anarchic order, and it is the national interest and psychology of egoism that shape foreign policy of a state. Applying this logic of the realist school, it would be unimaginable that a world-union would be possible. Perhaps the school of liberalism, which emphasizes interdependence for the fulfillment of national interests, is not diametrically opposite to the prospect of such a union.[3] However, the element of psychological union and sacrifice of national prejudices and idiosyncrasies that hinder the growth of an international outlook have not been emphasized in this school.

For Sri Aurobindo, IHU does not simply pertain to the world of ideas, but to the very world of practicality. It "has been born not only in the speculating forecasting mind of the thinker, but in the consciousness of humanity out of the very necessity of this new common existence." Although Sri Aurobindo hesitated to predict the particular form of world unity, he supposed that it would be gradually more unitary with nations as provinces of the world-state which will ensure to all "the great advantages of peace, economic well-being, general security, combination for intellectual, cultural, social activity and progress" (CWSA 1997, vol. 25, 562). As the state represents the will of the group within its territory, a World-State would represent the united will of all nations and the nation-states would not completely disappear in such a union even though the powers of lawmaking and defense would be concentrated in this World-State.

It is difficult to establish whether Sri Aurobindo's IHU directly influenced other scholars in other traditions, but similar ideas were developed by Western thinkers. One can trace similarities between the ideas of Sri Aurobindo and the French paleoanthropologist and philosopher Pierre Teilhard de Chardin.[4] Both possessed a profound belief in evolution, and believed that the current status of the world is a stage in this evolution toward an ultimate unity of mankind. W. B. Curry, in his *The Case for Federal Union*, appealed nation-states to come out of their narrow chauvinism to make the idea of federal union possible. For the survival of the civilization, Curry argued, "the groups which we call nations should become like other groups, less fierce, less exclusive, less aggressive, less dominating, admitting allegiance to, and submitting to some measure of control by the community consisting of mankind as a whole" (Curry 1939, 65). Clarence Streit argued for the establishment of a Union of the North Atlantic democracies, with scope for further expansion wherein national governments will have a separate existence. But the Union will provide "effective common government in ... those fields where such common government will clearly serve man's freedom better than separate governments," and "create by its constitution a nucleus world government capable of growing into universal world government peacefully and as rapidly as such growth will best serve man's freedom" (Streit 1939). Emery Reves in his *The Anatomy of Peace* wrote, "World government is not an 'ultimate goal' but an immediate necessity. It has been overdue since 1914" (quoted in Basu 1999, 4). The Parliament of World Religions in 1993 advocated for the adoption of the Golden Rule by the nation-states toward the evolution of a just and fair world (Giandomenico et al. 2001, 74). For Alexander Wendt, a world-state is inevitable (Wendt 2003). Wendt applies a teleological logic and argues that nation-states, working in the conditions of anarchy, would be motivated to participate in higher supranational institutions, including a possible world-state. This argument can be juxtaposed to Sri Aurobindo's concept of nation-soul which gives way for larger formations, in contrast to national ego which is narrow and rigid.

An international township, called Auroville (city of dawn), was established in the Indian city of Pondicherry (Puducherry) to give a shape to Sri Aurobindo's IHU.[5] In February 1968, it was formally declared with representatives from 124 states putting handfuls of soil from native lands in an urn located at the center of the city. Sri Aurobindo's collaborator, The Mother, laid the foundation stone for the township. Earlier in 1954, she laid out her "dream" of establishing an international township to give a shape to Sri Aurobindo's vision. She elaborated the dream: "A place no nation would claim as its sole property, a place where all human beings ... could live freely as citizens of the world...a place of peace, concord, harmony...a place where the relations among human beings, usually based almost exclusively upon competition and strife, would be replaced by relations of emulation for doing better, for collaboration, relations of real brotherhood" (Sri Aurobindo Ashram Trust 1977, 7).

How Does the UN Reflect IHU?

Do international organizations reflect ideal human unity? One of the bodies that is considered a primary vehicle of global governance, and also factored in Sri Aurobindo's writings, is the UN. The UN is the only international organization of which almost all nation-states are members. Thakur and Weiss argue that the universal character of the UN provides it legitimacy in formulating global public policy, and this legitimacy they term "precious asset" (Thakur and Weiss 1999, 20) and for Rosenau, besides the national governments, the UN is "central to the conduct of global governance" (Rosenau 1995, 13). The value of the UN as a global governance mechanism has been affirmed on many occasions. The 1992 Agenda of Peace under the leadership of then UN Secretary-General Boutros Boutros-Ghali embodied the post–Cold War concerns and argued for the necessity of international cooperation toward a peaceful world (United Nations 1992). The co-chair of the Commission on Human Security, Sadako Ogata, reiterated the message of the Agenda of Peace in the report Human Security Now, 2003, "In a world of growing interdependence and transnational issues.... United Nations stands as the best and only option available to preserve international peace and stability as well as to protect people, regardless of race, religion, gender or political opinion" (Commission on Human Security 2003, 4). *Crossing the Divide* written under the auspices of the UN in 2001 challenged the theories of "Clash of Civilizations" and "End of History" and posited hope on the UN for the resolution of the global problems (Giandomenico et al. 2001, 109–152).

Sri Aurobindo argued that the predecessor of the UN, the League of Nations, created to replace "old unjust Balances of Power and stumbling, quarrelsome Concerts" could have performed better had it not succumbed to "the natural egoistic instincts and rooted past habits of the international mentality." Although the League started with a hope for human unity, it was actually no more than "an instrument subservient to the policy of a few great Powers" (CWSA 1997, vol. 25, 430 note 1). Sri Aurobindo was of the firm belief that unless a deeper internal principle of unity evolves among nations, it is difficult to sustain an international organization merely on the basis of external mechanisms agreed by the members. The successor of the League, the UN, was mandated to provide avenues for the members to display their diversities in a harmonious way under one roof, where the differences among them could be resolved under the framework of international law applicable equally to all. The UN appeared more representative in comparison to its predecessor. The General Assembly comprised almost all states of the world (at present the number of the members is 193; in 1945, the year it was established, the number was 51). The Assembly works on the principle of one nation, one vote, which is designed to give equal voice to all nations, big or small, powerful or weak. Through its various bodies such as the United Nations

Educational, Scientific and Cultural Organization and the United Nations Children's Fund, the UN has expanded its activities globally.

Sri Aurobindo could foresee the possible future strains in the working of the international body. Even though he called the formation of the UN an "event of capital importance" supposed to create "a new era in world history," he expressed dissatisfaction at the nature of its formation and questioned its effectiveness for a just global order. The United Nations General Assembly, formed in 1945, could be argued as an approximation of world parliament as suggested by Sri Aurobindo. The preamble of the UN Charter affirms "faith in fundamental human rights, in the dignity and worth of the human person, in the equal rights of men and women and of nations large and small." One of the core assumptions of the Sri Aurobindo's IHU is that individual's interests can be best realized through international communities based on universal values of liberty, equality, and fraternity. This assumption expands status of the individual not merely as a citizen of a nation-state but as a member of the globalized world and this formulation chimes well with global governance. But is the UN, the apex international organization, capable of fulfilling its mandate keeping in view the "national ego" that continues to dominate international politics? Sri Aurobindo questioned the very structure of the UN and argued that a preponderant position of the five powers, or P5, weakens the hope of a permanent peace. In such an arrangement, small countries like "Honduras and Guatemala... may indulge themselves in some feeling of being lifted up to an equality with imperial England, America, the new arbiter of the world, and victorious France," but in reality "this is an illusion, *a trompe l'oeil*" (CWSA 1997, vol. 25, 643). Such arrangements carry in them ominous seeds of "own future mutability and perhaps dissolution" (CWSA 1997, vol. 25, 650) as is reflected in the functioning of the UN.Can the UN be considered an effective means toward ideal human unity? Coate and Murphy in their editorial note to the inaugural issue of *Global Governance* journal reflected the dilemma of how hopes for a revitalization of multilateral institutions in the post–Cold War world is belied by the strains on these institutions. They particularly referred to the UN in this context. To quote them, "The emerging global unity of purpose has allowed many of us to imagine revitalized multilateral institutions forging cooperative responses to global problems; still, the reality of the UN system straining under so many new demands makes most of us question whether such a renaissance is possible" (Coate and Murphy 1995, 1). International organizations, anchored in the state system inspired by realism, continue to remain constrained to emerge as truly global governance institutions. Weiss and Thakur argue, "the evolution of intergovernmental institutions to facilitate to robust international responses lags well behind the emergence of collective problems with transborder, especially global, dimensions" (Weiss and Thakur 2010, 4). While expressing dissatisfaction at the working of existing international institutions, Cox referred to their functioning as "sclerotic, politically biased and often malfunctioning," and argued it is necessary that international organizations encourage a learning process from different civilizations, and develop principles that can be acceptable to inter-subjectivity of each component parts of the organization. The aim of a world organization needs to "distill a kind of supra-inter-subjectivity from the distinct inter-subjectivities of its component parts," and this is a lengthy learning process from "experience in reconciling conflicts" (Cox 2002). Cox further argued it should be accepted that civilizations coexist, and there should be a dialogue between them, since "mutual comprehension" is "paramount" for harmonious co-existence. However, clash instead of dialogue appears to be a dominant trend in current international politics.

The working of the UN gives rise to the formulation that the system built more than seventy years ago has not developed needed resilience and flexibility to realize its mandate. Kofi Annan argues, "The new United Nations of the twenty-first century cannot afford to perpetuate such narrow nonintegrative thinking and approaches" (Annan 1998, 136). According to Rosenau, "in its performances the United Nations has not lived up to the surge of high hopes for it that immediately followed the end of the Cold War. Rather than sustaining the movement toward effective global governance, it foundered in Somalia, dawdled in Bosnia, and cumulatively suffered a decline in the esteem with which it is held by both governments and publics" (Rosenau 1995, 36). The crisis in Syria reflects the weakness of the body toward evolving a common framework to address the crisis.[6] Syria can be considered the latest humanitarian crisis that adds urgency to the debate on the effectiveness of the UN in maintaining international peace and security. The mammoth challenges emerging out of international conflicts, market economy and globalization, the north-south divide, the problems related to human rights and democracy have not been addressed by the world body effectively.

Rosenau argues that in the interdependent world, "global governance is conceived to include systems of rule at all levels of human activity—from the family to the international organization" (Rosenau 1995, 13). This integral view on global governance is in tandem with the basic argument of Sri Aurobindo that the actions from the levels of family to the level of inter-state have linkages, which Rosenau terms "micro-macro processes," that cannot be delinked. While in families individuals can be considered actors, at the international stage nation-states can be considered individual actors. The reluctance on part of the dominant to come out of their egos, to use Sri Aurobindo' terminology, and accommodate the aspirations of small actors has eclipsed the UN role as a driving force toward human unity. Cox argues that the UN as an institutional framework has the potential to represent a "multi-civilizational world," but it is not successful so far as it has been subject to competing interests of the major powers (Cox 2002, 184). The provision of veto power for the five permanent members of the Security Council has affected the prospects of the rise of an egalitarian world structure. Sri Aurobindo had cautioned against making the Security Council an elite group. According to him, the arrangement that provides "preponderant place to the five great powers in the Security Council" of the UN ensures a "strong surviving element of oligarchy" in the international body (CWSA 1997, vol. 25, 782). Moller reiterates this argument, "The five victorious nations decided that they should govern the world. Is that the best solution?" (Moller 2000, 173). Like Sri Aurobindo, he argues that a new international system cannot be built upon sovereign nation-states as participants but has to be built on a transfer of sovereignty from the nation-state to international institutions. Nation-states need to play active roles in international mechanism, but for the success of these mechanisms they have to partially transfer their sovereignty (Moller 2000, 146). For this to happen, some kind of "creative destruction" on the part of the nation-states needs to take place. Weiss and Thakur reflect this urgency, "states react, cope, and eventually agree under duress to construct institutions in the face of such challenges. Perhaps it has always been the case that too few institutions have developed too late. But in the twenty-first century, the urgent nature of many collective problems suggests that we must build more and soon" (Weiss and Thakur 2010, 4). The challenges confronted by the UN have given rise to speculations, or ideas of alternatives such as L-20 for a fair world order (Martin 2005). Thakur and Thompson point out that the L-20 idea reflects contemporary geopolitical and economic realities with a decisive break from past practices, and prospects of emerging as a defining global institution of the twenty-first century since the UN and many other existing international bodies have entered a period of stagnation (Thakur and Thompson 2006, 301).

Joseph Baratta in his work on world federalist movement, that was prevalent during the Cold War years, argues that though the movement has lost its momentum in the post–Cold War period, various movements toward global governance reflect the spirit of the federalist movement. He terms them post-federalist movements and argues that the ongoing movements for global governance are based on a "federalist culture" (Baratta 1999, 341). These movements need to be actively factored in the UN reforms for making this international organization a primary tool for raising "collective consciousness" for addressing the global problems. The measures such as the enlargement of the membership of the Security Council, financial autonomy, and giving wider recognition to the leadership of the Secretary General can be steps in this regard. Richard Falk makes the case for a Global People's Assembly, in which non-state actors and their concerns can be represented, and an Economic Security Council for the reform of the international body (Falk 2006). Thakur and Weiss talk about three UNs, adding one (comprising actors not formally part of the UN but are closely associated with it) to Inis Claude's two UNs: comprising member states and secretariats. They argue that all the three are essential for effective policy formulation at the UN (Thakur and Weiss 1999, 21).

One of the major challenges of global governance, Thakur and Thompson argue, is a double disconnect: the first disconnect between the distribution of hard and soft power in the real world and the distribution of decision-making authority within intergovernmental institutions. The second disconnect is between the number and type of actors playing expanding roles in national and international arenas and the concentration of decision-making authority within intergovernmental institutions (Thakur and Thompson 2006, 298). They refer to the 2004 report of the High Panel, appointed by the UN Secretary General, which argues that "the importance of international peace and security importantly depends on there being a common global understanding, and acceptance, of when the application of force is both legal and legitimate" (Thakur and Thompson 2006, 297). This argument is in consonance with Sri Aurobindo's assertion that for the development of a common global understanding it is necessary that the nation-states give up rigid thinking and policies. Rosenau's argument is somewhat similar to that of Sri Aurobindo as he adopts an evolutionary perspective on it and argues that governance does not happen suddenly as "circumstances have to be suitable, people have to be amenable to collective decisions being made, tendencies toward organization have to develop, habits of cooperation have to evolve, and a readiness not to impede the processes of emergence and evolution has to persist" (Rosenau 1995, 17).

For Sri Aurobindo, the underlying impulse behind IHU is the achievement of the highest possible world unity which may take any shape but what is more important is that the nation-states must come out of the confinements of national ego to participate in this unity. Hence, a world union can be neither rigid nor dogmatic nor subject to dictates of a particular state or group of states. It cannot succumb to hegemonic ambitions of any particular state because a true world union needs to be based on the "principle of equality in which considerations of size and strength will not enter" (CWSA 1997, vol. 25, 783). This world structure will be like a rich tapestry in which different shades of color are placed in their requisite places or like an ornament in which precious stones are placed in symmetry. In this arrangement there will be equal respect for diverse cultures and patterns of life with the principles of equality and distinction, not domination and disintegration, being all pervasive. The UN in its current functioning does not appear to reflect these principles.

Conclusion

For effective global governance, a change of consciousness—both individual and collective—is necessary, Sri Aurobindo would argue. He would further argue that for global governance it is necessary to have perspectives from various cultural traditions. The ideal human community has its roots not in one particular tradition but in many traditions. It is necessary to identify various sources as they help enrich the discourse on the subject, bring diverse perspectives on it, and contribute to the real goal of governance—a peaceful and harmonious world, in which, as Sri Aurobindo points out, all nation-states whether small or big, weak or powerful, will have an equal voice. Sri Aurobindo's distinction between national ego and nation-soul is quite crucial, and a key for a reflection on the ongoing discourse on global governance. His IHU has at its core an evolutionary perspective of human unity, in which nation-states adopt a broader perspective of national interest. This can be possible when nation-states see the wider side of nationalism—nation-soul—and act accordingly rather than seeing its narrow side—the national-ego—and act accordingly. He would not undermine the role of nationalism in the formation of a larger human unity, but nationalism that is rigid and narrow creates an obstacle for world unity. Aggressive nationalism was the chief reason behind the First and Second World Wars, and also behind the wars further past, and it must be transcended, toward larger human unity. In that sense, it can be argued nationalism can be an obstacle, and can be an aid; hence what aspects of nationalism a nation-state adheres to is quite critical. As his arguments on the values of liberty, equality, and fraternity have indicated, mere formation of associations or creation of laws may not help global governance, unless there is a deeper conviction on part of nation-states to follow the laws and abide by the ideal. His ideas about international organizations, particularly the UN, can be seen from this perspective.

Sri Aurobindo "seeks to answer the age long philosophical questions about the nature of the world, viz., how has the world been created, why has it been created and where lies its destination" (Trivedi 1971, 137). Also, the debate on global governance does not shy away from these age-long questions including the question how to reconcile narrow national interests, driven by psychological egoism, and broader world unity, driven by a consciousness that transcends egoism. From this point of view, Sri Aurobindo's ideas are relevant. Particularly his argument that insistence on formal mechanisms, without changing the internal approach or attitude toward international organizations, would not be sufficient to graduate the current world into an ideal human community. Kartus wrote in 1960, "The Western world knows far more of Marx's call to the working men to unite than it does of Sri Aurobindo's message to the humanity to unite. Yet it is a message such as that of Sri Aurobindo with which humanity must become familiar and which it must need in order attain human unity" (Kartus 1960, 314). A tremendous optimism is visible in Sri Aurobindo's writings throughout the pages of IHU. Sri Aurobindo was cognizant of the problems such as colonialism, the fragile character of international bodies such as the League of Nations, the preponderance of the few powers in the UN, chaotic distribution of power grapping the world in his time; he, however, sheltered a strong belief that the world is evolving toward a better future. Even if one does not take into account the evolution part of the main argument of Sri Aurobindo, his emphasis that there is a need for an internal change—a change in the rigid mindset and behavior—on part of the nation-states is of capital significance for a debate on international organizations and global governance.

Notes

1. For an overview of global governance and its various aspects see, for instance, Murphy (1995), Finkelstein (1995), Weiss and Thakur (2010), Rosenau (1995), and Weiss and Wilkinson (2014).
2. For a detailed exposition of Hegel's philosophy, see Cullen (1979), and Varma (1974). For a comparison between Hegel and Sri Aurobindo see Mahapatra (2007) and Maitra (1968, 237–371).
3. For an explication of the liberal school of IR see Keohane and Nye (1989). The opening sentence of the first chapter reads, "We live in an era of interdependence" (p. 1). The authors in the same page quoted Henry Kissinger, one of the earlier champions of realism in international politics. The quote is relevant for the main argument of this chapter: "The traditional agenda of international affairs—the balance among major powers, the security of nations—no longer defines our perils or our possibilities ... Now we are entering a new era. Old international patterns are crumbling; old slogans are uninstructive; old solutions are unavailing. The world has become interdependent in economics, in communications; in human aspirations."
4. For instance, see Zaehner (1971) and Sethna (1973).
5. For details of the Auroville city see its website http://www.auroville.org/ (Accessed June 14, 2016). The opening page of the website reads, "Auroville wants to be a universal town where men and women of all countries are able to live in peace and progressive harmony above all creeds, all politics and all nationalities."
6. In June 2015, the UN Secretary General, Ban Ki-moon, reflected the exasperation of the international community at the failure of the UN Security Council to develop a consensus on Syria. He urged, "It is time to find an exit from this madness." See

New York Times (2015). Earlier, then UN High Commissioner for Human Rights, Navi Pillay, had observed, "There will always be some disagreement within the international community on how to respond to a given situation; but when tens of thousands of civilian lives are threatened, as currently in Syria, the world expects the Security Council to unite and act." See United Nations (2013).

References

Annan, Kofi. 1998. "The Quiet Revolution." *Global Governance* 4, 2: 123–138.
Baratta, J. P. 1999. "The International Federalist Movement: Towards Global Governance." *Peace and Change* 24, 3: 340–372.
Basu, Samar. 1999. *The UNO, the World Government and the Ideal of World Union*. Pondicherry: Sri Aurobindo Ashram.
Coate, R. A. and Murphy, C. N. 1995. "Editors' Note." *Global Governance* 1, 1: 1–2.
Commission on Human Security. 2003. *Human Security Now*. New York: Commission on Human Security. Also available at http://www.unocha.org/humansecurity/chs/finalreport/index.html (Accessed June 14, 2015).
Cox, R. W. 2002. *The Political Economy of a Plural World: Critical Reflections on Power, Morals and Civilization*. New York: Routledge.
Cullen, Bernard. 1979. *Hegel's Social and Political Thought: An Introduction*. Bristol: Gill and Macmillan.
Curry, W. B. 1939. *The Case for Federal Union*. Middlesex: Penguin Book Ltd.
Falk, Richard. 2006. "The United Nations System: Prospects for Renewal." In Nayyar, Deepak ed. *Governing Globalization: Issues and Institutions*. New Delhi: Oxford University Press, 177–208.
Finkelstein, Lawrence. 1995. "What Is Global Governance?" *Global Governance* 1, 3: 367–372.
Giandomenico, Picco et al. 2001. *Crossing the Divide: Dialogue among Civilizations*. New Jersey: Seton Hall University.
Kartus, Sidney. 1960. "World Unity." In Chaudhuri, H. and Speigelberg, F. eds. *The Integral Philosophy of Sri Aurobindo*. London: George Allen and Unwin Ltd.
Keohane, R. O. and Nye, J. S. 1989. *Power and Interdependence*. Glenview, IL: Scott, Foresman and Company.
Mahapatra, D. A. 2007. "Political Philosophy of Hegel and Sri Aurobindo: A Comparison." *The Indian Journal of Political Science* 68, 3: 483–496.
Maitra, S. K. 1968. *The Meeting of the East and the West in Sri Aurobindo's Philosophy*. Pondicherry: Sri Aurobindo Ashram.
Martin, Paul. 2005. "A Global Answer to Global Problems: The Case for a New Leaders' Forum." *Foreign Affairs* 84, 43: 2–6.
Minor, R. N. 1979. "Sri Aurobindo's Integral View of Other Religions." *Religious Studies* 15, 3: 365–377.
Mohanty, J. N. 1993. *Essays on Indian Philosophy, Traditional and Modern*. Delhi: Oxford University Press.
Moller, O. J. 2000. *The End of Internationalism or World Governance?* Westport: Praeger.
Murphy, Craig. 1995. *International Organization and Industrial Change: Global Governance since 1850*. Cambridge, UK: Polity.

New York Times. 2015. "U.N. Chief: World Should Be Ashamed at Failure to End Syria Conflict," *New York Times*, June 30.
Rosenau, J. N. 1995. "Governance in the Twenty-first Century." *Global Governance* 1, 1: 13–43.
Ruggie, J. G. 2010. "Foreword." In Weiss, T. G. and Thakur, R. eds. *Global Governance and the UN: An Unfinished Journey*. Bloomington: Indiana University Press.
Sethna, K. D. 1973. *Teilhard de Chardin and Sri Aurobindo: A Focus on Fundamentals*. Varanasi: Bharatiya Vidya Prakasan.
Sri Aurobindo. 1997. *The Complete Works of Sri Aurobindo, vol. 25*. Pondicherry: Sri Aurobindo Ashram. The Complete Works are available at http://www.sriaurobindoashram.org/ashram/sriauro/writings.php (Accessed June 14, 2016).
Sri Aurobindo Ashram Trust. 1977. *The Mother on Auroville*. Pondicherry: All India Books.
Streit, C. K. 1939. *Union Now: A Proposal for a Federal Union of the Democracies of the North Atlantic*. New York: Harper & Brothers Publishers. Also available at http://www.constitution.org/aun/union_now.htm (Accessed May 1, 2018).
Thakur, R. and Thompson, A. S. 2006. "The L-20 in the Twenty-First Century." In English, J., Thakur, R. and Cooper, A. F. eds. *Reforming from the Top: A Leaders' 20 Summit*. Tokyo: United Nations University Press, 296–310.
Thakur, R. and Weiss, T. G. 1999. "United Nations 'Policy': An Argument with Three Illustrations." *International Studies Perspectives* 10, 1: 18–35.
Trivedi, Ramchandra. 1971. "The Philosophy of Sri Aurobindo: Its Epistemological and Conceptive Significance." *East and West* 21, 1/2: 137–154.
Uberoi, J. P. S. 2002. *The European Modernity: Truth, Science and Method*. New Delhi: Oxford University Press.
United Nations. 1992. "An Agenda for Peace." Available at http://www.un-documents.net/a47-277.htm (Accessed August 14, 2018).
United Nations. 2013. "Security Council Must Unite to Protect Civilians in Conflict Zones—UN Officials." Available at http://www.un.org/apps/news/story.asp?NewsID=44127&Cr=protection+of+civilians&Cr1#.UXRzYLXUd0s (Accessed August 14, 2018).
Varma, V. P. 1960–1961. "Sri Aurobindo and Greek Philosophy," *Philosophy East and West* 10, 3/4: 135–148.
Varma, V. P. 1974. *Political Philosophy of Hegel*. New Delhi: Trimurti Publications Pvt. Ltd.
Weiss, T. G. and Wilkinson, R., eds. 2014. *International Organization and Global Governance*. London: Routledge.
Weiss, T. G. and Thakur, R. 2010. *Global Governance and the UN: An Unfinished Journey*. Bloomington: Indiana University Press.
Wendt, Alexander. 2003. "Why a World State Is Inevitable." *European Journal of International Relations* 9, 4: 491–542.
Zaehner, R. C. 1971. *Evolution in Religion: A Study in Sri Aurobindo and Pierre Teilhard de Chardin*. Oxford: Clarendon Press.

Part Five

Vision of India

13

The Force behind the Indian Renaissance and the Crucial Significance of Auroville's Emergence

Aryadeep S. Acharya

On August 15, 1947, India attained her Independence from British rule. August 15, 1947, was also the seventy-fifth birthday of one of the early pioneers of the freedom movement, Sri Aurobindo. However, on that momentous day, he was not living in India proper but in what was then regarded as French India, more precisely, in the town of Pondicherry where he had been residing for the past thirty-seven years, in pursuit of what he increasingly came to regard as new vistas of world evolution. A request came to him from All India Radio, Tiruchirapalli (the modern Trichy), to give a message to the country. Sri Aurobindo termed his message a *"personal declaration"* and elaborated the five dreams he had been cherishing since long. Before elaborating the dreams, he wrote:

> To me personally it must naturally be gratifying that this date which was notable only for me because it was my own birthday celebrated annually by those who have accepted my gospel of life, should have acquired this vast significance. As a mystic, I take this identification, not as a coincidence or fortuitous accident, but as a **sanction and seal of the Divine Power which guides my steps on the work with which I began life.**
>
> (Sri Aurobindo 2006, 474)

My stress on the last sentence in the above passage is deliberate as my aim in this chapter is to first investigate briefly the presence, the action, the influence, or the intervention of the deeper or supraphysical factors that were at work in the lives of Sri Aurobindo and his colleague and co-worker, the Mother. Having done that, my second aim is to show how the Auroville Universal Township constitutes a visible, material, social climax of their lifelong experiments and explorations. Finally, my third aim is to show how Auroville, if she fructifies fully in the earth atmosphere, in terms of both material achievement and ideological success, could pave the way for India's supreme renaissance with a consequent impact on the world civilization.

The Deeper or Supraphysical Forces: Their Ways of Working and the Secret of India's Rise

At Pondicherry, Sri Aurobindo gradually developed his worldview, his philosophy of life, of evolution, of social progress. He dwelt at length on poetry, on art and culture, and on education. He also wrote extensively on India. To further his vision of new evolution, he also developed and elaborated the modus operandi of a new approach to and practice (sadhana) of yoga which he termed "Integral Yoga." In all that he wrote on the subject of yoga, there is one rare, seldom-noted sentence—in fact, it is only a part of a sentence, but it may help to understand or give glimpses of the ways of the workings of the deeper or supraphysical forces in human life. It reads: "the Divine gives the fruits, not by the measure of the sadhana but by the measure of the soul and its aspiration" (Sri Aurobindo 2013, 55). The words "the measure of the soul and its aspiration" suggest that a human soul has a measure! It has a size. It has its level of maturity, its stage of evolution, its height, its depth, its caliber, its reach, its scope, its strength. It has an aspiration for something higher, nobler, diviner. All these taken together impel the divine force to act, to "give fruits," irrespective of one's efforts, "sadhana." In other words, there are elements in an individual, quite separate from what she or he calls self, which have their own lives, their relevance, their "say" in the individual's destiny.

An intimate, unconditional rapport between the divine and "the measure of the soul and its aspiration" in the lives of Sri Aurobindo and the Mother could be found in various incidents and experiences that spontaneously occurred to them. In the year 1893, Sri Aurobindo landed at Bombay, today's Mumbai, after spending fourteen of his formative and academic years in England. Referring to it, he wrote in a letter fifty-six years later, in April 1949:

> Since I set foot on Indian soil on the Apollo Bunder in Bombay, I began to have spiritual experiences, but these were not divorced from this world but had an inner and intimate bearing on it, such as a feeling of the Infinite pervading material space and the Immanent inhabiting material objects and bodies. At the same time I found myself entering supraphysical worlds and planes with influences and an effect from them upon the material plane, so I could make no sharp divorce or irreconcilable opposition between what I have called the two ends of existence and all that lies between them.
>
> (Sri Aurobindo 2011, 233–234)

There is his reference to spontaneous spiritual experiences in another letter, written a decade earlier, in October 1935:

> The mind's canons of the rational and the possible do not govern spiritual life and experience (of)...the Self, the Adwaita, Vedantic. Atman.... my own first experience of the Self, long before I knew even what Yoga was or that there was such a thing, at a time when I had no religious feeling, no wish for spiritual knowledge, no aspiration beyond the mind, only a contented agnosticism and the

impulse towards poetry and politics... began in London, sprouted the moment I set foot on Apollo Bunder, touching Indian soil, flowered one day in the first year of my stay in Baroda, at the moment when there threatened to be an accident to my carriage.

(Sri Aurobindo 2011, 232–233)

A. B. Purani, one of his attendants, records from memory what Sri Aurobindo had said in the course of an informal conversation:

Once I visited Ganganath (Chandod) after Brahmananda's death when Keshwananda was there. With my Europeanized mind I had no faith in image-worship and I hardly believed in the presence of God. I went to Kernali where there are several temples. There is one of Kali and when I looked at the image I saw the living presence there. For the first time, I believed in the presence of God.

(Purani 1995, 609)

Below are two more extracts from Sri Aurobindo which explain the "measure of the soul and its aspiration":

Kashmir is a magnificent place, its rivers unforgettable and on one of its mountains with a shrine of Shankaracharya on it I got my second realization of the Infinite (long before I started Yoga).

(Sri Aurobindo 2011, 235)

When she (the Mother) was twelve or thirteen, every evening many teachers came to her and taught her various spiritual disciplines. Among them was a dark Asiatic figure. When we first met, she immediately recognized me as the dark Asiatic figure whom she used to see a long time ago. That she should come here and work with me for a common goal was, as it were, a divine dispensation.

(Sri Aurobindo 2012, 36)

The above quotes demonstrate that the soul personality in the person of Aravinda Ackroyd Ghosh *and Blanche Rachel* Mirra Alfassa, the names of Sri Aurobindo and the Mother in their youth, *was* so extraordinarily advanced, so evolved, so conscious, so missioned, so destined that they used to experience openings to incredible riches of consciousness—the marvels of the inner kingdoms—even before their minds came to comprehend the existence of such kingdoms, got interested in them, and asked consciously for them. And when they asked consciously for them, when they strove to realize those higher or diviner states of consciousness in their owns lives, Aravinda Ackroyd Ghosh, the intellectual youth, emerged in time as Mahayogi Sri Aurobindo, and Blanche Rachel Mirra Alfassa emerged as the Divine Mother. According to Sri Aurobindo, the Mother is "the consciousness and force of the Supreme" who was "inwardly above the human even in childhood" and who "comes in order to bring down the supramental" the descent of which "makes her full manifestation here possible" (Sri

Aurobindo 2012, 14, 32, 34). These two mighty "receptacles" then became the leaders of the human march and offered a grand vision of human destiny as well as the light and inspiration to walk on the path to realize that destiny.

One of the central affirmations of their vision and experience is that India is a living entity, a living soul. In fact, they regarded India much more than a soul—a Godhead, Mother India. India's journey, India's progress and evolution, India's future occupies a preeminent place in their world-vision. Their entire life and work, directly or indirectly, form a base to ignite and propel the Indian renaissance side by side with the world renaissance. One of the Mother's messages reads: "The Soul of India is one and indivisible. India is conscious of her mission in the world. She is waiting for the exterior means of manifestation" (The Mother 2004, 351). It can therefore be inferred that just as "the measure of the soul and its aspiration" are the paramount realities which invoke spiritual realizations, guide the steps, mold the lives, the work, the mission, and the destiny of deserving men and women, similarly, the soul of India too has its measure and its aspiration. It cannot but guide the steps, create the human instruments, create circumstances, and lead the country to her lofty mission. This inner soul reality of India, then, is the force behind the Indian renaissance. It is the perception of this inner soul reality of India that led an early prophet of the Indian renaissance Vivekananda to declare toward the end of nineteenth century: "None can desist India any more; never is she going to sleep any more; no outward powers can hold her back any more; for the infinite giant is rising to her feet" (Swami Vivekananda 2006, 765).

Auroville: Culmination of an Evolutionary Undertaking

There are many instances which convey that the vision of Sri Aurobindo and the Mother was not static but growing and evolving at a constant rapid pace. Sri Aurobindo once wrote in a letter to a disciple, "I used Savitri as a means of ascension. I began with it on a certain mental level, each time I could reach a higher level I rewrote from that level" (Sri Aurobindo 2004, 272). Referring to his pre-Pondicherry writings, he wrote in 1937, "My spiritual consciousness and knowledge at that was as nothing to what it is now" (Sri Aurobindo 2011, 7). In his essay "Indian Culture and External Influence" written in March 1919, he expressed serious concerns about India taking the path of European industrialism and consequently generating not only wealth but also "social discords and moral plagues and cruel problems" and "becoming the slaves of the economic aim in life and losing the spiritual principle of our culture." However, six and a half years later, in a casual conversion with the disciples, he changed his view to the effect that India must acquire wealth first of all by embarking on the path of large-scale industrial production and that the problems of industrialization could be addressed later and that they were bound to disappear (Sri Aurobindo 1997a, 46 and Purani 1995, 303, 304).

In her later years, the Mother had withdrawn from daily activities of the Ashram and confined herself to her room. On a few occasions, her answers to various questions that had been put to her about a decade and a half earlier were read out. On listening to them, she would say to Satprem—a French disciple and writer in whom she had confided most of the extraordinary experiences and experiments of her last years—

that some of her answers were "old," "cut-and-dried," "intended for children," and once even expressed surprise that she could have spoken those words. In 1967, on being shown a photo of hers at the Playground with some disciples when she was granted Indian Citizenship in 1954, she said:

> It's amusing. When I look back at all those things, I have a very acute sensation of looking at my childhood, it all seems to me so childish!... Still in the illusion of the world. And for how many years?... Since something like 1915, I felt—constantly felt—I was acting on the Command: the Command from above. The personal impulsion had disappeared. Since as long as that, 1915, and in that condition, there have been a whole evolution and transformation. And now, when I look back, not only all I used to do, but the way of looking at things, especially the way of looking at things... (seems to me childish). (The Mother 1981b, 44, 170, 239)

A few more extracts from the Mother's conversations with Satprem illustrate the point:

> ....when I had those gatherings (*at the Playground*), on some days I would feel the full Force like this (gesture of descent), and everything I said would come direct. At other times, it was the memory that spoke, and then it would be so flat!
> .... on certain days That would speak (gesture from above), and I would only feel my mouth move and hear the sound of my voice. At other times it was the whole storehouse of memories, and what was expressed was just worthless.
> And these things (showing the Playground Talk) are still too cut-and-dried. But I quite understand that if now I were to tell experiences like the one I had this morning, it would be almost incomprehensible—too far from (people's) consciousness. (The Mother 1981b, 44, 170, 239)

The above quotes indicate that unlike many spiritual teachers who realize a higher state of consciousness and then are known as realized beings, in the case of Sri Aurobindo and the Mother there was no full stop. They had reached a state of constant progress in their consciousness. It is important to grasp this point because Auroville, as a universal township, took shape during the last eight years of the Mother's life and, therefore, has the benefit of her lifelong explorations and experiences of the realities of the divine consciousness. The comprehensive concept of Auroville, the designs of the town, the organization of collective life, the approaches to various aspects of individual and collective life, the purposes of various Auroville projects, the very name of the universal township "Auroville," the names of some of the communities within Auroville, and, very importantly, the Charter of Auroville were all shaped by the Mother's latest perceptions and vision of what is needed for human progress and transformation. Earlier, she had developed the multifaceted community of the Sri Aurobindo Ashram at Pondicherry. She had also guided a dynamic new experiment in education. In both of these, she poured her time and energy and built a base for the collective application and practice of Integral Yoga. Auroville has, therefore, the advantage of integrating her latest experiences as well as the experiments and progress made at the Ashram. It could be argued that her vision of Auroville is a culmination of the exceptional undertaking that the Sri Aurobindo Ashram was and is. Just as the Mother regarded Sri Aurobindo's epic poem *Savitri* as "*supreme revelation of Sri Aurobindo's vision*," Auroville, too, could be regarded as a supreme revelation of the Mother's own latest knowledge, insights, illuminations, and vision of the most appropriate approaches to the diverse aspects of individual and collective life necessary to evolve and perfect itself.

It follows that in her vision of Auroville, too, one could trace the stamp of higher or diviner forces at work. For instance, the Charter of Auroville—a brief four-point document which has inspired the imagination of many youths and pioneers of Auroville—was written in moments of what I would call "consciousness action." Two disciples, probably Auroville workers in the field of education, had prepared two drafts of the charter and sent them to the Mother. Like a teacher who corrects worksheets sent by students, she went through them and improvised on them in a separate piece of paper. Then, some three weeks before the Auroville inauguration, in the course of her regular conversations with Satprem, she "unrolls a big parchment on her windowsill, facing Sri Aurobindo's Samadhi. (Then) perched on a low stool and armed with a huge black felt-pen that draws cuneiform-like letters, she starts copying Auroville's Charter while commenting on it." What was more striking and noteworthy was when she finished writing, she said, "It's not me who wrote all this … I noticed something so interesting: when it comes it's imperative, there's no room for arguing; I write it down—whatever I may be doing I am FORCED to write it down. But when it's not there, it's just not there! Even if I try to remember, nothing comes, it's not there! So it's clear that it doesn't come from here: it comes from somewhere above" (The Mother 1981c, 25–26). Viewed within these contexts, it could be argued that the Auroville Charter is an example of a collaborative outcome between the human and the divine! Two residents of Auroville wrote a draft and a consciousness beyond the human mind revised it through the Mother! The result was the birth of the first-ever-of-its-kind city charter in the history of mankind.

Auroville Charter

1. Auroville belongs to nobody in particular. Auroville belongs to humanity as a whole. But to live in Auroville one must be the willing servitor of the Divine Consciousness.
2. Auroville will be the place of an unending education, of constant progress, and a youth that never ages.
3. Auroville wants to be the bridge between the past and the future. Taking advantage of all discoveries from without and from within, Auroville will boldly spring towards future realizations.
4. Auroville will be a site of material and spiritual researches for a living embodiment of an actual Human Unity. (The Mother 2004, 193–194)

The stamp of the higher or divine power on Auroville had been emphasized by the Mother on many occasions. At the center of Auroville is the Matrimandir—a very distinct creation, not just an architectural creation but, like the Charter of Auroville, a revolutionary creation. One of the Mother's messages about the Matmandir reads: "*Matrimandir is directly under the influence of the Divine and certainly He arranges things better than we could do ourselves*" (The Mother 2004, 225). On another occasion, in course of a conversation with a disciple, she stressed:

> This birth of Auroville wasn't preceded by any thought; as always, it was simply a Force acting, like a sort of absolute manifesting, and it was so strong [when the idea of Auroville presented itself to Mother] that I could have told people, "Even if you don't believe in it, even if all circumstances appear to be quite unfavourable, I KNOW THAT AUROVILLE WILL BE. It may be in a hundred years, it may be in a thousand years, I don't know, but Auroville will be, because it has been decreed.
>
> (The Mother 1981a, 138)

A Major Dimension of Auroville: The Indian Renaissance

One of the major teachings of Sri Aurobindo and the Mother is that an individual is a microscopic representation of the macro-scope. By transforming his or her inner difficulties and imperfections, one can help in transforming the same difficulties and imperfections in other human beings. Similarly, India with her spiritual wealth and legacy and inner capabilities becomes, by the virtue of that legacy and capabilities, a representative of humanity propelling it to move further in its evolution. Just a few weeks before the inauguration of Auroville, when the Mother was asked for a message for a conference in Delhi, this subtle truth of things appeared to her with great force of clarity. She wrote: "India has become the symbolic representation of all the difficulties of modern mankind." And, "India will be the land of its resurrection—the resurrection to a higher and truer life." She elaborated further:

> And the clear vision: the same thing which in the history of the universe made the earth the symbolic representation of the universe so as to concentrate the work on one point, the same phenomenon is now taking place: India is the representation of all human difficulties on earth, and it is in India that the... cure will be found. And then, that is why—THAT IS WHY I was made to start Auroville.
> It came and it was so clear, so tremendously powerful!"
> ... It was very interesting. It remained the whole time, for more than an hour, such a strong and clear vision, as if suddenly everything became clear. I often used to wonder about it (not "wonder," but there was a tension to understand why things, here in India, have become such a chaos, with such sordid difficulties, and all of it piling up), and instantly, everything became clear, like that. It was really interesting. And immediately there was: "Here is why you have made Auroville."
>
> (The Mother 1981c, 17)

This strong experience of the Mother brings out an eternal link between India and Auroville. It creates a profound and powerful relevance of Auroville for India. Auroville as a torchbearer for India, as a role model for India—this is not just a revelation of the

Mother, but, viewed in context of India's rich spiritual legacy and Auroville's morning fresh adventure into the future, a necessary, an advisable, and a logical step for India. Of course, the actual success of this depends upon the residents, friends, associates of Auroville, and the disciples of Sri Aurobindo worldwide to live and to realize the ideals and spirit of Auroville—and their ability to convey and convince the Indian elite of this view.

How Can Auroville Contribute to the Building of a New India

So far, our study in this chapter has brought out the following points:

1. The lives of Sri Aurobindo and the Mother exemplify an extraordinarily dynamic action of an ever-growing consciousness.
2. The Indian renaissance has profound soul dimensions—India's destiny is not just to become a developed country among other developed countries but a new kind of country where the power of a truer consciousness has created a higher equilibrium.
3. Auroville, in essence, is an action of the same ever-growing true consciousness through the spiritually advanced instrumentality of the Mother, and the well-meaning and growing human instrumentality.
4. One of main purposes of Auroville is to propel India toward her true destiny—an India which has resolved within herself the difficulties that impede the further evolution of humankind with the help of Auroville's worldview, vision, ideals, aspirations, and approaches to individual and collective life.

How precisely can Auroville's worldview, vision, ideals, aspirations, and approaches to individual and collective life contribute toward India's rejuvenation? Here, three major ideas that anchor life in Auroville need specific attention:

Idea One: The Psychic Being as the Centripetal Power of All Life

The dominating idea of life in Auroville is that all life should be oriented toward the discovery of an all-knowing center, which is not a center but rather a new continent. Sri Aurobindo and the Mother call this the psychic being. The first point of a text written by the Mother "To be a true Aurovilian" reads:

> "The first necessity is the inner discovery in order to know what one truly is behind social, moral, cultural, racial and hereditary appearances.
> At the center there is a being free, vast and knowing, who awaits our discovery and who ought to become the active center of our being and our life in Auroville."
> (The Mother 2004, 207)

This collective aim helps create an environment to walk on, what Sri Aurobindo calls, the "sunlit path." According to the Mother, India needs this "sunlit path" to overcome the difficulties she is facing in contemporary times. Following is one of her messages, which she wrote toward the last phase of her bodily life, in 1970.

> India is the country where the psychic law *can and must* rule and the time has come for that *here*. Besides, it is the only possible salvation for this country whose consciousness has unfortunately been distorted by the influence and domination of a foreign nation, but which, in spite of everything, possesses a unique spiritual heritage.
> (The Mother 2004, 370)

This "psychic law" is the very first organizing principle of collective life in Auroville and it is this "law," so to speak, which can bring about the "salvation for this country." In other words, what could be the highest state of collective existence in India is being invoked, aspired for, aimed at in Auroville.

Idea Two: Progressive Realization of an Actual Human Unity

The earliest message of the Mother on Auroville reads,

> Auroville wants to be a universal town where men and women of all countries are able to live in peace and progressive harmony, above all creeds, all politics and all nationalities. The purpose of Auroville is to realise human unity.
> (The Mother 2004, 188)

Eighteen years earlier, in 1947, in his Independence Day message to India, Sri Aurobindo wrote: "A new spirit of oneness will take hold of human race." He wrote this while explaining the role that India could play in bringing *the countries of the world closer into some sort of a world union in which each country would retain its freedom while at the same time "forming the outer basis of a fairer, brighter and nobler life for all mankind"* (Sri Aurobindo 2011, 479). Viewed in this context, the presence of a universal township on Indian soil dedicated to the ideal of human unity can provide an inspiration for India, for India's leaders and activists in diverse fields, to be a catalyst for a world-union. One of the works of Sri Aurobindo is titled *The Ideal of Human Unity*. It was written almost fifty years before the founding of Auroville. In this book, Sri Aurobindo discussed the multiple possibilities and challenges for actualizing human unity. But always his conclusive stress was on the psychological unity which alone could provide a lasting base for unity in other spheres—political or social. Auroville in this sense is a laboratory of human unity, a nucleus that can grow and expand gradually on a wider scale and provide a sound basis for the healthy unity of humankind.

Idea Three: "Auroville, at last a place where one will be able to think only of the future"—the Mother

Futurism or futurology has recently gained international attention as a subject. Frequently, we see new publications about the emerging future, especially about the impact of new technological innovations on future life. More than fifty years ago, elaborating her concept of life in Auroville, the Mother stressed that Auroville is meant to be a city for studying, contemplating, and exploring the future. "Man is a transitional being"—this phrase is the cornerstone of the vision of Sri Aurobindo and the Mother. It is a revolutionary idea which, if understood fully, has the power to reorganize the social life of humanity on a new basis. Auroville is a laboratory to work out this idea and has the potential to set an example of a future human society beyond the divisions of religion, beyond capitalism and communism, beyond fixed intellectual beliefs and dogmas, beyond traditional spirituality and rigid uniformity.

Three Major Projects of Auroville

In this section, I will focus on the three major projects of Auroville and elaborate briefly their possible contribution to the Indian renaissance.

Project One: Matrimandir

Matri is a Sanskrit word for the Mother and *Mandir* is a Sanskrit word for temple. A deeper inquiry into the attributes and purpose of the Matrimandir would throw light on its significance. The main room or the inner chamber of the Matrimandir is the materialization of the vision of the Mother. A writer called it the "*world's loudest silence*." Such is the power of the higher consciousness pervading this Chamber for those who are open and receptive. The mini-rooms housed in the twelve petals of the Matrimandir carry the names of noble qualities needed to walk on the path of progress and evolution: Sincerity, Humility, Gratitude, Perseverance, Aspiration, Receptivity, Progress, Courage, Goodness, Generosity, Equality, and Peace. The twelve gardens surrounding Matrimandir are meant to be more than gardens. They are meant to be the wordless communication of various attributes of spirit. The attributes are: Existence, Consciousness, Bliss, Light, Life, Power, Wealth, Utility, Progress, Youth, Harmony, and Perfection. All these aspects and attributes of a built spot, whose etymology refers to something sacred in India, serve the purpose of opening the collective mind to what is beyond itself—the higher or the diviner things.

Project Two: International Zone

In his book *The Human Cycle*, Sri Aurobindo writes:

> The nation or society, like the individual, has a body, an organic life, a moral and aesthetic temperament, a developing mind and a soul behind all these signs and powers for the sake of which they exist. One may say even that, like the individual, it essentially is a soul rather than has one; it is a group-soul that, once having attained to a separate distinctness, must become more and more self-conscious and find itself more and more fully as it develops its corporate action and mentality and its organic self-expressive life.
>
> (Sri Aurobindo 1997b, 35)

The International Zone of Auroville is precisely meant to help nations "become more and more self-conscious," to find themselves "more and more fully," and to develop their "corporate action and mentality and its organic self-expressive life." It does this by identifying and encouraging distinctive strengths, qualities, aspirations, achievements, and attributes of each country. This research-based endeavor by means of national pavilions can draw out the best of each country and help make the collective human life a joyous, progressive, and greatly enriched existence. Such national pavilions in the International Zone of Auroville could reflect a new kind of United Nations and, in a sense, complement the existing United Nations based in New York. In Sri Aurobindo's vision, India and America represent two opposite poles of existence—the spiritual and the material—which must unite for a better and bright world order. From this perspective, it is only appropriate that there should be a kind of a complementary United Nations in India. Obviously, such a development would enormously strengthen India's international stature as a constructive force, and foster a positive international understanding and goodwill which could effectively thwart possibilities of deadly confrontations between nations. There is also another interesting side to the International Zone. Indian Prime Minister Narendra Modi suggested in a speech in the Indian parliament in 2017 that each state of India should have centers or pavilions of all other states of India so that they become familiar with and develop appreciation for the culture, language, history, best traditions, and contribution of each other. Obviously, this will not only enrich the cultural fabric of the country but also strengthen national unity and cohesiveness. This idea was already envisioned by the Mother in Auroville more than fifty years ago in the sense that Bharat Nivas in Auroville has the provision for each state of India to have its mini-pavilion.

The International Zone of Auroville at the time of this writing is at a nascent stage but there are few individuals who, either individually or in small groups, are keeping the flame alive by organizing various meaningful activities. Notable are the Pavilion of Tibetan Culture, and the Unity Pavilion which seeks to be the catalyst for further development and which houses one of the world's three Peace Tables, carved by the Japanese-American woodworker and architect, George Nakashima. Future emergence of the International Zone depends upon the collaboration, commitment, and creativity of workers, scholars, of national and international organizations, the government of India, and the members of the Auroville Foundation set up by the Government of India. So far, UNESCO and the Government of India are Auroville's time-tested friends. What is especially needed is to articulate the potentialities of the International Zone to create roadmaps for realizing those potentialities.

Project Three: Sri Aurobindo International Institute of Educational Research (SAIIER)

Drawing inspiration from the educational philosophy of Sri Aurobindo and the Mother, SAIIER is the umbrella organization that facilitates the educational, vocational, and cultural activities in Auroville. There are nine schools within the ambit of SAIIER, besides a sports grounds, publication section, and art section. The Cultural Zone of Auroville is a primary support of the educational activities of SAIIER. Additionally,

Savitri Bhavan—a building complex for fostering research and study of Sri Aurobindo's epic poem *Savitri*—is also part of SAIIER. Nirodbaran, who was often a scribe for Sri Aurobindo in transcribing *Savitri*, said while laying the foundation of Savitri Bhavan that it is a twin to Matrimandir. This is sufficient to point out its relevance. Savitri Bhavan is a significant psychological and physical support to all students and researchers of *Savitri* worldwide. Another section of SAIIER is known as the University of Human Unity, which is not a university in the conventional sense of the term, but it has emerged as an online resource of multiple scholarly researches and teaching programs. Educational set-up in the world is going to see many differences in years to come with the avalanche of new technologies. SAIIER can take advantage of this by spreading its wings and taking up distant education and skill training using these technologies. Just like the International Zone of Auroville, SAIIER and the Cultural Zone also have the potential to emerge as outstanding international platforms serving the growth of knowledge and peace in the world.

Conclusion

The Auroville vision and the human endeavor to realize it represent the "exterior means of manifestations" for India's soul to fulfill her great mission in the world. In a conversation with a disciple the Mother once remarked, "Auroville's modest appearances are quite out of proportion to its true role in the invisible" (The Mother 1981a, 219). Similarly, on another occasion she observed, "I tell people that the creation of a city such as Auroville has more weight in the history of the earth than all the groupings in the world" (The Mother 1981b, 253). These words provide ample evidence of the extraordinary significance of Auroville in the perception of one who had inwardly attained a state of constant progress—the Mother. They also provide a clear message to all forward-looking individuals irrespective of divisions of race, religion, language, color, and economic status. The message is: "Keep Auroville up," that is, continue to work for and serve the mission of Auroville despite all challenges. Then, as surely as the sun is to rise tomorrow, Auroville will emerge into what I like to call the "Earth-Queen"; "the Rose-flower of the earth"; "a new kind of United Nations"; "the cultural, educational, architectural, and all-round world Olympics, 365 days a year, for centuries to come."

February 2018 witnessed the fiftieth anniversary of the foundation of Auroville. Inaugurating the event at Auroville, the Prime Minister of India Narendra Modi said, "Auroville was conceived with the vision of enveloping the whole of humanity in one small area. This would show that the future would see an integrated world. The fourth founding principle of Auroville is that it will connect the spiritual and material approaches of the contemporary world. As the world progresses materially through science and technology, it will increasingly long for and need spiritual orientation for social order and stability... May Auroville serve as a beacon to the world. May it be the guardian which calls for breaking down narrow walls of the mind. May it continue to invite everyone to celebrate the possibilities of humanity's one-ness" (Modi 2018). The participation of India's foremost political leader in Auroville's golden jubilee and his message on the occasion signaled his and his administration's openness to the lofty purpose and vision of Auroville. This is perhaps a good omen. A true and perpetual emergence of Auroville means India's supreme renaissance with its implications for a "fairer, brighter and nobler life for all mankind" (Sri Aurobindo, 2006, 479).

References

Modi, Narendra. 2018. Text of PM's address at Auroville, Puducherry, on February 25, 2018. Available at https://www.auroville.org/contents/4419 (Accessed May 15, 2018).
The Mother. 1981a. *Mother's Agenda, vol. 7*. Paris: Institut de Recherches Evolutives.
The Mother. 1981b. *Mother's Agenda, vol. 8*. Paris: Institut de Recherches Evolutives.
The Mother. 1981c. *Mother's Agenda, vol. 9*. Paris: Institut de Recherches Evolutives.
The Mother. 2003. *Questions and Answers 1929–1931, Collected Works of the Mother (hereafter CWM), vol. 3*. Pondicherry: Sri Aurobindo Ashram.
The Mother. 2004. *Words of the Mother I, CWM, vol. 13*. Pondicherry: Sri Aurobindo Ashram.
Purani, A. B. 1995. *Evening Talks with Sri Aurobindo*. Puducherry, India: Sri Aurobindo Society.
Sri Aurobindo, 1997a. *The Renaissance in India, Complete Works of Sri Aurobindo (hereafter CWSA), vol. 20*. Pondicherry: Sri Aurobindo Ashram.
Sri Aurobindo. 1997b. *The Human Cycle, CWSA, vol. 25*. Pondicherry: Sri Aurobindo Ashram.
Sri Aurobindo. 2004. *Letters on Poetry and Art, CWSA, vol. 27*. Pondicherry: Sri Aurobindo Ashram.
Sri Aurobindo. 2006. *Autobiographical Notes and Other Writings of Historical Interest, CWSA, vol. 36*. Pondicherry: Sri Aurobindo Ashram.
Sri Aurobindo. 2011. *Letters on Himself and the Ashram, CWSA, vol. 35*. Pondicherry: Sri Aurobindo Ashram.
Sri Aurobindo. 2012. *The Mother with Letters on the Mother, CWSA, vol. 32*. Pondicherry: Sri Aurobindo Ashram.
Sri Aurobindo. 2013. *Letters on Yoga II, CWSA, vol. 29*. Pondicherry: Sri Aurobindo Ashram.
Swami Vivekananda. 2006. *Complete Works of Swami Vivekananda, vol. 3*. West Bengal, India: Ramakrishna Math & Ramakrishna Mission, Belur Math

14

Sri Aurobindo's Vision of India's Rebirth

Michel Danino

Sri Aurobindo's faith in India's rebirth took root when he was a student in England in the late nineteenth century, grew in Baroda as he explored India's ancient culture, and deepened during his revolutionary days in Bengal. It never wavered after his withdrawal in 1910 to Pondicherry (today's Puducherry), even as he drew attention to the considerable stumbling blocks and pitfalls on India's long road to freedom—and beyond.

In a message given in 1948, just two years before his passing, Sri Aurobindo spelt out the whole issue confronting free India:

> Ancient India and her spirit might disappear altogether and we would have only one more nation like the others and that would be a real gain neither to the world nor to us.... It would be a tragic irony of fate if India were to throw away her spiritual heritage at the very moment when in the rest of the world there is more and more a turning towards her for spiritual help and a saving Light. This must not and will surely not happen; but it cannot be said that the danger is not there. There are indeed other numerous and difficult problems that face this country or will very soon face it. No doubt we will win through, but we must not disguise from ourselves the fact that after these long years of subjection and its cramping and impairing effects a great inner as well as outer liberation and change, a vast inner and outer progress is needed if we are to fulfil India's true destiny.
>
> (Sri Aurobindo 2006, 499–504)

"A great inner as well as outer liberation and change, a vast inner and outer progress" is precisely an agenda for India's resurgence. Indeed, in the course of numerous speeches, articles, talks, and writings spanning almost sixty years,[1] Sri Aurobindo laid out a program for India to "rejuvenate the mighty outworn body of the ancient

---

This chapter is a revised and reworked version of my 2004 paper, "Sri Aurobindo's Vision of India's Resurgence." It was later published in *Dialogue* in 2015. See, Danino (2015).

Mother" (Sri Aurobindo 1998, 511). Is his vision merely idealistic or mystic—perhaps "mist-ic," as we often take the word to mean? Or does it offer actual solutions to the "numerous and difficult problems that face this country or will very soon face it"? India, as we know, is a maddeningly complex nation-cum-civilization; there shall be no simple roadmap to her rebirth. But we may attempt to extract a few essential lines from Sri Aurobindo's lifelong endeavor.

Breaking the Mold

Even as he fought for India's political freedom, Sri Aurobindo saw her colonial shackles as a necessary evil, one that would compel her to let go of outworn forms and reshape her culture and purpose. In 1909, he wrote in *Karmayogin*, a weekly he founded and edited:

> The spirit and ideals of India had come to be confined in a mould which, however beautiful, was too narrow and slender to bear the mighty burden of our future. When that happens, the mould has to be broken and even the ideal lost for a while, in order to be recovered free of constraint and limitation .... The mould is broken; we must remould in larger outlines and with a richer content.
> (Sri Aurobindo 1997a, 247)

Sri Aurobindo thus set himself as a non-traditionalist, yet one attached to the deepest values that went into defining India. The task of "remolding" remains unfinished, but today, it is not merely the mold of tradition in its corrupting or stagnant aspects (for tradition also has enriching and progressive sides); what India is still grappling with is the corrupt relic of colonial mold. Here too, Sri Aurobindo looked beyond India's political liberation: "What preoccupies me now," he wrote in 1920, "is the question what [the country] is going to do with its self-determination, how will it use its freedom, on what lines is it going to determine its future?" (Sri Aurobindo 2006, 256).

Despite the churning that preceded and followed India's liberation from the colonial yoke, the new nation's attempt at decolonization was less than half-hearted: its apparatus remained wedded to a British constitution, a British polity, a British judiciary, a British administration, and a British educational system—a prison that is about the antithesis of what Sri Aurobindo envisioned.

India's Mission

Before we examine a few symptoms of the malady, we must pause and go back to the fundamentals. If there is a thread running through Sri Aurobindo's vision of India, it is that she does not exist without a spiritual base and a spiritual mission in the world; she is the creator of "a profound and wide-spread spirituality such as no other can parallel" (Sri Aurobindo 1997b, 45). But Sri Aurobindo's view of spirituality is not an ascetic, world-shunning renunciation, the eyes fixed on some otherworldly goal; it is the full manifestation in life of the powers of the Spirit latent in every human being. He wrote, "it is an error to think that spirituality is a thing divorced from life" (1998: 12). It is, to him, a living power, a source of life and strength, and in India's case, the actual origin of her creativity, her ability to assimilate and integrate, and her unique cultural cement—therefore something wholly material in its manifestation.

About 1915, Sri Aurobindo, a refugee in Pondicherry for five years, broke his silence in a revealing interview given to a correspondent of *The Hindu*:

> I quite agree with you that our social fabric will have to be considerably altered before long.... Our past with all its faults and defects should be sacred to us; but the claims of our future with its immediate possibilities should be still more sacred.
>
> I am convinced and have long been convinced that a spiritual awakening, a reawakening to the true self of the nation is the most important condition of our national greatness.... India, if she chooses, can guide the world.
>
> It is more important that the thought of India should come out of the philosophical school and renew its contact with life, and the spiritual life of India issue out of the cave and the temple and, adapting itself to new forms, lay its hand upon the world. I believe also that humanity is about to enlarge its scope by new knowledge, new powers and capacities, which will create as great a revolution in human life as the physical science of the nineteenth century. Here, too, India holds in her past, a little rusted and put out of use, the key of humanity's future.
>
> (Quoted in Rishabhchand 1981, 410–411)

India was thus not to rise for her own sake: "The spiritual life of India is the first necessity of the world's future" (Sri Aurobindo 2002, 611). Such is ultimately India's mission. But to fulfill it, that "spirit" must first create a new body for itself:

> [India] can, if she will, give a new and decisive turn to the problems over which all mankind is labouring and stumbling, for the clue to their solutions is there in her ancient knowledge. Whether she will rise or not to the height of her opportunity in the renaissance which is coming upon her, is the question of her destiny.
>
> (Sri Aurobindo 1997c, 40)

A question that is today more acute than a century ago. Can something be done, individually or collectively, to hasten the process and shorten the birth pangs?

Spiritualizing All Life

In Sri Aurobindo's concept of spirituality, all aspects of life must be brought under its influence, its regenerative and integrative power:

> My idea of spirituality has nothing to do with ascetic withdrawal or contempt or disgust of secular things. There is to me nothing secular, all human activity is for me a thing to be included in a complete spiritual life.
>
> (Sri Aurobindo 2006, 255)

Indeed, irrespective of her various philosophical sects, schools, and doctrines, India more than any other civilization has insisted on spiritualizing all human life:

> Hinduism has always attached to [the organisation of the individual and collective life] a great importance; it has left out no part of life as a thing secular and foreign to the religious and spiritual life.
>
> (Sri Aurobindo 1997c, 181)

Here, we begin to see how unhappy Sri Aurobindo would be with clichés about "secularism" being the foundation of Independent India. Divorcing national life from religion has been Europe's historical development and definition of secularism—a necessary liberation from Christianity's straitjacket and political power, but also a failure to find deeper values and the actual source of liberty and fraternity, beyond both dogmatic religions and shallow humanism.

A regeneration of India can only begin with a frank rejection of the European concept as unsuited to the Indian temperament, and a full acceptance of India's principle of integration of spirituality in life—provided spirituality, again, does not mean a meditation removed from "worldly" affairs; it is a power, and as any other power, it needs instruments. Those are our mind, life, and body; and just as individual yoga involves bringing them under the central rule of the soul or spirit, national resurgence acquires its true meaning when the national mind, life, and body are shaped by the central Spirit of the land.

India's Intellectual Life

Sri Aurobindo often deplored the inability of Indians to think for themselves, the unhappy result of a crippling educational system and an intellectual subservience to the West. He wrote in 1920:

> I believe that the main cause of India's weakness is not subjection, nor poverty, nor a lack of spirituality or Dharma, but a diminution of thought-power, the spread of ignorance in the motherland of Knowledge. Everywhere I see an inability or unwillingness to think—incapacity of thought or "thought-phobia."
>
> (Danino 2018, 147)

We can still see it today. Most of India's intellectual life is second-hand, a tiresome collection of substandard slogans, preferably of Western origin, with no real grasp of the concepts involved and no creative power. Among the numerous maladies stemming from this, we may mention lethargy ("What can I do?"), complacency

("Don't worry, all will be well: *satyameva jayate*"), misplaced syncretism ("God is one and everything is the same"), lack of discernment ("All paths lead to the same goal"), inextricable confusion ("Hinduism is a way of life; its central teaching is tolerance and non-violence; for a casteless society, let us have caste-based reservations and parties; democracy is Britain's greatest gift to India; minorities are secular; secularism means tolerance"; etc., etc.), indifference ("Anyhow science and technology alone can make us progress"), or outright hostility ("You want to take us to the age of obscurantism and the bullock cart? Anyhow whatever knowledge India may have had was elitist, upper-caste, and excluded the lower classes of the society.")

The only way out of this morass is to relearn the art of original thinking:

> Our first necessity, if India is to survive and do her appointed work in the world, is that the youth of India should learn to think,—to think on all subjects, to think independently, fruitfully, going to the heart of things, not stopped by their surface, free of prejudgments, shearing sophism and prejudice asunder as with a sharp sword, smiting down obscurantism of all kinds as with the mace of Bhima.... We must begin by accepting nothing on trust from any source whatsoever, by questioning everything and forming our own conclusions. We need not fear that we shall by that process cease to be Indians or fall into the danger of abandoning Hinduism. India can never cease to be India or Hinduism to be Hinduism, if we really think for ourselves. It is only if we allow Europe to think for us that India is in danger of becoming an ill-executed and foolish copy of Europe.
> (Sri Aurobindo 1997d, 40–41)

To stimulate original thinking should have been the first task of education in free India. Instead, it retained a perverse system which had been designed to rob Indians of their thinking power. If anything, it made the system worse over the years, burdening it with more and more irrelevant data to be mechanically memorized and regurgitated. Around 1900, Sri Aurobindo was already complaining that "the mental training [provided in Indian Universities] is meagre in quantity and worthless in quality" (Sri Aurobindo 2003, 358). A few years later, he added:

> The Indian brain is still in potentiality what it was; but it is being damaged, stunted and defaced. The greatness of its innate possibilities is hidden by the greatness of its surface deterioration.
> (Sri Aurobindo 2003, 377)

Besides teaching students to think, Sri Aurobindo wanted education to enrich them with their rightful Indian heritage. Along with his co-workers in the Independence movement, he called this "national education" and outlined it thus:

> In India... we have been cut off by a mercenary and soulless education from all our ancient roots of culture and tradition (Sri Aurobindo 2003, 433).... The full soul rich with the inheritance of the past, the widening gains of the present, and the large potentiality of the future, can come only by a system of National

Education. It cannot come by any extension or imitation of the system of the existing universities with its radically false principles, its vicious and mechanical methods, its dead-alive routine tradition and its narrow and sightless spirit. Only a new spirit and a new body born from the heart of the Nation and full of the light and hope of its resurgence can create it.

(Sri Aurobindo 2003, 411)

Yet independent India chose to keep her culture and heritage more and more out of sight of students, as though it were something unimportant or perhaps shameful. Recent efforts to rectify this situation have been half-baked at best and drowned in irrationally hostile clamor: any attempt to introduce into the school curriculum positive elements of Indian culture or some knowledge of genuine accomplishments from various fields of knowledge has been dubbed "nationalistic," "chauvinistic," or worse.

Indian education is neither Indian nor an education. Only when it becomes both will a new class of intellectuals emerge, who will regenerate India's intellectual life not by looking up to, or down on, the West, but by having their feet firmly planted in the Indic worldview.

India's Vital Life

The intellect is an essential tool of India's resurgence, but the vital is often a better instrument, yielding more potent and quicker results. As Sri Aurobindo noted:

Indeed without this opulent vitality and opulent intellectuality India could never have done so much as she did with her spiritual tendencies. It is a great error to suppose that spirituality flourishes best in an impoverished soil with the life half-killed and the intellect discouraged and intimidated. The spirituality that so flourishes is something morbid, hectic and exposed to perilous reactions. It is when the race has lived most richly and thought most profoundly that spirituality finds its heights and its depths and its constant and many-sided fruition.

(Sri Aurobindo 1997c, 10)

A glance at classical India confirms that spiritual efflorescence as well as massive artistic creation often went hand in hand. The creation of new forms of Indian aesthetics, poetics, music, dance, sculpture, architecture, crafts, is therefore another important condition. It can be encouraged to some extent by intelligent official patronage and encouragement, but much more so, again, by education:

The system of education which, instead of keeping artistic training apart as a privilege for a few specialists frankly introduces it as a part of culture no less necessary than literature or science, will have taken a great step forward in the perfection of national education and the general diffusion of a broad-based human culture.... It is necessary that those who create, whether in great things or small, whether in the unusual master-pieces of art and genius or in the small common things of use that surround a man's daily life, should be habituated to produce and the nation habituated to expect the beautiful in preference to the ugly, the noble in preference to the vulgar, the fine in preference to the crude, the harmonious in preference to the gaudy. A nation surrounded daily by the beautiful, noble, fine and harmonious becomes that which it is habituated to contemplate and realises the fullness of the expanding Spirit in itself.

(Sri Aurobindo 2003, 453)

Considering the all-pervasive ugliness of modern India—our chaotic, polluted cities and towns, our garbage-ridden streets, our ugly and garish buildings, our gridiron offices, our concrete homes and pigeonhole apartment blocks—we are clearly far from the goal. In the field of art, the flood of third-rate artistic creations from the West has produced professional copycats reveling in tortured art and celebrated ugliness from which all beauty has been perverted away, while humanity's maladies are in full bloom.

Still, there are signs that the demand for genuine Indian art, be it classical music, dance, or traditional crafts, still exists—partly as a consequence of Western appreciation for them. But a mere ornamental addition of art in an otherwise beautyless and crude way of life will not suffice; what is required is a fusion of art in everyday life and activities: only then will Indian art recover its true function as a spiritualizing, enriching, and refining agent, as well as a powerful social cement and vehicle of culture.

India's Physical Life: The Polity

This brings us to the all-important physical organization of India's body politic. There is, first, the question of India's polity. As we know all too well, India's unquestioning adoption of the Westminster type of democracy has led a serious dysfunction of democratic mechanisms, massive corruption, criminalization of politics, and a host of other evils. Sri Aurobindo foresaw this long ago. In 1911, he wrote to a friend:

Spirituality is India's only politics, the fulfilment of the Sanatana Dharma its only Swaraj. I have no doubt we shall have to go through our Parliamentary period in order to get rid of the notion of Western democracy by seeing in practice how helpless it is to make nations blessed. India is passing really through the first stages of a sort of national Yoga.

(Sri Aurobindo 2006, 170)

Almost a century later, we are perhaps touching the end of this first stage. As I briefly stated earlier, the European concept of secularism has no real meaning or application in the Indian context: no pre-Islamic Indian king or emperor ever attempted—or perhaps desired—to turn his chosen creed into a "state religion." Conceivably, Ashoka could have tried to impose Buddhism on his empire; or Kharavela might have been tempted to make Jainism his kingdom of Kalinga's religion. But that would have run against the grain of India's ethos. Here, *dharma*, rather than "religion," was regarded as underpinning the polity and the organization of society at all levels. Wrongly equating Dharma with religion has resulted in divorcing Dharma from national life, which can be done only at the risk of losing what has held this nation together: diversity without the unifying center provided by Dharma is a sure road to fragmentation. Here is Sri Aurobindo's considered verdict (in 1920):

> I do not at all look down on politics or political action or consider I have got above them. I have always laid a dominant stress and I now lay an entire stress on the spiritual life, but my idea of spirituality has nothing to do with ascetic withdrawal or contempt or disgust of secular things. There is to me nothing secular, all human activity is for me a thing to be included in a complete spiritual life.... I believe in something which might be called social democracy, but not in any of the forms now current, and I am not altogether in love with the European kind, however great an improvement it may be on the past. I hold that India having a spirit of her own and a governing temperament proper to her own civilisation, should in politics as in everything else strike out her own original path and not stumble in the wake of Europe. But this is precisely what she will be obliged to do, if she has to start on the road in her present chaotic and unprepared condition of mind.
>
> (Sri Aurobindo 2006, 255–256)

The question remains what political system a resurgent India should build upon. In conversations with disciples, Sri Aurobindo remarked:

> The parliamentary form would be hardly suitable for our people. Of course, it is not necessary that you should have today the same old forms (as in ancient India). But you can take the line of evolution and follow the bent of the genius of the race (Danino 2018, 166–167).... Parliamentary Government is not suited to India. But we always take up what the West has thrown off.... (In an ideal government for India,) there may be one Rashtrapati at the top with considerable powers so as to secure a continuity of policy, and an assembly representative of the nation. The provinces will combine into a federation united at the top, leaving ample scope to local bodies to make laws according to their local problems.
>
> (Danino 2018, 213)

On the surface, this may look much like the present system, but there are crucial differences. The first lies in the quality and sincerity of the political effort. Sri Aurobindo had no illusions as regards our present ruling classes, whether Western or Indian:

> There is no guarantee that this ruling class or ruling body represents the best mind of the nation or its noblest aims or its highest instincts. Nothing of the kind can be asserted of the modern politician in any part of the world; he does not represent the soul of a people or its aspirations. What he does usually represent is

all the average pettiness, selfishness, egoism, self-deception that is about him and these he represents well enough as well as a great deal of mental incompetence and moral conventionality, timidity and pretence. Great issues often come to him for decision, but he does not deal with them greatly; high words and noble ideas are on his lips, but they become rapidly the claptrap of a party. The disease and falsehood of modern political life is patent in every country of the world and only the hypnotised acquiescence of all, even of the intellectual classes, in the great organised sham, cloaks and prolongs the malady, the acquiescence that men yield to everything that is habitual and makes the present atmosphere of their lives.

(Sri Aurobindo 1997e, 296–297)

The second essential difference is that in Sri Aurobindo's scheme of things, there would be no need or room for political parties, an institution which Sri Aurobindo consistently criticized in his talks and writings. In a single sentence, he spelt out the whole problem:

Certainly, democracy as it is now practised is not the last or penultimate stage; for it is often merely democratic in appearance and even at the best amounts to the rule of the majority and works by the vicious method of party government, defects the increasing perception of which enters largely into the present-day dissatisfaction with parliamentary systems.

(Sri Aurobindo 1997e, 456)

European democracy begins by dividing, pitting government against opposition, Right against Left, group against group. In smaller and simpler countries, it may work for a time—although Western masses are increasingly wearied by the merry-go-round in which everyone ends up with the same ideology and lies with equal skill. In a complex and endlessly diverse country like India, to assume that democracy cannot exist without political parties is a typical example of our inability to "think independently." It means that Independence came with little self-questioning or bold search for new lines suited to a free India—all the old and already decrepit colonial structures were seen as the *summum bonum* or a panacea that no one could or should try to improve upon. India is paying decades of lost time and energy on account of this refusal to "be Indian, think Indian." Western polity conceives of doing away with political parties and creating governments of national unity only in times of war or crisis; India, because of her long tradition of a unity underlying her diversity, should have shown that unity is not a freak phenomenon but a workable basis for new politics.

Another difference lies in the phrase "ample scope to local bodies." Sri Aurobindo elaborated in other conversations:

In ancient times each community had its own Dharma and within itself it was independent; every village, every city had its own organization quite free from all political control and within that every individual was free—free to change and take up another line for his development. But all this was not put into a definite political unit. There were, of course, attempts at that kind of expression of life but they were only partially successful. The whole community in India was a very big one and the community culture based on Dharma was not thrown into a kind of (political or national) organization which would resist external aggression.

(Danino 2018, 159–160)

That is what we see at work in India's early Republics (the Mahajanapadas) as well as in later kingdoms, such as the Cholas: an elaborate structure starting from village assemblies and built upward, with strict codes for candidates to those assemblies as well as to village courts. The system was dynamic and ensured actual participation at all levels. With necessary adaptations, a search for a genuine Indian polity should lie in this direction, for that is the native system that arose from India's complex society. Sri Aurobindo elaborated further:

> In India we had...a spontaneous and free growth of communities developing on their own lines.... Each such communal form of life—the village, the town, etc., which formed the unit of national life, was left free in its own internal management. The central authority never interfered with it. There was not the idea of "interest" in India as in Europe, i.e., each community was not fighting for its own interest; but there was the idea of Dharma, the function which the individual and the community has to fulfil in the larger national life. There were caste organizations not based upon a religio-social basis as we find nowadays; they were more or less guilds, groups organized for a communal life. There were also religious communities like the Buddhists, the Jains, etc. Each followed its own law—Swadharma—unhampered by the State. The State recognized the necessity of allowing such various forms of life to develop freely in order to give to the national spirit a richer expression.... The machinery of the State also was not so mechanical as in the West—it was plastic and elastic.
> ... The English in accepting this system have disfigured it considerably. They have found ways to put their hand on and grasp all the old organizations, using them merely as channels to establish more thoroughly the authority of the central power. They discouraged every free organization and every attempt at the manifestation of the free life of the community. Now attempts are being made to have the cooperative societies in villages, there is an effort at reviving the Panchayats. But these organizations cannot be revived once they have been crushed; and even if they revived they would not be the same.[2] If the old organization had lasted it would have been a successful rival of the modern form of government.... You need not come back to the old forms, but you *can* retain the spirit which might create its own new forms.

(Danino 2018, 170–172)

We will therefore refrain from attempting to spell out precise features of India's future polity, but in its broad lines it will surely move away from party politics, aim at simplification, decentralization, local empowerment, true participation, ruthless transparency, and a suppleness that remains responsive to evolving situations. Other institutions, such as the judiciary or the bureaucracy, the penal system and policing, would necessarily be part of this change, and their unwieldy structures, a source of misery rather than service to the common Indian, would have to undergo a major overhaul.

Let us add, as a word of caution, that even an ideal system, if at all there could be one, would not be able to solve human problems: "You can go on changing human institutions infinitely and yet the imperfection will break through all your institutions" (Danino 2018, 217), warned Sri Aurobindo in 1939. Again, the real foundation of the resurgence lies in a spiritual renewal—nothing less can wash away the immense corruption that has taken root in India's institutions and official machineries.

India's physical life cannot be healthy without a sound economy. Sri Aurobindo made a few important remarks in this connection:

> It is better not to destroy the capitalist class as the Socialists want to: they are the source of national wealth. They should be encouraged to spend for the nation. Taxing is all right, but you must increase production, start new industries, and also raise the standard of living; without that if you increase the taxes there will be a state of depression.
>
> (Danino 2018, 218–219)

That is exactly what happened in Nehruvian India and one reason for its economic stagnation. A second reason is the excess of control it indulged in, which stifled the Indian's natural sense of initiative:

> I have no faith in government controls, because I believe in a certain amount of freedom—freedom to find out things for oneself in one's own way, even freedom to commit blunders.... Without the freedom to take risks and commit mistakes there can be no progress.... Organize by all means, but there must be scope for freedom and plasticity.
>
> (Danino 2018, 211–212)

A degree of freedom of initiative having been restored in recent years (the so-called "liberalization," which is not yet liberal enough), India appears to have taken off economically. However, global mechanisms apart, complex social and environmental factors will decide the long-term evolution of India's economy. One such factor is caste, of course, which is intricately linked to community organization. Sri Aurobindo clearly wanted the caste system in its present decayed form to go:

> The spirit is permanent, the body changes; and a body which refuses to change must die.... There is no doubt that the institution of caste degenerated. It ceased to be determined by spiritual qualifications which, once essential, have now come to be subordinate and even immaterial and is determined by the purely material tests of occupation and birth. By this change it has set itself against the fundamental tendency of Hinduism which is to insist on the spiritual and subordinate the material and thus lost most of its meaning.
>
> (Sri Aurobindo 2002, 684)

Sri Aurobindo would therefore certainly not have approved of the clumsy caste-based reservation system, insofar as it has hardened caste differences, triggered a race to backwardness, encouraged mediocrity by compromising on academic and bureaucratic standards, and failed to uplift the weakest members of the society. At the same time, as stressed earlier, Sri Aurobindo recognized the importance of community organization (which is not the same as caste) in India's development, and much of the current boom in Indian enterprise can be shown to respect this pattern.

Another factor currently undergoing rapid evolution is the status of Indian woman, a key to change in most of the problems confronting today's India. Sri Aurobindo, always ahead of his times, regarded the marginalizing of woman as a major reason for India's degeneration. Around 1910, he went so far as to envisage that Indian woman's superiority to man "is no more impossible in the future than it was in the far-distant past" (Sri Aurobindo 1997d, 53). A few years later, he asserted, "Whenever women have been given opportunity they have shown their capacity.... We have to wait a few generations in order to see them at work" (Danino 2018, 174). Seeing the rise of woman in today's India in many fields—from village life to the spiritual world—we are tempted to say that the wait will soon be over. Then India's dormant energies will truly be unlocked.

The Intercommunal Problem

The so-called "communal" problem, the relationship of Hindus, Jains, and Sikhs with Christians and Muslims, remains unsolved. Here Sri Aurobindo was quite clear that Hinduism's tradition of tolerance posed no threat to non-Hindus, but needed to be reciprocated:

> You can live amicably with a religion whose principle is toleration. But how is it possible to live peacefully with a religion whose principle is "I will not tolerate you"? How are you going to have unity with these people? Certainly, Hindu-Muslim unity cannot be arrived at on the basis that the Muslims will go on converting Hindus while the Hindus shall not convert any Mahomedan. You can't build unity on such a basis. Perhaps the only way of making the Mahomedans harmless is to make them lose their fanatic faith in their religion.
>
> (Danino 2018, 161)

The same can be said today of aggressive Christian campaigns of conversion spread to the remotest corners of India with the massive support of foreign finance, aiming ultimately at the same conquest of India as militant Islam does. From the Morley-Minto reforms to the Lucknow Pact and the Khilafat movement, Sri Aurobindo opposed all measures aimed at giving a separate treatment to Indian Muslims, instead of regarding them as Muslim Indians—or simply Indians. He would have equally opposed the privileges extended to so-called minorities under the Constitution, since they reinforce rather than blur the divisive "minority identity" and are unfairly denied to the Hindus, in contradiction of the spirit of equal rights. In fact, the whole burden of "tolerance" is laid at the Hindus' feet; "minorities," portrayed as perennial victims, are not expected to share in the task; the "majority" alone is—even if there is in reality no coherent, monolithic Hindu majority. If, today, a few marginal groups have been indulging in criminal acts—while the vast chunk of Hindus remain peaceful and tolerant—such discriminations are partly to blame; they should have no place in a resurgent India.

The solution for India's communal problems was formulated long ago by Ashoka himself and may be summarized in three simple steps: do not praise your creed excessively (i.e. no fanaticism); do not criticize other creeds harshly; instead, study the positive elements of all creeds. However, in such a vision, there is no scope for religions claiming to be sole repositories of the truth (which Indic religions never did).

India and Nature

In the end, however, the above issues may be overtaken by the most silent of them all: the environmental degradation that is fast threatening the land's life-sustaining ability. The problem was not yet acute in Sri Aurobindo's time, although he once remarked that "the forests (in India) have to be preserved and also the wildlife. China destroyed all her forests and the result is that there is flood every year" (Danino 2018, 218). It was even less acute two millenniums ago, when Kautilya prescribed wildlife sanctuaries, assigned taxes to the use of various irrigation works, and enjoined penalties for the felling of trees.

Today, despite bountiful monsoons, the illusion created by the "Green Revolution" is reaching the end of its tether. India is in the grips of a severe water crisis, the result of decades-long mismanagement and incompetence. The drying up of river after river, the poisoning of earth, air, and water with toxic substances, the plunder of natural resources by industries, the extreme pollution of Indian cities will lead at the very least to a collapse of the health system, at worst to the demise of India's agriculture, traditionally her primary strength. The only silver lining is a growing awareness of the urgency, but that is yet to be reflected in long-term vision plans by the authorities. Only if this awareness grows exponentially and is absorbed by the rising grassroots movements will we be able to avoid a wide-scale catastrophe. The coming years will decide India's destiny at the most physical level.

Conclusion

Sri Aurobindo's vision of a rejuvenated India calls for nothing less than a national yoga—an effort of transformation in which a critical mass of Indians must consciously take part, those who happen to be in a position to change things as well as those who have been victims of the system. In fact, way back in 1910, he himself said so:

> The soul of Hinduism languishes in an unfit body. Break the mould that the soul may live.... If the body were young, adaptable, fit, the liberated soul might use it, but it is decrepit, full of ill-health and impurity. It must be changed, not by the spirit of Western iconoclasm which destroys the soul with the body, but by national Yoga.
>
> (Sri Aurobindo 2003, 552–553)

Going by the superficial signposts provided by the media, we might despair of this ever happening. "Hinduism" is not a fashionable word, to begin with, and many of our intellectuals seem to have developed a hatred for the core concepts and values of Indian civilization. Some of them even have even called Sri Aurobindo "communal"[3]— one of those convenient but reckless adjectives thrown at anyone who does not blindly subscribe to Western solutions or methods, or who has faith in India's inherent strengths.

However, circumstances speak a language and follow a path that are not intellectual. And discreet signs abound that we have entered a phase of change. Apart from the awakenings we have evoked above, or the calls for change in various fields from the educational to the ecological, the most important sign is the growing assertiveness of the masses. From self-help groups to village committees, women's and citizens' organizations, NGOs good and bad (mostly the latter), everywhere we can note attempts toward self-government, an organic phenomenon that has been a feature of Indian society since antiquity. Indians seem to have understood that there is no point waiting endlessly for the administration to do everything for them. Provided such groups do not fall back into the trap of politicization, they can change the grassroots pattern of India and effectively erode the system from below—for it is unlikely to change willingly from above.

Some of those endeavors for change have had a spiritual motive, in conformity with Indian history, which has seen the deepest social changes arising from spiritual impulses, from the Bhakti to the freedom movements. If this trend continues, the result will be not only lasting changes in Indian society, but also a welcome testimony that Indian spirituality is capable of tackling India's pressing social problems.

We may end where we began, by looking at the meaning of this strange curve in India's history from the time of the colonial conquest:

> Whatever temporary rotting and destruction this crude impact of European life and culture has caused, it gave three needed impulses. It revived the dormant intellectual and critical impulse; it rehabilitated life and awakened the desire of new creation; it put the reviving Indian spirit face to face with novel conditions and ideals and the urgent necessity of understanding, assimilating and conquering them. The national mind turned a new eye on its past culture, reawoke to its sense and import, but also at the same time saw it in relation to modern knowledge and ideas. Out of this awakening vision and impulse the Indian renaissance is arising, and that must determine its future tendency. The recovery of the old spiritual knowledge and experience in all its splendour, depth and fullness is its first, most essential work; the flowing of this spirituality into new forms of philosophy, literature, art, science and critical knowledge is the second; an original dealing with modern problems in the light of the Indian spirit and the endeavour to formulate a greater synthesis of a spiritualised society is the third and most difficult. Its success on these three lines will be the measure of its help to the future of humanity.
>
> (Sri Aurobindo 1997c, 15)

Sri Aurobindo regarded "the spiritual history of mankind and especially of India as a constant development of a divine purpose" (Sri Aurobindo 2012, 411). Which does not mean that the road to this divine purpose will be a smooth one. Sri Aurobindo often warned of "the perpetual danger of a barbaric relapse" for humanity (Sri Aurobindo 1997e, 77). Whether India will contribute to the relapse or will at last emerge from her long lethargy is the question now before her.

Notes

1   A selection of such texts can be found in Danino (2018).
2   That is why the attempt to revive "Panchayati Raj" has failed. However well-intentioned, it could only end up burdening the administrative structure further and dividing villages along party lines.
3   This trend was stated by Nurul Hasan, a Communist minister for Education in Indira Gandhi's government in the 1970s. A Marxist historian, Bipin Chandra, in *Modern India—A History Textbook for Class XII* (New Delhi: NCERT, 1990–2000, p. 207), held Sri Aurobindo's "concept of India as mother and nationalism as religion" to be a "step back" because it had "a strong religious and Hindu tinge." Recently, Jyotirmaya Sharma in his *Hindutva: Exploring the Idea of Hindu Nationalism* (New Delhi: Penguin Books India, 2003) holds Sri Aurobindo partly responsible for the rise of "Hindutva" (along with Dayananda Saraswati and Swami Vivekananda, among others), calls him a "pamphleteer," and accuses him of having "inspired a jihadi Hinduism and political Hindutva" (p. 69).

References

Danino, Michel. 2015. "Sri Aurobindo's Vision of India's Resurgence." *Dialogue* 17, 2: 83–101.
Danino, Michel, ed. 2018. *Sri Aurobindo and India's Rebirth*. New Delhi: Rupa.
Rishabhchand. 1981. *Sri Aurobindo: His Life Unique*. Pondicherry: Sri Aurobindo Ashram.
Sri Aurobindo. 1997a. *Karmayogin, The Complete Works of Sri Aurobindo (hereafter CWSA), vol. 8*. Pondicherry: Sri Aurobindo Ashram.
Sri Aurobindo. 1997b. *Essays on the Gita, CWSA, vol. 19*. Pondicherry: Sri Aurobindo Ashram.
Sri Aurobindo. 1997c. *The Renaissance in India, with a Defence of Indian Culture, CWSA, vol. 20*. Pondicherry: Sri Aurobindo Ashram.
Sri Aurobindo. 1997d. *Essays Divine and Human, CWSA, vol. 12*. Pondicherry: Sri Aurobindo Ashram.
Sri Aurobindo. 1997e. *The Human Cycle, The Ideal of Human Unity, War and Self-Determination, CWSA, vol. 25*. Pondicherry: Sri Aurobindo Ashram.
Sri Aurobindo. 1998. *Essays in Philosophy and Yoga, CWSA, vol. 13*. Pondicherry: Sri Aurobindo Ashram.
Sri Aurobindo. 2002. *Bande Mataram, CWSA, vols. 6 and 7*. Pondicherry: Sri Aurobindo Ashram.

Sri Aurobindo. 2003. *Early Cultural Writings, CWSA, vol. 1*. Pondicherry: Sri Aurobindo Ashram.
Sri Aurobindo. 2006. *Autobiographical Notes and Other Writings of Historical Interest, CWSA, vol. 36*. Pondicherry: Sri Aurobindo Ashram.
Sri Aurobindo. 2012. *Letters on Yoga—I, CWSA, vol. 28*. Pondicherry: Sri Aurobindo Ashram.

Index

Advaita Vedanta viii, x, 1, 15, 16, 19, 20, 22, 23, 27, 28, 30–2, 40–2, 83
agni 139, 144
Albrow, Martin 78–80, 87
Alfassa, Mirra 221
Ananda Math 44
Apollo Bunder 220, 221
Arjuna 42–43
Arya/Aryan v, 53–6, 59–66, 68–9, 71–3
Aryan Invasion Theory (AIT) 8, 53–6, 59, 61, 63, 65, 66, 68–70
Aryan Migration Theory (AMT) 65–7, 69, 70
Ashoka 239, 245
Ashram vii, viii, 12, 31–2, 51–2, 73, 88, 104–5, 119, 134, 151, 166, 184, 200–1, 208, 214–15, 222–4, 231, 247–8
atman 16–18, 82, 93–4, 96, 220
Auroville vi, vii, ix, 11, 51, 207, 213, 215, 219, 222–31
avatara 42
avidya 17, 111
Ayer, A. J. 4, 11–12

Bande Mataram 44, 188, 204, 247
Banga Mata 44
Bengal Renaissance v, 8, 33, 35–47, 49–51
Bergson 48, 83
Berkeley 84
bhadralok 35–6
Bhagavad Gita 86, 96
Bopp, Frantz 54
Brahman 16–20, 22–7, 41, 85, 109–11, 121–2, 126–7, 221
Brahmo movement 38
Bronze Age Civilization 60, 62
Buddha 33, 59, 84

Calcutta (Kolkata) 1, 26, 33, 35–6, 44–5, 52, 73, 107, 151, 188, 190
capitalism 77–8, 88, 228

Cartesian 21–3, 25; *also see* Descartes
Cesaire, Aime 69–71
Chaitya Purusha 193–4
Chardin, Pierre Teilhard de 82, 207, 215
Chattopadhyay, Bankim Chandra 39
Chola 242
civilizing mission 55, 69
Cold War 79, 203, 208–11
colonialism 5, 26, 35–6, 49, 51–2, 69–71, 76, 213
common ancestry theory 54
Comparative Philology 58–9, 69
cosmology viii, 15, 21, 30, 53, 58, 70
Cox, Robert 209–10, 214
cradle of the civilization 54, 56
creative destruction 210
Curry, W. B. 207, 214

dasyu 59
Deleuze, Gilles 43, 48, 52
Derozio, Henry Vivian 37
Derrida 48
Descartes 21, 31; *also see* Cartesian
Dharma 10, 41, 52, 154, 157–9, 189, 236, 239, 240–2
dohas 193
Dravidian 60
dualism 19, 21–3, 25, 204
dukka 17
Durga 44

Earth-Queen 230
ecosystems 78
ego 2, 5–6, 10, 16–17, 55, 68, 95, 98, 101–3, 122–3, 125–7, 129, 132, 157, 176, 191–4, 196, 199, 200, 205–7, 209, 212
Egypt 61, 67, 69
eliminativism 25
enlightened civilization 36

Enlightenment v, vii, 8, 21–3, 25, 33–9, 41, 43, 45–51, 58, 59, 191, 192, 199
ethical being 154, 157, 160, 163–4
ethical mind 196
ethics v, 1, 2, 9–10, 32, 84, 87–8, 107, 135, 153–65, 187, 196
Eurocentrism 75, 87
evolving humanity 139
experiential knowledge 139, 141

Fichte 23
First World War 205
five dreams 3, 6, 11, 219
fraternity 45, 190, 206, 209, 212, 236
Freud, Sigmund 8, 194
Fukuyama, Francis 47, 52

German philology 55
Ghaggar 62–3, 67
Giddens, Anthony 88
Gita 6, 37, 42, 52, 86, 88, 96, 154, 247; *also see* Bhagavad Gita
global age v, 8, 9, 13, 75–83, 85–7, 89
global governance vi, ix, 10, 203–5, 208–15
global harmony 187, 196
Global People's Assembly 211
globalization vii, 9, 75–82, 87–9, 210, 214
globaphobia 80
gnosis 111, 126, 146
God 1, 20, 24–5, 34, 39–40, 43, 47, 51–2, 61, 72, 85, 100, 110, 113, 115–16, 122, 124, 138, 142, 146, 148–50, 153–4, 158, 164, 187, 189, 192, 197–9, 221, 237
golden light 119, 137, 138
Golden Rule 207
Great Bath 63, 67
Green Revolution 245
guna 80
Gupta, Nolini Kanta viii, 115, 119, 120, 147

Hakra 62–3, 67
Halbfass, Wilhelm 39, 41, 52
Harappa 60–6, 72–3
Harvey, David 78, 88
Hegel 11–12, 23–4, 31–2, 47–9, 52, 204, 213–15
hegemony of Reason 180

Heidegger 33, 45, 49, 52
Heraclitus 15, 20, 204
Higher Mind 19, 26, 30, 111, 122, 124–5, 144–5, 150
Hindu-Muslim unity 244
The Human Cycle 1, 37, 49, 52, 88, 155, 200, 204, 228, 231, 247
human evolution v, 10, 153, 155, 157, 159, 161, 163, 165, 204
human unity vi, 1, 5–6, 10, 52, 76–7, 88, 146, 185, 187, 189–92, 195–201, 203–13, 215, 224, 227, 230, 247; *also see* Ideal of Human Unity
humanism 23, 34–5, 37, 39, 43, 236
Huntington, Samuel 79, 88

Ideal of Human Unity vi, 1, 6, 10, 52, 77, 88, 190, 195–6, 200, 203–7, 209, 211, 213, 215, 227, 247; *also see* human unity
idealism 19, 20, 23–6, 30, 37, 108, 159
ignorance 3, 4, 17, 42, 58–9, 94, 96–7, 101, 103, 108, 111, 113, 115–18, 122, 129, 161, 163, 166, 236
illumined mind 18–19, 111, 122, 125, 144, 145, 150
India vi–x, 3, 6–8, 11, 20, 31, 33, 35–8, 40–1, 44, 47, 49, 52–7, 59–62, 65–6, 69–73, 76, 79, 81, 83, 84, 88, 108, 140, 162, 187, 188, 190, 204, 215, 217, 219–20, 222, 225–31, 233–47
Indo-European languages 54, 64, 66
Indus 60, 62–7, 71–2
Indus-Saraswati Civilization 62
Industrial Age 179–80
Industrial-Consumerist society 179
infrarational 155
integral education v, vii, 10, 167–71, 173, 175–7, 179, 181–4
integral teacher 176, 178, 183
Integral Yoga vii, ix, 2, 7, 10, 93–5, 97, 98, 100, 102, 105, 145, 163, 174, 220, 223
intercommunal problem 244
international organization(s) vi, 10, 12, 203–5, 208–14, 229
intuition 18, 19, 27, 29, 34–5, 48, 122, 144–6, 148–50, 159, 163, 183, 194
intuitive mind 3, 38, 111, 138

involution 17, 19, 24, 32, 48, 110, 112, 123
inward progress 141
inward voyage 137
Islam, Kazi Nazrul 44

James, William 24–5, 30–1, 83
jivatman 93
Jones, William 53–4
jugupsa 81

Kali 40–1, 44, 221
Kalinga 240
Kant, Immanuel 1–2, 12, 23, 38, 49
karma 84, 103, 158, 160
Karmayogin 105, 189, 190, 234, 247
Katha Upanishad 193
Kautilya 4–5, 245
Kena Upanishad 84–5, 109
Kharavela 240
Khilafat movement 244
Knowledge Academy 35
Krishna 20, 32, 40–3

League of Nations 5, 10, 208, 213
liberation 9, 126, 130, 170, 179, 199, 233–4, 236
Liberty 77, 206, 209, 212, 236
life viii, x, 1–9, 11, 18–20, 22–4, 26, 27, 30, 32–3, 38, 40, 42, 48, 50, 52, 61, 76–7, 79, 82–6, 88, 94–8, 100–4, 107–11, 113–19, 121, 123–7, 129–31, 134, 137–8, 140, 144, 147–9, 154–69, 171–9, 182–4, 187–92, 194, 196–200, 204–6, 212, 219–20, 222–9, 231, 235–6, 238–47
The Life Divine 2, 4, 6, 9, 32, 42, 48, 52, 88, 110, 116, 121, 124, 130, 134, 141, 144, 147, 156, 166, 187
Lila 17, 19, 127
Lucknow Pact 244

mahajanapadas 242
Mahatma Gandhi ix–x, 5, 15, 188–9, 200
mantra 102, 138–40, 144, 146, 147
Marshall, John 60
Matrimandir 224–5, 228, 230
maya 17, 19, 84
Mayavadins 2, 109
McLuhan, Marshall 82
Mesopotamia 61, 67

metaphysics v, viii, 2, 4, 8–9, 15–17, 19–21, 23–7, 29, 31, 40, 48, 76, 86, 91
mindfulness 176
modernity 8, 21, 33–7, 39–41, 46, 50–2, 77–80, 87, 215
Mohenjodaro 60–5, 67
Morley-Minto reforms 244
The Mother vii, viii, 54, 97, 101, 103–5, 117–20, 145, 148–9, 189, 207, 215, 219–31
Muller, Max 51, 55

Nakashima, George 229
nation soul, nation-soul 205–7, 212
national education 237–8
national ego 5, 10, 196, 199, 205–7, 209, 212
national yoga 239, 245
nationalism 23, 36, 40, 44–5, 49, 52, 187–90, 197, 200, 204, 212, 247
Nature 1, 3, 5–6, 9, 15–17, 20–4, 29, 31–3, 44–5, 48–9, 57, 59, 65, 77, 79, 80, 82, 85–7, 93–100, 102–4, 108, 113, 115–19, 122–4, 128–31, 133, 137–8, 142, 144, 149, 153–65, 168, 170–3, 175–9, 189, 190, 192, 194, 196, 198, 199, 203–5, 209, 211, 212, 245
Neutral Monism 23–5
New Man 116
New Race 115
New World 89, 116–17, 167
Newtonian-Galilean science 21
Nietzsche, Friedrich 35, 38–40, 49, 52, 83
Nirodbaran viii, 101, 105, 230
nirvana 33, 51, 84
non-reductive physicalism 25

oneness v, vii, 9, 50, 77, 82, 111, 121–33, 156, 176, 190, 195, 198–9, 205, 227
othering 70, 81
overhead aesthetics 144–5
overhead planes 143–5, 150
overhead poetry 145–6, 150–1
Overman viii, 39
overmind 18–19, 80, 111, 122, 125–6, 143–50

Parabrahman 110
Parmenides 20
passive resistance 188–90

Peace Tables 229
physical education 119, 174
physicalism 19, 22, 23, 25–32
Plato 5, 20
Plotinus 20, 30
positivism 21, 70
post-Cold War 203, 208, 209, 211
postcolonial 44, 69
post-Enlightenment 8, 33, 36, 39, 41, 50–1
postmodernity 39, 79
practical spiritual philosophy v, 1–3, 5, 7–9, 11
pragmatic utilitarianism 179
pragmatism 23, 83, 88
Prakriti 96, 128
pre-Enlightenment 33
Proclus 20
The Problem of Rebirth 154
Proto-Indo-European languages 54, 68
psychic being v, 9, 49, 93–7, 99, 101–3, 105, 116, 118, 119, 121, 128, 129, 133, 191, 193–4, 196, 226
Purusha 93–4, 128, 149, 193–4
Pythagorus 20

Radhakrishnan, Sarvepalli viii, 15, 17, 20, 32, 42
rajas 80, 129
rationalism 21, 70
rationality 29, 34, 37–9, 43, 47–8, 172–3, 187
religio-ethical sense 155
Religion of Humanity 195–8, 206
Religion of Man 198, 201
renaissance v, vi, 8, 11, 33, 35–47, 49–51, 53, 70, 82, 88, 209, 219, 221–3, 225–9, 231, 235, 246–7
Rig Veda 56, 87
Rishi/s 3, 58, 81, 139, 140, 162
Rolland, Romain 8
Roy, Ram Mohun 38, 40

Sachchidananda 9, 109–11, 115, 121–2, 127, 131, 156
sacred fire 137, 139
sadhak vii, 98–102, 118–19, 163
sadhana 93, 95, 98, 100, 103, 142, 151, 220

Sahni, Daya Ram 60
Samrat 116
Sanatan Dharma 41, 52
sanskara 165
Saraswati 62–3, 67, 247
Sarvodaya 188
Satprem 103–5, 222–4
sattwa, sattva 80, 129
satyameva jayate 237
Savitri 4, 6–7, 80, 88, 132, 134, 146–9, 192, 198, 200, 222, 224, 230
Schelling 23, 54
Schlegel, A.W. von 54
Schrödinger, Erwin 84
scientism 23, 25, 28
Second World War 49, 61
shakti 37, 110, 129
Shankara 83–4
siddhi 95, 103
Simondon 48
socialism 23, 39, 77
soul 2, 9–10, 20–2, 30–2, 37, 46, 48–9, 51, 85, 93–6, 100, 102, 108, 114, 116, 128–31, 137–43, 147, 153–4, 169–71, 175, 178, 183, 193, 199, 205–7, 212, 220–2, 226, 228, 230, 236–7, 240, 245
Sri Ramakrishna ix, 40
Streit, Clarence 207, 215
subconscient 4, 101, 103, 122–3, 155, 165
Sumer 61
superhumanity 116
supermanhood 1
supermind 18–19, 22, 24, 26–7, 30, 38, 42–3, 48, 103, 111, 113, 115, 117, 118, 122, 126, 146, 149–51
supramental 4, 38, 42–3, 47, 50, 95, 103, 108, 113, 115, 117, 119–20, 122, 126–7, 145, 149, 221
supramental force 108, 120, 126
supra-nation 116
supreme social trinity 10, 206
swadharma 116, 242
Swami Chinmayananda 42
Swami Vivekananda ix, 5, 37, 39, 84, 222, 231, 247
swarat 116
The Synthesis of Yoga 6, 9, 11, 42, 52, 88, 109, 121, 134, 162, 166

Tagore, Abanindranath viii, 44
Tagore, Debendranath 38, 40
Tagore, Rabindranath viii, 38, 40, 44, 49–50, 193, 198, 201
Taittiriya Upanishad 85, 109
tamas 80, 129
Tennyson, Alfred 89
Theory-of-Everything 45
Truth-consciousness 9, 108, 119, 122, 144, 163

UNESCO 229
United Nations (UN) 5, 6, 10, 204–5, 208–15, 229–30
United Nations Security Council 5, 210–11, 213–15
universal humanity 157
Upanishad(s) 3, 21, 70, 81, 84–8, 109–10, 126, 134, 139, 162, 193, 200
Uttapara speech 41, 52

Vaishanavism 40
Vedanta viii, x, 2, 4, 7, 8, 15–16, 19–23, 26–8, 30–2, 37, 39–42, 52, 82–5, 94, 111
Vedantic monotheism 40
Vedas 46, 55, 57–60, 64–6, 126
Vedic history 58
Vedic seers 138, 193
vibhutis 108
Viswarupa 42–3

Wheeler, Robert Eric Mortimer 61, 63–4, 73
wholeness 80, 169, 195
Wilber, Ken 82, 89, 194, 201
world-state 77, 207

yoga iii, v–x, 2, 6–7, 9, 11, 16, 26, 31, 41, 43, 52, 86, 88, 91, 93–5, 97–8, 100–2, 104–5, 107, 109, 121, 134, 162, 163, 166, 174, 184, 193–4, 200, 220–1, 223, 231, 239, 245, 247–8

www.ingramcontent.com/pod-product-compliance
Lightning Source LLC
Chambersburg PA
CBHW072138290426
44111CB00012B/1905